**SAGE** was founded in 1965 by Sara Miller McCune to support the dissemination of usable knowledge by publishing innovative and high-quality research and teaching content. Today, we publish over 900 journals, including those of more than 400 learned societies, more than 800 new books per year, and a growing range of library products including archives, data, case studies, reports, and video. SAGE remains majority-owned by our founder, and after Sara's lifetime will become owned by a charitable trust that secures our continued independence.

Los Angeles | London | New Delhi | Singapore | Washington DC | Melbourne

# Hinduism in India

# Hinduism in India

## MODERN AND CONTEMPORARY MOVEMENTS

### Edited by
Will Sweetman
Aditya Malik

### Series Editor
Geoffrey A. Oddie

Los Angeles | London | New Delhi
Singapore | Washington DC | Melbourne

*First published in 2016 by*

**SAGE Publications India Pvt Ltd**
B1/I-1 Mohan Cooperative Industrial Area
Mathura Road, New Delhi 110 044, India
*www.sagepub.in*

**SAGE Publications Inc**
2455 Teller Road
Thousand Oaks, California 91320, USA

**SAGE Publications Ltd**
1 Oliver's Yard, 55 City Road
London EC1Y 1SP, United Kingdom

**SAGE Publications Asia-Pacific Pte Ltd**
3 Church Street
#10-04 Samsung Hub
Singapore 049483

Published by Vivek Mehra for SAGE Publications India Pvt. Ltd, typeset in 10.5/12.5pt Minion Pro by PrePSol Enterprises Pvt. Ltd, Haryana and printed at Chaman Enterprises, New Delhi.

**Library of Congress Cataloging-in-Publication Data**

Hinduism in India : modern and contemporary movements / editors Will Sweetman and Aditya Malik.
    pages cm
Includes bibliographical references and index.
  1. Hinduism—India. I. Sweetman, Will, editor.
BL1153.5.H56     294.50954—dc23         2016     2015032789

**ISBN:** 978-93-515-0099-5 (HB)

**The SAGE Team:** N. Unni Nair, Sandhya Gola, Rajib Chatterjee, and Ritu Chopra

*For*

*Nola*

## Bulk Sales

SAGE India offers special discounts
for purchase of books in bulk.
We also make available special imprints
and excerpts from our books on demand.

*For orders and enquiries, write to us at*

Marketing Department
SAGE Publications India Pvt Ltd
B1/I-1, Mohan Cooperative Industrial Area
Mathura Road, Post Bag 7
New Delhi 110044, India

*E-mail us at* **marketing@sagepub.in**

## Get to know more about SAGE

Be invited to SAGE events, get on our mailing list.
*Write today to* **marketing@sagepub.in**

This book is also available as an e-book.

# Contents

# Introduction: Hinduism in India

## Geoffrey A. Oddie

This book and *Hinduism in India: The Early Period* by SAGE Publications are examples of exploratory studies of major religions in the Asian region. They consist of original chapters contributed by a deliberate complement of elite and emerging scholars (i.e., the next generation of elite scholars). These are also international in their scholarly representation and interdisciplinary in scope, including, for example, chapters by historians, linguists, anthropologists, sociologists, religionists, and others.

The chapters contain a great deal of material that offers a fresh and original contribution to knowledge and understanding and which, in that sense, will supplement and update entries in existing encyclopedias. Clearly, it is impossible to deal with all the issues and topics that might be thought of as relating to Hinduism, especially as the term Hinduism is an ill-defined, somewhat amorphous concept about which there is no agreement and which, it could be argued, relates to a very broad range of different topics. Continuous research in archeology, anthropology, mythology, vernacular literatures, and history and the development of new movements has greatly increased an ever-expanding field of inquiry into the subject; and what we hope to do in these books is not to offer any kind of overall survey, but to highlight *some* of the issues and debates, to point to new research and interpretations, and to open up the field still more widely for further inquiries. For the latter purpose, we have included bibliographies, which should be useful not only for those wanting to develop a basic knowledge of Hinduism, but also for researchers doing original research and wanting to know the latest publications in their particular field of inquiry. Furthermore, some of the topics included here, such as Hinduism and the modern media and the urban Hindu arranged marriage, are seldom considered among entries on Hinduism. At the same time, some of the other chapters explore newly emerging and challenging methods of interpretation. Clear examples of this are Bailey's chapter on "mythology" in *Hinduism in India: The Early Period* (referred to as *The Early Period* hereafter in this section) in which he discusses "four modes of approach to the study of Hindu mythology" and here, in this book, Spurr's analysis of the different interpretations of the modern guru phenomenon.

The chapters here are intended *primarily* for those wishing to pursue further reading and, especially, research—for those already familiar with much in Hinduism, but who want to identify significant issues to become familiar with more recent publications and to extend and develop their own work. At the same time, it is expected that many of the chapters will also prove accessible and useful for others, such as students, workers in aid organizations, businessmen, and diplomats, wanting to gain further knowledge and a deeper understanding of major aspects of India's religious and cultural heritage. It is especially for their benefit that Bailey, in *The Early Period*, has included a commentary on some of the major and most influential concepts that emerged in the history of early Hinduism. It is also for the sake of those who are not well versed in Asian history that Sweetman, in this book, outlines some of the major changes, including the advent of colonialism and the increased influence of overseas communities, in shaping Hindu ideas and practice *in India* during the modern era.

Given that the topic of Hinduism is such an extensive and ever-expanding field of inquiry, it was decided that these studies should be restricted to developments in India itself. There might, for example, have been studies of Hinduism in Nepal or in different countries in Southeast Asia, such as Cambodia or Indonesia, or still further afield of Hinduism and the diaspora in places such as Britain, South Africa, Canada, Australia, or the USA. Furthermore, linked with the obvious need to restrict the number of chapters in the current publication was an important methodological consideration. This is the fact that in all studies of Hinduism, the actual context of developments is all-important. Detailed studies of Hinduism outside of India, while instructive, would have necessitated further discussion of the varied contexts in which Hindu ideas and practices were established, and perhaps changed, and have come to influence the lives of millions outside of India itself; and this discussion would have added greatly to the overall size of our project. Sweetman's overview of the growth of Hindu communities overseas (mostly during the period of the British Raj) is a relevant and timely contribution. Some additional references to Hindus overseas are for comparative purposes, for example, to illustrate differences in Hindu temple architecture in India and in Southeast Asia or to compare Hindu gurus, some of whom live and flourish in the USA. While these comparisons provide us with further insights into the nature of Hinduism in India, another important issue that is raised, for example, in Rao's chapter, is the part played by overseas Hindu communities in furthering particular views of Hinduism and in the development of Hindu nationalist organizations and ideology in India itself.

Our sense of the importance of the context not only influenced our decision to focus primarily on Hinduism in India alone, but also the decision to arrange chapters in two books—an arrangement that allows for the influence of a changing historical context including the sequence of events and developments over time. Hence, while *The Early Period* focuses *primarily* on Hinduism in early India, chapters in this book grapple with issues and changes that have taken place since about the end of the 18th century (a) during the period of increasing European contact and colonization and (b) in the postcolonial situation.

Another major consideration, apart from the context and clearly apparent in many of the contributions, is a concern with the process of continuity and change. The importance of continuities in the history of Hinduism, in Hindu philosophy and mythology, in teachings and rituals, and even in the social system, emerges in discussions in a number of chapters that follow. For example, one of the arguments in Rao's chapter is that while there have been enormous changes in methods of communication in modern times, continuities have enabled Hindus to communicate "more of the same." Also significant is Srivastava's reference to continuities in connection with caste, for example, the ongoing influence of ancient Hindu texts, including the idea of *varna* (caste [lit. "color"]), which continues to reinforce the status of brahmans in India today.

But while there has been, and there is, continuity, there is also modification and change—developments that took place in early India, as well as in subsequent centuries and up to the present time. Indeed, one of the more difficult challenges for scholars is to discover or identify what changes were evolving or taking place. Why did some traditions persist, while others were modified or disappeared? How do we explain the emergence of new ideas and practices including the particular conglomeration and complexities in what is called Hinduism today? In his chapter on the Mahabharata and Dharma in *The Early Period*, Bowles investigates changing ideas of dharma and sees these as reflecting the rise and influence of the Buddhism, Jainism, and other religious movements in early India. Spurr, in this book, also takes up the challenge of continuity and degrees of change in his analysis of Hindu gurus, while Lubin discusses the same process with respect to Hindu law in early India, under colonial rule, and in India since Independence in 1947.

The issue regarding the influence of non-Hindu religious traditions on Hinduism receives further attention in chapters by Oddie and Frykenberg. The former suggests that contact with Islam heightened a greater awareness among Hindus of their own religious traditions and also explores the part Evangelicals played in coining and popularizing the term Hinduism. Frykenberg examines the effect of the latter's activities on Hindu teachings and forms of organization also in the 19th century. These themes, including the ways in which Hindu traditions were created, modified, or changed as a result of religious movements emanating from outside as well as within the subcontinent, might have been explored still further, had it not been for the constraints of space in the present publication. Indeed, there might well have been further studies of the influence of other non-Hindu religious movements (including Islam) on changes in Hinduism—if space permitted.

However, it also needs to be kept in mind that the influence of non-Hindu religious ideas and movements was not the only reason for changes in Hindu religious thought and practice. Changes in Hindu ideas, teaching, and practice have been influenced not only by specific religious movements, but also by more general and broader developments that affected Indians. The internal migration of different people, invasions from outside as well as within the subcontinent, the emergence of different types of social structure and economic activity, changing tribal and organized political systems (including colonialism), and new types of transport and communication have all been important elements affecting religious practice and teaching.

To take the last in the list of these external factors affecting Hinduism, one might consider the impact of changes in transport and communication since the 1840s when the British pioneered the introduction of the Indian railway system. The idea of pilgrimage took on a new meaning, as pilgrims could travel more easily to holy sites throughout the subcontinent. Improvements in literacy, the advent of the newspaper, and, in still more recent years, the introduction of electronic media have all had effects in creating a greater awareness of the diversity of Hindu teachings and of Hinduism as an all-India system. Films and television and the advent of the global communications' revolution are not only affecting people in the cities, but also in villages and in the more remote parts of the country. Here, one might note Bailey's comment on the rise of "the mythological" in Bollywood cinema, and especially Rao's detailed analysis of recent developments in what she describes as "Media Hinduism." This includes the introduction and development of the mobile phone.

Another major issue that emerges in these books is the relationship between what the anthropologist Robert Redfield once called "the great and little traditions" or between brahmanic and folk Hinduism. Are these separate traditions or are they in some way interrelated and enveloped in an overarching whole? To what extent were village Hindus in early or pre-modern India, as well as later, participating in a wider world of Hindu mythology, rituals, and practice? Was there such a thing as an all-embracing India-wide entity (equivalent to what we now call Hinduism) during the pre-modern period?

The answer to these questions seems to depend partly on which aspect of Hinduism one is exploring. Hence Bailey, in his chapter on oral mythology in *The Early Period*, writes:

> [T]he themes found in such myths are pan-Indian to the extent they occur beyond vernacular sources in a variety of geographical areas. There is another pan-Indian mythology found in the Puranas, which is not localized yet shares common themes and motifs with localized mythology. Both are necessarily interrelated and establish India as a common mythological zone.

Furthermore, Branfoot, writing in the same book, notes the spread of common forms of iconographic representation and remarks that one of the striking features of early Hindu iconography is "the degree to which deities are depicted in a similar manner across great geographical distances" before modern communications. On the contrary, Michaels, also in *The Early Period*, is at pains to emphasize the enormous diversity of rituals and, at one point in his argument, notes that "regional theological tendencies are incorporated into traditional myths to create a mixed genre."

Oddie, in the first chapter of this book, notes some of the common assumptions among Hindu scholars, as well as commonalities in Hindu practices well before the term Hinduism was introduced and became current in the 19th century and in subsequent debate. And yet what becomes clearly apparent among reformers and others involved in subsequent discussion is the lack of agreement as to what Hinduism was all about. Ferrari, who writes on Hinduism and healing, also underlines diversity and lack of agreement among Hindus themselves. He remarks that even now "the deities, religious practices, customs and laws transmitted from Vedic times through textual and oral traditions as well as social conventions are understood in rather different ways across Hindus living in the Subcontinent." Hinduism is, in his opinion, "a fractured tradition emerging from many and diverse cultural stratifications." Furthermore, traditions that may seem to unite Hindus in a common pool of beliefs and practices are, in some cases, a reflection of an even wider world of beliefs and practices among people outside as well as within the subcontinent. For example, and as Schömbucher makes it very clear, spirit possession has had a long history in Europe as well as in India. Thus, while there may have been signs of increasing commonality across India during the precolonial period, there were also commonalties (including beliefs and practices) outside the boundaries of what we now call India.

These are considerations that need to be taken into account when dealing with the question of the emergence of the idea of Hinduism in the late 18th century. How far was there already an actual consciousness or sense of a shared ethos, as well as religious commonality among Hindus prior to the introduction and use of the term by British commentators in the late 18th and early 19th centuries? What effect did the notion of Hinduism have on religious, political, and other developments thereafter? Why is the term now used so widely in the postcolonial situation? Oddie explores these issues in the first chapter in this book that focuses on continuities as well as developments of Hinduism in India in the modern and contemporary periods.

Last, but not the least, are issues of women's status and role in Hinduism. Bowles, Bailey, and Lubin, all have something to say (even if briefly) about the subject, while Lahiri-Roy, in her essay dedicated explicitly to women's issues, explores the complexities and changing character and stresses of urban Hindu arranged marriages in the contemporary society. She argues that "certain traditional patterns are now being rearranged with the onset of urbanization, the influence of Westernisation and increasing levels of female education." But, she concludes, "on certain levels change [in the women's position] has not really occurred so much as the same pattern has merely refashioned itself along different lines."

These chapters illustrate the extraordinary richness of what is now called Hinduism, its religious and cultural diversity, including rituals, asceticism, and forms of devotion that have survived and been readapted to meet new challenges that have emerged throughout a very long history of over two millennia.

To extend even further the readers' sense of the complexity of Hinduism, we have a final chapter in this book by Srivastava on the relationship between Hinduism and caste—one of the basic issues in studies such as these.

Note: While some of the authors in what follows have continued the practice of using diacritics, others have chosen to dispense with the practice, especially when referring to more modern developments.

# Acknowledgments

These books are the result of a long-term and complex process involving close and constructive collaboration between me and all three editors (Greg, Will, and Aditya). Indeed, without the editors' enthusiasm, hard work, and flexibility, these books would never have seen the light of day. I also wish to thank all the contributors from different parts of the world. Many of them are not only researchers but are also busy teachers and administrators. Thanks are also due to Michael Allen for his encouragement and advice during the early stages of this endeavor, and to all those at SAGE Publications in New Delhi who have collaborated with us with suggestions and in the production process. They include Ashok Chandran, Rekha Natarajan, Sutapa Ghosh, and N. Unni Nair. For technical assistance, thanks to Robin Ford. Last but not the least, very special thanks are due to my wife, Nola, for her encouragement, love, and support, for hosting a special weekend meeting between me and all the three editors at Killcare on the central coast in New South Wales during the early stages of this project. I also wish to thank her for her suggestions and proofreading of my own material.

**Geoffrey A. Oddie**

# Chapter 1

## The Emergence and Significance of the Term "Hinduism"

Geoffrey A. Oddie

Implicit in all of the chapters and discussion throughout these books is the ever recurring question of what is "Hinduism"? Bailey's comment that it comprised "a religious, cultural, and social system" provides a solid basis for discussion on its rise and consolidation in early Indian history. And what (more precisely) is meant by "Hinduism" in this sense is the substance of much of what follows in both books. However, the question still remains, when was the term "Hinduism" first used? What did it mean when it was first developed and introduced? And why has the term (apparently not used until the late 18th century) become so popular, sacrosanct, and central in so much of the debate about India's history and society today?

The most widely accepted meaning of the term "Hindu" in the pre-modern period of Indian history was a person or thing of Indian origin. Both words, "Hindu" and "Indian," used interchangeably in some travel accounts, were coined by outsiders. The river Indus was known in Sanskrit as "Sindhu," and the Persians, who found difficulty in pronouncing an initial "s," called it "Hindu"—a word which, as Heinrich von Stietencron explains, was applied "both to the river and to the country through which the Indus flows." Thus, for the Persians the "Hindus" were the local or indigenous inhabitants who lived in the vicinity of the Indus river. Later still, the term Hindu was extended in meaning to include native inhabitants of the entire subcontinent. In the meantime, the Greeks, who invaded and settled in parts of northern India in the 3rd century BCE, coined the word India. Borrowing the Persian word Hindu for the Indus river, they called it Indos and the country through which it flowed, India. Thereafter the terms Hindu and Indian were synonymous, indicating the people and their place of origin, or the things, such as language, customs, or artifacts associated with them.[1]

Subsequent Arab and European travelers and commentators on Indian society had, therefore, a ready-made interchangeable terminology. For example, if the translation is correct, the 8th-century Arab commentator Al Masudi referred to Indians in one part of his description and to Hindus in another (Elliott and Dowson, 1867). This practice was followed by Arab and Muslim travelers' writing about India from the 10th to the 13th centuries (ibid., vol. I: 27, 28, 97, 98) and also by European observers of a later date. Among these were Francois Bernier and Jean Baptiste-Tavernier (the well-known French travelers and commentators on India in the 17th century) and the Englishman, John Ovington, who following the same trend in his account of his visit to Surat in 1689—referred to Indians in some parts of his book and to "Hindoes" in other places (Ovington, 1929).

Use of the term "Hindu" for natives or inhabitants of India, even including Indian Christians, persisted well into the 19th century. In the introduction to his "Lectures on Tinnevelly Missions" delivered in 1857, the well-known bishop and linguist, Robert Caldwell, declared that he would be endeavoring to give a fair estimate of "Hindu Christianity" (Caldwell, 1857 : 14) and in later comments remarked that the Tinnevelly Christian community might be expected to occupy an eminent position hereafter among "Hindu Christians"[2] (ibid.: 65). The term "Hindu Christian" was also adopted by Indian Christians themselves keen to emphasize the Indianness of their faith. For example, in the very first issue of *The Bengal Christian Herald* (first published in 1870), the joint editors Kali Charan Banerjea and J. G. Shome declared that

> In having become Christians, we have not ceased to be Hindus. We are Hindu Christian, as thoroughly Hindu as Christian. We have embraced Christianity, but we have not discarded our nationality. We are as intensely national as any of our brethren of the native press can be. (Baago, 1969)

## Outsider Comments

For a number of non-Indian commentators, and from a very early period, use of the term "Hindu" or "Hindoo" came to imply even more than "native" or "inhabitant of India." It was recognition that Hindus were a distinctive people and led inevitably to further ideas about their having a distinctive culture, including rituals and ways of life. The term therefore began to take on additional and more complex overtones. Indeed, Arvind Sharma, has, for example, argued that there was, from a very early period, a certain degree of ambiguity in the use of the word "Hindu" and that, while one has to acknowledge "the primacy of territorial meaning," at least one early Buddhist traveler in India seems to have used the term "Hindu" with some kind of "religious" connotation (Sharma, 2002).

For some Muslim commentators, the Hindus generally were a classic example of "the other" in a very broad sense—a potent reminder that they were everything Muslims were not. This point was made abundantly clear in the early years of the 11th century by the Muslim scholar and traveler, al-Burini, who accompanied Mahmud into northern India. In his account, al-Burini explained to his readers that they should always bear in mind that "the Hindus entirely differ from us in every respect." They differed from Muslims in their language, and in "all manners and usages … to such a degree as to frighten their children with us, with our dress, our ways and our customs." Furthermore, in al-Burini's view, Muslims believed in nothing in which Hindus believed "and vice versa." And, while Hindus seldom debated theological issues, they directed "all their fanaticism" against all foreigners. "They call them *mleccha*, that is, impure, and forbid having any connection with them, be it by intermarriage or any other kind of relationship, or by sitting, eating, and drinking with them, because thereby they think they would be polluted." Lastly, adverting to what he claimed were the peculiarities of the Hindu "national character," he remarked that

> [w]e can only say, folly is an illness for which there is no medicine, and the Hindus believe that there is no country but theirs, no nation like theirs, no kings like theirs, no religion like theirs, no science like theirs. They are haughty, foolishly vain, self-conceited, and stolid. (Embree, 1971)

For Europeans too, the idea of "the Hindu" was beginning to imply much more than "the inhabitants or people of India." Indeed, a belief that the "Hindus" were the founders of a distinctive *civilization* preceding the Muslim incursions was the basis of considerable

European literature in the 18th and early 19th centuries. Orientalist scholars such as Sir William Jones, Alexander Dow, and William Robertson, and governors and administrators such as John Malcolm and Mountstuart Elphinstone, all thought and wrote about the history of the Hindu people and the nature of Hindu civilization, including their language, religion, and social institutions. But though religion was discussed, the Hindu was not defined solely on the grounds of his or her religious allegiance (Marshall, 1970; Robertson, 1804; Malcolm, 1970; Elphinstone, 1849). The comparison was more between the Hindus and people of other ancient civilizations (such as those of Egypt, Greece, and Rome) than it was between Hindus and the followers of other faiths. In other words, nationality, residence, or citizenship, rather than religion, continued as the primary European focus and basis of definition.

This territorial, racial, and general cultural notion of the Hindu was also reflected in the 19th-century comment (Oddie, 2003) and in English and French dictionary definitions, even when the more limited (specifically religious) idea of the Hindu as "the follower of Hinduism" was becoming increasingly popular. British dictionaries even as late as the middle of the 19th century continued to insist on a basic territorial and racial definition. Thus, according to *Barclay's Universal English Dictionary* published in 1848, Hindus were "the people inhabiting Hindustan, also called gentoos"—gentoo being a Portuguese term for gentile or heathen.[3] In the words of the author of the entry in the *Imperial Dictionary* published in 1851, Hindoo or Hindu referred to "an aboriginal of Hindoostan or Hindostan"[4] (Ogilvie, 1851). However, while these dictionaries limited themselves to the territorial and racial definition, the notion of "the Hindu" in some other references was beginning to change. Colange in *The People's Encyclopedia* published in 1875 described the Hindu as "a native of Hindostan," and in an article on Hindustan, made three further points: (a) the great bulk of the inhabitants of Hindustan are Hindus, (b) they are followers of the Brahmanical religion, and (c) they are separate and different from the Muslims (Colange, 1875). Comment on their religion was an increasingly important ingredient and an indication of the way in which the concept of the Hindu was continuing to develop especially in Britain.

## The Hindu in Hindu Self-understanding

If these are the comments of outsiders, what were the feelings and views of the "Hindus" themselves? To what extent were they developing a self-conscious sense of their own cultural, social, or religious identity? In particular, was there a growing belief that they had common religious traditions or a faith different from that of Europeans and other outsiders?

There has been extensive comment on these issues in recent years, and any detailed analysis of the arguments and evidence advanced is not possible here. Suffice it to say that as a result of the work of a range of scholars, it is now possible to see more clearly general trends and regional variations and to suggest some very tentative conclusions. First, studies focusing on different parts of the subcontinent such as those of Nainar Jagadeesan, von Stietencron, and Sanjay Subrahmanyam have highlighted the extent of religious diversity and fragmentation that appears to have prevailed among people subsequently described as "Hindus" in different parts of the subcontinent prior to the coming of Islam (Jagadeesan, 1997). Especially well documented is the intensity of the Vaishnavite–Saivite conflict in south India, which, it has been argued, is best thought of as between two mutually exclusive and distinctive "religions." Moreover, not only does there appear to have been an absence of Hindu religious unity during the centuries prior to the appearance of Muslims, but according to Andre Wink in particular, when the Muslims first arrived, they collaborated with the locals so that any alliance system that developed tended to cut across the foreign versus indigenous peoples division (Wink, 1990). In other words, rivalry was between class or special interest groups rather than between clearly defined religious communities comprising the incoming "invaders," on the one hand and the local people (Hindus) on the other.

Recent research does, however, suggest that after the initial stages of Islamic conquest and settlement in different parts of India, and for reasons that may or may not be related to the stimulus of these events, Hindu scholars, including those who created Hindu texts, were beginning to develop a sense of Hindu religious unity—at least at a philosophical or intellectual level. In his book *Unifying Hinduism*, Andrew

Nicholson tells the story of what he describes as "a remarkable shift," arguing that the seeds were planted for the now familiar discourse of Hindu unity by a number of influential philosophers in late medieval India (Nicholson, 2010).

Alongside this ongoing philosophical development as described in Nicholson's work was the further pressure of outsiders, encouraging, among all kinds of Hindus, a further sense of the religious difference between themselves as "insiders" or residents of India and the foreigners. This process was accelerated by the introduction of what Cantwell Smith has described as the more formal, rigid, and structured form of Islam, culminating in the policies of Aurangzeb in the 17th century (Smith, 1981). Indeed even before the introduction of these measures that heightened Hindu awareness and helped to undermine the status and position of Hindus within the Mughal administration, there is some evidence that indigenous commentators and writers were beginning to think of themselves as "Hindus." Talbot's work on Telugu inscriptions associated with the rulers of Vijayanagara, Joseph O'Connell's examination of Bengali Gaudiya Vaishnava texts dating from the second half of the 16th century, and Balkrishna Gokhale's discussion of Marathi devotional literature produced during the period of Shivaji's conflict with Mughal rulers, shows that during the 16th and 17th centuries, usage of the term "Hindus" by Hindus was gradually spreading as they began to compare themselves with Islamic intruders (Gokhale, 1984; O'Connell, 1993; Talbot, 1995).

This sense of difference was not always based on what might be described as religious markers—recognition of difference also being based on language, dress, housing, forms of social organization, and so on. O'Connell in his study of the Bengalis' use of the term "Hindu" goes so far as to argue that none of the references to the term really reflect a sense of corporate religious or confessional identity separating Hindus as a whole from the Muslims among them. The result of Gokhale's research on the situation in western India during the period of Shivaji's encounter with Mughal rulers is, however, very different. In his study, Gokhale notes the cumulative effect of Mughal policy on Hindu religious life and practice and the effect this had on Marathi commentators who reflected increasingly their own sense of religious identity and difference that separated them from Muslim opponents. Alongside this research and these developments that are documented especially in Gokhale's study of Hindu responses to the Muslim presence in Maharashtra are comments by insiders such as Kabir (1440–1518) (Vaudeville, 1974: 186) and Guru Arjun (1563–1606) who used the term "Hindu" and "Muslim" in a religious sense but who denied they belonged to either camp (Oberoi, 1994).

While these developments suggest that, at least among some Hindus, there was an emerging consciousness or sense of being Hindu in a religious sense, it is still not clear just how far this consciousness was confined to certain classes or groups of people in the population of people. There were the Hindu scholars, and others influenced by their ideas (the type of people referred to in Nicholson's work) who recognized the connection between different schools of philosophy or practice in different parts of India. And, as we have argued, contact and conflict with outsiders was also an important factor in raising awareness of the importance and value of one's own religious ideas and customs. But how common was contact with outsiders (including Muslims) in the life of ordinary, lower caste, or tribal people throughout the subcontinent? And, what about those who were not well versed in Hindu theology or speculation and who were not participants in the life of "the reflective few"? Scholars may point to phenomena like the great India-wide pilgrim routes throughout the Indian subcontinent and to similarities in Hindu rituals, mythology, and worship in many different parts of the subcontinent.[5] But again similarity in stories, rituals, and practice is not the same thing as "an awareness" that other Hindus all over India speaking different languages were sharing in the same thing. A far greater and more widespread conscious conviction (or feeling) that Hindus all over India were indeed sharing in a similar corpus of tradition, practice, and belief did, however, develop especially among the Western-educated classes during the period of colonial rule. Indeed, to fully understand this growing conviction, including the coining of the term "Hinduism," and its increasing usage by both Europeans and Western-educated Indian elites during the period from Ram Mohan Roy to Independence in 1947 and after, it is necessary to briefly examine developments in Europe—especially during what has been described as the European "Age of Discovery."

## Europe and the Indian Ocean

One of the key European concepts of the 17th and 18th centuries was the idea of religion.[6]

The term religion comes from the Latin *religio*. For the Romans *religio* or religion meant "ceremony, custom, or tradition." Among early Christians, religion was not merely outward practice or custom but implied certain attitudes and belief, especially inner conviction. However, this stress on inner conviction was eventually matched, or even overshadowed, by a long process of objectification—religion became something, which could be expressed objectively in written creeds, doctrine, or stated belief.

This notion was bound up with the idea of a foundational scripture or written text. Each religion was supposed to have its priests or scholars who could interpret and guide its followers.

During the European Enlightenment, religion was thought of (perhaps even more generally) as an objective reality—rather like natural objects (rocks, animals, and plants) that could be explored, compared, and classified through scientific enquiry. A religion was "a system" with shape and boundaries—one religion being clearly divided from another.

An illustration of this approach can be seen in William Carey's influential pamphlet *An Enquiry into the Obligation of Christians to Use Means for the Conversion of the Heathens*, first published in 1793. Carey divides the world among followers of different religions and presents the reader with four basic categories: Judaism, Christianity, Islam, and Heathenism—the latter being seen in Africa, the Americas, and Asia—including Australia and New Zealand (Oddie, 2006: 14).

## Age of Discovery

In the meantime, other developments were taking place as a result of the European discovery and exploration of the new world. As Europeans gained a greater knowledge of new regions and extended their power and influence, especially eastward, their somewhat vague and generalized idea of "Paganism" proved less and less satisfactory. This is because there seemed to be differences between Paganism in for example between India and Africa, or between India and China, or between other regions and the South Sea Islands. Hence, there was an increasing need to differentiate between the different types of Paganism or Heathenism. Ultimately for many early travelers,

readers of the burgeoning genre of travel literature,[7] officials, and
missionaries who were attempting to describe religions in India,
it was not good enough to use unqualified general terms such as
"Paganism" or "Heathenism." What was needed was the evolution
of a further and more precise system of terminology—such as
"Indian paganism," "Hindu idolatry," or "the Hindu system," and
from the notion of an Indian or Hindu system, it was but a small
step to the idea of "Hindooism"—a term that was eventually spelled
as "Hinduism."

## First Use and Significance of the Term "Hindooism" or "Hinduism"

The evidence so far uncovered shows that Europeans (or rather
Britons) used the word "Hindooism" at least 29 years before Ram
Mohan Roy (the first well-known modern Indian reformer) used it in
1816.[8] Charles Grant, an Evangelical and subsequently a Director of
the East India Company, employed the term in a letter written from
Calcutta to a friend in England in 1787. He also used it a number
of times in his well-known *Observations* written in 1792. Grant was
not only a convert to Evangelical Christianity, but was closely allied
with Protestant missionaries, including the Baptist missionaries who
settled in Serampore in 1793. Some years after Grant used the term
"Hindooism" in both his private and official capacity as a Company
employee, William Ward of the Baptist mission employed it in his
diary in 1801. Joshua Marshman, another member of the Serampore
trio, also used it (as an alternative to "the Hindoo system") in his
diary in 1802. Indeed, evidence that Ram Mohan Roy met with
William Yates, another Baptist missionary, in 1815 and visited the
Baptist mission at Serampore in the following year leaves open the
intriguing possibility that he (Ram Mohan Roy) borrowed the term
"Hindooism" from the Baptists.

The adoption and increasing use of the term "Hindooism" (later
Hinduism) was significant especially for the Hindus themselves as it
was a clear acknowledgement by Europeans writers and others that
Indian religion could be compared with the other four religions of

the world. According to Europeans, "Hinduism" was part of the same genus and could be classed with Christianity and other religions. The criteria that applied to Christianity as a religion could also be applied to "Hinduism" as well as to Islam and Judaism. And just as one could define Christianity by its characteristics, one could define "Hinduism" in the same way too. India's religion was therefore acknowledged, even by foreigners, as one of the units in a comparative and global religious approach. Indeed, the emergence of the term "Hindooism" was one further step in the growth of the notion of "comparative religion." In fact, it was the basis of an idea that could be carried even further and used by members of rival Indian elites wanting to establish the superiority of their own particular tradition by claiming for it a status as one of the great "religions of the world." One of the beneficiaries of this idea was, for example, J. M. Nallasvami Pillai (an exponent of *Saiva Siddhanta*). As Bergunder has so clearly shown, Pillai argued that his tradition, as well as Hinduism, could be considered a global and universal religion alongside the other great religions of the world (Bergunder, 2010).

Furthermore, embedded in the notion that Indian religion or "Hinduism" was one among a number of world systems was the idea that it shared with them certain common characteristics. It was first and foremost an objective "system," which like all religious systems was an echo of the Christian model. All religions including "Hinduism" had boundaries that separated them from other rival systems; and marking the boundaries between "Hinduism" and other religions eventually became one of the functions of the census commissioners of a later date. Religions were unified systems internally coherent with parts, which depended on each other, so, for example, "Hinduism" involved inner-workings such as one might find in the workings of a clock—and a missionary like Dr Alexander Duff could argue that if you undermined or destroyed one part of the system, the whole mechanism would cease to function.[9] In all religions, according to this view, there were elites (usually priests) who controlled everything *from the top down.* There were sacred texts or writings (which priests or indigenous scholars could interpret) and there was a belief system or a "creed," including something like an essence or hard core of belief (in the case of "Hinduism," usually "Pantheism") that was its chief characteristic. But also, according to Europeans, religions had their particular institutions and were also responsible for the tone and kind of values permeating society.

While the European idea of "Hinduism" incorporated long held brahmanical views of the overall system, it also introduced less familiar features drawn from Christian experience and history. This was the emphasis on creedal belief. Europeans in the census and other writings often used the term "creed" as a substitute for religion and Indians themselves began to describe "Hinduism" in the same way. Hence, Bengali reformer Debendranath Tagore published in his paper a "confession of faith" and Lala Lajpat Rai (1865–1928) who founded a new branch of the Hindu reform association known as the Arya Samaj, included, in his account of the movement, "Ten Principles to which every Arya is required to subscribe" (Rai, 1967). This he assured his readers is "the simplest of creeds, to which no Hindu, at any rate should have any difficulty in subscribing." Gandhi and other Hindus also used the term "creed" in their speeches and writing.

Furthermore, the European emphasis on "a creed," as one of the central components of religion, began to influence indigenous Indian terminology so that by the end of the century, a term like "dharma" that had come to have almost the same meaning as religion or "religious creed." It is perhaps sufficient to quote the words of Bankimchandra Chatterji, the well-known author and patriot who, writing at the end of the 19th century, declared that "the word dharma has been used with different meanings. Several of the meanings have no use for us. The meaning in which you now use the word dharma that is simply a modern translation of the English word Religion. It is no indigenous thing" (Brekke, 1999) [10]

In addition to the influence that the idea of "Hinduism" had on indigenous concepts associated with religion, was its importance for individual as well as corporate identity. It gave to Hindus, especially to those who were becoming better educated, a fresh new India-wide sense of identity—a stronger sense of belonging to an India-wide movement, which could be compared with other systems elsewhere. Individuals became proud of being "Hindu" in a religious sense, even though they were not necessarily sure of its meaning.[11] Indeed, it might even be argued that the term helped unite Hindus in feeling and sentiment in a way they hadn't been united before. And yet, paradoxically, and at the same time, it also created division. While, on the one hand, Hindu leaders in the newly emerging colonial society all felt they were followers or even champions of "Hinduism," they disagreed, sometimes vehemently, as to what it really meant. Indeed, use of the term played an important part in the process of sectional religious, political, and other forms of mobilization. It was a deep-seated and sometimes emotive label that could easily be used as a tool or slogan by both Indians and Europeans in propaganda and in efforts to gain support and influence others. As V. D. Savarkar, a consummate propagandist and exponent of the idea of "Hindutva," pointed out, "When various things get mystically entwined with the word that signifies it, the name seems to matter as much as the thing itself" (Savarkar, 1942).

When out preaching and in their books and pamphlets, missionaries used the term for comparative purposes, comparing Christianity with "Hinduism" to the detriment of the latter.[12] In Britain and the USA, the term was also a very effective instrument in propaganda— missionary societies for much of the 19th century contrasting all that was diabolical in "Hinduism" with the purity of the Christian faith. A constant stream of missionary material representing "Hinduism" as something like a chamber of horrors, underlined the urgent need for social reform and evangelism that would save the poor heathen from the consequences of a truly horrific religious system.[13] Furthermore, the perceived contrast between "Hinduism" and Christianity was one of the factors that encouraged young men and women to participate in missionary activities.

East India Company officials used the term to consolidate British rule along the lines suggested by the editors of *The Invention of Religion* (2002) when they observe that colonial officials formalized religious practices and doctrines "in order to define political constituencies and claim authority" (Peterson and Walhof, 2002). In India many of them thought of "Hinduism" as Brahmanism, and could bask in the idea that they were not only consolidating British rule but were helping to forge a grand India-wide unity symbolized by "Hinduism." This was to be done through the maintenance of Hindu temples and ceremonial and by endorsing the efforts of scholars dedicated to uncovering and explaining "Hinduism's" ancient teachings.

# Use of the Term in Ongoing Hindu Public Controversy

As noted in earlier comments, the term "Hinduism" had its special uses in different types of conflict within Indian society. In the first place, the Brahmans had their own reasons for welcoming a greater use of this type of terminology. They could argue that of course they were the custodians of India's entire religion, namely "Hinduism," and that they knew what its texts and tenets were, and what needed to be preserved in Hindu tradition. Indeed, the increasing use of the term, together with the widespread assumption that "Hinduism" was in fact "Brahmanism," probably strengthened the overall control of the Brahman elite who were so often the consultants employed in socio-religious as well as legal affairs.

Second, there was the increasing ease with which Hindu religious and political leaders more generally used the term "Hinduism" in their bid for power and support and in the elimination of rivals. Two trends are clearly apparent from the time of Ram Mohan Roy through to Independence. One tendency was to take the high ground and claim that one's own particular version of "Hinduism" was the correct one and that all other versions were wrong. The other approach was to brush over differences and use the idea of "Hinduism" to unify all Hindus in the struggle against the missionaries and British rule.

1. *Divisive religious models.* Ram Mohan Roy, who founded the Brahmo Samaj in 1828, drew a distinction between the "real Hindooism," which he promoted through his reform movement and "the superstitious practices that deformed the Hindoo religion," and that had nothing to do with "the pure spirit of its dictates."[14] Lala Lajpat Rai, one of the leaders of the Arya Samaj founded in 1875, was equally emphatic in claiming to represent the true form of "Hinduism," while Gandhi, who was not always thought of as a religious reformer, also developed his own special definition of "Hinduism." Indeed it was his idea of "Hinduism" as moral action which, as Jordens has argued,

distinguished him from many other Hindus involved in the nationalist movement.[15] The particular and crucial moments during which his adherence to his own model of "Hinduism" furthered division rather than building unity among Hindus are a topic for further investigation.

2. *Unifying models.* In contrast to these more divisive models was the notion of an inclusive and all-India religious system, which could be used to unite people against foreign missionary intervention and also colonial rule. One example of this approach can be seen in pamphlets published by the Hindu Tract Society. An aggressive and increasingly influential organization founded in Madras in 1887 to defend "Hinduism" against Christian missionaries, it placed a great deal of emphasis on the need for unity. For example, the writer of Tamil tract No. 2 asked readers if the missionaries converted Moslems to Christianity. Replying to his own question he remarked that

> the Moslems realize that the danger to the Moslem is a danger to all of them and thus safeguard their religion. Is it not due to this realization and unity among them that the Moslems are not converted to Christianity ... Hereafter Hindus should not fight among themselves, calling themselves Thenkalais, Vadakalais, Saivites, Vaishnavites, Advaitins, Visistavaitins and Dvaitins; they should act as one man and oppose the Christian religion.[16]

As is well known, Vivekananda also used the idea of "Hinduism" in his campaigns in ways that tended to unify Hindus of all traditions and from all walks of life.[17] His central message, emphasizing the universality of the Hindus' spiritual yearning for God, irrespective of social status or religious sophistication, not only eliminated differences within "Hinduism," but nurtured in Hindus a sense of pride that European colonizers and even Christian missionaries could learn from them.

Finally, there were at least two general developments encouraging the high caste Hindus' sense of belonging to "Hinduism" and the need to defend it from all its enemies.

One of these was an ongoing conflict with Christian missionaries and fear of conversion especially through mission schools. In the mid-19th century, for example, the conversion of high caste individuals, usually young men in mission schools, created enormous upheaval and ferment especially in cities such as Calcutta, Bombay, and Madras. The local English language papers were increasingly concerned with the task of defending what they described as "Hinduism."[18] Furthermore, this fear of conversion was heightened by a suspicion that the colonial government itself was implicated in a sinister attempt to bring "Hinduism" crashing down. Measures such as the suppression of sati, legislation giving converts the right to retain ancestral property, and the attempted introduction of the Bible in government schools were seen by some Hindus as a widespread and common threat and solid proof of the government's evil intention of destroying what was now coming to be called "Hinduism." Newspapers, tracts, and pamphlets all tended to reflect this new polarity between Christianity on the one hand and "Hinduism" on the other.

Another factor in heightening communal awareness and in promoting the idea of an India-wide "Hinduism" was the introduction of the Census in British territory in 1871 and also into the Princely states 10 years later.

Religions were classified in the usual British way—the people being put in boxes and clearly divided from one another. There were now clear lines of division between people of different religions.

The method of counting Hindus in particular was highly problematic. According to the Census Commissioner in 1891, this was done through "the process of successive exclusion" whereby "Hinduism" was defined as "the large residuum that is not Sikh, or Jain, or Buddhist, or professedly animistic, or included in one of the foreign religions, such as Islam, Mazdaism [Zoroastrianism], Christianity or Hebraism."[19]

But in spite of their problematic nature, especially of the figures on the number of Hindus, the returns were taken very seriously by a growing number of politically conscious Hindus in the 1920s and 1930s. They became increasingly alarmed by figures that seemed to suggest a decline in the number of Hindus as a result of conversion to Christianity and Islam. One outcome of this was the establishment of the All-India Hindu Mahasabha. It was founded in 1915 specifically to defend Hindu interests and in opposition to the secular and religiously inclusive Indian National Congress.[20]

But while there were Hindus who were becoming increasingly conscious of the need to defend "Hinduism," there were still millions of others who didn't know what "Hinduism" was all about. Indeed, it appears to have been the higher castes and educated (and usually urban classes) who were those mostly influenced by British categories and the notion of religion.

In his introduction to the Madras Census of 1921, the Census Commissioner remarked that

> the chief hindrance to the obtaining of accurate returns is the fact that the terms used to classify the religions are unfamiliar to the people of the country, and do not really suggest what is meant in common parlance by religion. The worst instances are the terms "Hindu" and "Animist". No Indian is familiar with the term "Hindu" as applied to his religion. If asked what his religion is, he usually replies with the name of the sect (e.g., Saivite), to which he belongs ... the word "Hindu" implies not only certain religious beliefs but also a certain nationality and almost necessarily a certain social organization.[21]

## Postcolonial Debates and Ideas of Hinduism

Since Independence, the idea of being "Hindu" or of "Hinduism" has remained problematic—the meaning of these concepts being hotly debated not only among scholars but also among Indian people more generally—for practical as well as for religious and other reasons.

One practical issue has been the new central government's criteria for assisting the "backward" sections in Indian society through what is sometimes called a policy of "compensatory discrimination."[22] The new rules involving an assessment of who is or is not a Hindu were applied to both the scheduled castes (including people who are now called *dalits*) and the scheduled tribes. The most frequent and widespread disputes have been in relation to both central government and, more recently, state government policies of educational and other forms of assistance for *dalits*. While Hindus, Sikhs, and now Buddhists are considered eligible for grants, Christians and Muslims are not (Smith, 1981: 234; Oliver and Vicziany, 1998). This means that unless several million Christian *dalits* and many more millions of

Muslim *dalits* declare themselves "Hindus," they are in no position to receive assistance.[23] This policy, which has been described as essentially "discriminatory," has in recent years been somewhat modified in some parts of the subcontinent. But the essential point here is that for very practical reasons one's stated religious affiliation, including the term "Hindu," has now become even more important than it was under colonial rule.[24]

In the meantime, some tribals (now *adivasis*) have also been politically active—resisting the way they are represented as Hindus in the Census. In 1951, the government of India dropped the separate category for "tribals," listing them as "Hindus": a practice that has been followed ever since.[25] This change in official policy has focused further attention on the question of how far the various tribal groups do in fact think of themselves as "Hindus" or followers of "Hinduism." Referring to the results of his recent research in Jharkhand, in central India, the anthropologist Alpa Shah (2010) notes that "Fearful of the Hindu nationalists who seek to incorporate *adivasis* into mainstream Hinduism, Jharkhandi activists have been ... promoting a separate indigenous religion comparable to Christianity, Islam, and Hinduism that is sometimes called Sarn and sometimes Adi-dharam". The persistent rejection of what some tribals regard as a false category is also reflected in one of the more recent incidents when representatives of some *adivasi* organizations met in West Bengal in January 2011. They demanded that a distinctive religious code be organized for them in the census—some of them claiming, for example, to be followers of Sari Dhorom or some other tribal (non-Hindu) religion.

Apart from the census and these practical issues, a second development, much of it since Independence, has been the increasing level of debate, especially among both Indian and non-Indian scholars (anthropologists and others) interested in the nature and boundaries of "Hinduism" in its postcolonial or contemporary environment. Even if there is still no consensus, these controversies have certainly helped refine new ways of looking at the phenomena as a whole. Redfield's thesis that civilizations, as distinct from primitive societies and cultures, are made up of distinctive but interrelated parts is widely accepted and reflected in the notion of "the great" and "little tradition"—the great tradition being associated with the specialists and dominant elite and the little tradition with the peasantry and "unreflective" many. This idea of levels is also reflected in the work of M. N. Srinivas (a brahman) who put forward his well-known thesis involving what he described as the process of "Sanscritization" whereby tribals and lower caste Hindus adopt the practices and beliefs of higher caste Hindus. While there can be little doubt that this process is continuing to happen, commentators would do well to reflect on the opposite process whereby tribals or lower caste Hindus influence religious ideas and rituals from below (Hardiman, 1987). One clear example of this was the practice of "hook-swinging" in the 19th century (Oddie, 1995). Though it was apparently introduced in a much earlier period and practised very largely by tribals and lower caste Hindus, it was eventually adopted and performed by some higher caste Hindus.

Among other somewhat different attempts to overcome difficulties in defining "Hinduism" Heinrich von Stietencron stresses, not the notion of levels in Hinduism, but the idea of separate parts. He writes,

> [w]hat we call Hinduism, is a geographically defined group of distinct but related religions, that originated in the same region, developed under similar socio-economic and political conditions, incorporated largely the same traditions, influenced each other continuously, and jointly contributed to the Hindu culture. Therefore, it is only by distinguishing the various Hindu religions from "Hinduism" that comparability with other historical religions can be ensured. (Sontheimer and Kulke, 1991)

While this is certainly a helpful way of looking at the different Hindu religious traditions, it raises the question of what is meant by "Hindu culture" and how one distinguishes Hindu culture from Indian culture more generally. How does Hindu culture differ from Christian and Muslim culture in India? If, for example, Muslims recite some of the same folk tales as Hindus, does this make them Hindus?[26] And what of Christian theologians and others who incorporate Hindu practices in their forms of worship?[27] There may be certain common forms of culture in India, but this doesn't necessarily make them "Hindu" in a strictly religious sense.

A third development, and one that is especially important for the way in which Indian people perceive themselves and interpret notions of "Hindu" and "Hinduism," is the breath-taking scale and rapidity of social, economic, and other changes. As a result of increasing literacy, improvements in road and rail connections, the activity of modern political parties (which debate aspects of Hinduism as well as Hindutva), and especially the revolution in communications, including the use of television and mobile phones, the isolation endured by village people is rapidly breaking down. Issues of identity or self-definition in an increasingly complex (even amorphous) world are perhaps more important than ever. Indeed one suspects that when the census takers recently revisited the villages and asked the usual question about religious affiliation (for the Census of 2011), there was a higher proportion of people either *conscious* of being "Hindu" in a religious sense or familiar with the term than there had been when the Madras census was taken in 1921. It is also likely that the term "Hinduism," once largely restricted to the Indian elites, is now much more widely known and used among ordinary people.

## Notes

1. For these and other details, see especially Basham (1954, 1975). See also Von Stietencron (1991).
2. The term "Hindoo Christian" was also used by non-Christian Hindus in a petition published in *UK Parliamentary Papers, Commons* 436(27): 1852–1853.
3. For comments on the meaning of the term "Gentoo," see especially Grose (1772) and Hamilton (1828).
4. The similarity in the meaning of "Hindu" and "Indian" is implied in other contemporary observations. Thus according to James Forbes, author of *Oriental Memoirs.* (1834) the "Hindoos" were "the aborigines of Hindostan," vol. 1, p. 236 (London: Bentley).
5. For comment on Hindu mythology, see *Hinduism in India: The Early Period*, Chapter 3.
6. See especially Smith (1991), Harrison (1999), Oddie (2006).
7. For readers of travel literature which illustrated and discussed different forms of "Paganism" see especially, Masuzava (2005).
8. For the details which follow see especially Oddie (2006: 71–72, 171) and Killingley, Dermot. 1993. *Rammohan Roy in Hindu and Christian Tradition*, the Teape Lectures (1990) Newcastle upon Tyne: Grevatt and Grevatt, Ch. 4.
9. On Duff's views of Hinduism, see especially Oddie (2006), Ch. 6.
10. See also Oddie in Frykenberg (2003: 163).
11. On one occasion at the University of Sydney one of the Indian students said to me "Sir, I'm a Hindu, but tell me, what do I believe?" He was proud to be a follower of "Hinduism" even though he was not sure what it was.

12. Oddie in Frykenberg: 164–166. However, it needs to be kept in mind that not all Protestant missionaries either propounded or shared in these views. For missionary criticisms of the dominant view that Hindus shared one holistic system, see, for example, the remarks of Robert Caldwell in Oddie (2006), Ch. 9.
13. See especially "Hinduism in Missionary Society Literature," in Oddie (2006), Ch. 7.
14. Killingley, op. cit.
15. See especially Jordens (1998).
16. Tamil Tract, No. 2, July 1887, "What Hindus Should Carefully Consider," Hindu Tract Society Pamphlets: Theosophical Society Archives, Adayar, Chennai.
17. *The Complete Works of Swami Vivekananda*, Calcutta: 1958–1963. See especially his address on "Hinduism" at the Parliament of Religions, vol. 1, pp. 6–21.
18. See especially, Oddie in Frykenberg (2003: 166–173).
19. *Census of India*, 1891, Vol. 1, India, Report, 157. The same problems and method of exclusion were referred to in the Census of 1921. See *Census of India*, 1921, Vol. 1, India, Report, 108–113.
20. For the origin and meetings of the Hindu Mahasabha, see especially the *Indian Annual Register*, 1924–1940.
21. *Census of India*, 1921, Vol. X111, Madras, Part 1, Report, p. 57.
22. For details, see especially Webster (2009).
23. For Christian reactions to this policy, see, for example, *Christianity Today*, February 9, 2011.
24. In his otherwise impressive study of popular Hinduism and Society in India during the postcolonial period, Christopher Fuller (like many others) is unquestioning in his attitude toward census figures on the number and proportion of Hindus in India's population in 1981 and somewhat later (see Fuller, 2004). However, what is not known and needs to be established, is the actual number of Christian and Muslim *dalits*—perhaps millions—who, for the sake of social and other benefits, declare themselves "Hindus" in the official records.
25. From 1881 to the Census of 1911 there was a separate category for "Primitive" who in 1911 were said to represent nearly 3.24 percent of India's total population. In the census of 1921 this category was abolished being replaced by "Tribal." In 1941 "Tribal" became "Tribes" when it was claimed that they numbered more than 25 million representing 6.59 percent of the total population. See Oddie (1991).
26. See Malik's findings as reported in this book.
27. See especially Baago, Kaj, op.cit. and Boyd (1969).

# References

Baago, Kaj. 1969. *Pioneers of Indigenous Christianity*, 3. Bangalore: Christian Institute for the Study of Religion and Society.
*Barclay's Universal English Dictionary* (New Ed.). 1848. London: James S. Virtue.
Basham, A. L. 1954. *The Wonder That Was India*, vol. 1, 1. London: Sidgwick and Jackson.

Basham, A. L. (ed.). 1975. *A Cultural History of India*, vol. vii. Oxford: Clarendon Press.

Bergunder, M. 2010. "Saiva Siddhanta as a Universal Religion: J. M. Nallasvami Pillai (1864–1920)" and "Hinduism in Colonial South India." In Michael Bergunder, Heiko Frese, and Ulrike Schroder (eds), *Ritual, Caste and Religion in Colonial India*. Verlag: Halle.

Brekke, T. 1999. "The Conceptual Foundation of Missionary Hinduism." *Journal of Religious History* 23: 203–214.

Boyd, R. 1969. *An Introduction to Indian Christian Theology*. Madras: The Christian Literature Society.

Caldwell, R. 1857. *Lectures on Tinnevelly Missions*, 14. London: R. Clay.

Colange, L. (ed.). 1875. *The People's Encyclopedia*. London: John G. Murdoch.

Elliott, H. M. and J. Dowson. 1867. *The History of India as Told by Its Own Historians*, vol. 1, 19–20. London: Trubner & Co.

Elphinstone, M. [1841] 1849. *The History of India* (3rd ed.). London: John Murray.

Embree, Ainslie T. 1971. *Alberuni's India* (Tr. Edward C. Sachau), Abridged edition, 17–22. New York: Norton, W.W. & Co.

Frykenberg, R. E. (ed). 2003. *Christians and Missionaries in India: Cross-cultural Communications since 1500*, 155–182. Michigan: Eerdmans.

Fuller, C. J. 2004. *The Camphor Flame. Popular Hinduism and Society in India*, Revised and expanded edition, 5. Princeton and Oxford: Princeton University Press.

Gokhale, Balkrishna Govind. 1984. "Hindu Responses to the Muslim Presence in Maharashtra." In Yohanan Friedmann (ed.), *Islam in Asia*, vol. 1, 146–173. Colorado: Boulder.

Grose, J. H. 1772. *A Voyage to the East Indies*, 231. London: (Printed for S. Hooper).

Hamilton, W. 1828. *The East India Gazetteer*, vol. 2, 724. London: (Printed for Parbury, Allen).

Hardiman, David. 1987. *The Coming of the Devi: Adivasi Assertion in Western India*, 82. New Delhi: Oxford University Press.

Harrison, P. 1999. *"Religion" and Religions in the English Enlightenment*. Cambridge: Cambridge University Press.

Jagadeesan, N. 1997. *History of Sri Vaishnavism in the Tamil Country (Post-Ramanuja)*, 230–239. Madurai: Koodal.

Jordens, J. F. T. 1998. *Gandhi's Religion: A Homespun Shawl*, Ch. 3–4. New York: St Martin's Press.

Malcolm, John. [1823] 1970. *A Memoir of Central India*, 2 vols. Delhi: Sagar Publications.

Marshall, P. J. (ed.). 1970. *The British Discovery of Hinduism in the Eighteenth Century*. Cambridge: Cambridge University Press.

Masuzava, Tomoko. 2005. *The Invention of World Religions or How European Universalism Was Preserved in the Language of Pluralism*, 48–63. Chicago and London: University of Chicago Press.

Nicholson, Andrew J. 2010. *Unifying Hinduism: Philosophy and Identity in Indian Intellectual History*, Paperback edition, 2014. New York: Columbia University Press.

Oberoi, Harjot. 1994. *The Construction of Religious Boundaries: Culture, Identity and Diversity in the Sikh Tradition*, 57. New Delhi: Oxford University Press.

O'Connell, Joseph T. 1993. "The Word Hindu in Gaudiya Vaishnava Texts." *Journal of the American Oriental Society* 93(3): 340–344.

22    Geoffrey A. Oddie

Oddie, G. A. (ed.). 1991. *Religion in South Asia*, Second Revised & Enlarged Edition, 256–260. New Delhi: Manohar.

———. 1995. *Popular Religion, Elites and Reform: Hook-Swinging and Its Prohibition in Colonial India, 1800–1994*. New Delhi: Manohar.

———. 2003. "Constructing 'Hinduism': The Impact of the Protestant Missionary Movement on Hindu Self-Understanding." In R. E. Frykenberg (ed.). *Christians and Missionaries in India: Cross-cultural Communications since 1500*, 155–182. Michigan: Eerdmans.

———. 2006. *Imagined Hinduism: British Protestant Missionary Constructions of Hinduism, 1793–1900*, Ch. 1. Delhi: SAGE Publications.

Oliver, M. and M. Vicziany. 1998. *The Untouchables. Subordination, Poverty and the State in Modern India*, Ch. 4 and Ch. 7, p. 234. Cambridge: Cambridge University Press.

Ovington, J. 1929. *A Voyage to Surat in the Year 1689*, 85, 183, 190, 195, 199, 201, 204, 220. London: Oxford University Press.

Peterson, D. R. and D. R. Walhof (eds). 2002. *The Invention of Religion. Rethinking Belief in Politics and History*. New Brunswick, New Jersey, and London: Rutgers University Press.

Rai, L. 1967. *A History of the Arya Samaj*, Revised, Expanded and Edited by Sri Ram Sharma, 79–80. Bombay: Orient Longmans.

Robertson, William. [1791] 1804. *An Historical Disquisition Concerning the Knowledge Which the Ancients Had of India* (4th ed.) London: T. Cadell and W. Davies.

Savarkar, V. D. 1942. *Hindutva*, 2nd ed. Pune: World Book Centre.

Shah, A. 2010. *In the Shadows of the State. Indigenous Politics, Environmentalism, and Insurgency in Jharkhand, India*, 109. Durham and London: Duke University Press.

Sharma, Arvind. 2002. "On Hindu, Hindustan, Hinduism and Hindutva." *Numan* 49: 1–36.

Smith, Wilfred Cantwell. 1981. "The Crystallization of Religious Communities in Mughal India." In his *On Understanding Islam: Selected* Studies, 177–196. The Hague and New York: Mouton Publishers.

Smith, W. C. 1991. *The Meaning and End of Religion*, Ch. 1–3. Minneapolis: Fortress Press.

Sontheimer, G. D. and H. Kulke (eds). 1991. *Hinduism Reconsidered*, 20. New Delhi: Manohar.

Talbot, C. 1995. "Inscribing the Self: Hindu Muslim Identities in Pre-Colonial India." *Comparative Studies in Society and History* 37(4): 699.

Thapar, Romila. 2002. *Early India from the Origins to AD 1300*, xxix, 438–440. New Delhi: Penguin Books.

Vaudeville, Charlotte. 1974. *Kabir*, vol. 1, translated from Hindi with an introduction and notes. New Delhi: Oxford University Press.

Von Stietencron, Heinrich. 1991. "Hinduism: On the Proper Use of a Deceptive Term" and Frykenberg, R. E., "The Emergence of Modern Hinduism." In G. D. Sontheimer and H. Kulke (eds), *Hinduism Reconsidered*, 11–12 , 30. New Delhi: Manohar.

Webster, J. C. B. 2009. *The Dalit Christians: A History*, 4th ed, Ch. 4. Delhi: ISPCK.

Wink, A. 1990. *Al-Hind: The Making of the Indo-Islamic World*, vol. 1, *Early Medieval India and the Expansion of Islam 7th to 11th Centuries*, 196–201. New Delhi: Oxford University Press.

# Chapter 2

## Hinduism and Modernity

Will Sweetman

All religions change over time, but in the modern period the pace of change has accelerated greatly. While never static, Hinduism has changed more rapidly in the last two centuries than in the preceding two millennia. In this section of the book, Tim Lubin, Thomas Birtchnell, Robert E. Frykenberg, and Ursula Rao examine how these changes have played out in the realms of law, economics, politics, and the media, and Michael J. Spurr examines the role in the modern period of the gurus who have often been at the forefront of changes in Hindu practice.[1] This introduction will set the scene for their chapters by considering some aspects of the modern world, which have provoked profound shifts in Hindu thought and practice. For India in the modern period, it is inevitable that we should have to consider the impact of colonialism upon the forms of Hindu practice. Similarly, although migration—both within and beyond India—has long been a factor shaping Hinduism, migration of Hindus in the modern period, often facilitated by colonialism, has occurred on an unprecedented scale and it is therefore important to examine the consequences, particularly within the Hindu diaspora in Asia.

## Colonialism

The British East India Company first gained power in Bengal in the second half of the 18th century and gradually extended their control across India. For a period of almost two centuries, the British were the dominant political force in India. This had profound implications for Hinduism, not least because the king had traditionally played an important role in Hindu religion. At Independence in 1947, the Indian subcontinent was divided along religious lines, with the creation of the Muslim states of Pakistan and Bangladesh. The legacy of colonial division has also been important within India itself, as we shall see, and so the effects of colonialism on Hinduism have endured beyond the end of the colonial period.

The emphasis on the importance of colonial rule and its effects carries with it the danger of neglecting other causes of change in the modern period. In the modern period, there has been a strong tendency for both Hindus and others to present Hinduism as an ancient and unchanging tradition. When colonial rule was being established in the late 18th century, European observers often represented Hinduism as an ancient religion whose development had been arrested at an early stage, so that it had failed to progress in the way that other religions had. Modern Hindus often refer to Hinduism as *sanātana dharma*, translating *sanātana* as "eternal" and emphasizing its unchanging essential character. Ironically, the widespread use of the expression in this sense is itself a modern phenomenon. While the expression appears in ancient sources, it is only in the 19th century that it came to be used as a way of referring to Hinduism as a religion (Halbfass, 1988: 344), and those who popularized the terms were in fact very active in reformulating Hinduism in response to the challenges of the modern world (Dalmia, 1997: 2; cf. Zavos, 2001).

This image of Hinduism as unchanging, or unchanged until the onslaught of colonialism, does not cohere with the historical evidence. For example, around the turn of the 16th century, three teachers had emerged in different parts of India, and founded movements that changed the religious landscape of India not only then, but also subsequently. In Bengal the Vaiṣṇava teacher Caitanya (1486–1533) revived devotion to Viṣṇu; in western India, in Gujarat and the surrounding states, Vallabhācārya (1473–1531) founded another Vaiṣṇava bhakti tradition and at the same time the first Sikh Guru, Guru Nānak (1469–1539) was active in Punjab. Andrew Nicholson has recently argued that one important development that has widely been taken to be an effect of colonial rule—the idea of Hinduism as a unified religion—was in fact already underway in the work of late medieval Hindu doxographers who sought to defend the unity of orthodox Hindu philosophical traditions over against Jain and Buddhist heterodoxies (Nicholson, 2010).

Not only is colonialism not the only source of change, but its effects—and those of Caitanya, Vallabhācārya, Nānak and the doxographers—were also limited, and in many places Hindus continued to carry out rituals according to centuries-old handbooks and to express devotion in ways, which would be recognizable to the compilers of those texts. There are important parallels in Hindu thought between the god and the king, and the same word, *deva*, is used to refer to both. The supreme deity is often imagined as the king of the gods, with other deities forming his court. The rituals for anointing a human king are similar to those for consecrating a divine image, and the king's role in upholding order and ensuring divine protection of the kingdom depended in part on his place as the patron of ritual. The displacement of the king by colonial rulers and then by the secular government of independent India therefore had a profound impact on Hinduism.

It is important to note, however, that in many parts of India, Hindu kings had already been displaced earlier by Muslim rulers. A series of Muslim rulers of Turkish and Central Asian origin had begun conquering parts of north India from the 11th century. By the 13th century, their successors had established the Delhi Sultanate, which was to dominate much of India until the rise of the Mughals in the 16th century. While Hindu kingdoms survived in some parts of India, notably the south, for many parts of India rule by non-Hindus had been the norm for centuries.

To differing degrees, the Mughals had taken on aspects of the traditional ritual functions of Hindu kings, and when in the 18th century the British began to emerge as the dominant force in India they too took on some of these roles. From the late 17th century onward, Company officials in Madras participated in public religious festivals, processing through the streets together with local notables in the manner of both Hindu gods and kings (Frykenberg, 2000: 6).[2] The Company also seems to have made attempts to legitimize its rule by invoking traditional authorities. Coins minted by the Company in Madras from the mid-17th century bore an image of Śrī Veṅkaṭēśwara, the form of Viṣṇu worshipped at the great temple at Tirupati to the north of Madras. The coin was known as a "pagoda" from a Portuguese word which, while its derivation is obscure, was also widely used to refer to Hindu temples (Deyell and Frykenberg, 1982). An 18th-century Sanskrit document includes Europeans among those who made endowments to temples in Madras (Frykenberg, 1988). In 1805, the Company agreed to requests from officials and priests of the Jagannāth temple in Orissa, recently added to the Company's territories, to administer a tax on pilgrims to the temple as the Mughals and Marathas had done before them (Cassels, 1972).[3] In the following decade, the Company passed regulations in both Bengal (1810) and the south (1817) making it responsible for the administration of all public religious institutions—from temples and monasteries to pilgrim rest houses—and the endowments, which supported them. While the regulations required only that the Company's agents ensure that the endowments were properly managed and applied to those purposes for which they had been intended by those who established them, in practice this meant that the Company became responsible for superintending the management of tens of thousands of temples and other religious institutions (Frykenberg, 2000: 8–9).

As the Company's territorial possessions and administrative responsibilities had grown in the later part of the 18th century, its leaders had become convinced that the loyalty of its Hindu and Muslim subjects depended upon the assurance of freedom in the exercise of their religion. In 1772, the first Governor General of Bengal, Warren Hastings, recommended that Hindus and Muslims should be governed according to their own laws in matters of marriage, inheritance and religion, and this became law from 1780 (Rocher, 1993). Subsequent Governor Generals extended and reaffirmed this policy of "non-interference." This policy was nevertheless to have a number of important, if indirect, consequences for Hindus.

In order to be able to administer Hindu law, Hastings commissioned a group of Hindu scholars to produce a summary of the principles of Hindu law contained in the *dharmaśāstras*. A group of Hindu scholars prepared a Sanskrit document, which was then summarized in Persian, the language of Mughal administration, before being translated into English in 1776. This text marked the beginning of a series of scholarly works undertaken with the support of the Company and in pursuit of its goals. It was followed in 1794 by a direct translation from Sanskrit into English of the *Mānavadharmaśāstra* by a judge of the Supreme Court at Calcutta, William Jones. Jones, famously, complained at having to rely in administering Hindu law on the advice of Hindu scholars whom he believed to be biased, and therefore learned Sanskrit in order to be able to read Hindu law for himself.

While the nature of these texts made them unsuitable for the practical administration of law, they represent a shift from oral authority (and the authority of custom) to written and printed authority, which was to have important consequences not only for Hindu law but for Hindu religious practice as a whole. Davis notes that in classical and medieval India, the "first order of practical legal discourse" was ācāra, customary law, and not the texts of Dharmaśāstra (Davis, 2008). Rocher argues that the accepted customs that constituted ācāra were preserved orally in the form of precepts in the vernaculars of different regions. Although these sayings are the ultimate source of the often contradictory collections of statements on different topics in the Sanskrit Dharmaśāstra, Rocher argues that the dharmaśāstras were "divorced from the practical administration of justice" (Rocher, 1993: 267). Thus the British despite attempting to administer Indian law in the manner in which they believed their Indian predecessors had done, in fact elevated the dharmaśāstras to a position that they had never previously held. While the practical difficulties in ruling by Dharmaśāstra meant that in fact it was not until 1864 that the British were able to dispense with the services of the Hindu scholars whom Jones so mistrusted, nevertheless the new primacy of textual authority was of the greatest importance as we shall see below in relation to the debates on satī.[4]

The formal study of Indian religious and legal literature by Britons in the employ of the East India Company also had another equally important, if less direct, impact on Hinduism. The works of Jones and others in his circle inaugurated a tradition of formal study of Hinduism, which was to change the Hindus' understanding of their own past. The picture of Indian religious history, which eventually emerged from this tradition of study, has been influential even among the many modern Hindus who reject some of its basic features.

Frykenberg has argued that the Company's involvement in the administration of Hindu temples, the codification of Hindu laws and other sacred texts, helped create Hinduism as a public religion, and one that was "heavily brahmanical in its orientation," not least because the textual tradition, which it privileged was largely brahmanical (Frykenberg, 2000: 11).He concludes that the "euphemism of "religious neutrality" (or "non-interference")" masked a de facto "Hindu Raj" (Frykenberg, 2006). In the early decades of the 19th century, there was certainly a growing body of opinion in Britain that saw matters in this light, regarding the Company's involvement with Hinduism as a "connexion with idolatry" intolerable for a Christian government. Since the late 1780s, the Company had resisted efforts to require it to provide official support for Protestant missions in India. As the campaign gathered strength after the turn of the century, its supporters increasingly drew attention to aspects of Hindu practice tolerated by the Company, which they knew would excite disapproval at home. The pitch of debate was raised considerably following the shock of the Vellore Mutiny in 1806, which resulted in the death of about a hundred Europeans. Although the immediate cause of the mutiny by Indian soldiers in the Company's Vellore garrison in Tamil Nadu was changes in dress regulations, the Court of Directors found that the deeper cause was the troops' fear that "the next step would be, to force them to become Christians."[5] Opponents of missionary activity were quick to point out that any sign of official support for missionaries would give credence to these fears. Missionaries and their supporters responded vigorously, giving rise to a pamphlet war in which the Company's involvement with Hinduism was subjected to intense scrutiny (Fisch, 1985).

In 1811 Claudius Buchanan, a former chaplain to the Company in Bengal, published an account of his travels in India, which contrasted the "obscene" and bloody rites of Hindus in Bengal with the "moral conduct, upright dealing, and decorous manners of the native Christians" converted by German missionaries in south India (Claudius, 1811). His lurid account of the death of a Hindu who had sacrificed himself beneath the wheels of the huge festival car of the Jagannāth temple concludes by noting that the temple remained a source of revenue for the East India Company, demonstrated by an extract from the official accounts of the temple's expenses. An eyewitness account of the burning of three wives of a Brahman, one of whom had to be carried to the pyre, concludes by laying the blame on the Company for their acquiescence, claiming that their Muslim predecessors had not hesitated to intervene in similar circumstances.

When its charter was renewed by parliament in 1813, the Company was forced to accept the establishment of an Anglican bishopric in Calcutta and the insertion in its charter of a "pious clause," first framed 20 years earlier, insisting that the country had a duty to promote the "religious and moral improvement" of the Indians. While the Company retained the right to expel from its territories anyone it considered unfit, and continued to restrict the activities of missionaries, especially in the Madras Presidency and in border areas, the passing of this clause was celebrated by the supporters of mission as a victory and the next 20 years saw significant growth in the number of mission stations, if not of conversions (Carson, 1991). Nevertheless, the "pious clause" also contained a caveat, which enshrined in the Company's charter for the first time "the principles of the British Government on which the Natives of India have hitherto relied for the free exercise of their Religion," requiring that they "be inviolably maintained."[6]

The significance of this caveat can be seen in relation to *satī*, which the Company moved to regulate in the same year as the principle of religious freedom was safeguarded in its charter. Against the claims of opponents of the practice, both British and Indian, the Company asserted that *satī* was "recognized and encouraged by the doctrines of the Hindoo religion." Acknowledging the "fundamental principle of ... the most complete toleration in matters of religion" the Company decided that it could not prohibit Hindu women from committing *satī*, but that it should seek to ensure that they did so only "in those cases in which it is countenanced by their religion; and to prevent it in others." Thus, in 1813 the Company instructed its magistrates to issue directions to the police, which noted that according to "the expositions of the Hindoo law, delivered by pundits ... the burning a woman pregnant, or one having a child of tender years, or a girl not yet arrived at full age, is expressly forbidden in the Shasters; and also, that intoxicating a woman for the purpose of burning her, and burning one without her assent, or against her will, is highly illegal, and contrary to established usage."[7] It is notable here that alongside the opinions of Hindu scholars, and "established usage," the Company's directive invokes the authority of the śāstras. Textual authority, and especially that of "the most ancient laws of the Hindoos," notably the *Mānavadharmaśāstra*, was again invoked in 1828 when the Company drafted a regulation to ban *satī* altogether.[8] The British may thereby have been able to satisfy themselves that they had not "interfered" with the religious practices of their Hindu subjects, but many Hindus saw the matter differently.

Their sense that Hindu tradition was under threat grew later in the century when the British legislated again on matters, which many Hindus now regarded as part of their religious practice protected by the policy of non-interference. The most contentious issues were those which related to women, notably the legalization of remarriage for Hindu widows in 1856 and the raising of the age of consent in 1891. Although there were a number of aspects of Hindu tradition, which the British presented as evidence for the degraded state of Hinduism and its need of the civilizing mission of colonialism,[9] increasingly it was the condition of Indian, and especially Hindu, women that became emblematic for both the colonizers and the colonized. For the British, the plight of Indian women was a sign of the need for their enlightened rule; in the domestic sphere Indian men denied their women the freedom they demanded for themselves in the political sphere, thereby—according to the British—revealing themselves to be unworthy of it. While Indian reformers used similar arguments, Tanika Sarkar has argued that for them the condition of women represented also "a possibility for self-transformation and self-fashioning which was absent in all other realms of life in which the state ruled arbitrarily" (Sarkar, 2001a: 551).

For those who resisted reform, early marriage, and a ban on remarriage were important in order to guard the purity of offerings made to ancestors, and thus formed an essential part of the free exercise of their religion. From the 1870s, their arguments also took on a nationalist tone. Women came to represent the only part of Indian culture untouched by colonial rule, a realm in which custom had to be preserved if Indians were to retain any autonomy and authenticity. In 1873, in the wake of a court decision that confirmed some implications of the 1856 Widow Remarriage Act, which seemed to Hindus to undermine their understanding of marriage, one Hindu wrote:

> We are but a half-civilised, poor, sorrowful, subjected, despised nation. We have but one jewel, our chaste women, and that is the treasure of seven realms, a priceless jewel ... this so-called subjection of our women produces this sacred jewel of chastity which still glows radiantly throughout the civilized world, despite centuries of political subjection (Sarkar, 2001: 557).

Tanika Sarkar notes the growing colonial dominance of all spheres of public life and enterprise in the latter part of the 19th century and argues that the resultant "shrinking scope for self-expression through 'male' enterprise, alongside the militant nationalist self-organization of the late nineteenth century, gave the Age of Consent debates their extraordinary charge [and produced] the first stirrings of a modern anti-colonial agitational nationalism" (Sarkar, 2001b: 229–230). She finds the roots of the momentous political changes that began in this period in the "immunity enjoyed by personal laws" that was a consequence of the policy of non-interference. In independent India, Hindu nationalists have continued to present women as the custodians of an authentic Hinduism besieged now not by the colonial state, but by the secular state, which was its legacy.[10] In the late 1980s, as Hindu nationalists moved closer to political power at the national level, these claims were played out in public around the death of a young Rajasthani woman on her husband's funeral pyre.

## Migration

Sea-borne trade and military expeditions, notably under the Chola kings of South India, took Hindus to Southeast Asia where they left archaeological evidence and traces of cultural influence. In later times too, communities of traders established themselves in various places around the Indian and Pacific oceans, including East Africa. There was nevertheless a taboo on crossing the seas for high-caste Hindus and a powerful attachment to India as a pure land, lying at the center of the cosmos, surrounded by concentric seas. Despite these historical instances of Hinduism spreading beyond the Indian subcontinent, and the survival of communities in parts of Southeast Asia—notably Bali (Ramstedt, 2004)—large-scale migration of Hindus is for the most part a modern phenomenon and, initially at least, was very closely bound up with the history of the British empire (cf. Sinha, 2005: 19–20). In the 19th century, following the abolition of slavery, many Hindus and other South Asians moved within the British empire to Southeast Asia, Africa, the Caribbean, and the Pacific region, mostly to work as contract or indentured laborers but also in some cases to pursue commercial and educational opportunities. In the early 20th century, migration from India slowed, but following the Second World War, many members of Hindu communities outside India undertook a second migration, most to Britain. In the 1950s and early 1960s many moved from the Caribbean to Britain, largely for economic reasons, and in the late 1960s and early 1970s many Hindus left East Africa in the wake of the policies of Africanization followed in countries that were themselves newly independent of the imperial power. From the mid-1970s, migration to Britain slowed, consisting largely of the reuniting of families as wives and other dependent relatives followed Hindu men to Britain. There has also been some other movement of Hindus and other South Asians from Britain and other places to the USA, Canada, and Australia. The number of Hindus in the USA grew rapidly following the lifting of immigration restrictions in 1965, primarily through migration of professionals, and the number of Hindus there (including converts to Hinduism, who would be in the minority) has recently been estimated at more than 1.2 million, now more than twice the number in Britain, which once had the largest population in the Western world. Later smaller waves of migration came about as a result of political upheavals in various parts of the world, notably the military coups in Fiji in the late 1980s, and the conflict in Sri Lanka. Since the 1970s, there has been a further significant movement of skilled and semi-skilled Indian laborers to work in the oil industry and related infrastructural development in several countries around the Persian Gulf. The vast majority of these have come from the southern states of India, especially Kerala. For the most part, these countries have not allowed Indian workers to obtain citizenship, so the diaspora communities here have a different character than those elsewhere.

Steve Vertovec emphasizes that Hindu practice outside of India differs not only from practice within India, but also from place to place outside India (Vertovec, 2000). This reflects the different histories of the communities, their different regions of origin within India, as well as differences in the new cultural context within which they have developed. Even within one country, the differences among Hindu groups can be significant, for the same reasons. Despite sharing a history of twice migrating, Indo-Caribbean Hindu migrants to Britain differ from those who migrated from East Africa. Among the latter group, Gujarati-speaking Hindus differ from Punjabi speakers, even though both are mostly engaged in small- to medium-scale businesses. Both groups would have different practices from more recent direct migrants—many of them professionals—from other parts of India. It is nevertheless possible to identify some common strategies that have emerged among these very different groups, not least a heightening of the importance of religious adherence as an element of identity and the emergence of a kind of "ecumenical" Hinduism, which is only found outside of India. A number of scholars have challenged the tendency to regard diaspora Hinduism as a departure from an idealized Indian Hinduism regarded as normative. Not only are diasporic communities sometimes more conservative in practice, but they deserve also to be taken seriously as religious communities in their own right, and not only as off-shoots of a more "authentic" Indian Hinduism.

We will here briefly survey some of the patterns that scholars have identified in different diasporic communities, before considering how far these patterns are to be found in the Hindu diaspora in Asia.

## New Homelands

With the exception of some countries with long-established communities such as Nepal, Hindus outside of India live as minority communities. Only in Mauritius, Fiji, and two Caribbean countries, do Hindus constitute more than 10 percent of the population. In a study of these countries, and other communities constituted primarily by movement of indentured laborers in South and East Africa, Paul Younger characterizes the development of Hinduism as the construction of "new homelands." These new complexes of rituals, values, and mythic stories developed quickly for two reasons. First, in each country there were concentrations of migrants from particular regions of India who shared a common religious culture. Second, the relatively weak colonial administration of the plantations opened up spaces for the development of religious institutions. By contrast with later migrants to Europe and North America who have sought a continuity of practice with Indian traditions, and with migrants to regions closer to India, the isolation and—in some cases—loss of language forced upon these earlier migrants created a more decisive break with "ritual routines" (including the ritual order of caste) of India (Younger, 2010 : 11).

*Five Strategies of Adaptation*

As emphasized earlier each diaspora community—and even each group within those communities—has developed differently. Raymond Brady Williams has identified five strategies of adaptation, which he argues are characteristic of Indian religious groups in the USA (Williams, 1992). Although not directly applicable to other diaspora communities in the West, the typology is useful, and similar strategies have also been identified by scholars working on those communities.[11] The earliest migrants to the USA mostly came alone, and lived where there were few other Indian migrants. Williams characterizes their religious practice as individualism, whether through private acts of devotion or through a disregard for religious practice altogether. As numbers of migrants increased, associations based on national identity were formed following the model of many earlier migrant groups to the USA. Although these organizations were primarily secular in nature, the pervasiveness of Hindu elements in Indian culture and arts meant that Hinduism became in many respects "the unofficial religion of many of these associations," even if this was contested by some members of the association. Williams nevertheless characterizes this as a national strategy of adaptation and distinguishes it from an ecumenical strategy, which emerges when explicitly Hindu associations began to develop. In the centers and temples established by such groups,

> Emphasis is placed upon all-India Hindu "great tradition," on devotion to major deities, and upon some elements of the Sanskrit tradition. Study and devotional groups use universally accepted Hindu texts, such as the Bhagavad Gita and the Ramayana. Languages used are Sanskrit for rituals and English for instruction, commentary, and business. Sectarian leaders on tour from India are incorporated as guests during the annual calendar of events, but primary leaders are developed from within the immigrant group. The sacred festivals observed are those from the calendar observed throughout India. (Williams, 1992: 239)

As the numbers of migrants increased, it became possible for groups defined by ethnic (regional–linguistic) differences to emerge. Shared language, cuisine, dress, and forms of religious practice gave an ethnic strategy of adaptation a powerful appeal, particularly for first-generation migrants. Finally what Williams characterizes as a hierarchical strategy is based on "loyalty to a living religious leader who provides a unity for the group beyond ethnic or national loyalties" (Williams, 1992: 241). As in the case of ISKCON or Sai Baba groups, devotion to the guru draws members with ethnic and national backgrounds, but the unity of such groups is dependent on the presence of the guru or successful negotiation of the period following the guru's death.[12]

## The Hindu Diaspora in Asia

Within Asia, the most significant Hindu diaspora communities are in the "old diaspora" countries on the Malay peninsula.[13] In absolute terms Hindus in Malaysia, where over 80 percent of the 2 million ethnically Indian Malaysians are Hindus, constitute the largest of the Hindu diaspora communities formed in the modern period. The number of Hindus in Singapore is much lower in absolute terms, but the 150,000 Hindus there constitute a similar proportion of the total population (5 percent in Singapore, 7 percent in Malaysia).

The Indian diaspora communities on the Malay peninsula were largely formed during the century between the abolition of slavery in the British empire in 1834 and the Indian government's ban on migration of unskilled labor in 1938. The majority of migrants were poor, low-caste, rural Tamils recruited to work on rubber plantations. There were, however, also Tamils from the higher-status vēḷāḷa caste in both India and Sri Lanka who filled lower-level clerical positions in the colonial administration, the railways, and on the plantations. A third Tamil group was the Ceṭṭiyār entrepreneurs who acted as financiers, traders, and also investors in the plantations and other enterprises. Small numbers of Tamil brahmins had also migrated to Singapore and Malaysia from the late 19th century. From the 1920s, the rise of the anti-brahmin movement in Tamil Nadu greatly increased the numbers of Tamil brahmins migrating to many parts of the world, including Southeast Asia (Clothey, 2006 : 10–11, 118–120), and their prominence among highly mobile professional groups has sustained their growth. Although there have also been migrants—mostly merchants—from other religious groups and from other parts of India, a substantial majority of the Hindu diaspora in Malaysia and Singapore have long been Tamil Hindus, and a substantial part of the remainder—Telugus or Keralites—are also of South Indian origin. Religious practice has been a key element in the strategies by which Tamil Hindu migrants have sought both to maintain their identity as Tamil Hindus in a new cultural context and to make sense of their new identities as Malaysians or Singaporeans. The construction of temples, in the distinctive South Indian style, has been central to these processes. Temples serve not only as highly visible manifestations of the presence of a community, but they also create a space, both literally and symbolically, for the community to express its self-understanding. In Tamil Nadu, temples play a central role in defining habitable space and hence constituting a village as a place. The construction of permanent temples in Malaysia and Singapore thus reflects not only the size and financial strength of the diaspora communities that erect them, but also the incorporation of their new—and now permanent—place of residence into an established and sacralized cosmos. While temples continued to serve some of the same functions as they had in India—notably as "sites for displaying and constituting dominant social hierarchies" (Mines, 2005 : 18), they also took on new significance. In Malaysia and Singapore, life-cycle rituals are performed less often or in attenuated forms, but when they are performed the primary site for their performance has become the temple, rather than the home. Participation in temple activities is also a way for those approaching the age of marriage both "to be visible to prospective partners and to be seen as apt embodiments of the tradition from which a partner is being sought" (Clothey, 2006: 25). As elsewhere in the diaspora, temples have also served as cultural centers, where language is passed on and traditional arts are celebrated.

The designation of one of the Batu Caves, just north of Kuala Lumpur, as a shrine to Murukaṇ has also served to incorporate the Malaysian peninsula within the Tamil sacred geography. The Tai Pūcam festival, celebrated in January–February, has also served as a way for Hindus to stake a claim in the public sphere. The festival is a public holiday in four Malaysian states (although not a federal holiday), and is prominent in official attempts to promote tourism in Singapore. The incorporation of other Hindus, and also some non-Hindus, in the festival contributes also to the sense that this is a Malaysian and Singaporean, and not merely a Hindu, event. Although Tai Pūcam, like other Hindu festivals, expresses a broader sense of participation in a Malaysian or Singaporean identity, it also reveals a hierarchical ordering within the Tamil community in a manner that is similar to that of festivals in Tamil Nadu (Younger, 2002 : 7–9).

Although in general caste consciousness is greatly attenuated in the diaspora, and the more so the further in space and time communities are removed from their place of origin in India, caste or caste-like social stratifications remain relevant for Tamils in Malaysia and Singapore—especially in relation to the choice of marriage partners—and this hierarchical ordering is also reflected in festivals there, including Tai Pūcam. Ceṭṭiyār merchants, who had become devotees of Tanṭāyutapāṇi (Murukan at Palaṇi) in India and established temples for him in Singapore and Malaysia, have been patrons of the festival since its early days. The temple car in Kuala Lumpur makes a stop outside the Ceṭṭiyār Taṇṭāyutapāṇi temple, although the festival is formally sponsored by the Mahāmāriyammaṇ temple. Like many such temples, this is controlled by pillais or vēḷāḷas, in alliance with other groups such as tēvars and kauṇṭars, who had served as recruiters or administrators on the plantations. Those who participate most fervently in the ritual vows for which the festival is renowned—carrying kāvaṭi and other forms of sacred wounding, or inviting possession by the deity—are mostly drawn from the descendents of the *dalit* or adi-dravida groups who came as unskilled laborers to work on the plantations. In the early period of migration, the latter groups were refused admission to temples controlled by the higher castes.[14] Despite their inclusion in the festival, debates have continued over which forms of religious devotion represent "authentic" Tamil Hindu tradition. Both Ceṭṭiyār and the orthodox Śaiva Siddhānta Jaffna Tamils, who sought to distance themselves from "the more extreme forms of penitential participation," (Clothey, 2006: 190) and reformers from the 1940s to the 1990s, have tried and mostly failed to dissuade the predominantly low-caste devotees from piercing their skin. A similar process of the partial dissolution of caste boundaries, but also continuing struggle for control among different groups, can be seen in the gradual transformation of Muniānṭi, a fierce god traditionally worshipped by low castes, into Muniśvaran, a form of Śiva (Sinha, 2005; Clothey, 2006: 69; Collins and Ramanathan, 2014: 23). Religion thus remains central to the attempts of Tamil Hindus in the diaspora to work out their identity both within and outside their own communities.

# Notes

1. David Miller argues for the centrality of the guru in shaping change in Hinduism: "The dynamic, sacred center of Hinduism, is, in fact, the enlightened guru, whose charismatic leadership creates the institution for philosophical, religious, and social change" (1977: 527).
2. Frykenberg has documented many examples of this sort in articles over more than 20 years.
3. Cassels notes that the Company had first authorized collection of a pilgrim tax in 1784, but that the Jagannāth tax was the first time this was done as a matter of policy.
4. Textual authority has remained important in legal decisions in independent India, although customary practice is also authoritative. See Fuller (1988).
5. Papers relating to East India affairs, p. 4. *Parliamentary Papers* 1812–1813 (194).
6. Bill for continuing in East India Company Possession of British Territories in India with certain Exclusive Privileges, p. 14. *Parliamentary Papers* 1812–1813 (327) II. 1239.
7. Papers relating to Hindoo Widows and Voluntary Immolations, pp. 31–33. *Parliamentary Papers* 1821 (749) XVIII. 295.
8. Correspondence relative to Burning of Hindoo Widows on Funeral Piles of their Husbands, p. 130. *Parliamentary Papers* 1830 (178) XXVIII. 783. The actual regulations, passed in Bengal in 1829 and Madras in 1830, note only that *satī* is "no where enjoined by the religion of the Hindoos as an imperative duty."
9. For example, hook-swinging, which the British sought to discourage in various ways before banning it in Bengal in 1865 and Madras in 1894. The debates over hook-swinging reprise a number of the themes in the debates over *satī*. See Oddie (1995).
10. As Lubin notes below, they have also charged the state with being only "pseudo-secular," citing its failure to intervene similarly in the cases governed by Muslim personal law.
11. See the chapters on South Asians in Australia, Britain, and Canada in Hinnells (1997).
12. For a discussion of the issues in the case of ISKCON, see the essays by Jan Brzezinski and Irvin H. Collins in Bryant and Ekstrand (2004). The death of Sathya Sai Baba in 2011 will likely raise similar issues for his organization. For a study of Sai Baba movement in Malaysia, see Kent (2007).
13. There are, of course, significant numbers of Hindus in other South Asian countries (Pakistan, Bangladesh, Sri Lanka, and Myanmar), but these are not considered here as the history and experience of these communities is different from those who were constituted by migration in recent times. (For overviews of Hinduism in these countries, see the chapters on them in Jacobsen, 2009.) The Ministry of Overseas Indian Affairs uses the term "old diaspora" to distinguish communities established in the colonial era from those "new diaspora" countries which were largely formed by migration after Indian independence.

14. In 1935, the Hindu Mahajana Sangam, which had fought for temple entry, gained control of the Queen Street Māriyamman temple and a nearby hilltop temple where the festival procession ended (Collins and Ramanathan, 2014).

# References

Bryant, Edwin F. and Ekstrand, Maria L. (eds). 2004. *The Hare Krishna Movement: The Postcharismatic Fate of a Religious Transplant.* New York: Columbia University Press.

Buchanan, Claudius. 1811. *Christian Researches in Asia: With Notices of the Translation of the Scriptures into Oriental Languages.* Cambridge: J. Smith.

Carson, Penelope. 1991. "Missionaries, Bureaucrats and the People of India, 1793–1833." In Nancy Gardner Cassels (ed.), *Orientalism, Evangelicalism and the Military Cantonment in Early Nineteenth Century India: A Historiographical Overview,* 125–155. Lewiston: Edwin Mellen Press.

Cassels, Nancy Gardner. 1972. "The 'Compact' and the Pilgrim Tax: The Genesis of East India Company Social Policy." *Canadian Journal of History* 7(1): 37–49.

Clothey, Fred W. 2006. *Ritualizing on the Boundaries: Continuity and Innovation in the Tamil Diaspora.* Columbia: University of South Carolina Press.

Collins, Elizabeth Fuller and K. Ramanathan. 2014. "The Politics of Ritual Performance and Ritual Authority among Murugan's Malaysian Devotees." In Tracy Pintchman and Linda Penkower (eds), *Hindu Ritual at the Margins: Innovations, Transformations, Reconsiderations,* 83–105. Columbia: University of South Carolina Press.

Dalmia, Vasudha. 1997. *The Nationalization of Hindu Traditions: Bharatendu Harischandra and the Ninteenth-Century Banaras.* New Delhi: Oxford University Press.

Davis, Donald R. 2008. "Law and 'Law Books' in the Hindu Tradition." *German Law Journal* 9(3): 309–325.

Deyell, John S. and Robert Eric Frykenberg. 1982. "Sovereignty and the 'Sikka' under Company Raj: Minting Prerogative and Imperial Legitimacy in India." *The Indian Economic and Social History Review* 19(1): 1–25.

Fisch, Jörg. 1985. "A Pamphlet War on Christian Missions in India, 1807–1809." *Journal of Asian History* 19(1): 22–70.

Frykenberg, Robert Eric. 1988. "The Myth of English as a 'Colonialist' Imposition Upon India: A Reappraisal with Special Reference to South India." *The Journal of the Royal Asiatic Society of Great Britain and Ireland* (2): 305–315.

———. 2000. "The Construction of Hinduism as a 'Public' Religion: Looking Again at the Religious Roots of Company Raj in South India." In Keith E. Yandell and John J. Paul (eds), *Religion and Public Culture: Encounters and Identities in Modern South India,* 3–26. Richmond: Curzon.

Fisch, Jörg. 2006. "Christians and Religious Traditions in the Indian Empire." In Sheridan Gilley and Brian Stanley (eds), *The Cambridge History of Christianity*, 473–492. Cambridge: Cambridge University Press.

Fuller, C. J. 1988. "Hinduism and Scriptural Authority in Modern Indian Law." *Comparative Studies in Society and History* 30(2): 225–248.

Halbfass, Wilhelm. 1988. *India and Europe: An Essay in Understanding*. Albany: State University of New York Press.

Hinnells, John R. (ed). 1997. *A New Handbook of Living Religions*. Oxford: Blackwell.

Jacobsen, Knut A. (ed). 2009. *Brill's Encyclopedia of Hinduism*, vol. 2. Leiden: Brill.

Kent, Alexandra. 2007. *Divinity and Diversity: A Hindu Revitalization Movement in Malaysia*. Singapore: Institute of Southeast Asian Studies.

Miller, David. 1977. "The Guru as the Centre of Sacredness." *Studies in Religion/Sciences Religieuses* 6(5): 527–533.

Mines, Diane P. 2005. *Fierce Gods: Inequality, Ritual, and the Politics of Dignity in a South Indian Village*. Bloomington: Indiana University Press.

Nicholson, Andrew J. 2010. *Unifying Hinduism: Philosophy and Identity in Indian Intellectual History*. New York: Columbia University Press.

Oddie, Geoffrey A. 1995. *Popular Religion, Elites, and Reforms: Hook-Swinging and Its Prohibition in Colonial India, 1800–1894*. New Delhi: Manohar.

_____. 2003. "Constructing 'Hinduism': The Impact of the Protestant Missionary Movement on Hindu Self-Understanding." In R. E. Frykenberg (ed.). *Christians and Missionaries in India: Cross-cultural Communications since 1500*, 155–182. Michigan: Eerdmans.

Ramstedt, Martin. 2004. *Hinduism in Modern Indonesia: A Minority Religion between Local, National, and Global Interests*. London: RoutledgeCurzon.

Rocher, Ludo. 1993. "Law Books in an Oral Culture: The Indian 'Dharmaśāstras'." *Proceedings of the American Philosophical Society* 137(2): 254–267.

Sarkar, Tanika. 2001a. "Enfranchised Selves: Women, Culture and Rights in Nineteenth-Century Bengal." *Gender and History* 13(3): 546–565.

_____. 2001b. *Hindu Wife, Hindu Nation: Community, Religion, and Cultural Nationalism*. Bloomington: Indiana University Press.

Sinha, Vineeta. 2005. *A New God in the Diaspora?: Muneeswaran Worship in Contemporary Singapore*. Singapore/Copenhagen: Singapore University Press/NIAS Press.

Vertovec, Steven. 2000. *Hindu Diaspora: Comparative Patterns*. London: Routledge.

Williams, Raymond B. 1992. "Sacred Threads of Several Textures," In Raymond B. Williams (ed.) *A Sacred Thread: Modern Transmission of Hindu Traditions in India and Abroad*, 228–257. Chambersburg: Anima Publications.

Younger, Paul. 2002. *Playing Host to Deity: Festival Religion in the South Indian Tradition*. Oxford: Oxford University Press.

_____. 2010. *New Homelands: Hindu Communities in Mauritius, Guyana, Trinidad, South Africa, Fiji, and East Africa*. Oxford: Oxford University Press.

Zavos, John. 2001. "Defending Hindu Tradition: Sanatana Dharma as a Symbol of Orthodoxy in Colonial India." *Religion* 31(2): 109–124.

# Chapter 3

## Hinduism and Law

Timothy Lubin

## Introduction

Hinduism—the web of distinctive devotional traditions in South Asia and the Brahmanical institutions and theology that have provided a systematizing influence over the centuries—has at every stage in its history intersected with the legal realm. In antiquity, in law as in religion, the Brahmanical priesthood sought to unify and systematize what where otherwise oral norms and customary practices, setting themselves up as authorities. As Brahmins promoted themselves as officials and advisors to rulers, their earlier focus on ritual and personal conduct was broadened to include precepts on administrative, civil, and criminal law; while continuing to acknowledge the validity of customary rules observed by particular groups or in certain regions, which probably operated without written codes and quite independently of Brahmin dharma professionals. Although the resulting system, which came to be called *Dharmaśāstra*, the "Science of What Is Right," was probably not usually invoked directly outside of high-caste circles and the royal courts, it provided a durable and refined model of law that influenced legal practices across India and had an impact beyond the subcontinent as well.

Under Muslim kingdoms from the 13th century, and later during the age of European colonial intervention, a growing swath of affairs—especially criminal and administrative law—was brought under newly introduced legal systems. The consequence of this is that indigenous legal traditions, including those of the Sanskrit *Dharmaśāstra*, came more and more to be associated with the cultural mores and religious commitments of those whom the Muslims and then the Europeans classed as "Hindu." This was particularly so because the jurisdiction of this indigenous law was restricted to the adjudication of disputes and the ritual rehabilitation of wrong-doers within Hindu groups, and the administration of Hindu religious institutions. The colonial British courts encouraged this trend by attempting to codify Hindu law (or aspects thereof) in the manner of English Common Law, relying at first on Brahmins and the *Sanskrit Dharma* canon, but gradually seeking to purge Hindu society of what the British viewed as cruel or immoral customs by legislating against them.

Independent India's secular law today has inherited from colonial law both a certain ambivalence in its approach to matters of religion and a commitment to progressive social reform and multiculturalism. This has been steadily resisted by a countervailing political movement that idealizes *Hindutva* ("Hinduness") as a national ethos that should be publicly and legally recognized (an idea formulated by Savarkar [1923]). In various ways, the notable court cases and landmark enactments reflect this contest between those who would remodel the polity to reflect a unified modern "Hinduness" and those committed to a religiously neutral, pluralist, and egalitarian political ideal. The struggles of Hindu communities outside India to secure their legal status and rights, and at the same time their distinctive social identity, have favored the consolidation of a more uniform transnational form of Hinduism, and have inclined many diaspora (and convert) Hindus to sympathize with the Hindutva movement in India.

In what follows, I shall briefly review the interaction between religion and law in premodern periods before presenting in more detail the complex developments since the 17th century up to the present day. This will include the creation of "Anglo-Hindu" law, colonial administration of justice (including the legal treatment of disapproved Hindu practices), and the gradual restriction of Hindu law to matters of family law; legal treatment of Hindus and Hindu institutions under secular law in modern India and Nepal; and Hindu religion under modern secular law outside South Asia. Throughout, the emphasis will be on the fruits of research from the last 30 years or so, especially current developments.

## *Dharmaśāstra* and Premodern Indic Law

In its origins, *Dharmaśāstra* resulted from a progressive broadening of scope in the canonization of rules (*sūtras*) of proper action. The earliest such rulebooks (the *śrautasūtras*) dealt only with high Vedic liturgy, then all the rites and ceremonies of household life were similarly codified (in the *gṛhyasūtras*). Finally, the tradition produced rulebooks governing all aspects of the personal conduct and social relations. These *dharmasūtras*, are also the first works to prescribe rules of royal conduct and state policy. These became the starting point for a vast, highly textualized scholastic discipline that produced compendia of versified maxims, commentaries, digests, and treatises, constituting almost the only juristic literature in South Asia.[1] In spite of its orientation to the concerns and values of the Brahmin priestly class, *Dharmaśāstra* was intended to apply to all "civilized" people (as defined in terms of those very values).

Thus, *Dharmaśāstra* resulted from the fusion of two distinct spheres of Brahmanical activity: ritual codification and political science. From the former, it took its sacral character, its focus on correct action, its deference to the Veda, its ethical foundations, and many other traits; from the latter, it adopted an ideal of kingship and the state, and most of its approach to legality and the legal process. The circumstance of this fusion cannot be known in detail, but it appears to have happened in the last couple of centuries BCE as Brahmin preceptors sought to define roles for themselves in the royal courts of urbanizing north India. Brahmins indeed succeeded in being accepted by most rulers and much of the social elite as authorities in judicial and administrative affairs well beyond the temple sanctuary, and they were commonly appointed to office in these spheres. It is said religious and legal ideals and obligations became thoroughly interwoven precisely because Brahmins were broadly able to define the terms of legitimacy in both theology and jurisprudence.

Turkic forays into north India after 1000, culminating in the establishment of the Mamluk kingdom at Delhi in 1206, meant that Islamic law began to constitute another textualized, religiously grounded law being practiced in India. The precise impact of this development is difficult to trace, but it is noteworthy that from about this period, a new genre appears within *Dharmaśāstra*: the topically arranged digest. Works of this type would have been useful both in *śāstric* education and as a reference work for those called upon to give an opinion on a particular legal or moral question. If nothing else, this may reflect a heightened awareness of *Dharmaśāstra* as a canon to be treated encyclopedically in a way similar to the treatment of classical authorities in Islamic law. More explicit signs of interaction between Hindu and Islamic law appear in the late medieval period. One example is the self-conscious "restoration" of Hindu legal institutions under the Marāṭhas in the 17th century largely involved a translation of the legal and administrative institutions of the Muslim Bāhmānīs who preceded them into *Dharmaśāstra*-based analogs (Gune, 1953). In this period at least, Islamic courts are known to have invoked customary Hindu law in cases involving Hindus, in one case agreeing to a "change of venue" to a *dharmasabhā* (Brahmin court) in Paithan (Smith and Derrett, 1975; discussed by Eaton, 2005: 145–150).

The most exhaustive treatment of *Dharmaśāstra* will long remain P. V. Kane's eight-part *History of Dharmaśāstra* (1962–1975). Lingat's one-volume survey (1972) also remains a useful point of departure, but in the last 30 years many of the core texts have been revisited on the basis of more manuscript material and innumerable advances in our knowledge of Indian history (esp. Lariviere, 1981, 1989a; Olivelle, 2000, 2005a, 2009; Rocher, 2002). Olivelle (2010) has reassessed the chronology of this literature based on his critical studies of several major texts. Mathur (2007) has made an interesting, if overreaching, argument that the medieval *dharmaśāstra* writers helped make the classic dharma tradition responsive to changes in society and legal practice, and established *vyavahāra* (judicial process) as a secular legal system.

The articles collected by Nanda and Sinha (1997) attempt to draw classical Hindu law into comparative discussions of legal theory. More recent studies of particular topics have dealt with the scriptural bases and conceptual framework of legal authority (Lubin, 2007, 2010; McCrea, 2010), the ritual aspects of *Dharmaśāstra* (Yelle, 2010), and the complementary political roles of literature and *Dharmaśāstra* in a medieval Indian court (Cox, 2010). Two scholars have worked simultaneously on a set of medieval Sanskrit texts dedicated to expounding dharma for Śūdras, the lowest of the four ideal social ranks in *Dharmaśāstra* (Benke, 2010; Vajpeyi, 2010), and Aktor (2008, 2010) had sought out the śāstric foundations of "untouchability."

In sum, the Brahmin proponents of *Dharmaśāstra*, along with their patrons in the political and social domains, were the chief architects of an overarching vision of moral and legal rectitude (dharma), theoretically grounded in revealed sacred knowledge (viz., *śruti* or the "Veda").

Hence, the *Dharmaśāstra* literature carefully subsumes customary norms (recognized as broadly valid) and elements of civil law (drawn largely from the tradition that produced the *Arthaśāstra*, plus prescriptions for the production of legal documents) within a fundamentally religious framework, in which Brahmin authority (derived in principle from the Veda itself) is deemed preeminent. The state, in the person of the king, is assigned the highest executive and judicial authority, but *Dharmaśāstra* asserts that the authority is constrained by the king's duty to rely on Brahmin advisers and to adhere to the dictates of dharma, which transcend human wisdom. Violation of that duty—of the "king's dharma"—was said to entail grievous consequences according to the operation of the universal law of karma.

We do not know how widely *Dharmaśāstra* was applied "according to the letter of the law"; probably its maxims were invoked verbatim mainly in Brahmin circles, though hardly any direct evidence of this survives. However, *Dharmaśāstra* certainly attained wider influence as an ideal of sacred moral authority and legal principle. As such, it managed to establish a conceptual and even terminological structure that permeated legal practice through most of South and Southeast Asia, and continued to resonate through the 19th century in India (Lariviere, 1996, 1997) and Nepal (Michaels, 2005). Legal traditions in these regions that reflect the influence of *Dharmaśāstra* (directly or indirectly) tend today to be called "Hindu law" (Davis, 2010a).

## State Law and Customary Law

As influential as *Dharmaśāstra* was, especially in providing a cosmopolitan idiom and conceptual framework for law "on the ground," much of the work of law could be and surely was done without it (see the studies in Kölver, 1997; Davis, 2010b, which attempts a historical overview). Public administration was regulated on different levels by different authorities: local affairs and private disputes were handled by local and regional councils; caste assemblies and trade guilds, governed by customary norms and oral maxim; matters of state and appeals in "hard cases" were dealt with by state-appointed officials, including Brahmin judges. Litigation over land rights and commercial or financial transactions relied on the testimony of witnesses and (increasingly) on documentation. Such documents might be produced on palm leaf, cloth, bark, or paper; in certain cases, copies were also inscribed on stone or copper plates, and most surviving examples of older records are of this type. Where concrete evidence was lacking or as a last-ditch appeal to a "divine witness," oaths and ordeals were recognized as legally valid (Lariviere, 1981).

This "civil law" mostly remained uncodified, with the single and very important exception of the *Arthaśāstra* ("Treatise on Polity") attributed to the legendary Brahmin minister of the third-century BCE king Chandragupta Maurya (but dating in its current form probably to the first or second century CE). Kangle (1965–1972) remains authority on the *Arthaśāstra*, providing a good text, translation, and Scharfe's (1993) analysis of its political system refines earlier estimates of the work's date and composition, and refers to the 12th-century Malayalam commentary. As for the *Arthaśāstra*'s treatment of religion, Olivelle (1987) notes the social roles (instead of their spiritual attainments) of ascetics, including the possibility of employing them for espionage and undercover intelligence. Through a nuanced analysis of the work's textual structure, McClish (2009) shows that it initially lacked those sections which promote "Brahmin exceptionalism," which were inserted at a later stage as "part of a broad re-assertion of Brahmanical privilege in a new political context."

Both *Dharmaśāstra* works and Kauṭilya's *Arthaśāstra* recognize the validity of customary norms and of the non-Brahmin, non-state institutions that apply them. Direct evidence of specific instances, however, comes mainly from inscriptions. The scholarly literature on the epigraphy is vast but surprisingly little of it discusses the legal functions or effects of such records. Nagaswamy (1978) was one of the first to look at south Indian inscriptions as legal records, though his essays are thinly annotated and greatly overstate the degree to which the epigraphy reflects śāstric models. More nuanced work in this direction has been done by Davis (1999, 2002, 2004a, 2004b, 2005). Karashima (1984, 2008) has greatly refined our understanding of Tamil epigraphical legal and administrative terminology. Lubin (2010) attempts to clarify the authority and distinctive legal functions of inscriptions and legal records. In late medieval India, compilations of model legal documents began to circulate. One of these, the *Lekhapaddhati* from Gujarat, has recently been studied in illuminating detail (Strauch, 2002; Prasad, 2008). An archive of legal documents preserved in Nepal has been published by Kölver and Śākya (1985).

Valuable and sometimes contrasting epigraphical evidence is also available from many parts of mainland and coastal Southeast Asia, to which Hinduism and Indian legal models spread beginning around the seventh century CE. In Indonesia, Burma, and Thailand this spread also gave rise to the composition of "*Dharmaśāstras*" composed in the local languages and codifying local customary law (inflected by Buddhist ideas in Burma and Thailand). For Javanese and Balinese materials, Hoadley and Hooker (1981, 1986) and for Khmer epigraphy, Ishizawa (1986) offer useful overviews. This is being improved upon now by Creese (2009a, 2009b) and Griffiths and Soutif (2010–2011).

Non-śāstric evidence of legal practice, including the adjudication of disputes, is also available from the 17th through the 19th centuries, especially for western India, thanks to the Marāṭha "Daftar" records. Many of these cases have been examined by Wagle (1970, 1980, 1982, 1987, 1995, 1998, 2005) and O'Hanlon (2009). Even today, some examples of the persistence of non-official law have been noted (e.g., Galanter, 1981, 1989; Vincentnathan, 1992; Bavinck, 1998), and some Hindus still treat the temple as a "court of last resort," seeking divine justice when human justice falls short (e.g., Malik, 2010).

## Hinduism and Law in the Colonial Era

The beginning of the colonial era marks the most important rupture in Indian law and in religious life. On the one hand, the East India Company of London, and other European trading companies, competing for influence in the subcontinent, gradually brought more and more territory under direct or indirect control. The eventual centralization of rule and law under the British set in motion a radical change in the relationship between Hinduism and law. It was in this period that Hinduism was first explicitly conceived of as a single religion of that name, a religion, moreover, possessing its own system of law. The dominant perspective on law in India during and just following the colonial period was set by Marc Galanter, J. Duncan, M. Derrett, and Ludo Rocher. Galanter, in a series of articles from the 1960s, argued that British law was able to thoroughly displace and supplant the indigenous forms of law, despite being dissonant with social mores and traditional structures. Even the separate personal law codes developed for Hindus and certain other religious groups on the assumption that they would provide continuity with indigenous norms ended up being a major change. Rocher (1972) explained this by noting that Indians found ways to take advantage of the new system, which at least had the merit of resulting in speedy, clear-cut decisions enforced by the state.

Werner Menski reaches almost diametrically opposite conclusions: he argues that traditional "Hindu law"—not Anglo-Hindu personal law, but a coherent indigenous tradition—survived and remained vital during the colonial period by going "underground, populating the realm of the unofficial law" (2003: 24). Menski's depiction of the Hindu law is highly idealized and based on an interpretation of the classical tradition that has been pointedly criticized by many reviewers (see especially D. Davis, 2004c).

The Judicial Plan of 1772 established the policy objective of governing the Hindus by their own laws so far as those could be known. The British cast about for something that looked like a law book and settled on *Mānava-Dharmaśāstra*, which was duly translated into English by Sir William Jones, a judge in the Supreme Court of Judicature in Calcutta, published in 1794 under the title *Institutes of Hindu Law: or, the Ordinances of Menu*. Generally referred to thereafter as the "Laws of Manu," this most venerable work of *Dharmaśāstra* became overnight the basis for a system of black letter law administered to Hindus by the colonial government (Rocher, 1993). British authorities thus treated the Sanskrit maxims as if they were a code of statutes and applied them to all "Hindus" in place of the customary norms that they were used to, and then (partly realizing their error) attempted to codify Hindu customary law through the principle of judicial precedent, and the exigencies of court-driven social reform. The extraordinary confection that emerged was gradually refined and merged into an adaptation of English law, eventually providing the basis for the legal system of independent India.

After the revolt of 1857, the British crown formally absorbed India into the Empire. This change brought a shift in administrative policy. The British abandoned the earlier effort to codify a sort of Indian common law, and enacted uniform criminal and civil codes for the whole land. Only one area of the law was exempted from this: that portion of colonial (and contemporary) Indian law that bears the name "Hindu law" are the statutes and decisions pertaining to Hindu marriage, annulment, divorce, adoption, succession, and inheritance. Only in this domain was it felt necessary to defer to the customary norms of the population. Sturman (2010) notes that, in essence, "religious" law was reduced to family law. Sturman sees in this the seeds of the politicization of family law and Hindu law that would follow, continuing to the present day.

Apart from this special codification of Hindu family law, Hindu religious institutions and practices were (and are) regularly subjected to legal process, both criminal (in the case of practices deemed corrupt, immoral, or otherwise illegal) and civil (in the case of disputes over caste status and rights, administration of religious endowments, Hindu personal, and family law, etc.). The government after 1858 set out to suppress customs and religious practices that it regarded as unsavory or socially disruptive. Accordingly, laws were passed in various jurisdictions regulating or criminalizing "suttee" (the putative self-immolation of a widow—the *sati* or "good wife"—on her husband's funeral pyre: Mani, 1998), the giving of girls to temples to dance before the image of the deity, to whom they are "wedded" (called by the British "temple prostitution" because of the dancers' non-marital relations with priests and others: Parker, 1998; Kodoth, 2001; Jordan, 2003), and "hook-swinging" (a votive act of suspending oneself by hooks in one's skin, a common form of collective piety during festivals: Oddie, 1995; Dirks, 1997).

Recent studies have elucidated the legal aspects of the colonial preoccupation with "thuggee" (*thagī*). Historians had by the 1990s demonstrated that what British authorities depicted as ritualistic acts of murderous Kali-worship was really just a form of gang banditry. Singha (1993) suggests that this spectacular issue provided a "providential" opportunity to introduce new legal mechanisms and commit greater resources to deal with other forms of banditry. Lloyd (2006) analyzes the evidence offered by William Sleeman, General Superintendent of the Thuggee Department in the 1830s, that thuggee constituted a form deviant religion; he shows that Sleeman's lurid descriptions of thug-gee devotion to Kali picked up on contemporary characterization of Hinduism as grotesque, immoral idolatry. Wagner's special contribution (2007) is his attempt to disclose the thugs' perceptions of themselves (or self-representations, anyway) by studying the personal accounts of some convicted thugs who became informants ("approvers") for the British.

## Hinduism and Law in Independent India

Following partition of British India into the independent states of India and Pakistan, the vast majority of Hindus found themselves governed by a newly created secular state that recognized the cultural and religious diversity of the population. The British colonial legal regime was largely carried over intact, but it Immediately began to be modified in accordance with the aspirations of the new government. The Constituent Assembly, elected just prior to Independence, had as one of its main tasks the drafting of a constitution. Although the resulting Indian Constitution (1950) explicitly ensures "the right freely to profess, practice and propagate religion" (Article 25), this provision was a matter of bitter debate in the Assembly from the start. Some members, such as Lokanath Misra and K. M. Munshi, strenu-ously opposed a right to propagate, seeing such a right as "paving the way for the complete annihilation of Hindu culture, the Hindu way of life and manners" (Misra, in *Constituent Assembly Debates* 7: 824). Munshi at first proposed legal restrictions on conversion, although he gradually came to accept the right to proselytize provided that no force, deception, or "enticement" be used.

## India's Constitutional Secularism

Although the word "secular" was not added to the description of the Indian state in the preamble of the Constitution until 1976, the document was shaped by secularist ideals (as described by Mitra and Fischer, 2002). Those ideals differ somewhat from American constitutional secularism in that the state is empowered to interfere in religious affairs so long as it shows "equal respect" to all religions. The ideal is often expressed as "fairness toward all religions" (*sarvadharma-samabhāva*) and "religious neutrality" (*dharma-nirapekṣatā*). Unlike the American model, which strives to minimize government involvement in matters of religion by declaring the state to be neutral in such matters, India's secularism accepts legal intervention so long as it is even-handed (Mahajan, 2008). Galanter (1965, 1971) has noted that, in practice, what this means is that American courts end up favoring religions in which commitment is a private, voluntary matter, tolerant of the presence of other religions in India, the state is openly willing to make normative judgments to deal with the greater presence of groups for whom religion is a determining factor in public practice and social organization, though it is supposed to apply those overriding norms even-handedly to all religions.

Jacobsohn (2003) calls this conception of constitutional secularism "ameliorative" in the sense that the machinery of law is empowered to interfere in religious matters only where religion impedes social progress (as in caste prejudice, the treatment of women, and "communalism," the fostering of conflicts between social groups, especially where those groups are religiously defined).

All along, and increasingly since the 1980s, however, India's secularism has been sharply criticized by certain commentators and politicians on the political right. A group of essays edited by Rajeev Bhargava (1999, 2008), Baird (1993/2005), and a recent essay by Amartya Sen (2005) have cataloged the wide range of attitudes to secularism in the Indian context. Cossman and Kapur (1999) argue that "the debate over the meaning of secularism is very much a debate over the meaning of equality." Because of this, even the Hindu nationalist movement has "staked out its own claim to secularism" by downplaying the religious foundations of *Hindutva* and faulting the Congress Party for undermining its own ideal of religious neutrality by favoring religious minorities.

Hence, many on the Hindu right insist that India should be officially recognized as Hindu, based on its heritage and its national character. Some go so far as to charge that the state is in fact "pseudo-secular," that is, anti-Hindu, systematically favoring minorities, especially Muslims. The chief examples cited of this lack of neutrality are the rewriting of Hindu law according to social reformist criteria while neglecting to reform Muslim personal law in the same way; exempting Muslim-majority Kashmir from numerous laws; and bowing to pressure from

Muslim groups (e.g., rescinding the Shah Bano decision, protecting the Babri mosque in Ayodhya from being destroyed and replaced by a temple to Rama; Narula, 2010).

Rajeev Dhavan, a prominent Indian jurist, noting India's extreme religious and ethnic diversity, identifies the three basic ingredients of secularism: "religious freedom, celebratory neutrality, and reformatory justice." At the same time, he recognizes that it is an ideal that is always being negotiated in a changing and often volatile political environment, in the context of a fraught history, and that India is in a position to "lead the way for the rest" of the world in the quest for viable secularism (Dhavan, 2001: 320). R. Sen (2007, 2010) offers perhaps the most comprehensive and balanced assessment of Supreme Court's role in interpreting India's secular constitution. In deciding cases involving religion, the judges have not hesitated to offer their own readings of India's religious history and doctrines. Lariviere (1989b) has gone so far as to argue that they have usurped the role of the pandits.

## The Hindu Code Bills

The vague echoes of *Dharmaśāstra* and Hindu customary law that were still discernable in "Anglo-Hindu law" under British rule faded soon after Independence. The Indian National Congress had reluctantly consented to retain the separate "personal law" codes for Hindus (including Sikhs and Jains), Muslims, Christians, Jews, and Parsees, but one of the first projects after passage of the Constitution was to reform the Hindu Code. The debates, beginning in 1952, were heated, and it was decided to break the proposed bill into four parts, which were eventually passed: The Hindu Marriage and Divorce Act, 1955; and the Hindu Succession Act, the Hindu Minority and Guardianship Act, and the Hindu Adoptions and Maintenance Act, all of 1956 (Sontheimer, 1964a). Williams (2010; more extensively: 2006) argues that the national discourse on modernizing reform focused on protections for women, which in turn had the effect of reconstructing Hindu law (and national identity) "in gendered terms" (p. 119), and exclusively by means of the apparatus of the state. Agnes (1999) and Solanki (2011) offer contrasting assessments of the broader question of women's rights under religious personal laws.

The personal law codes became a charged political issue again after the *Shah Bano* judgment,[2] in which the Supreme Court's opinion (written by a Hindu judge) made so bold as to interpret Islamic scripture to propose a reinterpretation of Muslim law, in the process awarding a divorced woman additional financial support. Following an outcry from Muslim groups, the government back-pedaled by passing the Muslim Women (Protection of Rights on Divorce) Act, 1986, which exempted Muslims from Section 125 of the criminal code, and so nullified the *Shah Bano* decision. Since then, many Hindus (with the encouragement of Hindu nationalist groups) have cited this as another example of "appeasing" religious minorities, to the detriment of "oppressed" Hindus, who docilely accepted the earlier rewriting of the Hindu Code (Narula, 2010). Since this controversy, Hindu nationalists have campaigned vigorously for passage of a uniform personal law code as a way of depriving Muslims of their special dispensation in this area. The essays collected in Larson (2001) examine the Hindu law code in the larger context of the separate personal laws and the problems they pose to a secular state.

## Religious Status and Conversion

One of the most vexed areas of Indian law on religion is the regulation of religious identity and affiliation. Personal religious status become legally salient in three interconnected ways: in the application of the "personal laws," in determining who can benefit from affirmative action quotas ("reservations") (Jenkins 2010), and in the legal treatment of proselytization. The greatest difficulties arise where change of religion, or more than one status, is involved.[3] Viswanathan (1998) in fact observes that debate about conversion in India has largely been about civil and political rights, and the colonial and Indian courts have seen fit to define the terms of membership in one religious status or another.

The Constitution explicitly protects the right to "profess, practice, and propagate" religion. In the late 1960s, however, several states began to pass legislation that in effect restored the restrictions on conversion that had been proposed by K. M. Munshi and then dropped. These laws, rather disingenuously and ironically called "Freedom of Religion Acts," criminalized proselytization alleged to rely on "force," "allurement," or "fraud" (under Articles 295A and 298 of the Indian Penal Code). Orissa and Madhya Pradesh were the first to introduce such laws in 1967 and 1968, respectively.[4] Such laws in effect distinguish between the intransitive and transitive uses of the verb "convert": anyone is free to convert to another religion, but strict limits are placed on how one can convert someone else, that is, bring about (or abet) a conversion.

These laws were challenged in *Rev. Stanislaus v. State of MP* (AIR 1977 SC 908). A Christian priest alleged that the state did not have authority to make such a law, and that it infringed on the rights guaranteed by Article 25; another petitioner had made the same claims about the Orissa law. The Madhya Pradesh High Court had upheld their act; the Orissa High Court had found "inducement" too vague and agreed that Article 25 was infringed. The Supreme Court, however, affirmed the right of the state governments to pass the acts for the overriding purpose of maintaining "public order," and found that Article 25 was not infringed. The latter finding, as explained in Chief Justice A. N. Ray's opinion, relied on an eccentric and poorly reasoned distinction between "propagating" (an "effort to transmit or spread the tenets of his religion," presumably among those already belonging to it) and "converting" someone to one's own religion (likewise "by an exposition of its tenets"), on the grounds that the latter impinges upon the "freedom of conscience" guaranteed by Article 25 (*Stanislaus*, p. 911).

In the Freedom of Religion laws, the criteria of force, fraud, and inducements were applied very loosely, treating the promise (explicit or implied) of social or material benefits, or even the promise of heavenly rewards, as inducements or fraudulent promises violating the spirit of true conversion and even constituting a form of force in themselves.

A recent development is a ruling by the Madras High Court recognizing as valid for the purposes of affirmative action a woman's claim to be Hindu on the basis of her Hindu religious practices, despite her having been born a Christian.[5] This decision is interesting because it does not rely upon any sort of institutional confirmation of her acceptance by a Hindu group, but validates her personal actions. Moreover, unlike most judicial tests of religiosity, the judgment gives probative force to the performance of rites, rather than focusing on professed beliefs. In any case, R. Sen (2010) concludes that the net effect of the

Niyogi report, state-level legislation, and court decisions has been to "attenuate" the rights promised by Article 25.

## Caste Panchayats

Prior to the penetration of British legal institutions during the colonial period, most legal cases were handled in the first instance by one of a variety of local bodies, collectively referred to as panchayats (*pañcāyat* in Hindi). Article 40 of the Constitution, included as a sop for Gandhians in the Constituent Assembly, who were keen to preserve an element of local self-governance, attempted to institutionalize an element of local justice by creating "justice councils" (*nyāy pañcāyats*) intended to mirror the old traditional village or caste panchayats. These hybrid institutions failed, mainly because the hearing format too closely matched that of the standard courtroom, and government-driving staffing policies clashed with traditional leadership patterns (Galanter, 1972).

At the same time, the traditional "folk law" panchayats survived in some places as a court of first resort. Studies over the last few decades have shown that such institutions were most likely to remain vital in villages remote from urban centers, especially those in which the lower castes continued to find employment in their traditional occupations, and in single-caste villages (whatever their location) (Hayden, 1984; Vincentnathan, 1992: 68–71).

Over the last decades, there has been a resurgence of caste panchayats (and *khap* panchayats, regional assemblies of representatives from local panchayats) in certain parts of rural north India as a means of resisting a trend toward the loosening of taboos on intercaste marriage. This resistance is framed in terms of the defense of sacred tradition and the preservation of values and purity. In a series of highly publicized cases, *khaps* have handed down death sentences leading to extra-judicial killings carried out by caste members and families of the condemned. One person was quoted as saying: "Khaps are like gods. They can do no wrong" (Luthra, 2010).

Some *khap* leaders have looked beyond the immediate aim of enforcing caste rules, and have called for the abolition of the Hindu Marriage Act, which (in their eyes) has undermined the authority of their own ethical standards and customary law. In particular, they urge that marriage within *gotra*, and "love marriage" in general, should be prohibited by law (Chowdhry, 2004, 2009; Baxi et al., 2006).

## Temple Administration

As the British took over as the rulers of India, they inherited some functions they might not have chose for themselves. One of these was responsibility maintaining and administering large temples formerly endowed by the local ruler. Beginning with Regulation VII of 1817, the government took upon itself the duty "to interfere summarily" to ensure that the endowments of temples and mosques were administered and used properly (Sontheimer [1964b] analyzes the legal principles, both traditional and modern, invoked to resolve disputes over Hindu religious endowments). In spite of growing pressure during the 19th century from Christian groups in Britain to "withdraw" the government's "patronage" of Hindu religion (in the form of funds allotted to temples and the presence of officers at Hindu festivals), the Madras Presidency at least was reluctant to cede its role. The shift to favoring self-government after the end of World War I led to the formation of the Hindu Religious Endowments Board in 1926, a move that was controversial because it centralized management of all Hindu religious institutions in the Presidency under an independent agency by government mandate.

In a monograph treating the situation in Tamil Nadu, Presler (1987) examines the Hindu Religious and Charitable Endowments (Administration) Department (formed in 1952 to succeed the HRE), and its efforts to change the authority and prerogatives of temple personnel, to standardize temple landholdings and land use, and to centralize ecclesiastical administration under the direction of the state.

A similar situation developed outside of India as well. The first law passed by the British administration in the Straits Settlements (Singapore, Penang, and Malacca) was the Mohammedan and Hindu Endowments Ordinance of 1905, which created a board to manage religious institutions of those traditions, a task earlier performed by temple panchayats. Heretofore, disputes within the Hindu communities over control and administration of temples were brought before the British courts for arbitration (Sinha, 2011).

Legal control of temple administration in India was also taken as an opportunity for progressive social reform. Large temples administered by the state were considered to be public institutions and thus open to all castes (Galanter 1964). Hence, when independent India's Constitution was drafted, Article 25 protecting the free exercise of religion was qualified: "(2) Nothing in this article shall affect the operation of any existing law or prevent the State from making any law … (b) providing for social welfare and reform or the throwing open of Hindu religious institutions of a public character to all classes and sections of Hindus." Courts have also been called upon to ensure that non-Brahmin priests are allowed to officiate.

The most contentious temple-related litigation in recent times has been the long-running dispute over the Babri Masjid (Mosque) in Ayodhya, otherwise known as the Ram Janmabhumi ("Birthplace of Lord Ram"). A series of court orders had divided the space so that Muslims could worship in one area while Hindu services were performed in another by a court-appointed priest. This status quo broke down in the early 1990s when the Bharatiya Janata Party, campaigning on a Hindu nationalist agenda, revived the dispute as a national issue, leading to the destruction of the mosque by a mob of activists in 1992, allegedly in collusion with the BJP-controlled state government. A study by the Archaeological Survey of India provided expert testimony that the mosque was built over the ruins of a temple (although the study stopped short of asserting that the temple indeed marked the birthplace of Ram, an incarnation of the Hindu deity). The case was finally resolved by a 2010 decision by the Allahabad High Court, which effectively handed a victory to the Hindu side.

It was in the context of this dispute that The Places of Worship (Special Provisions) Act (No. 42 of 1991) was passed to outlaw the "conversion" of places of worship from one religion to another. Another recent legal intervention saw the Andhra Pradesh High Court issuing a stay order to prevent the gold-plating of the sanctum of the famous Tirumala Temple on the grounds that it would damage artwork of historical value on the walls.

## The "Hindutva Judgments"

Closely related to the controversy and social unrest generated by the Ayodhya dispute was a series of cases in which Hindu nationalist politicians were charged with campaigning on an explicitly religious platform and fostering interreligious hatred, "corrupt practices" prohibited by Section 123(3) of the Representation of the People Act (RPA, 1951). The law survived an early challenge on free-speech ground in 1954. Decisions in a series of subsequent cases had the effect of weakening the law however, as the courts gave candidates latitude in how they express themselves on the stump, and found that the mere presence of religious symbols did not necessarily constitute an appeal to religious prejudice.

This trend reached its apogee with a set of seven cases decided by the Supreme Court in 1996 (Cossman and Kapur, 1999; R. Sen, 2007; Narula, 2010). In these cases, members of Hindu nationalist parties, including Bal Thackeray, head of the Shiv Sena and Manohar Joshi, chief minister of Maharashtra, were charged under Section 123 for campaigning on the basis of "Hindutva." Thackeray was found guilty of encouraging voters to support his candidate because he was Hindu, and of denigrating Muslims, but Joshi was exonerated despite his having publicly declared that the first Hindu state would be established in Maharashtra.

Of more consequence was the court's acceptance of the Hindu nationalists' defense that Hindutva is a cultural ethos, a "way of life" distinctive of Indian culture, rather than a religion, strictly speaking. This is the very argument made by Savarkar (1928), although J. S. Verma, writing for the court, did not allude to him directly. The significance was not lost on Arun Shourie, a minister in the BJP-led government and a prominent spokesman for the movement: "The Court accepted, indeed adopted in to the definition of Hindu, of Hindutva which the RSS and BJP have been maintaining is what they have meant whenever they have used these expressions" (quoted in R. Sen, 2010: 24). Verma's decision has been criticized for undermining the intent of the RPA and giving official endorsement to a divisive political ideology, but it was also hailed by some liberals, including Ronald Dworkin, on free-speech grounds.

# Hinduism beyond South Asia

Encounters between Hindu religion and the law happen not just in South Asia but in many parts of the world. The last few centuries have seen a Hindu diaspora emerge. These movements of population happened in waves, for different reasons at different times. During the colonial era, the major cause was indentured servitude: Indians were sent to far-flung parts of the British Empire as laborers. Their descendents comprise large segments of the population of Fiji, Singapore, Malaysia, South Africa, parts of East Africa, Guyana, and Trinidad. Since Indian independence, South Asians have migrated voluntarily to England, various Commonwealth countries (especially Canada and Australia), and increasingly the United States. In each of these settings, Hindus must negotiate the local legal system, both as regards their personal status and the status of their religion. Krishnan (2010) provides a compact survey of the subject.

While sociological and ethnographic studies are available for many of these cases, works treating the legal situation directly are relatively rare (Menski, 2007 is a recent exception). Younger (2011) provides a good general account of the Indian communities in several parts of the diaspora, focusing on social and religious patterns, including the ways in which the self-representation of Hindus in these countries contributed to the formation of a transnational form of Hinduism as a world religion. Younger includes some discussion of the legal dimensions of this process. He notes, for instance, that the legal recognition of Hindu marriage laws from the 1850s helped north Indian Hindus in Mauritius "live in their own world" more than other immigrant populations there (p. 51). Hindu religious leaders in Guyana in 1927 sought and won official recognition for a Council of Pandits, which performed legal weddings, secured the legalization of cremation, and eventually came to represent the interests of the Indian community more broadly (pp. 80–84); the Sanatana Dharma Maha Sabha founded in 1952 in Trinidad played a similar role (pp. 108–110). Gandhi's legal activism in colonial South Africa is well-known; among other things, it led to the passage of the Indian Relief Act of 1914, which legally recognized Hindu and Indian Muslim marriages. In East Africa too, Anglo-Hindu law remained in effect long after it had been replaced in India (Derrett, 1963).

A unique monograph on law and Hinduism in the diaspora was inspired by Presler's work on the administration of South Indian temples (1987). Sinha (2011) provides a detailed study of the legal position of Hindu religious institutions in the Malay peninsula and in independent Singapore.

A quite different situation is found in Indonesia, where the tiny Hindu minority (concentrated today in Bali and parts of Java) dates back more than a thousand years, to the period when Hinduism was adopted as the state religion by local rulers under the influence of Indian traders settled in ports on the coasts of Java and Sumatra. Living today in a country that is 99 percent Muslim, Indonesian Hindu leaders have sought official recognition for their traditions (known as *adat hindu*) by formulating a formal "religion" (Agama Hindu) that can be regarded as legitimate in light of Islamic criteria (monotheism, revealed scripture, etc.) and recognized in the courts (Ramstedt, 2004).

Religion meets law in other ways for "second-wave" immigrant Hindus in places like the United Kingdom and the United States. Hindus have recourse to host countries' laws to establish religious institutions, gain sanction for religious practices (such as an ill-fated attempt to have open-air cremations allowed in England), and settle marital disputes based on Hindu-law marriages sanctified in India. Women married in India under Hindu marriage law and wishing to bring criminal charges in India against a spouse for alleged harassment or fraud under Section 498A of the Indian Criminal Code may first seek a civil ruling against him in American family court, which can then provide a *res judicata* to support the criminal charges (*Chhibber v. Nangia*, Henrico County Circuit Court of Henrico County, Virginia, 2011).

But the law can also provide a venue for Hindu groups to try to win official recognition for a particular representation of their religion. For example, groups affiliated to the Hindu American Foundation filed suit in 2005 against the California State Board of Education to make changes to sixth-grade textbooks' depiction of Hinduism and Indian history (Kurien, 2007: 204–206).

Besides diaspora Hindus, converts to Hinduism in the West also sometimes have recourse to the law to seek accommodation for their religious practice. In one case in England, members of ISKCON (the "Hare Krishnas") argued that their public Krishna *lila* should be permitted because it was more "like a nativity play" than mere "public entertainment" (Sullivan, 2006).

# Notes

1. The Buddhist monkhood produced extensive codes of rules and a comparably vast jurisprudential literature but it was limited in jurisdiction to members of the order, dealing almost exclusively with internal discipline and institutional administration.
2. *Mohammed Ahmed Khan v. Shah Bano Begum* (AIR 1985 SC 945).
3. An early Supreme Court case, *Chatturbhuj Vithaldas Jasani v. Moreshwar Parashram* (1954 SCA 395), overturned the disqualification of a candidate for a seat reserved for Scheduled Castes due to his conversion to the Mahanubhav Panth.
4. They were followed by Arunachal Pradesh (1978), Tamil Nadu (2002, repealed 2004), Gujarat (2003), Chhattisgarh (2003), Rajasthan (2006), and Himachal Pradesh (2006). Similar laws had been passed in some princely states prior to Independence. Unsuccessful attempts were made to pass anti-conversion bills at the federal level (1954, 1978).
5. *Chandra v. M. Thangamuthu & Anr.* 2010 INSC 705 (September 7, 2010).

# Bibliography

Agnes, Flavia. 1999. *Law and Gender Inequality: The Politics of Women's Rights in India.* New Delhi: Oxford University Press.

Aktor, Mikael. 2008. *Ritualisation and Segregation: The Untouchability Complex in Indian Dharma Literature with Special Reference to Parāśarasmṛti and Parāśaramādhavīya.* Corpus Iuris Sanscriticum et fontes iuris Asiae Meridianae et Centralis, 9. Torino: CESMEO.

———. 2010. Untouchability in Brahminical Law Books: Ritual and Economic Control. In Mikael Aktor and Robert Deliège (eds), *From Stigma to Assertion: Untouchability, Identity and Politics in Early and Modern India*, 31–63. Copenhagen: Museum Tusculanum Press.

Baird, Robert (ed.). 1993. *Religion and Law in Independent India.* New Delhi: Manohar; expanded second edition 2005.

Bavinck, Maarten. 1998. "'A Matter of Maintaining Peace': State Accommodation to Subordinate Legal Systems: The Case of Fisheries along the Coromandel Coast of Tamil Nadu, India." *Journal of Legal Pluralism* 40: 151–170.

Baxi, Pratiksha, Shirin M. Rai, and Shaheen Sardar Ali. 2006. "Legacies of Common Law: 'Crimes of Honour' in India and Pakistan." *Third World Quarterly* 27(7): 1239–1253.

Benke, Theodore. 2010. "The *Śūdrācāraśiromaṇi* of Kṛṣṇa Śeṣa: A 16th Century Manual of Dharma for Śūdras." Doctoral dissertation, University of Pennsylvania.

Bhargava, Rajeev (ed.). 1999. *Secularism and Its Critics.* New Delhi: Oxford University Press.

———. 2008. *Politics and Ethics of the Indian Constitution.* New Delhi: Oxford University Press.

Chowdhry, Prem. 2004. "Caste Panchayats and the Policing of Marriage in Haryana: Enforcing Kinship and Territorial Exogamy." *Contributions to Indian Sociology* 38: 1–42.

_____. 2009. "'First Our Jobs Then Our Girls': The Dominant Caste Perceptions on the 'Rising' Dalits." *Modern Asian Studies* 43(2): 437–479.

Cossman, Brenda and Ratna Kapur. 1999. *Secularism's Last Sigh? Hindutva and the (Mis)Rule of Law*. New Delhi: Oxford University Press.

Cox, Whitney M. 2010. "Law, Literature, and the Problem of Politics in Medieval India." In Timothy Lubin, Donald R. Davis, Jr., and Jayanth K. Krishnan (eds), *Hinduism and Law: An Introduction*, 167–182. New York: Cambridge University Press.

Creese, Helen. 2009a. "Old Javanese Legal Traditions in Pre-colonial Bali." *Bijdragen tot de Taal-, Land- en Volkenkunde (BKI)* 165(2/3): 241–290.

_____. 2009b. "Judicial Processes and Legal Authority in Pre-colonial Bali." *Bijdragen tot de Taal-, Land- en Volkenkunde (BKI)* 165(4): 515–550.

Davis, Donald R., Jr. 1999. "Recovering the Indigenous Legal Traditions of India: Classical Hindu Law in Practice in Late Medieval Kerala." *Journal of Indian Philosophy* 27: 159–213.

_____. 2002. "Dharma, Maryāda, and Law in Early British Malabar: Remarks on Words for 'Law' in the Tellicherry Records." *Studien zur Indologie und Iranistik* 23: 51–70.

_____. 2004a. *The Boundaries of Hindu Law Tradition, Custom and Politics in Medieval Kerala*. Corpus Iuris Sanscriticum, 5. Turin: CESMEO.

_____. 2004b. "Dharma in Practice: Ācāra and Authority in Medieval Dharmaśāstra." *Journal of Indian Philosophy* 32(1): 813–830.

_____. 2004c. "Traditional Hindu Law in the Guise of 'Postmodernism': A Review Article" [of Menski 2003]. *Michigan Journal of International Law* 25: 735–749.

_____. 2005. "Intermediate Realms of Law: Corporate Groups and Rulers in Medieval India." *Journal of the Economic and Social History of the Orient* 48(1): 92–117.

_____. 2007. "Hinduism as a Legal Tradition." *Journal of the American Academy of Religion* 75: 241–67.

_____. 2008. "Law." In Gene Thursby and Sushil Mittal (eds), *Studying Hinduism: Key Concepts and Methods*, 218–29. London: Routledge.

_____. 2010a. *The Spirit of Hindu Law*. New York: Cambridge University Press.

_____. 2010b. "A Historical Overview of Hindu Law." In Timothy Lubin, Donald R. Davis, Jr., and Jayanth K. Krishnan (eds), *Hinduism and Law: An Introduction*, 17–27. New York: Cambridge University Press.

Davis, Richard H. 2010. "Temples, Deities, and the Law." In Timothy Lubin, Donald R. Davis, Jr., and Jayanth K. Krishnan (eds), *Hinduism and Law: An Introduction*, 195–206. New York: Cambridge University Press.

Derrett, J. Duncan M. 1961. "The Administration of Hindu Law by the British." *Comparative Studies in Society and History* 4(1): 10–52.

_____. 1963. *Introduction to Modern Hindu Law*. Bombay: Oxford University Press.

_____. 1968. *Religion, Law and the State in India*. London: Faber and Faber.

Dhavan, Rajeev. 2001. "The Road to Xanadu: India's Quest for Secularism." In Gerald James Larson (ed.), *Religion and Personal Law in Secular India: A Call to Judgment*, 301–329. Bloomington: Indiana University Press.

Dirks, Nicholas B. 1997. "The Policing of Tradition: Colonialism and Anthropology in Southern India." *Comparative Studies in Society and History* 39(1): 182–212.

Eaton, Richard M. 2005. *A Social History of the Deccan, 1300–1761: Eight Indian Lives.* The New Cambridge History of India, I.8. New York: Cambridge University Press.

Galanter, Marc. 1964. "Temple-Entry and the Untouchability (Offences) Act, 1955." *Journal of the Indian Law Institute* 6(2–3): 185–195.

———. 1965. "Secularism East and West" [review article on Smith, *India as a Secular State*], *Comparative Studies in Society and History* 7: 133–159. Reprinted in Bhargava 1998.

———. 1971. "Hinduism, Secularism and the Indian Judiciary," *Philosophy East & West* 21: 467–487. Reprinted in Galanter 1989 and Bhargava 1998.

———. 1972. "The Aborted Restoration of 'Indigenous' Law in India," *Comparative Studies in Society and History* 14: 53–70. Reprinted in Galanter 1989.

———. 1981. "Justice in Many Rooms: Courts, Private Ordering and Indigenous Law." *Journal of Legal Pluralism* 19: 1–47.

———. 1984. *Competing Equalities: Law and the Backward Classes in India.* New Delhi: Oxford University Press.

———. 1989. *Law and Society in Modern India*, edited with an introduction by Rajeev Dhavan. New Delhi: Oxford University Press.

Griffiths, A. and Soutif, D. 2010–2011. "Autour des terres de Loñ Śrī Viṣṇu et de sa famille: Un document administratif du Cambodge angkorien, l'inscription K. 1238," *Bulletin de l'École française d'Extrême-Orient.*

Gune, Vithal Trimbak. 1953. *The Judicial System of the Marathas: A Detailed Study of the Judicial Institutions in Maharashtra from 1600–1818 AD, Based on Original Decisions Called Mazhars, Nivadpatras and Official Orders.* Deccan College Dissertation Series, 12. Pune: Deccan College.

Hayden, Robert M. 1984. "A Note on Caste Panchayats and Government Courts in India." *Journal of Legal Pluralism* 22: 43–52.

Hoadley, M. C. and Hooker, M. B. 1981. *An Introduction to Javanese Law: A Translation of and Commentary on the Agama.* Tucson: Univ. of Arizona Press/Association for Asian Studies.

———. 1986. "The Law Texts of Java and Bali." In M. B. Hooker (ed.), *The Laws of South-East Asia. Volume 1: The Pre-modern Texts*, 241–346. Singapore: Butterworth & Co.

Ishizawa, Y. 1986. "Remarks on the Epigraphy of Angkorian Cambodia." In M. B. Hooker (ed.), *The Laws of South-East Asia. Volume 1: The Pre-modern Texts*, 205–240. Singapore: Butterworth & Co.

Jacobsohn, Gary J. 2003. *The Wheel of Law: India's Secularism in Comparative Constitutional Context.* UK: Princeton University Press.

Jenkins, Laura Dudley. 2010. "Contemporary Caste Discrimination and Affirmative Action." In Timothy Lubin, Donald R. Davis, Jr., and Jayanth K. Krishnan (eds), *Hinduism and Law: An Introduction*, 215–233. New York: Cambridge University Press.

Jordan, Kay K. 2003. *From Sacred Servant to Profane Prostitute: A History of the Changing Legal Status of the Devadasis in India, 1857–1947.* New Delhi: Manohar.

Kane, Pandurang Vaman, 1968–75. *History of Dharmaśāstra*, 2d ed., 5 vols. in 8 parts. Pune: Bhandarkar Oriental Research Institute.

64    Timothy Lubin

Kangle, R. P. 1965–1972. *The Kauṭilīya Arthaśāstra*, 2d ed., 3 vols. Bombay: Bombay University; reprinted. New Delhi: Motilal Banarsidass.

Karashima, Noboru. 1984. *South Indian History and Society: Studies from Inscriptions, A.D. 850–1800.* New Delhi: Oxford University Press.

Karashima, Noboru. 2008. "Temple Land in Chola and Pandyan Inscriptions: The Legal Meaning and Historical Implications of *Kuḍinīṅga-dēvadāna*." *Indian Economic and Social History Review* 45(2): 175–199.

Kodoth, Praveena. 2001. "Courting Legitimacy or Delegitimizing Custom? Sexuality, Sambandham, and Marriage Reform in Late Nineteenth-Century Malabar." *Modern Asian Studies* 35(2): 349–384.

Kölver, Bernhard (ed.). 1997. *Recht, Staat und Verwaltung im klassischen Indien/The State, the Law, and Administration in Classical India.* Schriften des Historischen Kollegs, 30. Munich: Oldenbourg Wissenschaftsverlag.

Kölver, Bernhard and Hemrāj Śākya (eds). 1985. *Documents from the Rudravarṇa-Mahāvihāra, Pāṭan 1: Sales and Mortgages.* Sankt Augustin: VGH Wissenschaftsverlag.

Krishnan, Jayanth K. 2010. "Legally and Politically Layered Identities: A Thumbnail Survey of Selected Hindu Migration Patterns from South Asia." In Timothy Lubin, Donald R. Davis, Jr., and Jayanth K. Krishnan (eds.), *Hinduism and Law: An Introduction*, 252–265. New York: Cambridge University Press.

Kurien, Prema A. 2007. *A Place at the Multicultural Table: The Development of an American Hinduism.* Piscataway, NJ: Rutgers University Press.

Lariviere, Richard W. 1981. *The Divyatattva of Raghunandana Bhaṭṭācārya: Ordeals in Classical Hindu Law.* New Delhi: Manohar.

_____. 1989a. *The Nāradasmṛti*, 2 vols. Philadelphia, PA: University of Pennsylvania, Department of South Asia Regional Studies.

_____. 1989b. "Justices and *Panditas*: Some Ironies in Contemporary Readings of the Hindu Legal Past." *Journal of Asian Studies* 48(4): 757–769.

_____. 1996. "Dharmaśāstra: Its Present Value and Relevance." In K. Satchidananda Murty and Amit Dasgupta (eds), *The Perennial Tree: Select Papers of the International Symposium on India Studies*, 176–189. New Delhi: Indian Council for Cultural Relations.

_____. 1997. "Dharmaśāstra, Custom, 'Real Law' and Apocryphal Smṛtis." In Bernhard Kölver (ed.), *Recht, Staat und Verwaltung im klassischen Indien/The State, the Law, and Administration in Classical India*, 97–110. Munich: Oldenbourg Wissenschaftsverlag Reprinted in Olivelle 2004a: 611–627.

Larson, Gerald James (ed.). 2001. *Religion and Personal Law in Secular India: A Call to Judgment.* Bloomington, IN: University of Indiana Press.

Lingat, Robert. 1973. *The Classical Law of India*, trans. J. Duncan M. Derrett. Berkeley: University of California Press.

Lloyd, Tom. 2006. "Acting in the 'Theatre of Anarchy': The 'Anti-Thug Campaign' and Elaborations of Colonial Rule in Early Nineteenth-Century India. *Edinburgh Papers in South Asian Studies*, 19.

Lubin, Timothy. 2007. "Punishment and Expiation: Overlapping Domains in Brahmanical Law." *Indologica Taurinensia* 33: 91–120.

Lubin, Timothy. 2010. "Indic Conceptions of Authority." In Timothy Lubin, Donald R. Davis, Jr., and Jayanth K. Krishnan (eds), *Hinduism and Law: An Introduction*, 137–153. New York: Cambridge University Press.

————. 2013. "Legal Diglossia: Modeling Discursive Practices in Premodern Indic Law." In Vincenzo Vergiani and Whitney Cox (eds), *Bilingual Discourse and Cross-Cultural Fertilisation: Sanskrit and Tamil in Mediaeval India*. Collection Indologie, 121. Paris and Pondicherry: Institut français de Pondichéry/École française d'Extrême-Orient.

————. 2015. "Writing and the Recognition of Customary Law in Premodern India and Java." *Journal of the American Oriental Society* 135(1).

Luthra, Parikshit. 2010. "Khaps Defiant, Say Honour Killings Will Continue." CNN-IBN/IBNLive. July 12. Online at http://ibnlive.in.com/news/khaps-defiant-say-honour-killings-will-continue/126456-3.html (accessed on November 23, 2010).

Mahajan, Gurpreet. 2008. "Religion and the Indian Constitution: Questions of Separation and Equality." In Rajeev Bhargava (ed.), *Politics and Ethics of the Indian Constitution*, 297–310. New Delhi: Oxford University Press.

Malik, Aditya. 2010. "In the Divine Court of Appeals: Vows Before the God of Justice." In Timothy Lubin, Donald R. Davis, Jr., and Jayanth K. Krishnan (eds), *Hinduism and Law: An Introduction*, 207–214. New York: Cambridge University Press.

Mani, Lata. 1998. *Contentious Traditions: The Debate on Sati in Colonial India*. Berkeley, CA: University of California Press.

Mathur, Ashutosh Dayal. 2007. *Medieval Hindu Law: Historical Evolution and Enlightened Rebellion*. New Delhi: Oxford University Press.

McCrea, Lawrence. 2010. "Hindu Jurisprudence and Scriptural Hermeneutics." In Timothy Lubin, Donald R. Davis, Jr., and Jayanth K. Krishnan (eds), *Hinduism and Law: An Introduction*, 123–136. New York: Cambridge University Press.

McClish, Mark Richard. 2009. "Political Brahmanism and the State: A Compositional History of the *Arthaśāstra*." Doctoral dissertation, University of Texas at Austin.

Menski, Werner. 2003. *Hindu Law: Beyond Tradition and Modernity*. New York: Oxford University Press.

————. 2007. "Law, Religion and South Asians in Diaspora." In John Hinnells (ed.), *Religious Reconstruction in the South Asian Diaspora: From One Generation to Another*, 243–264. New York: Palgrave Macmillan.

————. 2008. "Recent Developments in the Uniform Civil Code Debates in India." *German Law Journal* 9(3): 212–250.

Michaels, Axel. 2005. *The Price of Purity: The Religious Judge in 19th Century Nepal. Containing the Edition and Translation of the Chapters on the Dharmādhikārin in Two (Mulukī) Ains*. Corpus Juris Sancriticum et fontes iuris Asiae Meridianae et Centralis, 6. Turin: CESMEO.

Mitra, Subrata and Alexander Fischer. 2002. "Sacred Laws and the Secular State: An Analytical Narrative of the Controversy over Personal Laws in India." *India Review* 1(3): 99–130.

Mudaliar, Chandra Y. 1974. *The Secular State and Religious Institutions in India: A Study of the Administration of Hindu Public Religious Trusts in Madras*. Wiesbaden: Franz SteinerVerlag.

Nanda, Ved P. and Surya Prakash Sinha (eds). 1997. *Hindu Law and Legal Theory.* International Library of Essays in Law and Legal Theory; Legal Cultures, 12. New York: New York University Press.

Narula, Smita. 2010. "Law and Hindu Nationalist Movements." In Timothy Lubin, Donald R. Davis, Jr., and Jayanth K. Krishnan (eds), *Hinduism and Law: An Introduction,* 234–251. New York: Cambridge University Press.

Oddie, Geoffrey. 1995. *Popular Religion, Elites and Reform: Hook-Swinging and Its Prohibition in Colonial India, 1800–1894.* New Delhi: Manohar.

O'Hanlon, Rosalind. 2009. "Narratives of Penance and Purification in Western India, c. 1650–1850." *The Journal of Hindu Studies* 2: 48–75.

Olivelle, Patrick. 1987. "King and Ascetic: State Control of Asceticism in the Arthaśāstra." *Adyar Library Bulletin* 51: 39–59.

———. 1993. *The Āśrama System.* New York: Oxford University Press.

———. 2000. *Dharmasūtras: The Law Codes of Āpastamba, Gautama, Baudhāyana, and Vasiṣṭha.* New Delhi: Motilal Banarsidass.

———. (ed.) 2004a. Dharma: Studies in Its Semantic, Cultural, and Religious History. Special double issue of the *Journal of Indian Philosophy* 32.

———. 2005a. *Manu's Code of Law: A Critical Edition and Translation of the Mānava-Dharmaśāstra,* with the editorial assistance of Suman Olivelle. New York: Oxford University Press.

———. 2005b. "Power of Words: The Ascetic Appropriation and the Semantic Evolution of Dharma." In *Language, Texts, and Society: Explorations in Ancient Indian Culture and Religion,* 121–135. Florence: University of Firenze Press.

———. 2009. *The Law Code of Viṣṇu: A Critical Edition and Annotated Translation of the Vaiṣṇava-Dharmaśāstra.* Harvard Oriental Series, 73. Cambridge, MA: Harvard University Press.

———. 2010. "Dharmaśāstra: A Textual History." In Timothy Lubin, Donald R. Davis, Jr., and Jayanth K. Krishnan (eds), *Hinduism and Law: An Introduction,* 28–57. New York: Cambridge University Press.

Parker, Kunal M. 1998. "'A Corporation of Superior Prostitutes': Anglo-Indian Legal Conceptions of Temple Dancing Girls, 1800–1914." *Modern Asian Studies* 32(3): 559–633.

Prasad, Pushpa. 2007. *Lekhapaddhati: Documents of State and Everyday Life from Ancient and Early Medieval Gujarat.* New Delhi: Oxford University Press.

Presler, Franklin A. 1987. *Religion under Bureaucracy: Policy and Administration for Hindu Temples in South India.* South Asian Studies, 38. Cambridge: Cambridge University Press.

Ramstedt, Martin (ed.). 2004. *Hinduism in Modern Indonesia: A Minority Religion Between Local, National, and Global Interests.* London: Routledge Curzon.

Rocher, Ludo. 1969. "'Lawyers' in Classical Hindu Law." *Law and Society Review* 3: 383–402.

———. 1972. "Indian Response to Anglo-Indian Law." *Journal of the American Oriental Society* 92(3): 419–424.

———. 1993. "Law Books in an Oral Culture: The Indian *Dharmaśāstras.*" *Proceedings of the American Philosophical Society* 137: 254–267.

———. 2002. *Jīmūtavāhana's Dāyabhāga: The Hindu Law of Inheritance in Bengal.* Oxford: Oxford University Press.

Rocher, Ludo. 2012. *Studies in Hindu Law and Dharmaśāstra*, Donald R. Davis Jr (ed.). London and Delhi: Anthem Press.

Rocher, Rosane. 2010. "The Creation of Anglo-Hindu Law." In Timothy Lubin, Donald R. Davis, Jr., and Jayanth K. Krishnan (eds), *Hinduism and Law: An Introduction*, 78–88. New York: Cambridge University Press.

Savarkar, Vinayak Damodar. 1923. *Hindutva*. Nagpur: V. V. Kelkar. Originally published under the pen-name 'A Maratha'; reissued in 1928 under the author's real name as *Hindutva: Who Is a Hindu?*

Scharfe, Hartmut. 1993. *Investigations in Kauṭalya's Manual of Political Science.* Wiesbaden: Harrassowitz Verlag. Revised English version of *Untersuchungen zur Staatsrechtslehre des Kauṭalyas* (Wiesbaden: Harrassowitz, 1968).

Sen, Amartya. 2005. "Secularism and Its Discontents." In *The Argumentative Indian*, 294–316. New York: Farrar, Straus & Giroux.

Sen, Ronojoy. 2007. *Legalizing Religion: The Indian Supreme Court and Secularism.* Policy Studies, 30. Washington: East-West Center.

_____. 2010. *Articles of Faith: Religion, Secularism, and the Indian Supreme Court.* New Delhi: Oxford University Press.

Sinha, Vineeta. 2011. *Religion–State Encounters in Hindu Domains: From the Straits Settlements to Singapore.* Dordrecht: Springer.

Smith, Graham, and J. Duncan M. Derrett. 1975. "Hindu Judicial Administration in Pre-British Times and its Lesson for Today." *Journal of the American Oriental Society* 95(3): 417–423.

Solanki, Gopika. 2011. *Adjudication in the Religious Family Laws: Cultural Accommodation, Legal Pluralism, and Gender Equality in India.* New York: Cambridge University Press.

Sontheimer, Günther-Dietz. 1964a. "Recent Developments in Hindu Law." *International and Comparative Law Quarterly Supplement* 8: 32–45.

Sontheimer, Günther-Dietz. 1964b. "Religious Endowments in India: The Juristic Personality of Hindu Deities." *Zeitschrift für vergleichende Rechtswissenschaft* 67(1): 45–100.

Strauch, Ingo. 2002. *Die Lekhapaddhati–Lekhapañcāśikā. Briefe und Urkunden im mittelalterlichen Gujarat. Text, Übersetzung, Kommentar.* Berlin: Dietrich Reimer.

Sturman, Rachel. 2010. "Marriage and Family in Colonial Hindu Law." In Timothy Lubin, Donald R. Davis, Jr., and Jayanth K. Krishnan (eds), *Hinduism and Law: An Introduction*, 89–104. New York: Cambridge University Press.

Sullivan, Winnifred Fallers. 2006. "Comparing Religions, Legally." *Washington and Lee Law Review* 63: 913–928.

*The Constituent Assembly Debates 7 (4 Nov. 1948–8 Jan. 1949). 1989.* New Delhi: Lok Sabha Secretariat.

Trautmann, Thomas R. 1971. *Kauṭilya and the Arthaśāstra: A Statistical Investigation of the Authorship and Evolution of the Text.* Leiden: Brill.

Vajpeyi, Ananya. 2010. "*Śūdradharma* and Legal Treatments of Caste." In Timothy Lubin, Donald R. Davis, Jr., and Jayanth K. Krishnan (eds), *Hinduism and Law: An Introduction*, 154–166. New York: Cambridge University Press.

Vincentnathan, S. George. 1992. "The Social Construction of Order and Disorder in Two South Indian Communities." *Journal of Legal Pluralism* 32: 65–102.

Viswanathan, Gauri. 1998. *Outside the Fold: Conversion, Modernity and Belief*. Princeton: Princeton University Press.

Wagle, N. K. 1970. "The History and Social Organization of the Gauda Sarasvata Brahmanas of the West Coast of India." *Journal of Indian History* 48(1): 7–25.

_____. 1980. "A Dispute between the Pancal Devajna Sonars and the Brahmans of Pune regarding Social Rank and Ritual Privileges: A Case Study of the British Administration of Jati Laws in Maharashtra, 1822–1825." In N. K. Wagle (ed.), *Images of Maharashtra: A Regional Profile of India*, 129–159. London: Curzon Press.

_____. 1982. "The Candraseniya Kayastha Prabhus and the Brahmans: Ritual, Law and Politics in Pune, 1789–90." In G. D. Sontheimer and P. Aithal (eds), *Indology and Law: Studies in Honour of Professor J. Duncan M. Derrett*, 303–328. Wiesbaden: Franz Steiner.

_____. 1987. "Ritual and Change in Early Nineteenth Century Society in Maharashtra: Vedokta Disputes in Baroda, Pune and Satara, 1824–1838." In Milton Israel and N. K. Wagle (eds), *Religion and Society in Maharashtra*, 145–181. Toronto: University of Toronto.

_____. 1995. "On Relations amongst Bhūts, Gods, and Men: Aspects of Folk Religion and Law in Pre-British Maharashtra." In Günther-Dietz Sontheimer (ed.), *Folk Culture, Folk Religion, and Oral Traditions as a Component in Culture and Society*, 181–220. New Delhi: Manohar.

_____. 1998. "Women in the Kotwal's Papers, Pune, 1767–1791." In Anne Feldhaus (ed.), *Images of Women in Maharashtrian Society*, 15–60. New York: SUNY Press.

_____. 2005. "Customary Laws among the Non-Brahman Jātis of Puṇe, 1824–1826." In Aditya Malik, Anne Feldhaus, and Heidrun Brueckner (eds), *In the Company of Gods: Essays in Memory of Günther-Dietz Sontheimer*, 283–328. New Delhi: Manohar.

Wagner, Kim A. 2007. *Thuggee: Banditry and the British in Early Nineteenth-Century India*. Basingstoke (UK): Palgrave Macmillan.

Williams, Rina Verma. 2006. *Postcolonial Politics and Personal Laws: Colonial Legal Legacies and the Indian State*. New Delhi: Oxford University Press.

_____. 2010. "Hindu Law as Personal Law: State and Identity in the Hindu Code Bill Debates, 1952–1956." In Timothy Lubin, Donald R. Davis, Jr., and Jayanth K. Krishnan (eds), *Hinduism and Law: An Introduction*, 105–119. New York: Cambridge University Press.

Yelle, Robert A. 2010. "Hindu Law as Performance: Ritual and Poetic Elements in Dharmaśāstra." In Timothy Lubin, Donald R. Davis, Jr., and Jayanth K. Krishnan (eds), *Hinduism and Law: An Introduction*, 183–192. New York: Cambridge University Press.

Younger, Paul. 2011. *New Homelands: Hindu Communities in Mauritius, Guyana, Trinidad, South Africa, Fiji, and East Africa*. Oxford: Oxford University Press.

# Chapter 4

## Hinduism and Economics

Thomas Birtchnell

## Introduction

The question "what is Hinduism?" has been asked and answered about as many times as the question "what is Economics?" so that it appears doubly brave to try to broach the two together. In this survey, an open view of Hinduism and economics is encouraged that sees both as composed of complex institutions, exchanges, customs, beliefs, and people. Of course facets of religion, like ritual or scripture, are not contingent on social, political, and economic change; however, people and their everyday lives are equally interconnected with both economics and religion so that both can co-exist and act upon each other (Flood, 1996). A starting point in this summary is that economics includes infrastructure, well-being, charity, philanthropy, and other "soft" factors. While it is true that economists have dabbled in religion, as inputs in economic modeling or as values in quantitative surveys, these efforts have tended toward understanding religion as a closed phenomenon outside of economic activity. Yet, in the case of India, as Deepak Lal has documented in detail in *Hindu Equilibrium* (2005), what might appear to be economic stagnation by some accounts—principally neoliberal—is in fact evidence of the ongoing social order and continuity of a Hinduism spanning over millennia. According to Lal, this social equilibrium was in many ways disrupted by the colonial order and sensitivity is demanded in appraising Hinduism from this longitudinal perspective.

There is now a large and respectable body of historical work that paints a graphic, in depth and scholarly picture of the changes wrought by colonialism and the origins and adaptations of the many scriptures and encounters that informed popular ideas of Hindu practices and beliefs. But Hinduism is also a religion that continues to be practiced; a religion that is vivid, colorful, and engrossingly complex. Hinduism is visible across India and throughout the world and is composed of interlocking, mutual beliefs, and practices. The cosmopolitan mediators and gurus that are the faces of this sprawling religion are not only religious icons, but political and economic agents. For example, there is a real connection between the global circuits of religious celebrities and the transnational identities of gurus and other religious elites in the popular imagination.

Academic projects that pursue thematic understandings of religion and economics are now informed by major shifts in the social sciences landscape that offers new techniques for understanding "how truly *social* economic life" is (Centeno and Cohen, 2010: 3). As Ninian Smart has made clear a broader, thematic approach to surveying aspects of Hinduism agrees with a "dimensional analysis" of religion that includes "economics" as one part of a number of dimensions within religious systems that are not only constituted by texts (Bowen, 1998).

Much recent work involving economics and Hinduism is contained within the scope of "Hindu nationalism" on one side and "Asian values" on the other. While incredibly useful and fruitful these areas are only a small part of a bigger picture that moves beyond the conceptual geopolitical boundaries of the State [India] or even of regions [Asia].

Scholarly opinion is being recast away from India or Asia as the only geographical spaces for Hinduism. Instead there are many "novel articulations" arising from the global context, in the diasporas and also in popular culture reworkings in the West (Coleman, 2010). Thus, while much research focuses on Hinduism as indigenous and nationalist, embedded in "civilizational territories," a growing body is also looking at Hinduism as a value system that is global and "deterritorialized" through global migration and flows of ideas and people (Casanova, 2011). These reworkings also include management and business contexts and (re)imaginings of how economics and Hinduism relate to one another.

Recent ideas of "Indovation" (Lamont, 2010), "consumptionomics" (Nair, 2011), "spirinomics" (S. K. Chakraborty and D. Chakraborty, 2007) and a whole other range of portmanteau words all point to a convergence of religious and economic values across geopolitical and knowledge borders. Work seeking to excite and fuse aspects of Hinduism with aspects of economics, business, and management make an elegant balance to critical, academic work on chauvinism, values, and Hindu nationalism.

From this big picture perspective, the economic aspects of Hinduism shape flows not only of finance and currency but also of ideas and beliefs. In this survey, four areas that represent the current state of play in Hinduism and economics have been identified and reviewed: infrastructures, values, mediators, and developments.

First, it is now widely recognized that infrastructures order religion. Within India infrastructures, like the Ayodhya temple complex, are central focus points for dispute and worship. But beyond this orthodox idea of infrastructure is a whole array of economic considerations: planning and logistics of events, exchanges, and pilgrimages; these all involve trade, finance, money, and investments.

Second, economists have engaged with the values of Hinduism in order to understand alternative management, business, and corporate practices as ways of modern, economically prudent, living. Hinduism has not only traveled through migrant track ways via itinerant labor flows to key diasporas, but also via the media, elites, popular culture, and fashion. The Asian values genre recognizes that alternative ways of living have economic values. It is no coincidence that with the surge of economic valency in India and China, there has been heightened attention to cultural and spiritual values. With this growing attention has arisen forecasting of how issues, including 'energy use' sustainability, and climate change might be articulated and even tackled through spiritual practices such as austerity, asceticism, vegetarianism, and care for the environment, acted out by the rising and aspirational middle classes.

Third, much has changed in assessments of how Hinduism is practiced by key actors and, often cosmopolitan, mediators between religion and economics. In one of the first assessments of Hindu practices and religious beliefs Nirad C. Chaudhuri's *Hinduism* describes quite vaguely, but cannily in a section titled "Gain from Religion" how those who "left the world and adopted a religious life or vocation lost nothing by giving up worldly occupations and cutting themselves adrift from society ... on the contrary they ensured an alternative means of livelihood ... which brought even substantial wealth to many of them" (1979: 303).

Much recent work embellishes and gives weight to the characters who not only derive incomes and livelihoods from their Hindu practices, but as well shape dialogues and discourses; lobby for economic and social equalities; and influence how economic and religious interests are tolerated, reported, and protected.

Fourth, development, charity, and philanthropy are major aspects of global economic activity and are in many cases channeled and enacted through religious means. Religious beliefs also serve to mobilize and bring attention to development issues in global contexts among overseas communities, diasporas, and informal networks.

Starting off, the next section surveys recent work on the economic aspects of logistics and events that take place in religiously primed "sacred" infrastructures. These spaces, while not always obviously sacred, underpin religious activity and in turn economic flows, providing a context in social space for religious expressions and values. Sites such as the Vatican, for example, not only serve to focus and house religious entities, but also are economic states in their own right.

## Sacred Infrastructures

Sacred infrastructures are zones of activity where economic and divine considerations overlap and intermingle in organized, logistical, and coordinated ways. In these infrastructures, the practices of religion take place and are facilitated. People's practices serve both divine and pragmatic ends, for instance to "change the circumstances of their lives—the quest for better jobs, educational opportunities, etc. are often expressed ritually" (Clothey, 2006: 197). As urbanization encroaches within India on what was once rural, the sacred and the civic are becoming interstitial and class and religion are no longer fixed. Instead, India's economy resembles what Barbara Harriss-White calls "tessellation" (2004), with only a small proportion of society involved in the high status occupations of trade or other religious functions.

What was strictly demarcated as religious, the temple or ghat, is now in many cases breached by urbanization. Furthermore, many religious Hindu infrastructures that appear eccentric and anachronistic, in fact are in many ways insulated from economic and political power and elites, or at least have some sense of control over their own resources and status (Milner, 1994). Smriti Srinivas offers in *Landscapes of Urban Memory* (2001) many engaging examples of how these infrastructures play out in urban conurbations such as Bangalore, where temples and places of worship are dispersed around the residential, industrial, and economic landscape. Temples and shrines sit side by side and are dwarfed by high rises, bus terminals, and sports complexes. Here then the sacred is also a "contested" space in the way nature is imagined for leisure, work or industry (Macnaghten and Urry, 1998).

Many popular tourist destinations also constitute sacred infrastructures as areas where different rules and economies play out and where religious expressions are not only sought, but also provided for. Rishikesh, Hardwar, and other pilgrimage towns are all examples of sacred infrastructures where the touristic imagination stands side by side with "locals" or "pilgrims." Tourist boards are well aware of the economic draw cards that these sacred infrastructures pose.

Donations and gifts constitute important economic flows in Hindu sacred infrastructures. Hindu religious sites are concentrated areas for exchange between worshippers and deities. Goods including words, texts, goods, and gifts are freely transacted and require logistics. These economic exchanges can be sources of power and influence for mediators such as priests, politicians, and kings; these entities are governed in turn by the "ethics of reciprocity" (Mines, 2008: 144). Thus, temples are not just sites of worship but also contain complex economic processes that spread out into wider society and politics.

Sondra Hausner in her ethnography *Wandering with Sadhus* (2007) traces the movements of *sādhus* around the extensive "pilgrimage circuits" that exist to India's major religious centers. Hausner highlights that the long held notion that these individuals lead ascetic lives pays no heed to the financial transactions and donations that they subsist off. Gathering in particular ashrams, centers with explicitly religious functions, *sādhus* can become involved in large sums of transfers, holding bank accounts, and deriving business from tourists and pilgrims.

Sacred hubs have long attracted mendicants seeking a living as well as attention to their religious practices. Under British rule, Caleb

Wright describes devotees moving to Benares to become *sādhus* "in order to secure a livelihood, as well as a large stock of religious merit" (1853: 70). Sacred infrastructures like Hardwar become micro-economies that harvest incomes from tourists and pilgrims. At crucial points in the religious calendar, such as the Kumbh Mela, the sprawling arrays of competing land use and patterning are overwhelmed and become sacred infrastructures that are composed of a myriad of economic units. These units facilitate both sacred and mundane commodities. Pilgrims constitute clients in these vast sacred infrastructures where donations are collected, converted, divided, and exchanged for food, clothing, water, and dwelling. Hausner describes the processes by which *sādhus* negotiate with "Mela administration" in order to sponsor construction of tents, buy firewood, and pay for feasts for officials.

Lucy Norris's *Recycling Indian Clothing* (2010) provides just such a compelling account of how religious practices, such as donation and charity—which appear to be personal and strictly non-secular—can in fact be tied to complex economic systems of tourism and manufacturing based on reciprocity and trust. Clothes are both highly symbolic and functional and have different meanings in touristic and religious contexts. Furthermore, clothes serve as catalysts for trade as religious goods in themselves. Thus, away from the temple emerge pilgrim sites that also serve as touristic sites: these are "new religious architectures" that include stores, online tourist guides as well as online and physical distribution networks.

The idea of "new religious architectures" corresponds with the growth in transnational and online avenues of religious organization and collaboration that allow global, flexible, networked "religiosity," including economic trade, as an alternative or complement to physical temple-going or worship. Peggy Levitt introduces the term for the activities of transnational migrants and indicates not only physical structures that are often the "be all and end all" of religious architectures in civic space, but the hidden and anonymous exchanges that occur on websites; across chat forums; and also in spaces like airport prayer rooms, where new sets of rules govern conduct according to different hierarchical standards.

In new religious architectures, online moderators, site designers, and community mediators play just as important a role as priests. Hinduism is thriving in cyberspace (Scheifinger, 2008) and in the process new standards of politics and hierarchy within religious organizations are emerging. But access to the Internet, let alone English language skills, is the privilege of only a minority of Hindus in India—thus new religious architectures benefit most the affluent, cosmopolitan, and globally mobile middle and upper class and urban groups (Chopra, 2006). Online communities occur profoundly to facilitate demand by migrants and overseas diasporas, so they can stay "connected" with India. Satisfying a similar audience, other types of economies have emerged to meet this demand in diasporic hubs. Vineeta Sinha describes a surge in local trade of religious objects and paraphernalia that has emerged with the growing popularity of a local deity "Muneeswaran" in Singapore's "Little India" district. As one businessperson claims, "Muneeswaran is good for business" (Sinha, 2005: 182). Traders in this industry, the majority not devotees, become religious experts in the same way as the moderators of online forums discussed above, advising followers on the details of religious devotion.

## Rebranded Values

It has widely been considered that "South Asian religions have, since the 19th century, been structured by Westerners in opposition to capitalist values and economic culture" (Mines and Lamb, 2010: 219). Indeed, many early commentators, mostly missionaries, were convinced that a pervasive unworldly indolence was manifest in India, stymieing economic growth and a productive work ethic and demanding intervention.

The "indolence in which they are destined to spend their lives, renders them totally useless to society" (Staughton, 1811: 133) a character "attributable to the climate, to indolent habits engendered by the heat, and to the impure histories of their gods" (ibid.: 216). More scholarly, authoritative and detailed accounts also adopted this perspective on Indian "character." *Sketches of Native Life and Character in Southern India* describes the Madras Sepoy, whom while courageous, was undisciplined suffering from "laziness, want of smartness etc." that stemmed from the otherworldly "gift" of "indifference to life" (1869: 23). Caleb Wright adopted this idea in his *Lectures on India* noting that Hinduism stemming as it did from customs instituted by the gods are "therefore incapable of improvement" and the "effect of this belief is to keep everything stationary. There is no progress in knowledge—no change for the better in any department of life" (1853: 52).

These accumulated ideas about India's indolent work ethic bled into US foreign policy in the mid-20th century informing decisions about aid and development as well as notions of economic potential, such as the "Hindu Rate of Growth" (Birtchnell, 2009). With India's dramatic economic growth in the 1990s, interest grew in articulating Hinduism as a productive work ethic by globally mobile elite in the diasporas and by the rising middle class in South Asia, aligning it with other religious value framings. Local, everyday practices of "making do" like *jugaad* have been dramatically reappraised from risky, unsafe, corrupt values to management and business contexts that demand a "can do" approach (Birtchnell, 2011). As well, *jugaad* has encouraged the Indian middle class to celebrate values that are exercised at the base of the pyramid and to try and export them as an Indian approach to living and working.

Excitement about Asian economies has seen an institutionalization of studies of religious, philosophical and spiritual values and practices and new interests in how they might relate to business and economics. For instance, there has been a surge of new investments in branded "Confucius institutes" in universities globally, cropping up in elite institutions across Europe, Britain, America, Argentina, Brazil, Australia, Israel, and New Zealand. These global clusters represent official recognition of the value framings presented by globalized economists and management thinkers but also a rebranding of Asia's religions from nationalist contexts to global ones. Organizations such as the India Council for Cultural Relations as well as various M. K. Gandhi-themed institutes, most notably the Gandhi Institute of Technology and Management, emerging from within India point to similar potential trends in future around Hindu values.

In the 1990s, a considerable debate emerged around "Asian values," a term that really reflects growing awareness of the impact of culture on economics, business, and management contexts. Part of this debate was a direct challenge and reorientation of classic ideas that religious values and practices in Asia negatively affect economic values and practices. Interest in Asian values accompanied the opening up of India and China to the global economy and complemented forecasts of changing demands of affluence, consumption, living standards, and well-being across Asian middle classes. Taking a lead from this interest, many experts now combine predictions of a faltering US hegemony with the renaissance of multicultural states like Singapore and Malaysia as producers of cosmopolitan mediators between China, India, and the "West."

There are many arguments that dispute whether Asian values are a real-world phenomenon, instead pointing out that religions and national values often cause divisions across and within regions; that Asian values are in many cases also Western values; economic change can be due to deeper processes; and that promoting Asian values debates often tacitly supports chauvinism, insularism, and nationalist agendas (Winter and Chang, 2008: 25). Hinduism occupied a minor but important place in this debate. A principle idea was that understanding certain national, regional, or cultural values might unlock the secrets of new markets, including India's, with values including "filial piety, collectivism, consensus-seeking, discipline, and respect for authority" (Beugelsdijk and Maseland, 2011: 70). These indigenous values indicated to some analysts alternative [non-Western] forms of modernity and development pathways, growth models, and ultimately global economic futures.

A key player in the Asian values debate where Hinduism is concerned is Kishore Mahbubani, the past Singapore Ambassador to the UN. Mahbubani, sensing the emerging interest and theoretical investments taking place in overseas diasporas around the array of Chinese values from Guanxi to Confucianism in management and business thinking, has sought to construct a pan-Asian values system sympathetic to Hinduism. Rather than skirting around internal religious tensions in India, Mahbubani cites these divisions or what he terms "Balkanization" (Mahbubani, 2009), as evidence of coordination and coexistence that demonstrates India's cohesion rather than division and Hinduism as a unifying force in the diasporas.

Hinduism is portrayed as compatible with this pan-Asian values debate due to its presence alongside a range of other religions internally and for its compatibility with democracy. Within India's nationalist discourses, Hinduism as a political force is necessarily balanced with more pragmatic, economic considerations, of "urban shopkeepers, white-collar workers, and the post-liberalization upper middle class" as "too much rioting and looting is bad for business" (Lutgendorf, 2007: 327).

As John Zavos has made clear, Hinduism, while tied up with nation-hood, has developed as a modern religion resting on an interaction and overlap of ideas that are also mutually informative not only to Indians, but also to a global audience (2005). Hinduism was exported very early on to the US in its modern development by key mediators like Swami Vivekananda and exemplified for its scope over the "outer" domain of materialism and the "inner" domain of the spirit.

Ideas of Hinduism as a productive, pan-Asian, globally important set of "Asian values" go hand in hand with other global "hybrids" of Hinduism that impact upon flows and circuits of people, ideas, and finances from outside of India but distanced from nationalist discourses. These "hybrids" include spiritual exercises like yoga and meditation that are seen as productive, particularly in occupational settings (van der Veer, 2007). Global hybrids that reference Hindu beliefs and practices, but do not share chauvinist overtones, interestingly have also found a place in the development of indigenous management and business settings that imagine Hinduism as a global "value" and as a global "hybrid". In short, these two areas of interest both represent a "rebranding" of Hinduism to be compatible with economics.

But this debate has represented a sea-change for economists and management experts concerned with Hinduism's relations to economic development, productivity and work values, and Hinduism as a "way of life." A concerted effort to critique classic notions that Hinduism was anathema to economic growth emerged in the late 1980s and it became acceptable to assert "Hinduism is not a blockade in material progress but actually aids it" (Madan, 1989: 58). It is now common in business and management research to assert that Hinduism "acts as a buffer to absorb stress and the other negative fallouts of the globalization process" for employees and workers and that "reflections on religion, and religious scriptures need to be assimilated with the values of industrial democracy to make Indian organizations more effective" (Rai, 2005: 388). Some research even shows that business people are directly influenced by Hindu spiritual beliefs and practices in their decision-making and daily work performance (Fernando and Jackson, 2006). Therefore, Hinduism is not now banished to private life or "compartmentalized" (Singer, 1972) but instead is pragmatically integrated into personal practices as well as institutional programs and relationships.

The rebranding of Hinduism indicates it is no longer understood as oppositional to consumerism and material accumulation: "the focus upon materiality, though here in the form of accumulation, is therefore just as strong in economics as it is in Hinduism" (D. Miller, 2005: 2): practitioners of Hinduism are as equally likely to accumulate "stuff" as anyone else (D. Miller, 2009: 69). The rebranding also represents a new relationship between spirituality and affluence within India. As former CEO of Procter and Gamble India, Gurcharan Das highlights in *The Elephant Paradigm*:

> During the 1990s, Indians seem to grow more religious, despite rising prosperity. The growing middle classes seemed avidly preoccupied with a rising standard of living, social mobility and the pursuit of material goods, pushed relentlessly by the global economy and communications. At the same time they continued to vigorously pursue their age-old spiritual paths towards living the meaningful life. I happened to meet a large number of young entrepreneurs during the 1990s, and I discovered, to my surprise, that almost all had a serious religious side to them. It is a mistake to think that people must necessarily grow less religious with prosperity. (2002: 86)

The rebranding is in part due to global manifestations of popular practices like yoga and meditation and rise of sacred infrastructures to facilitate these interests. Thus in modern India even a "big businessman ... a tall, clean-shaven, middle-aged man in a three-piece suit" with a Mercedes and a real estate business can be a "highly advanced *yogi*" (Ali, 2004: 138).

These popular Hindu practices are not only limited to *yogis*, CEOs of major corporations also draw on these virtues. Vijay Eswaran, Executive Chairman of the Qi Group, wrote *In the Sphere of Silence* (2005) drawing on his background as "a Malaysian who grew up in a meditative Hindu tradition that reflected his family's Indian origins" (Maidment, 2007: 1). The book promises both personal development and economic success through a technique not dissimilar to the *mouna vratham* that Eswaran learnt on his grandfather's knee.

The work of the Calcutta Indian Institute of Management's (IIM) Center for Human Values is a profound example of the use of Hindu ideas and practices in management contexts. Financed by donors and grants from a range of Indian institutions, including the House of Tatas, the introduction of indigenous ethics courses into mainstream MBA syllabuses at IIM demonstrates that there is local demand for contextual ethics. Thus, Hindu "indigenous culture was now a resource to be tapped for the long-term success of an organization" (Iterson, 2002: 165).

S. K. Chakraborty proposes the introduction of a Vedantic management system based on, though not limited to, scriptures such as the Vedas, the Smritis, and the Puranas, and the writings of Gandhi, Vivekananda, Tagore, and Aurobindo. Distilled into a concrete system of values, which he dubs "Spirinomics," Chakraborty believes that this rich cultural heritage has the capacity to "transform the workplace into a spiritual/moral gymnasium" to revolutionize management ethics and to promote positive leadership behavior "through sacred sadhana" (1998: 152).

Recent observers of Hinduism acknowledge that ritual and belief blend seamlessly with a cosmopolitan lifestyle and modern work ethic. It is far from reality that Hinduism impacts negatively upon productivity, diligence, and the other attributes required in the Protestant worldview associated with capitalism. Just like other religious practices, Hinduism is just another part of everyday life and even complements it as the case of Ramachandran illustrates:

> The purpose of his weekly temple visit is over, and Ramachandran must return home quickly. Once there he changes out of his dhoti and shawl and puts on the black pants and white buttoned shirt of his work attire. After drinking only a glass of water he mounts his bicycle to ride to the shop where all day he repairs the computers that are so essential to maintaining business in contemporary India. As he solders the memory boards of broken mainframe hardware, he is content in the memory of his link with his Goddess and with the rituals that bring balance to his life. (Hawley and Narayanan, 2006: 36)

As this example shows the early writers on Hinduism and economics greatly exaggerated the deleterious impacts the value system had on a work ethic. Furthermore, Hinduism is not only a source of conflict and chauvinism in modern India, it also provides meaning and continuity to everyday life. But, the notion that Hindu values might benefit an everyday working life needs to be greeted with caution as well, as it is also overstated in recent attempts to marry management with religion.

What is really at stake in this discussion of Hindu values and economic life is the shift to cosmopolitanism in India and China (Tyfield and Urry, 2009) and the surge in transnational movements, particularly among elites. The next section looks at how these elites have shaped global understandings of Hinduism and "mediated" with communities and nudged its acceptance and appreciation.

## Cosmopolitan Mediators

In 2010 a scandal arose around US "Tea Party" political leader Mark Williams's comments on plans to build a 13-story mosque and Islamic cultural center at Park Place and Broadway close to the site of the 2001 attacks on the World Trade Centre buildings. Williams made the bizarre statement that the "monument would consist of a Mosque for the worship of the terrorists' monkey-god" (Hutchinson, 2010: 1). When criticized in the media for this diatribe, however, Williams was quick to apologize—but only to Hindus:

> I described the "god" worshiped by terrorists as "a monkey god". I was wrong and that was offensive. I owe an apology to millions of Hindus who worship Lord Hanuman, an actual Monkey God. Moreover, Hanuman is worshiped as a symbol of perseverance, strength and devotion. He is known as a destroyer of evil and to inspire and liberate. Those are hardly the traits of whatever the Hell (literally) it is that terrorists worship and worthy of my respect and admiration not ridicule. So, again, to my Hindu friends I offer my sincerest apologies for my horrible lapse and my insensitivity. It was unintentional, inexplicably ignorant and I am ashamed at my offense toward you. (Goldsmith, 2010: 1)

What this excerpt shows is that despite many theological and ecclesiastical differences between Hinduism and Christianity (polytheism, animism, etc.), there is a wider sense of tolerance in the US around Hinduism.

However, this has not always been the case. In the 19th and early 20th century, considerable anxiety was expressed about Hinduism in the US media and by commentators such as Thomas H. Kennedy in *The Wrathful Patriot* in an invective not dissimilar to Williams'. It was an economic as well as moral threat highlighted in accounts of "vicious customs," "wresting pittance" and the taking of "some poor domestic's place" by "the heathen Hindoos [that] menace all the West" (1914: 18).

Wendell Thomas observed that Hinduism was "invading America" not only through the growing presence of "swamis and yogis" but also "a goodly throng of academic lecturers and organization directors ... slowly but surely conducting Hindu ideas into the very center of American culture" (1930: 13). Thomas also noted that the practice of yoga and Vedanta was popular among businesspeople and not at all incompatible, instead advocates preaching compatibility with "modern business methods and financial ambition for success" (ibid.: 167).

Yet as cosmopolitans followed these itinerant flows of labor, the landscape began to shift and Hinduism played an important role in this change. Many religious celebrities, championing Indian political causes, were sponsored by academics and religious studies scholars in the US and the UK. Fora were provided that combined both debate about India's political and economic independence as well as more esoteric, religious concerns.

In 1955, Phillip Ashby of Princeton University wrote in the US journal *The Christian Century*

> a respected and eminent Indian Christian, high in the councils of world Christianity, recently said to me that he is convinced the Hindu ... argument that all religions are equally valid may sweep the world in the next twenty-five years. He found this thesis congenial to the contemporary European and modern mind ... [The Hindu] considers himself to be the representative of 20th Century understanding, and the Christian, along with the Moslem, to be the epitome of the religious exclusiveness and bigotry which much disappear in the modern world. (*Life Magazine*, 1955: 80)

Hinduism in India changed as well to accommodate this global vision of modernity and religion. Even in the early 20th century, as Patricke Wolfe reminds us, elite globally active mediators like Tagore were key players acting "as a conduit between enlightened Europe and a regressive Brahmin elite, who were awakened and vitalized by his campaign to reform Hinduism" (2005: 238). And in more modern settings, like the Malaysian diasporic context, the increasing political role of the middle class in the US and West has seen an increase in secularism and a decline in religion. However, in India this is far from the case; the middle class has instead been shaped by caste, region, language, and religion (Fernandez, 2006).

The religious principles of Indian community groups in the US are diverse and scholars have grouped them into five rough categories: secular Hinduism, non-sectarian Hinduism, Bhakti or Devotional Hinduism, Reformist-Nationalist Neo-Hinduism, and Guru-Internationalist-Missionizing Neo-Hinduism (Larson, 2009: 193). Within these groupings are also many exceptions and attempts at a pan-American identity. For instance, the Northern California Hindu Businessman's Association published the "Nine Beliefs of Hinduism" as a summary of views accepted by all types of Hinduism in America (Eck, 2000: 234). But this does not account for divergent groups that maintain orthodox views apart from the mainstream, but also continue to grow globally.

Indian migrants recognize the ISKCON movement as a global religion making it impervious to many of the conflicts stemming from minority politics in Hindu migrant communities. ISKCON's integrative strategies put it in stark contrast to the recent confrontations between conservative Australian Hindu organizations and the Gay and Lesbian Mardi Gras over cultural appropriation of Hindu imagery and symbolism (Velayutham and Wise, 2001). ISKCON is, in this sense, a transnational organization that does not suffer from the nationalist and political ambivalence of officialized Hindu organizations. Indian migrant professionals have played a key role in championing ISKCON in the US by providing funding and drawing attention away from donation scandals that plagued its initial inception (Vande Berg and Kniss, 2008).

The internal tolerances to a contemporary lifestyle as well as its pre-existing place in US society—the movement was founded in America by an Indian immigrant—has made ISKCON a popular option for many Indian migrants to satisfy their desires for religious fulfillment as well as remaining true to cosmopolitan US identities. At the root of ISKCON's current manifestation is its tolerance and inclusion of outsiders, particularly Westerners, in its pursuit of global conversion and universalistic recruitment goals. Its worship of one god, Krishna, makes it more amenable to Christian groups in adopted countries. From this perspective ISKCON temples have become "locations for micro-level transnational interactions and processes" that have led to "new innovations in religious identities and practices for Western devotees, Indian immigrants, and for ISKCON itself" (Vande Berg and Kniss, 2008: 99).

Apart from ISKCON, there are other unorthodox "new age" cosmo-politan streams of Hinduism. Helweg describes migrant US entrepreneur Rajiv Malhotra's start-up based on his observation that Americans are fascinated with Indian religion as well as the cultural consumption in the US of things in "packages." Arbitrage is the capitalization of the imbalance between a price differential between two or more markets. Thus management consultants are "individuals who span national and cultural boundaries capitalizing on the arbitrage of knowledge from one country or culture to another" (Semadeni, 2001: 44). In this respect, cosmopolitan mediators become "culture arbitrageurs" of Hinduism (Birtchnell, 2013). For example, utilizing his family business networks in India Malhotra created "Guru kits," collections of wood sandals, incense, saffron, wood beads, and an Instruction Book on how to meditate, with names and addresses of Gurus and ashrams. The merging of cultural attractions takes advantage of the fact that "migrants and people with extensive contacts outside their realm of influence are most likely to be entrepreneurial" (Helweg, 2004: 24).

Mediation does not only occur though obvious religious representatives (priests, kings, acolytes), but through community, political, and social elites who can lobby and acquire vested interests in order to "nudge" for policies that favor religious issues (Thaler and Sunstein, 2009). "The Hindu gods of metropolitan Washington D.C., like the Hindu gods of the cities of Houston or Pittsburgh or Nashville, live in a substantive holy house that nonetheless is and yet is not at home on the land on which it stands" (Orsi, 1999: 105). Therefore, cosmopolitan middle classes are themselves mediators of Hindu values and practices.

> Hindu nationalism is helping unify the new bourgeoisie ... who make up the neo-rich in the countryside. The new entrants to the modern economy are increasingly getting linked to global economic institutions, especially since the beginning of liberalization in 1991. It is these newly upwardly mobile classes/castes, caught between their traditional inhibitions and modern allures, that are largely responsive to Hindutva's calls for a 'Hindu modernity.' (Nanda, 2003: 32–33)

On a global scale there are many important economic considerations to the "guru phenomenon" that has accompanied the spread of Hinduism to the West. As David Smith describes, gurus are often defined through key historical and political moments: the peace movement and the Vietnam War, the Beatles discovery of Indian music and the spread of drug culture in the West (2003: 168). It is within all of these movements that economic transactions and trade occur, often through global networks.

Many "new age" alternative values are linked to cosmopolitan transnationals who combined political will with religious values, like M. K. Gandhi (Birtchnell, 2012). Chandrashanker Shukla shows in *Gandhi's View of Life* that he drew not only on his teachings but also the philosophical thought of Walt Whitman, Victor Hugo, Oscar Wilde, and Will Durant, to list a few; binding them together as a complete pragmatic set of ethics. These ethics include "plain living," "voluntary simplicity" rejection of the "ideal of the High Standard of Living," and the idea that "superabundance of wealth tends to cramp the soul" the abatement of which will be "not merely for the individual good, but for corporate good also" (1956: 121).

Lisa McKean makes the reciprocal link between Hinduism and economics explicitly in *Divine Enterprise*, an ethnography of mendicancy in India:

> Gurus—spurious or genuine—are key players in the business and politics of spirituality. The activities of many gurus and their organizations during the 1980s and 1990s are related to the simultaneous expansion of transnational capitalism in India and growing support for Hindu nationalism in India and abroad … as producers and purveyors of spiritual commodities, gurus assist in propagating Hindu nationalism, an ideology that relies on referents to Hindu India's unparalleled spiritual prowess and moral authority. (1996: 1)

The "guru phenomenon" is also a story of global mendicancy. Hugh B. Urban's depiction of Osho the "Guru of the Rich," or Bhagwan Shree Rajneesh's, failed business enterprise based on his spiritual teachings demonstrates the global contexts of the guru phenomenon. Osho found considerable success and scandal in the US before returning to India. He clearly demonstrates that many renderings of Hinduism are detached from orthodoxies and institutional religions or political agendas unique to India, instead allied more to "spiritual logics" of late capitalism framed by the global capitalist market (2005). Many well-known "gurus" are concerned with the application of Hinduism, and ideas that stem from or reference it, to modern life including management and business contexts.

Many gurus attempt to ally the underlying moral and ethical tenets in Hindu contexts to the modern ailments and conditions viewed as globally detrimental to health, productivity, and the environment. The Maharishi Mahesh Yogi's ideas have been tailored to economic and business contexts as Transcendental Meditation (TM) by its advocates. According to Jack Forem "the evidence is convincing that TM increases a person's effectiveness in his chosen field of work" and that Hindu practices and philosophies like meditation, yoga, and scripture can have real "economic" consequences (1973: 164). Here, unlike Shukla's integration of Gandhi's thought to the modern condition described above, TM and Maharishi Yogi's values offers methods (self-actualization) for those seeking rather than rejecting higher standards of living, such as "high-ranking executives" of "multinational corporations" (1973: 174).

Another grade of management and business advocate is the pragmatic guru Deepak Chopra, who combines religious ideas in books like *the Seven Spiritual Laws of Success* (2009), heavily sourced from Hinduism, with management teachings. Chopra is an entrepreneur in his own right, the CEO of an international brand that revolves around his teachings and workshops for senior business people, which yield considerable profits. Chopra very successfully mediates for a secularized version of Hinduism, a "Hindu lite" (Raj, 2008) that is decontextualized from nationalism and includes many unorthodox "new age" practices: meditation, yoga, and metaphors that draw on modern life and concerns. Like many economic elites Chopra is also an active philanthropist. The next section explores further the links between philanthropy, business, and Hinduism through a focus on "development devotees."

## Development Devotees

In Hinduism giving is part and parcel of an implicit code of behavior defined by values of generosity, hospitality, philanthropy, and charity that mobilize faith-based communities as means for spreading faith and facilitating religious recruitment (Maharaj et al., 2008: 85). Development is part and parcel of economic flows and religion plays a pivotal role in structuring and facilitating development goals. Religious representatives engender and foment trust in the community in the performance of their duties; crucially, this is why their ranks are drawn from the political, social, and economic elite. Such affordances mean they also are involved in formidable economic transactions.

As well as administrating financial flows key players attract and motivate sources of wealth, in many cases around major events in the social conscience. In the 2005 tsunami many religious NGOs facilitated community activities in accordance with Hindu rituals of death (G. Miller, 2005). Organizations like the Hindu Forum Disaster Relief Task Force as well as ISKCON raised large amounts of donations in disaster appeals (BBC News, 2005). The religious philanthropic sector represents a huge source of support and a main driver of economic effort in crises. It is no coincidence that many NGOs in India, and in the rest of the world, are also religiously affiliated and work alongside official aid organizations. A database of Worldwide Hindu Development Organizations available from the International Information Resource Centre shows there are more than 5000 such NGOs worldwide (Gulzaar, 2009).

Hindu religious organizations are also sources of donations and philanthropy within their own activities for a range of causes, secular and non-secular. Crucially they are also recipients of economic flows through development channels. Smriti Srinivas highlights the vast spiritual networks of the global Sai organization, which consolidates wealth through over 9,000 official centers of devotion in India and 2,000 in over 130 countries outside of India. Religio-urban complexes, including Puttaparthi in Bangalore attract considerable regional and transnational economic flows. The key guru in the Sai organization, Sai Baba, received support, funds, and materials from many business donors throughout his career: bestowers from coffee planters and real estate developers to the Hard Rock Café franchise's Isaac Tigrett. The funds that derive from local and international devotees are fed through the conduit of the Sai organization into a whole platform of causes: housing development, hospitals, and museums (Srinivas, 2008: 63).

# Conclusion

To claim that one is a student, researcher, or commentator on both Hinduism *and* economics is to apparently betray interests so diffuse that they appear hopelessly irreconcilable. Surely Hinduism is all about asceticism, otherworldliness and in short non-economic activities? Is not Hinduism much too diverse and complex to sustain compelling generalizations? Are not economics, management and business the preserve of secular, professional, and other irreverent pursuits?

As demonstrated in this chapter, a concerted effort to understand the bigger picture of Hinduism cannot ignore economic aspects. Rejection of the juxtaposition of Hinduism to economics has now a lineage that is irrefutable, well debated, and authoritative. There is thus a great arsenal against simple notions of what constitutes religious identity. However, in many instances in the contemporary world this apparent or real juxtaposition has been the key to the spread and perpetuation of many beliefs, customs, and scriptures associated with Hinduism amongst many different national, community, and ethnic interests. Not only this, but non-secular interests still play a role in how investments are made, in motivations for economic activities, and in the structure and spread of diasporas and communities outside of national boundaries.

The successful mobility, flows and circuits of knowledge, talent, capital, and people to and from South Asia and the consequent companionship of many non-secular interests perhaps explains why there is a new and urgent demand for clarity in how these apparently disparate areas relate. That the linkages of religion and finance can spread by repeated and progressive exposures—often documented in popular culture—globally to alternative ways of being stemming from the Indian subcontinent is a great lacuna that has only recently been broached.

As powerful community groups and diasporas have dispersed and formed across the world so too have advocates of Hinduism petitioned for equality, freedom to worship, and formal recognition. It is no coincidence that many of the first migrants in the 20th century from India to the US and the UK were on religious tours aimed at informing both a keen academic and popular audience. Temples have been built and communities come together. But as well underneath these very obvious signs of religion have been personal and quasi-secular interests that have only spread tacitly and awkwardly. These tacit interests need equal weight in analyses of religion and business.

Hinduism, like any other "religion" or belief system, is not only about traditions, scriptures, and myths, but key players, practitioners, movements, and fashions. It is also about creative and academic commitments and expressions as well as merely pragmatic concerns for the sustaining of tradition and family obligations. Further, beliefs are not only present in long lineages of kinship and community bounded by caste, class, or region; but also present in collisions between cultures, alternative practices, and lived experiences. A great deal of what many commentators might deem "Hinduism" is instead explorations and inquiries into how personal beliefs that stem from traditional values, and often are not incompatible with formal religious expressions and communities, can be combined with secular interests and indeed lives that are bound to business obligations. There are radical beliefs and pedestrian ones, intensely personal and also communal ones. Just as those who might be identified as "Christian" might be evangelists, members of the *Twelve Tribes of Israel*, or simply Sunday church-goers or religiously demarcated school students; those identified with Hinduism are equally mixed, complex, and difficult to cluster.

It is now not enough to understand Hinduism and economics through traditional community and caste origins and the extant research on "the old association of business with an exclusive Vaishya order" (Damodaran, 2008: 3). Portrayals of Hinduism as a rarefied, detached, kinship-oriented, and exotic set of practices too often ignore the considerable presence the belief system has in communities, politics, and certainly economic relations globally. Once the methods within Hinduism might have been seen as "getting away from the world" (or otherworldliness) for colonial officials, missionaries and many scholars who, like Voltaire, Max Mueller, or Max Weber, had never travelled to India (Birtchnell, 2009). Hinduism now represents in popular imaginings and practices a method for being *in* the world, living in the moment and "finding oneself" and in so doing making oneself more productive and capable of living in the world. It is also an avenue to *traveling* to India. Therefore, it is vital that research on Hinduism and economics is sensitive to both contemporary and traditional threads.

While much of the excellent scholarly, historical research is valuable, there is much to be gained through an optic that centers on recent transitions to a global business order; new and recast technologies of communication, mobility and finance; and the affordances that stem from anonymous, long distance networks in the diasporas. The refocusing represents a starting point for a much more pertinent approach to how issues of livelihood, well-being, investment, finance, management, and development revolve around or involve Hinduism as collective or individual acts of devotion and avocation.

To identify with "Hinduism" is to be defined as "Hindu" by census lists, government reports, management groups, community organizations and a whole gamut of other political, economic and demographic human and non-human interests. Therefore of interest are not only the translations and interpretations of scriptures such as the *Bhagavad Gita* but also volumes of sales or numbers of reprints globally, not in terms of the spread and diffusion of Hinduism, but in terms of economic expenditures and commitments by organizations and individuals. Furthermore, artworks and practices within temples are indeed valuable subjects, but so too are the distributions of temples in key financial districts in the US or UK, their geotagging and clustering on business-oriented websites, and the support networks and economic financings derived from economic elites.

While the explosion of concern and media attention toward Islam and "Islamification" in Britain, America, Germany, and Australia has not been matched by the definition and classification of Hinduism as a distinctly threatening or imposing social force, there remains still specific bodies of people that are not spared the rigorous demarcations of demographics, measuring both income and religious affiliation, and who find themselves so treated by default rather than choice. The formal, bureaucratic binding and defining of individuals according to religious identity—and strategies to avoid this attention—is also another area that demands research.

The student or researcher of the links between Hinduism and business can be reassured that there are indeed many overlaps and new areas that historical abridgments fail to capture. In surveying the tacit and overt "sceneries" of global Hinduism through the optic of economics it becomes immediately obvious that sacred infrastructures are sites of business activity, a focus for financial investments, and areas of community exchange. Globalized acolytes are key players in business and management philosophies and at the same time profoundly spiritual benefactors; and development disciples' visions of equality, education, and common dignity often overlap with economic interests. Business elites, government representatives, talented migrants and celebrities are as important if not more in spreading Hinduism outside of South Asia as part of their life-projects. Much recent academic interest in Hinduism and economics has been in bridging these apparently irreconcilable domains.

Alongside debates about the production of a coherent and stable catalogue of Hindu laws, sects, and ritual practices is an interest in the same so-called laws, beliefs, and practices as methods of personal fulfill-ment and aesthetic interest (Pennington, 2005). Thus, the organized demonstrations of Hare Krishna devotees in a London street or the spiritual revelations of the Beatles can be linked to economic groups of practitioners, volunteers, donations and investments of time, energy, talent, and income. And it is these sorts of unpackings that much re-cent work in the social sciences has fruitfully pursued, in the areas of history, sociology, anthropology, and cultural studies.

# Bibliography

Ali, M. 2004. *Deeper Aspects of Hinduism: Jewel in the Lotus*, New Delhi: Sterling Publishers Pvt. Ltd.

BBC News. 2005. Asian Disaster: How to Help. *BBC*. Available at: http://news.bbc. co.uk/1/hi/world/africa/4131881.stm (accessed on April 21, 2011).

Beugelsdijk, S. and R. Maseland. 2011. *Culture in Economics: History, Methodological Reflections and Contemporary Applications*, Cambridge: Cambridge University Press.

Birtchnell, T. 2009. From "'Hindolence' to 'Spirinomics': Discourse, Practice and the Myth of Indian Enterprise." South Asia: Journal of South Asian Studies 32(2): 248–268.

_____. 2013. *Indovation: Innovation and a Global Knowledge Economy in India.* Basingstoke: Palgrave Macmillan.

_____. 2011. "Jugaad as Systemic Risk and Systematic Innovation in India: 'Hindolence' or 'Indovation'?" *Contemporary South Asia* 19(4): 357–372.

_____. 2012. "Elements, Elites and Events: Practice Theory and Scale." *Journal of Transport Geography* 24: 497–502.

Bowen, P. 1998. *Themes and Issues in Hinduism.* New York: Continuum International Publishing Group.

Casanova, J. 2011. "Cosmopolitanism, the Clash of Civilizations and Multiple Modernities." *Current Sociology* 59(2): 252–267.

Centeno, M. A. and J. N. Cohen. 2010. *Global Capitalism.* Cambridge: Polity.

Chakraborty, S. K. 1998. *Values and Ethics for Organizations: Theory and Practice.* Oxford: Oxford University Press.

Chakraborty, S. K. and D. Chakraborty. 2007. "The Economic Function In The Hindu Worldview: Its Perennial Social Relevance." *International Journal of Social Economics*, 34(10): 714–734.

Chaudhuri, N. C. 1979. *Hinduism: A Religion to Live By.* Oxford: Oxford University Press.

Chopra, D. 2009. *The Seven Spiritual Laws of Success: A Practical Guide to the Fulfillment of Your Dreams (Easyread Large Edition).* ReadHowYouWant.com.

Clothey, F. W. 2006. *Religion in India: A Historical Introduction.* London: Routledge.

Coleman, S. 2010. "Recent Developments in the Anthropology of Religion." In B. S. Turner (ed.), *The New Blackwell Companion to the Sociology of Religion*, 103–122. London: John Wiley and Sons.

Damodaran, H. 2008. *India's New Capitalists: Caste, Business, And Industry in a Modern Nation*. New York: Palgrave Macmillan.

Das, G. 2002. *The Elephant Paradigm: India Wrestles With Change*. New Delhi: Penguin Books.

Eck, D. 2000. "Negotiating Hindu Identities in America." In H. G. Coward, J. R. Hinnells, and R. B. Williams (eds), *The South Asian Religious Diaspora in Britain, Canada, and the United States*, 219–238. Albany NY: SUNY Press.

Eswaran, V. 2005. *In the Sphere of Silence*. Hong Kong: RYTHM House.

Fernandez, L. 2006. *India's New Middle Class: Democratic Politics in an Era of Economic Reform*. London: University of Minnesota Press.

Fernando, M. and Jackson, B. 2006. "The Influence of Religion-Based Workplace Spirituality on Business Leaders' Decision-Making: An Inter-Faith Study," *Journal of Management and Organization* 12: 23–39.

Flood, G. D. 1996. *An Introduction to Hinduism*. Cambridge: Cambridge University Press.

Forem, J. 1973. *Transcendental Meditation; Maharishi Mahesh Yogi and The Science Of Creative Intelligence*. New York: Dutton.

Goldsmith, S. 2010. Tea Party Express Leader Mark Williams Says "Sorry"—To Hindus—For Slamming Muslim's "Monkey God"—New York Daily News. *New York Daily News*. Available at: http://articles.nydailynews.com/2010-05-20/local/27064921_1_hindus-muslims-monkey-god (accessed on April 4, 2011).

Gulzaar, S. 2009. Hindu NGO's Worldwide. *Hindu NGO's*. Available at: http://hind-ungos.blogspot.com/ (accessed on April 21, 2011).

Harriss-White, B. 2004. "India's Informal Economy: Facing the Twenty-First Century." In K. Basu (ed.) *India's Emerging Economy: Performance and Prospects in the 1990s and Beyond*, 265–292. Massachussets: MIT Press.

Hausner, S. L. 2007. *Wandering with Sadhus: Ascetics in the Hindu Himalayas*. Bloomington: Indiana University Press.

Hawley, J. S. and Narayanan, V. 2006. *The Life of Hinduism*. Ewing: University of California Press.

Helweg, A. W. 2004. *Strangers in a Not-So-Strange Land: Indian American Immigrants in the Global Age*. Belmont: Wadsworth.

Hutchinson, B. 2010. Tea Party Leader Mark Williams Says Muslims Worship A "Monkey God," Blasts Ground Zero Mosque. *New York Daily News*. Available at: http://articles.nydailynews.com/2010-05-19/local/27064852_1_muslims-ibrahim-hooper-ground-zero (accessed on May 19, 2010).

Iterson, A. van. 2002. *The Civilized Organization: Norbert Elias and the Future of Organization Studies*. Amsterdam: John Benjamins Publishing Company.

Kennedy, T. H. 1914. *The Wrathful Patriot: A Satire On National Evils*. San Fransisco: T. H. Kennedy.

Lal, D. 2005. *The Hindu Equilibrium: India c. 1500 B.C.–2000 A.D.* Oxford: Oxford University Press.

Lamont, J. 2010. The Age of "Indovation" Dawns. *FT.com*. Available at: http://www. ft.com/cms/s/0/993f319c-7814-11df-a6b4-00144feabdc0.html#axzz1I0Po5FM4 (accessed on March 29, 2011).

Larson, G. J. 2009. Hindusim in India and in America. In J. Neusner (ed.), *World Religions in America: An Introduction*, 179–198. Louisville: Westminster John Knox Press.

*Life Magazine*. 1955. "Change an Challenge: Hinduism Begins to Adapt to the Modern Age and Competes with the World's other Faiths." *Life Magazine*, 79–80.

Lutgendorf, P. 2007. *Hanuman's Tale: The Messages of a Divine Monkey*, New York: Oxford University Press.

Macnaghten, P. and Urry, J. 1998. *Contested Natures*. London: SAGE Publications.

Madan, G. R. 1989. Social Institutions and Economic Development. In G. R. Madan & R. Mukerjee (eds), *Economic Problems of Modern India: Problems of Development*. Bombay: Allied Publishers.

Maharaj, B. et al. 2008. Religion and Development. In A. Habib and B. Maharaj (eds), *Giving and Solidarity: Resource Flows for Poverty Alleviation and Development in South Africa*, 79–121. Cape Town: HSRC Press.

Mahbubani, K. 2009. *The New Asian Hemisphere: The Irresistible Shift of Global Power to the East*, Public Affairs.

Maidment, P. 2007. Book Review The Sound Of Silence. *Forbes.com*. Available at: http://www.forbes.com/2007/03/22/meditation-management-eswaran-lead-ceo-cx_pm_0322bookreview.html (accessed on April 21, 2011).

McKean, L. 1996. *Divine enterprise: Gurus and the Hindu Nationalist Movement*, Chicago: University of Chicago Press.

Miller, D. 2005. *Materiality*, Durham: Duke University Press.

———. 2009. *Stuff*, Cambridge: Polity.

Miller, G. 2005. "The Tsunami's Psychological Aftermath." *Science* 309(5737): 1030.

Milner, M. 1994. *Status and Sacredness: A General Theory of Status Relations and an Analysis of Indian Culture*, Oxford: Oxford University Press.

Mines, D. P. 2008. "Exchange." In S. Mittal (ed.) *Studying Hinduism: Key Concepts and Methods*,139–154. Oxford: Taylor & Francis.

Mines, D. P. and Lamb, S. E. 2010. *Everyday Life in South Asia*, Bloomington: Indiana University Press.

Nair, C. 2011. *Consumptionomics: Asia's Role in Reshaping Capitalism and Saving the Planet*, Oxford: Infinite Ideas.

Nanda, M. 2003. *Prophets Facing Backward: Postmodern Critiques of Science And Hindu Nationalism In India*, New Brunswick: Rutgers University Press.

Norris, L. 2010. *Recycling Indian Clothing: Global Contexts of Reuse and Value*, Bloomington: Indiana University Press.

Orsi, R. A. 1999. *Gods of the City: Religion and the American Urban Landscape*, Bloomington: Indiana University Press.

Pennington, B. K. 2005. *Was Hinduism Invented? Britons, Indians, and Colonial Construction of Religion*, Oxford: Oxford University Press.

Rai, H. 2005. The Role of Hinduism in Global India. In N. Capaldi (ed.), *Business and Religion: A Clash of Civilizations?*, 379–389. M & M Scrivener Press.

Raj, J. 2008. *A Biblical Approach to Indian Traditions and Beliefs*, Singapore: Armour Publishing Pte Ltd.

Scheifinger, H. 2008. "Hinduism and Cyberspace." *Religion* 38(3): 233–249.

Semadeni, M. 2001. Toward a Theory of Knowledge Arbitrage. In A. F. Buono (ed.), *Current trends in management* consulting, 43–70. Charlotte: Information Age Publishing Inc.

Shukla, C. 1956. *Gandhi's View of Life*, Bombay: Bharatiya Vidya Bhavan.

Sinha, V. 2005. *A New God in the Diaspora? Muneeswaran Worship in Contemporary Singapore*, Singapore: Singapore University Press.

Smith, D. J. 2003. *Hinduism and Modernity*, Oxford: Wiley-Blackwell.

Srinivas, S. 2008. *In the Presence of Sai Baba: Body, City, and Memory in A Global Religious Movement*, Leiden: Brill.

_____. 2001. *Landscapes of Urban Memory: The Sacred and the Civic in India's High-tech City*, Minnesota: University of Minnesota Press.

Staughton, W. 1811. *The Baptist Mission in India: A Statement of the Physical and Moral Character of the Hindoos, Their Cruelties, Tortures and Burnings, with a Very Interesting Description of Bengal, Intended to Animate to Missionary Co-operation*, Pennsylvania: Hellings and Aitken.

Thaler, R. H. and C. R. Sunstein. 2009. *Nudge: Improving Decisions about Health, Wealth and Happiness*, London: Penguin.

Thomas, W. 1930. *Hinduism Invades America*, New York: Kessinger Publishing.

Tyfield, D. and J. Urry. 2009. "Cosmopolitan China? Lessons from International Collaboration in Low-Carbon Innovation." *The British Journal of Sociology* 60(4): 793–812.

Urban, O. B. 2005. "Osho, From Sex Guru to Guru of the Rich: The Spiritual Logic of Late Capitalism." In T. A. Forsthoefel and C. A. Humes (eds), *Gurus in America*, 169–192. New York: SUNY Press.

Vande Berg, T. and Kniss, F. 2008. "ISKCON and Immigrants: The Rise, Decline, and Rise Again of a New Religious Movement." *Sociological Quarterly* 49(1): 79–104.

van der Veer, P. 2007. "Global breathing: Religious Utopias in India and China." *Anthropological Theory*, 7(3): 315–328.

Velayutham, S. and Wise, A. 2001. "Dancing with Ga(y)nesh: Rethinking Cultural Appropriation in Multicultural Australia." *Postcolonial Studies* 4(2): 143.

W, F. E. 1869. *Sketches of Native Life and Character in Southern India*, Madras: Higginbotham and Co. Available at: http://www.archive.org/details/cu31924024114906 (accessed on June 21, 2011).

Winter, T. and T. C. Chang. 2008. *Asia on Tour: Exploring the Rise of Asian Tourism*. New York: Taylor & Francis.

Wolfe, P. 2005. "Islam, Europe and Indian Nationalism Towards a Transnational Perspective." In A. Curthoys and M. Lake (eds), *Connected Worlds: History in Transnational Perspective*, 233–266. Canberra: ANU E-Press.

Wright, C. 1853. *India and Its Inhabitants*. Cincinnati: J. A. Brainerd. Available at: http://www.archive.org/details/indiaitsinhabita00wrigrich.

Zavos, J. 2005. "The Shapes of Hindu Nationalism." In K. Adeney and L. Sáez (eds), *Coalition Politics and Hindu Nationalism*. New York: Routledge.

# Chapter 5

## The Sacred in Modern Hindu Politics: Historical Processes Underlying Hinduism and Hindutva*

Robert Eric Frykenberg

Between the logic of an integrating constitutional pluralism and the more fissiparous logic of a sacralizing, if not totalizing, kind of "civic" religion, operating within both parliamentary and extra-parliamentary processes, political structures of India as a secular state have suffered dangerous stresses, and yet have survived—so far. Stresses and tensions, between what Romila and Romesh Thapar (Thapar, 1997) called "Syndicated Hinduism"—a modern construction or "invented" tradition that required a special kind of secular pluralism leading to the increasing political integration and stability of the India Republic—and a no less modern or "invented" tradition linked to Hindutva, the Sangh Parivar, and militant Hindu nationalism, have produced profound contradictions within political systems of South Asia. The roots of these contradictions—from both analytical and historical perspectives—lie deeply imbedded in ancient lore. The historiography of these opposing logics, and mentalities and rationalities arising therein, are the focus of this chapter.

Two classic paradigmatic logics can be seen as reflecting traditions of political life in India since ancient times. One is irenic, diplomatic, inclusive, contractual, structurally integrating, resorting to force only as a last resort, and the other is aggressive, exclusive, violently expansive,

---

* In some measure, ideas expressed herein are inspired by Griffin (2008). This chapter is a condensed recension of my contribution to the volume in which Griffin's work appears (Frykenberg, 2008).

and voracious, relying on force rather than consent, contract, or law. The historiography of these countervailing processes, or tendencies in political logic, has ever been in a dialectical tension with each other. They are epitomized in the polar opposition of two ancient concepts: *mandala-nyāya* ("logic of circles or spheres") and *matsa-nyāya* ("logic of fish") (Spellman, 1964: 156–159).[1] The first was a formula for socio-political inclusion and integration by means of persuasion and brokered agreement. The second was a formula for political absorption, conquest, and dominion, by means of aggressive force and violent subjugation. These polarities serve as useful paradigms for understanding the parallel historiographies of Hinduism and Hindutva. Both were "Hindu" in the elemental or generic sense of the term. Both pertained to anything and/or everything "native" to the Indic continent (or subcontinent). All cultures, ideas, and institutions lying within lands surrounded by the continent's walls of mountains and moats of oceans were, are, and have always been inherently "Hindu."

Initially, the term "Hindu,"[2] itself an alien designation, was a label for all things located in the land beyond the Indus. First used by Persians and Greeks (Yavanas), and then by Muslims and Europeans, the term was adopted by the British from the 1770s onward, eventually coming into nearly universal (if vague) usage. They came into vogue at about the same time as, or soon after, the Government of India was first formed in 1772. Now universally recognized, albeit not always with consistent or precise meanings, they can be seen as consequences of the parallel processes by which the over-arching political systems of India (or South Asia) were gradually and painstakingly molded together under the shade of a single imperial umbrella. These events provide a framework for understanding the historiography for both Hinduism and Hindutva, as we now know these terms.

## The Historiography of "Syndicated" Hinduism

The historiography of events leading to an inclusive, modern, and tolerant "syndicated" Hinduism that, by its inner logic, was reflected in peculiarly Indian forms of "non-interference," "religious neutrality," and "secularism," which can be seen within a series of parallel and interlocking processes, both intellectual (ideational or ideological) and institutional or structural.

## Intellectual and Ideological Integration: Indology or Indian Orientalism

India's first Governor General, Warren Hastings (1773–1785), the only person ever to hold that position in the next 174 years of British rule who was not from British nobility, launched one of the most ambitious ventures of cultural exploration and recovery in all of history. He gave personal encouragement and official support to this vast enterprise. This became known as "Orientalism"—or, to be more precise, "Indology."[3] Out of this enterprise came some of the earliest constructions of such concepts as "Hindu" and "India." Hosts of scholars, *both* European and Native Indian, became avidly engaged in this venture of discovery—a project of uncovering, describing, surveying, preserving, and studying the entire corpus of artifacts, which constituted the cultural heritage of India's ancient civilization, a heritage that R. C. Majumdar would later claim had been all but forgotten. Later, after Napoleon's conquest of Egypt, this kind of venture would also be extended to exploring other civilizations of Asia and the Near East. Modern "Orientalism",[4] as a by-product of the Enlightenment, gained worldwide recognition and academic respectability. Chairs of "Indology" and Sanskrit were established at major universities around the world. "Hindoo" then became a generic label for describing all manifestations of life—social, ritual, or cultural—within the Indian continent. While it was mainly applied to "high" cultural and religious traditions, as defined by Brahmans within the Sanskritic (and Vedic) literatures, the term also came to include any and all forms of ritual and social practices, institutions, and values "native" to India.[5]

As far as can be determined, the earliest actual use of the term "Hinduism" (originally spelled "Hindooism") dates from the 1770s. Geoffrey Oddie traces the term "Hindooism" to the year 1787, and to the writings of Charles Grant.[6] Whether or not anyone, European or Indian, had previously ever conceptualized the possibility of there being a single and unified pan-Indian system of religious ideologies and institutions, remains a matter of controversy and debate. Charles

Grant was already occupying a high seat, as chair of the Company's Court of Directors in London, when, two decades later, a manuscript describing "Hindu Manners, Customs, and Ceremonies" arrived from Madras and when, a decade later, it appeared in print. This manuscript has long been linked to the Abbé Dubois, a French missionary of Pondicherry. But, thanks to the late Sylvia Murr (1987),[7] we now know that this manuscript, *Mœurs, Institutions et Cérémonies des Peuples de l'Inde*, so long attributed to the Abbé, for which the East India Company's Madras Government of Lord William Bentinck paid 2000 Star Pagodas in 1806/7 and first published under the title *Description of the Character, Manners, and Customs of the People of India; and of their Institutions, Religious and Civil, Translated from the French Manuscript, London, 1817*, was in fact plagiarized. This fact in itself, however much Dubois may have personally benefited, makes this work all the more significant, for instead of dating from the reign of Louis XVIII, it actually dates from that Louis XV, a full century earlier. Indeed, thanks to Murr, we know that it was the work of Gaston-Lauren Cœurdoux, an earlier missionary who also worked in South India. Yet, the question of whether this remarkable work ever suggested the pre-existence in India of an ancient and single and universal system of religious and social institutions or whether there only existed a fractured collection of segmented religious and social institutions remains one that was never answered. Nor, even now, is this a question that is settled with finality. What does emerge from Cœurdoux's work is a perspective revealing that whoever claimed to rule, whether Hindu or Muslim, "all posts of confidence were held by Brahmins" (Dubois, 1906: xxiii). As such, the work remains a valuable apologetic for ideological and institutional integration of all India under the sway of single authority.

Behind all that was "Hindu," in the sense of the high traditions being uncovered by Indologists stood the influence of twice-born (*dvīja*) scholars. Most of these were servants of the Company or local gentry from high-born families related to Company officials. All, from the very beginning, had long been connected, in one way or another, with the rise of the Indian Empire. Champions and defenders of all things "Native" (i.e., "Hindu" or "Indian"), these persons came, at least initially, from that class of indigenous notables which best understood the cultural and social foundations of political power. No class was more intimately involved in the pursuit of Indology than they. Having already long served as official *"dubashis," "munshis,"* and *"vakils,"* it

was they who played a vital role as teachers and translators for each
new generation of European servants of the Company.[8] As diplomatic agents, go-betweens, and interpreters between the Company and
various levels of Indian rulership, from the highest of lordly princes
(Mughals and Maharajas) down to petty village zamindars, they played
a pivotal part in the construction of both the Empire and of modern
"Hinduism." This Warren Hastings well understood.

Not surprisingly, therefore, it was also from the ranks of Indians
themselves, mainly Brahmans, that many if not most advances in
Orientalist and Indological understanding came. In concert with
Indologists and Sanskritists around the world, Indian scholars cease-
lessly unearthed, translated, interpreted and published fresh findings.
In fields of ancient history, philosophy and religion, the "wonder that
was India" was constantly being rediscovered.[9] Epitomized by Max
Müller's *The Sacred Books of the East*, a huge series of 50 volumes that
began to emerge between 1879 and 1910, over a century after Warren
Hastings had first launched such efforts; this project came to fruition in
the work of such scholarly giants as R. C. Majumdar, K. A. Nilakantha
Sastri, and Sarvepalli Radhakrishnan. These scholars symbolized hosts
of nameless predecessors whose works of collection, transcription, and
translation provided a vast corpus of intellectual and philosophical
substance for a newly reifying high religion now called "Hinduism."
More than that, since political logic called for eclectic and syncre-
tistic impulses necessary for continuing processes of imperial (and
national) integration, this official (Orientalist) Hinduism emphasized
and hallowed doctrines of restraint and tolerance. Unveiled by Swami
Vivekananda before the Parliament of World Religions at Chicago in
1893, this newly discovered or invented "Hinduism" achieved recognition among theologically liberal thinkers in the West; and legitimation
as a full-fledged "World Religion" (Ziolkowski, 1990: 11–12).

*Institutional Integration: State Administration of
Sacred Sites and Temples*

The second process, no less significantly, arose out of legislation
decreeing that, henceforth, imperial governments in India would take
direct responsibility for the care, maintenance, and support of all *pukka*

Native ("Hindoo") religious and charitable institutions. The imperial Raj, even as the shadow of its authority reached across the entire Indian Ocean, made itself the guardian of all endowments, temples, places of pilgrimage, sectarian academies (*mutths*), ceremonies, and festivals (Frykenberg, 1977). Bengal Regulation X of 1810 and Madras Regulation XVII of 1817, and a comparable Regulation for Bombay Presidency, brought many scores of thousands of proper temples, pilgrimage centers and monastic institutions (*mutths*), great and small, under official protection, management, and tax exemption. By this means, almost unbeknownst to Britain, the Indian Empire became, for all practical purposes, a *de facto* "Hindu" Raj. This officially (if "silently") sponsored policy of "Hinduization" (or what would now be called "nationalization") of all cultural and religious institutions in India, was later assailed by opponents in London. Subsequently modified by legislation in 1863 and 1926, it was never ended and, in many respects, still continues to be in force to this day (Presler, 1987).

Government-appointed officials administered temple endowments (*devasthanams*, etc.). They made temple repairs or renovations, and oversaw rituals (through the agency of *dharmakartas*, *pujaris*, and *stanikars*). They bestowed homage and worship (*puja*), and also official recognition and titles (such as *rasika* or *sampradayika*) on each deity. Europeans and Indians alike made generous private donations to deities, contributing to ostentatious public observances. Ceremonies conducted within temples, under the direct or indirect supervision of the state auditors, silently if not formally, legitimized the Hindu cosmic order (*dharma*) of separate temple calendars. In the South, neither the largest and oldest temples, such as those of Tirupati, Srirangam, Madurai, Kanchipuram, or Cuddalore, nor the meanest and tiniest of new shrines springing up beside dusty roadways and thoroughfares escaped close attention. Colonial officials, who were Hindu, not only controlled temple revenues and expenditures, but watched over ritual practices.

Soldiers of the empire, including Christians, Muslims, and Sikhs, stood on parade and saluted local deities, attended blood sacrifices, and marched in processions (*yatras*), remaining prominently visible at all great religious festivals (often in defiance of private consciences). Civil officials collected tolls from pilgrims and taxes at fairs and festivals, and commandeered huge drafts of involuntary labor from hundreds of thousands for the pulling of enormous temple cars (*rathas*), turning their heads when someone, propitiously, "happened" to be crushed beneath the huge wheels of Lord Jagganatha.[10] Even temple dancing, music, and prostitution, involving hundreds of thousands of *devadasis*, came under the eye of the government. All these activities came, at least in some measure, within the rubric of this second or "official" kind of Hinduism.

## The Historiographies of Reform and Reaction

Two other processes, in reaction to the two processes just described, can be seen as giving rise to the sacralized political religion of Hinduism, as we know it today. The first of these, initiated and supported by forward-looking Europeans (Westerners) and Indians alike, was progressive and reformist. The second, radically romantic and reactionary, was revivalist as well as militantly nationalistic and potentially totalistic, leading directly to the rise of Hindutva and allied movements of the Sangh Parivar.

*Hindu Reform: Toward an Inclusive Humanity,*
*Neutrality, and Secularity*

Well before the Company's Raj gained full paramountcy over the subcontinent, there were leaders in India, both European and Native, who denigrated what they saw as inhuman practices, and protested against human sacrifice, infanticide, and widow burning. Enlightenment ideologies and impulses, both religious and secular, led a radical ideal that every segment of mankind on earth, whatever its current condition and wherever this existed, shared cardinal features of a common humanity shared and ought, therefore, to enjoy certain fundamental human rights. This radical conception—seeing a common humanity within all mankind—was given further impetus by revolutionary movements in the West. However different in nature and origin, both the American and the French Revolutions stemmed from Enlightenment ideals, both religious and secular, that in turn harked back to Reformation ideals and policies of religious toleration evolving out of the Peace of Westphalia in 1648.

One branch of social protests in India was religious. It was a by-product of the modern missionary movement, generated by the Evangelical Christian awakenings in the West. Whereas earlier pioneer missionaries, inspired by the irenic ideals of German Pietism, had been loath to interfere with local customs and traditions that they encountered, later missionaries were more intrusive, striving for what they saw as "human" rights. While still lacking official support for their work from the East India Company, later generations of missionaries cautiously joined Indian Christians in protesting against practices that they felt were intolerably "inhuman" and against oppressive behaviors perpetrated by its local officials. Even before the Company was finally forced by Parliament, in 1813, to accept the inclusion of the so-called "pious clause" in its charter making the "religious and moral improvement" of the Indians incumbent upon the Company,[11] there were some European officials in India who wanted to bring about cultural and moral, if not social, reforms. Charles Grant and John Shore (aka Lord Teignmouth), themselves recent converts to Christianity who had risen to high positions (within the Company's Court of Directors and the Government of India), argued that official support for Christian missionaries into Company domains would help to bring about a moral transformation in India. Claudius Buchanan, a Company chaplain of Evangelical sentiments within the Church of England, did the same. As the first Vice-Provost of the newly founded Fort William College, he had been ordered to investigate moral conditions throughout India, His report, *Christian Researches in Asia*, published in 1811 (and in later editions), was critical of "Hindoo" (i.e., "Native") institutions. But, among various architects of "Hindooism" as a vast and monolithic system of religion, no individual did more than William Ward. This member of the "Serampore Trio"[12] produced a four volume work entitled *Account of the Writings, Religion, and Manners of the Hindoos, including translations from their principal works*. In this work, published at Serampore in 1811, and reappearing in a third edition in 1817–1820 not long before his death, he systematically "constructed," or "invented," "Hinduism" that had never before existed (Oddie, 2003, 2006). Responding to this work, Raja Ram Mohan Roy and other progressive notables among the Calcutta gentry (bhadralok) joined officials and missionaries in a campaign to eradicate decadent "Hindoo" customs and institutions, especially female infanticide and widow burning. Roy, in reacting to Orientalist scholarship and negative views of "Hindooism" strove to redefine high religious traditions of India in grand, Brahmanical, and monistic, if not monotheistic, terms, doing so through organizing a progressive reform society known as Brahmo Samāj (1828). Such was his influence that he is still credited with being "the father of modern India."[13]

It is useful to recall that, prior to the 1790s, Christians already had a long history in India. Thomas (Syrian and/or Orthodox) Christians of Kerala had flourished as integral parts of local, indigenous cultures for nearly 18 centuries. "Hindu" forms of Christianity had been deeply rooted in the Indian soil long before critical attitudes among some missionaries from the West gained currency. Moreover, some among the most gifted earlier generations of missionaries from Europe, both Catholic and Protestant, had made acculturating contributions to indigenous (Hindoo) cultures, customs and institutions, doing so in comprehensive and positive terms.[14] Leaders among newer Christian movements in South India at the end of the 18th century—located in Tarangambadi (Thanjavur), Tirunelveli, or Thiruvananthapuram (Travancore)—petitioned Parliament for protection from persecution by government officials. This they did as "Hindu" (or "Native") Christian subjects of the Company.

For the most part, however, attacks against official support for the "Hindu Establishment" within the Company-ruled Indian Empire came to nothing. In one remarkable case, several hundred European (Christian) officials who were outraged by what they saw as government participation in "heathen" practices and rituals organized a formal protest. Their "mutinous conspiracy" brought an immediate and swift response. The Anglican Bishop of Madras (Daniel Corrie) was sharply reprimanded; the commanding general in Madras (Peregrine Maitland) was forced to resign; and scores of other devoutly Christian European officials, civil and military, were obliged to leave the country. Some of the dissidents who returned to London organized the "Anti-Idolatry Connexion League" and launched a pamphlet campaign against the evils of the Company's "Hindu" empire. Years of lobbying for "religious neutrality" followed (Carson, 2012). Such concessions as were made, in legislation of 1863 and 1926, turned out to be hardly more than cosmetic. Various "Hindu Charitable and Religious Endowments Boards" that exist in India today are the products of this long process of amalgamation, and of modest reforms that came in its wake.

A number of other, similar reformist movements in India followed, not all of which can be traced here. These included cultural, educational, and social reform movements. In South India, these included the Madras Literary Society, the Madras Native Society, the Madras Hindu Association, and the Madras Mahajana Sabha. Prominent in Western India was the Prarthana Samaj of Ranade. During the 1880s, the gentry of Madurai launched a reform movement for the "reform," if not abolition, of all *devadasi* institutions, and endowments, within Hindu temples. Among Telugu gentry of what we now know as Coastal Andhra, Kandukuri Veerasalingam led movements for the amelioration and liberation of women, especially higher caste widows, from various forms of thralldom (Leonard, 1991). As newer forms of voluntarism entered "public life," voices became more strident. Against reform movements, reactionary "Hindu" forces mounted campaigns for the preservation of "*Sanāthana Dharma*"—the "Old [Hallowed] Religion" (or "Established Tradition").

## Hindu Reaction: Toward Exclusivist and Militant Communal Dominance

But it was yet another kind of process that redefined the concept of "Hindu" much more radically.

Responding to, and building upon, the developments described above, and growing in tandem with them, were movements that became the true progenitors of modern Hindutva. Extremely conservative, but also romantic, reactionary, and revivalist in character, they were defensive, chauvinistic, and xenophobic, especially in response to Western influences and negative attitudes of some foreign missionaries and officials, as well as Indian social reformers, toward ancient and hallowed "Hindu" cultures. These kinds of movements arose despite the fact that some European (British) officials enthusiastically propitiated local deities and made endowments to local temples, that some missionaries, such as theological liberals and Unitarians, enthusiastically embraced "Hindu" ideas and philosophies, and that Indian social reformers were themselves often attached to cultural legacies inherited from India's past. What really disturbed reactionary traditionalists were radical conversion movements and social reform movements that threatened ritual purity and hallowed customs of social apartheid, not only in distinctions between clean and polluting (untouchable) castes and tribes, but also between men and women of the same caste. Conversions and social reforms, in short, undermined traditional social structures (*varṇāśramadharma*: "color-ranking-order") upon conceptions of ritual purity (free of pollution) and sacred blood and earth.

Increasingly aggressive, especially after the 1920s, the most extreme of this collection of movements, now known as the *Sangh Parivar* (i.e., roughly: "Family or Kindred Societies"), would eventually exhibit what may even be seen as fascist and fundamentalist tendencies. Responding to what were interpreted as invidious attacks against indigenous institutions and against the purity of sacred birth and sacred earth, some high-born elites, especially Brahmans of Maharashtra and of regions in the north, resorted to various forms of resistance, both overt and covert. Activist, agitative and aggressive, and organized in defense of the "old order" (*sanathana dharma*), local and regional leaders formed voluntary associations. They initiated and organized petition drives (*arzi-s*), launched public protests (*hartals*), and formed violent forms of unrest (riots, insurrections, etc.). In doing so, even as they demonstrated, they discovered latent strengths hitherto never fully realized, enabling them to mobilize resources of political power within traditionally dominant social elites. In so doing, they embarked upon programs of constructing, defining, and then demonstrating a new kind of "Hindu" consciousness. This was a new kind of self-conscious "Hinduism" such as had never before existed, at least in quite the same form.[15] Those who did these things came from reactionary elements among the very same classes of notables and some of the very same families that, in earlier generations, had served the Raj, either directly, as officials, or as providers of financial and professional services that were essential sinews of the Empire. They reacted against any and all efforts to tamper with social customs or to undermine traditions, especially in matters pertaining to family practices and rituals. These were "Hindus" in a new sense. They sharply defined and increasingly emphasized salient features of the world that they themselves had helped to build—a system that they now wished to preserve and reify. What they saw endangered and threatened were sacred elements of their own birthright and their own native land.

These militantly nativistic kinds of "Hindu" reaction became, simultaneously and more avowedly, "political" and "religious." Borrowing methods from those Christian missionary societies which they viewed as most threatening, they mobilized as many supporters as possible. They took concerted actions *against* anything and everything which disturbed local sensibilities or local traditions, especially *against* what they saw as government interference in indigenous ceremonies, customs, institutions, or rituals. Established customs and traditions that had long held sway within each high-caste or "twice-born" birth group (*jati*), each domestic or sectarian community, especially those that had held sway within families and local domains—domains too sacred and sensitive to be "touched," or "polluted," by outsiders—were precisely what they felt most needed to be defended. Strangely, these were the much endowed "Hindu" charitable and religious institutions described above, that the government had taken under its administration since 1810 and 1817.

The first glimmers of this kind of reaction can be seen as early as 1799, when dominant elites in Tirunelveli Country, aided by local warlords and Marava clubmen from Shivaganga, tried to stop to massive conversions to Christianity that were taking place among the lowly Shanar (later known as Nadar) community. When whole villages had turned Christian, converting village temples into prayer-school halls, some violators of the old order were stripped and driven into the jungle to die. Surviving refugees, in turn, established separate "villages of refuge" for Christians. These defensive enclaves, in the face of further pogroms, multiplied and prospered. Prominent among movements of "Hindu" reaction that organized during the 1820s, 1830s, and 1840s, were the Vibuthi Sangam (Sacred Ashes Society) in Tirunelveli, the Chatur Veda Siddhanta Sabha (or Salay Street Society) of Madras, and local branches of the Dharma Sabha (from Bengal). Later movements in Western and Northern India such as the Arya Samaj (1875) of Swami Dayanand Saraswati and the Nagari Pracharini Sabha (1893) of Shyam Sundar Das, Ram Narayan Mishra, and Shiv Kumar Singh (Jones, 1976; King, 1994). Late 19th-century movements, in turn, inspired militant anti-cow-killing campaigns in Bengal, Maharashtra, and Punjab, the extremist rhetoric of Bankimchandra Chattopadhyay, the ideas of Swami Vivekananda (Narendranath Datta), the symbols of Bal Gangadhar Tilak, and the mystic spirituality of Shri Aurobindo (Ghose).

The most militant kind of reactionary "Hinduism," embracing a monolithic "Hindutva community" was also a modern invention. Envisioning a "Hindu consciousness" hitherto unimagined, it arose, in Romila Thapar's view, "when there was competition for political and economic resources between various groups in a colonial situation" and "a need to change from a segmental identity to a community which cut across caste, sect, and religion" (Thapar, 1989: 229).[16] What emerged out of movements of the 19th century was a growing sense of community that became increasingly self-conscious about its anxieties and aggressive about its aspirations. Leaders of this "imagined community" then claimed to be sole representatives of India's "majority." With India's "sacred destiny" as its legitimizing legacy and its sole possession, militant "Hindus" demanded dominion over all other communities in India. "Hinduism" as a "Hindu community" and "India" as a Nation-State thus became modern by-products of the Raj. Thus it was that the mobilizing of new systems of loyalty, forged out of the same "Hindu" elements previously used by the East India Company for constructing the Imperial State served to buttress post-imperial constructions of the National (or Nation) State in two forms: one secularizing (in uniquely Indian ways) and another sacralizing. The latter, in turn, threatened and undermined many of those contractual substructures of obligation which had previously served to construct and undergird the socio-political constitution of modern India itself: Hindutva *matsya nyāya*, in short, threatened to devour the local and All-India structures of a secularizing Hindu *mandala nyāya*.

Proto-Hindutva forms of Hindu reaction to reform movements led to ever more militant Hindu ideologies and organizations. None of them were, initially or explicitly, "Hindutva" (at least as that term later became known). Yet, these earlier reactionary movements led, step by step, in that direction.

## The Historiography of Hindutva

At its heart, Hindutva or "Hinduness" became a reactionary political religion—a sacralizing form of Hindu fundamentalism and/or militantly Hindu nationalism. The first openly fundamentalist Hindu agency was the "Hindu Sabha." This Punjabi association, "ardent and watchful in the interests of the Hindu community," was formed in 1907. This was followed by the Hindu Mahasabha in 1916 and the Rashtriya Swayamsevak Sangh (RSS) in 1925. Two new institutions served as preconditions: (1) the All-India Census and (2) the rise of representative government. These, together, hastened self-conscious movements of social mobilization that, in turn, led to communalism and to nationalism.

The earliest censuses, begun in the 1820s, were local. From 1871 onward, the decennial All-India Census, defined, refined and standardized communal, occupational, social, and religious categories (Barrier, 1981). Actually administered by local cadres of the civil service, most of whom were Brahmans, it codified and ossified the stratified social structures (*varnashramadharma*) so that virtually all who were not Christians, Jews, or Muslims, became "Hindus" by default. Altogether, twice-born (*dvija*) castes—Brahmans, Kshatriyas, and Vaishyas—made up hardly more than 15 percent of the population (5 percent in each category). Shudras throughout the subcontinent came to between 35 and 40 percent; and polluting (*avarna*) and aboriginal/tribal (*adivasi*) or peoples came to some 20 percent; and Muslims, Christians, and Jews came to another 20 to 25 percent of the total population of the empire. Census figures revealed, for all to see, that the "pure," "twice-born," or "Aryan" castes, were a minority whose hitherto dominant position with a representative system of governance could become precarious. Census categories and concepts, therefore, were manipulated in such a way as to include hitherto excluded untouchables and tribals as "Hindus" and to exclude hitherto included culturally respectable communities of Indian Christians and Muslims. By such arbitrary means, an immutable and permanent "Hindu majority community" was created. Census definition "inclusion" or "exclusion" from the "Hindu fold" became a powerful instrument that, in turn, exacerbated a growing "communalism" (Barrier, 1976).

The second process raised the unthinkable specter of a possible subjection of the high-born. The evolution of constitutional institutions promising democratically elected representative self-government, first in local councils and then, progressively, to higher levels made clear this possibility. By the 1870s and 1880s, Indians were already beginning to gain seats in Parliament, in Executive and Legislative Councils, and on the benches of various High Courts. The time was coming,

Sir Sayyed Ahmad Khan pointed out, when "representative Indians" who were predominantly "caste Hindus" would rule the land and when most of these would be militantly anti-Muslim. Census figures and democratic elections, taken together, could spell trouble. Thus, both Hindu elites and Muslim elites, could sense the possibility of future conflict. What punctuated such concerns was a newly rising incidence of Hindu–Muslim riots.

Perhaps no single person was more influential, or symptomatic of rising Hindu militancy, than Vinayak Damodar Savarkar. It was he who re-discovered and re-invented the term "Hindutva" or "Hinduness." Savarkar was a Chitpavan Brahman of Maharashtra who, after going to England to study law at Grey's Inn, had engaged in revolutionary activities and written a book about the 1857 Mutiny or Rebellion of North India entitled *The Indian War of Independence* (London: 1909). Arrested in 1910 after being implicated in the assassination of a British official, he had been transported for life to the Andaman Islands and remained in Indian prisons for 27 years. It was while incarcerated in Ratnagiri Prison (1922) that he penned his most famous work. *Hindutva: Who Is a Hindu?* (first published in 1923 but not appearing in English until 1942 and still in print), which became the Hindutva bible. By the time of his release in 1937, Savarkar had acquired a near cult-like status as a *rishi* among his devoted followers.

The All-India Hindu Mahasabha, a reaction to formation of the All India Muslim League, came into being in 1915/16, as an adjunct (or caucus) of the Indian National Congress (which, at that time, allowed multiple memberships).[17] By the 1920s, despite the Lucknow Pact (1916) and concessions on "separate electorates" made by the INC, *jihads* of the Khilafat movement and Mappilla massacres of Hindu landlords in Malabar provoked violent Hindu reactions. Hindutva disenchantment with Gandhi increased after the killing of 22 policemen by Hindu mobs at Chauri Chaura in early 1922, which led him to call off his non-violent *satyagraha* (or campaign of non-cooperation). In 1923, Pandit Madan Mohan Malaviya called for "means to arrest the deterioration and decline of Hindus and to effect an improvement of the Hindus as a community." From Varanasi, he called Hindus to demonstrate *kshatriya* valor and to develop academies (*akharas*) for training in martial skills. Lala Lajpat Rai worried that Gandhi's tactics were only weakening Hindu solidarity and engendering a "slave mentality." Hindu–Muslim riots kept mounting in scale, intensity and violence throughout the 1920s.

It was Savarkar who, while in prison, re-discovered or developed the ideology of "Hindutva" or "Hinduness." Hindutva became synonymous with militantly chauvinistic and nativistic nationalism. What emerged was a truly fundamentalist and modern political religion *par excellence*.[18] Centered in sacred cultures and countries, peoples and places, Hindutva defined essentials of an extremely militant nationalism and fount of inspiration. Hindus, Savarkar proclaimed, were the original people of the land. Aryan blood had forever formed a single nation (*rashtra*). Sacred "birth" and "earth" had made India (*Hindusthan*). Fundamentals of "Hindu*tva*," had been imprinted within genetic codes of sacred blood and sacred soil which, indeed, evoked cosmic sacred sound from whence all being and knowledge (*veda*) originated. Any true Hindu would feel the pulse Hindutva's timeless "antiquity" and "unity" (*sanghatan*). This "inner text" bound India's peoples to their divine fatherland (*pitrubhu*) and divine country (*punyabhu*). This "holy land," watered by eternal rivers (Indus, Ganga, Brahmaputra, Yamuna, Saraswati, Narmada, etc.) flowing from the holy "Home of Snows" (Himalayas), reached down to where three eternal and sacred seas mingled at Kanya Kumari.

What Savarkar preached, Kesnav Baliram Hedgewar, another Chitpavan Brahman, practiced. He founded Rashtriya Swayamsevak Sangh, or "RSS", in 1925. What India lacked, in his view, were overarching Hindu institutions that could build Hindu solidarity throughout India. Linguistic, regional, and social fragmentation had opened the country to Muslim and European subjugation. Disillusioned with tactics of non-violent non-cooperation (*ahimsa* and *satyagraha*) underlying Gandhi's campaigns, he dedicated himself to restoring "essential unity" (*sanghatan*).[19] This could only be done by inspiring deeper cultural, psychological, and religious changes within society. This called for a carefully planted and deeply rooted movement of totalistic transformation within the entire society. To bring about radical commitment to profound, if not radical, transformations within each person's heart and mind, he began building a local "brotherhood" of "national volunteers" (*sevaks*) made out of totally dedicated individuals (Frykenberg, 1980, 1988, 1993, 1994). True believers had to be able to transcend personal agendas and petty or narrow-minded rivalries. Each carefully built cadre of totally transformed and committed persons would serve as foundation stones for slowly building a totally new kind of organization, something truly national and revolutionary. Only by awakening a new self-consciousness—through rigorous self-discipline and a new sense of community of "Hindus"—could this be accomplished.

Following suggestions made by Sister Nevedita,[20] he decided that each small squad would "congregate and pray together for 15 minutes every day, and Hindu society will become an invincible society."[21] He recruited teenage schoolboys and college youths, idealistic lads not yet corrupted by worldly concerns nor preoccupied with domestic burdens—picking them carefully after scrutinizing their capacity for total, unquestioning loyalty and obedience. Each coterie of utterly dedicated followers was then trained in martial style and rigorously indoctrinated. Bound to each other by exceptionally strong emotional and political ties, each peer group grew up together in such a way as its own shared memories and sentiments would last a lifetime.

The first *sevaks* trained at a fencing academy or gymnasium (*akhara*) in Nagpur. All were Maratha Brahmans who nursed historical traditions of having once been great warriors and rulers. At the Hedgewar Bhavan, the RSS headquarters, Hedgewar personally supervised prayers, body-building exercises, martial drills, and textual learning. Stories about exploits of great Hindu heroes, such as Shivaji, Rana Pratap, or Nana Sahib, were told and retold. Emotional ties were deepened by means of outings, picnics, and sporting events. Each person was meant to gain an élan, a sense of self-importance, and proud independence; and, as the group sensed its superiority, it was disciplined to do anything on command, at the beck and call of the supreme commander.

The first regimented *shakha* (brigade or "branch") came into being in 1926. Other *shakhas* followed, each composed of "enlightened" *swayamsevaks* ("dedicated-servants" or "volunteers"). The number of *akharas*, martial arts academies extolling *kshatriya* ideals, jumped from 230 to 570 (Anderson and Damlé, 1987: 35). Each new *shakha*, disciplined in daily "character-building" exercises designed to be physically, mentally, and spiritually rigorous, learned to use hand weapons (brass-bound quarter-staffs, swords, daggers, and spears); and took part in forced marches, forest camps, and weekly discussions. Each was to reflect warrior (*kshatriya*) ideals and norms, mandating instant readiness for "action" or "service" (*seva*) and to take part in daily oaths, prayers, and salutes. A few of the very best and most dedicated were given "life oaths" and rituals of fealty before the Guruji or Supreme Sangh Guide (*Sar-Sanghchalak*), the saffron-colored Banner (*Bhagva Dwaj*),[22] and the Maruti Deva (Hanuman), as well as to Shivaji's guru Ramdas Swami.

Formally inaugurated during Dasara (September) 1925, on the annual festival for celebrating Rama's victory over Ravana, the name Rashtriya Swayam Sevak was publicly proclaimed at the Ram Navami of 1926. At that event, uniformed volunteers of the first *shakha*, in knee-length khaki shorts, white shirts, black hats, and quarter-staffs (*lathis*) marched, sang verses from Ram Das, poured drinking water for thirsty pilgrims, and drove away corrupt pandarams and sadhus. But the public reputation of the RSS did not become fixed until 1927, after the first training camp for *swayamsevaks* and after the outbreak of communal rioting in Nagpur. Circulating "news" that Muslims were planning an attack, 16 RSS squads moved into "respectable" neighborhoods to provide "protection." When not a single Hindu locality was attacked, Hindutva's reputation for valor was established. The Hindu Mahasabha then invited uniformed RSS brigades to its Bombay session. Thereafter, number of *swayamsevak* recruits multiplied and *shakha* brigades proliferated. Between 1931 and 1939, the number of *shakhas* grew from 60 to 500, with 60,000 active members (roughly half Marathi speakers). After 1929, an elaborate hierarchy of RSS leaders and officials began to emerge. These came by promoting elite *swayamsevaks*, ranked by year, to squad leaders (*gatanayaks*), ordinary and superior instructors (*gata-* and *mukhya shikshaks*), secretaries (*karyavahs*), celibate staff commanders (*pracharaks* of different ranks: local, regional, national), and directors (*sanghchalaks*: city/district and regional). All were under the ultimate authority of the RSS's Supreme Guide (*Sar-Sanghchalak*).

Despite all its political activism and regimentation, the RSS scrupulously avoided involvement in provincial or national politics. Indeed, outcries of consternation, criticism, and disappointment over avoidance of involvement in electoral politics did not disappear until after Independence. Savarkar, after his release from prison in 1937, expressed his disgust over this "purely cultural" agenda and predicted that the RSS would never amount to much. Anna Sohani resigned after uniformed RSS squads were ordered to avoid provocatively marching in front of mosques on Fridays so as not to incite violence, especially when Muslim paramilitary groups, such as the Khaksars, were being violently provocative, as also Akali Dal Sikh forces. When one General Secretary (G. M. Huddar) resorted to armed robbery and landed in prison, he was reprimanded. When the RSS refused to join the Hindu Mahasabha in agitations against the Nizam's Dominions in 1938–39, relations cooled. When the RSS avoided overt anti-British actions during World War II, refusing to militarize Hindus or to undermine loyalty within the Indian Army, Hindutva relations deteriorated still further.

Hedgewar died in 1940. He was succeeded by Madhav Sadashiv Golwalkar. The new Supreme Leader (*Sar-Sanghchalak*), being an ascetic ex-teacher and ex-*sunnyasi*, was even less interested in open politics. His *We, or Our Nationhood Defined*, a 1938 summary of Savarkar's *Rashtra Mimansa*, spelled out Hindutva ideology:

> The non-Hindu people in Hindustan must either adopt the Hindu culture and language, must learn to respect and hold in reverence Hindu religion, must entertain no idea but glorification of the Hindu race and culture: i.e., they must not only give up their attitude of intolerance and ungratefulness towards this land and its age-old traditions, but must also cultivate a positive attitude of love and devotion… In a word, they must cease to be foreigners, or must stay in this country wholly subordinated to the Hindu nation, claiming nothing, deserving no privileges, far less any preferential treatment, not even citizen's rights. (Golwalkar, 1947: 55–56)

After Independence in 1947, Hindutva suffered a severe setback. Gandhi's assassination (January 30, 1948) by a former *sevak* (Nathuram Vinayak Godse)[23] the RSS was outlawed and many thousands of members jailed.[24] Golwalkar strove thereafter to improve the public image and restore the strength of the RSS. RSS *kar sevaks* aided thousands of refugees during the Partition and wars with Pakistan (1950, 1965, and 1971) and China (1962). They assisted Vinobha Bhave during his agrarian campaign of persuading landlords to give land to the landless. The Emergency of 1975–1977 came as a boon. Despite again being outlawed, the RSS went underground and expanded rapidly. After Indira Gandhi's return to power in 1980, communalist difficulties mounted, she played the "Hindu card" by consulting *sadhus*, going to pilgrim sites, and extolling "Hindu hegemony." Her assassination in 1984—following the release of Sikh Sant Bindrranwale from prison in October 1981, militant Sikh capture of the Golden Temple in Amritsar, and military violation of the Akal Takht in Operation Blue Star—provoked a wave of Hindu revivalism ("Hindu *jagaram*"). But, unable to surmount Rajiv Gandhi's landslide "sympathy" victory at the polls, RSS forces bided their time, gathered recruits, and sharpened their political weapons.

By 1989, the RSS could claim that it commanded over 1.8 million disciplined *kar sevaks*, distributed in over 25,000 well-drilled *shakhas*, and 18,800 urban and rural centers. By then, Hindutva forces were ready to bid for greater political power. The successors of Hedgewar and Madhav Sadashiv Golwalkar, had formed subsidiary agencies, including the Bharatiya Jana Sangh (1951), the Vishwa Hindu Parishad (1964), the Bharatiya Janata Party (1980) that would win control over the Government of India from 1998 to 2004, and the ever more violent Bajrang Dal youth movement of the 1990s. Most of these agencies were led by Chitpavan Maratha Brahmans of Puné and Nagpur, one exception being the Non-Brahman Shiv Sena (Shiva's Army), led by Bal Keshav Thackeray. This anti-Muslim movement, coming to prominence in the 1960s, gained control of Mumbai (Bombay); and, with the BJP, of Maharashtra. In 1984, all Hindutva organizations joined together to form the *"Dharma Samsad"*—or "General Dharmic Council," with the aim of establishing the Righteous Realm, Reign and Rule of Ram Rajya. These agencies then began to speak of themselves as belonging to the *"Sangh Parivar"* (or the "Family of Societies").

From 1989 onward, Hindutva campaigns were led, step by step, toward a major climacteric. Their aim was to demolish the Babri Masjid in Ayodhya and to replace it with a Rama Mandir, on what was purported to be the sacred birthplace of Lord Rama. A gigantic Sri Ramjanmabhumi Mukti Yagna was mounted, with huge *rath yatras* using processions of modern vehicles to circulate around all of India so as to demonstrate Lord Rama's sovereignty over all the continents. Tens of thousands of *kar sevaks* (service volunteers) marched brandishing swords and tridents (*trishuls*). Despite the assassination of Rajiv Gandhi, and the ineffectual accession of the Congress "Old Guard" of P. V. Narasimha Rao, forces of the Sangh Parivar were confident that their day was coming.

This dawned on December 6, 1992. A wave of new Ayodhya campaigns culminated in the demolition of the Babri Masjid. On the morning of December 6, a throng of over 200,000 *kar sevaks* arrived at the site. In the early afternoon, well-drilled groups of *kar sevaks* began to systematically demolish the mosque. The small numbers of policemen who had been posted at the mosque by the BJP state government stood aside. By evening, the destruction had been completed and the mosque no longer existed. The event shook the whole country, both governing structures and people, as nothing in a half century (Hansen, 1999: 181–185). The Prime Minister of India, P. V. Narasimha Rao, never erased the stain of having done nothing to stop the carnage. An Aruvelu Niyoji Brahman Telugu scholar from Karimnagar (Andhra Pradesh) who had faithfully served Indira and Rajiv, his inaction spoke more loudly than anything he could say. Terrible killings followed: Hindutva-engineered pogroms, euphemistically labeled "riots" soon broke out across the land. How many tens of thousands died, mainly from poorer and weaker Muslim *bastis*, will never be fully known. World media recorded the grisly details in all their misery. Muslim and Christian communities throughout the land, especially the weak who lived in remote villages and shanty-towns, suffered the most. Brimming with new confidence, Hindutva forces believed that the day of Ram Rashtriya was about to arrive.

This day came, at least partially, with the election of 1999. The BJP was able to form a coalition government called the National Democratic Alliance. It gained control of key portfolios such as the Home, Finance, Education, and Foreign ministries. During the next five years, a totalistic, majoritarian, and authoritarian agenda of "saffronization" aimed to "Hinduize" all institutions and to bring minority people "into the Hindu fold" by whatever means necessary. Hindutva historians, insisting that all forms of life, including mankind (*manusha*) and Aryan people and civilization itself, had originated in the Indo-Gangetic plain, attempted to re-write all school textbooks. Marginal people, including aboriginal or polluting communities, were to be forced to remain in that perpetual submission from which they had so long tried to extricate themselves. People incapable of being "saffronized"—for example, Muslims and Christians—were demonized. India was to be cleansed from all alien, or non-Hindu, elements. Those refusing to submit would suffer. This campaign came to a climax in February 2002. Some 10,000 Muslims of Gujarat, mainly inhabitants of Ahmedabad, were done to death. The future of Christians and Muslims in India looked bleak. What might have happened had not an over-confident BJP-led government sought a new electoral mandate in 2004 can only be imagined.

How, then, can Hindutva be assessed as a political religion? As a movement it was totalizing, if not totalitarian, in its impulses and inner structures. This sacralization of politics can be seen, not just in Savarkar extolling of Hitler's cultural nationalism, but in how he was outdone by words of Golwalkar:

> German national pride has now become the topic of the day. To keep up the purity of the nation and its culture, Germany shocked the world by her purging the country of the semitic races—the Jews. National pride at its highest has been manifested here. Germany has shown how well-nigh impossible it is for races and cultures, having differences going to the root, to be assimilated into one united whole, a good lesson for us in Hindustan to learn and profit by Golwalkar. (1947: 27)

> From this standpoint ... the non-Hindu people in Hindustan must either adopt the Hindu culture and language, must learn to respect and revere Hindu religion, must entertain no idea but the glorification of the Hindu nation. They must not only give up their attitude of intolerance and ingratitude toward this land and its age-long traditions, but must also cultivate the positive attitude of love and devotion instead; in one word, they must cease to be foreigners or may in the country wholly subordinated to the Hindu nation, claiming nothing, deserving no privileges, far less preferential treatment, not even a citizen's rights. (Golwalkar, 1947: 52; Basu et al., 1993: 26)

Between Hindutva and European Fascism, especially in Italy and Germany, but less clearly in Spain and Soviet Russia, one can see differences. Not until fascists fully took control of a state apparatus could fascist agendas be fully realized. Yet, by 1945, the totalistic fascism achieved in Italy and Germany, had self-destructed. Hindutva, in contrast, grew gradually over 80 years. To date, it has never achieved totalitarian power. We have yet to see what Hindutva forces might do if they gained an absolute majority and total control. India, founded on a pluralistic and "secularistic" foundation, has retained its constitutional structures and federal states. These have functioned within such highly segmented and plural cultures that total authoritarian control was very difficult to achieve. No resorts to extra-constitutional action, mobilizing mass agitations and riots, have succeeded in bringing totalitarian close to successful attainment of such goals. M. K. Gandhi perfected the tools for mobilizing extra-constitutional campaigns of "non-violent" protest. Yet, from 1919 onward, not one of his campaigns ended without outbreaks of violence; and ultimately, he was murdered in 1947 for having betrayed Hindutva by making concessions to the Muslim community.[25] Thus, despite threads of fascism harking back to the beginnings of Hindutva, these were never woven into a country-wide fabric of authoritarian, or totalistic, governance—perhaps because Hindutva forces never gained total control over the machinery of governance.

Taking the long view, it is the language of this "reconstituted tradition" that forged political instruments of ruler, colonial and national alike. "Traditionalization"—starting with Indological ventures and "Hindu Raj" at the end of the 18th century—began "by assuming an overriding hegemony of Brahmanical texts over Indian society, and firmly incorporating that hegemony into the law-making process" (Rajagopal, 2003: 394). This repeatedly made it possible for regimes to revaluate and "reform" cultural, social and political structures. Raised to the next level by Hindutva forces, this enabled them to develop and refine an ideology designed to assure Brahmanical hegemony within Ram Rajya.

Yet, in reshaping public consciousness so as to conform to Hindutva vocabulary, Hindutva governments became riddled with complexities and contradictions. Events leading from *rath yatras* to Ayodhya, Bombay riots, and Gujarat pogroms, were managed to the advantage of Hindutva. By skillfully deploying resources and tactics so as to occupy spaces left vacant by less active, less attentive, less visionary or less ruthless opponents, Hindutva forces pursued their vision of Hindu Rashtriya (or Ram Rajya). Taking possession of central squares of Indian politics, they deployed double-edged, Janus-faced, and apparently contradictory tactics. Using tactics perfected by Gandhi during the 1920s, they tried to create a "parallel nation" and a "parallel state" apparatus along with a vocabulary for its utilization. They strove to capture institutions of civil society (e.g., communications, education, entertainment, media, etc.) so as to broaden their hegemony. Despite shifting tactics, directors of Hindutva managed to hold together divergent voices, at least enough to meet each challenge; and, at least, for a time.

# Notes

1. These ideas, intricately elaborated in Kautilya's *Arthasastra*, as well as in the *Danda Niti* and the *Sukra Niti*, juxtapose the two primary principles—"the enemy of my enemy is my friend, etc." vs "larger fish devour smaller fish and smaller fish devour still smaller fish, and so on ad infinitum."
2. Its twin, "India," comes from the same root.
3. Not coincidentally, it was Hastings who not only encouraged such "bright young men" as Charles Wilkins (1770), Nathaniel Brassey Halhed (1772), and Jonathan Duncan (1772), but also Sir William Jones (1746–1794), founder of Asiatic Society (Calcutta, January 15, 1784), a venture that encompassed studies of virtually everything concerning both man and nature within the geographical bounds of the continent.
4. Irwin (2006) traces "Orientalism" during earlier ages going all the way back to the Greeks, including under Alexander the Great.
5. Romila Thapar, writing about pre-modern India, points out the mistake of assuming some sort of "inclusive Hinduism" existed when "the reality perhaps lay in looking at it as a cluster of distinctive sects and cults, observing common civilizational symbols, but with belief and ritual ranging from atheism to animism and a variety of religious organizations identifying themselves by location, language, and caste" (Thapar, 1989: 229). No sense of community bound the population together. Small communities, birth groups and religious sects—now explained in Brahmanism, Shramanism, Shakti-ism, Puranic Shaivism and Vaishnavism, Bhaktism, etc.—separated "high" or textual cultures from innumerable local, "low" or popular religious cultures: a "mosaic of distinct cults, deities, sects, and ideas" adjusting and distancing themselves from each other. What bound communities to each other, if at all were manufactured structures of Statecraft. These, while often positive and supportive of local religious and sectarian institutions, had to remain "impartial," "neutral," or "secular." In this logic, Kautiliya's ideas find much in common with ideas of Machiavelli and Hobbes.
6. Oddie (2006: 72). Cf. Grant (1812–13). Citing Morris (1904: 105, 110), Oddie indicates that, in a 1787 letter to Thomas Raikes, Grant assumes that he understands the term "Hindooism."
7. Alas, for revealing that the authorship claimed by Jean-Antoine Dubois was a hoax, she suffered years of academic banishment (by Louis Dumont).
8. Raghavan (1957, 1958). This Sanskrit text, "Sarva Deva Vilāsa" (translated as "The Celebration of the Gods"), described how the Raj itself was a product of divine intervention, as seen in endowments made by Company dubashis.
9. Basham (1967: xxi, 568) reflects this view. This process of "unearthing" India's antiquity is still going on, despite its having been so hotly contested by disciples

of Edward Said. A thorough and incisive dismissal of Edward Said's *Orientalism* is found in Irwin (2006). It is time for this "unfairly maligned honourable pursuit" to be restored to its former honor and respectability.

10. The very term "juggernaut," coming from Jagannath, Lord of the Universe and avatar of Vishnu, entered the English vocabulary, denotes any relentlessly destroying vehicle, force or object of devotion, whereby devotees sometimes immolated themselves beneath giant wheels the deity's Great Car at Puri.

11. For the text of the clause, see Carson (2012: appendix 4).

12. These were the British Baptist missionaries—William Carey, Joshua Marshman, and William Ward—who were instrumental in inspiring missionary voluntarism throughout the English speaking world.

13. Robertson (1995) is the best comprehensive and penetrating study to have emerged so far. Both Roy's Brahmo Samaj (Brahma Society), and the Prarthana Samaj (Prayer Society, 1868), of Mahadev Govind Ranade were nativist precursors of an inclusivistic, and tolerant, Hinduism. Neither was a precursor of more militant and exclusivist Hindutva.

14. Two examples exemplify this perspective. The first is Dubois (1817). As *Hindu Manners, Customs and Ceremonies* (Dubois, 1906), translated again and edited with notes, corrections, and biography by Henry K. Beauchamp; with a prefatory note by F. Max Müller, it remains a classic. The late Sylvia Murr has shown that this work was plagiarized from the much earlier 1776–1777 work of the Jesuit Gaston-Laurent Cœurdoux entitled *Mœurs et Coutumes des Indiens*. cf. Murr (1977) and Sweetman (2003: 125–153). The second is Bartholomäus Ziegenbalg's manuscript, *Genealogie der malabarischen Götter*, sent to Copenhagen, Halle and London in 1713 which reveals an open appreciation for South Indian institutions and learning (Jeyaraj, 2005).

15. Marathas, led by Maharashtrian Brahmans (Chitpavans), perhaps recalled resistance against Mughals in the name of Ram Rajya under the banner of Shivaji (who proclaimed himself Chhatrapati of such a realm).

16. Bayly (1985) examines the role of religious difference in communal conflicts arising from shifts in political and economic power in the pre-colonial and early colonial period from 1700 to 1860.

17. For those who, all along, felt that the Hindu Mahasabha was not "orthodox" enough or who felt offended by the reformist appeals of the Arya Samaj, there was the Sanathana Dharm Sabha; or, later on, the Ram Rajiya Parishad.

18. A radical and militant, albeit selective, reaction to changes perceived as threats (from an alien, hostile, modernist, secularistic forces) which are seen as contradicting "The Truth" (of a world view) found within a literal or strict interpretations of a scriptural text. In this case, this text was imprinted in genomes and in cosmic sounds of Brahma (stemming from the *Rigveda*, as conveyed from the mouths of sages or prophets). See Andersen and Damlé (1987: 76) and Hansen (1999).

19. Hingle (1999) provides a later review of his life.

20. Alias Miss Margaret Elizabeth Noble, author of *Web of Indian Lives* (New York: 1916), an Irish nationalist and feminist, who was also one of Swami Vivekananda's noteworthy disciples.

21. From an interview with G.S. Sudarshan, General Secretary of the RSS, given to Tapan Basu et al. (1993: 16, 54).

22. This symbol, allegedly belonging to Ram and used by Shivaji in his "proto-nationalist" campaigns against Mughals, gave the movement a strongly Maratha bent.
23. Godse felt that Gandhi had insulted the Hindu Nation, weakened it by advocating *ahimsa*, and, by his fasts, had catered to Muslim fanatics (Andersen and Damlé 1987: 51; from 1969 interview with Gopal Godse by Damlé).
24. We now know from Noorani (2002) that Savarkar himself was complicit in the planning of this assassination.
25. Noorani (2002: 95–139) convincingly shows that Savarkar, who very carefully orchestrated the assassination, cleverly remained in the shadows and, as much as possible, hid tracks that might lead to him. This work is dedicated "to the victims of the Pogrom of Gujarat 2002, and to the media, print and electronic, which did India proud."

# References

Andersen, W. K. and S. D. Damlé. 1987. *The Brotherhood in Saffron: The Rashtriya Swayamsevak Sangh and Hindu Revivalism*. Boulder: Westview Press.
Barrier, N. G. 1976. *Roots of Communal Politics: The Cawnpur Riot Commission Report*. Columbia: South Asia Books.
_____. 1981. *The Census in British India: New Perspectives*. New Delhi: Manohar.
Basham, A. L. 1967. *The Wonder That Was India*. London: Sidgwick & Jackson.
Basu, T., P. Datta, S. Sarkar, et al. 1993. *Khaki Shorts and Saffron Flags*. New Delhi: Orient Longman.
Bayly, C. A. 1985. "The pre-history of 'communalism'? Religious conflict in India, 1700–186." *Modern Asian Studies* 19: 177–203.
Carson, P. 2012. *The East India Company and Religion 1698–1858*. Woodbridge: The Boydell Press.
Dubois, J-A. 1817. *Description of the Character, Manners, and Customs of the People of India; and of their Institutions, Religious and Civil*. London: Longman, Hurst, Rees, Orme, and Brown.
_____. 1906. *Hindu Manners, Customs and Ceremonies*, Oxford: Clarendon Press.
Frykenberg, R E. 1977. "The Silent Settlement in South India, 1793–1853: An Analysis of the Role of Inams in the Rise of the Indian Imperial System." In R. E. Frykenberg (ed.), *Land Tenure and Peasant in South Asia*, 37–53. New Delhi: Orient Longman.
_____. 1980. "On the Study of Conversion Movements: A Review Article and a Theoretical Note." *The Indian Economic and Social History Review* 17: 121–138.
_____. 1988. "Revivalism and Fundamentalism: Some Critical Observations with Special Reference to Politics in South Asia." In J. W. Bjorkman (ed.), *Fundamentalism, Revivalism , and Violence in South Asia*, 20–39. Riverdale: Riverdale Press.
_____. 1993. "Hindu Fundamentalism and the Structural Stability of India." In M. E. Marty and R. S. Appleby (eds), *Fundamentalisms and the State: Remaking Polities, Economies, and Militance*, 233–255. Chicago: University of Chicago Press.

Frykenberg, R E. 1994. "Fundamentalisms in South Asia: Ideologies and Institutions in Historical Perspective." In M. E. Marty and R. S. Appleby (eds), *Accounting for Fundamentalisms*, 591–617. Chicago: University of Chicago Press.

———. 2008. "Hindutva as a Political Religion: An Historical Perspective." In R. Griffin, R. Mallett and J. Tortorice (eds), *The Sacred in Twentieth Century Politics: Essays in Honour of Professor Stanley G. Payne*, 178–220. New York: Palgrave Macmillan.

Golwalkar, M. S. 1947. *We, or Our Nationhood Defined*. Nagpur: Bharat Prakashan.

Grant, C. 1812–1813. *Observations on the State of Society among the Asiatic Subjects of Great Britain,* particularly with respect to morals; and on the means of improving it. Written chiefly in the year 1792. Appendix to Report from the Select Committee on the Affairs of the East India Company with Minutes of Evidence Volume I, Parliamentary Papers, 1831– (734) VIII.

Griffin, R. 2008. "Introduction: The Evolution and Convolutions of Political Religion." In R. Griffin, R. Mallett, J. and Tortorice (eds), *The Sacred in Twentieth Century Politics: Essays in Honour of Professor Stanley G. Payne*, 1–18. New York: Palgrave Macmillan.

Hansen, T. B. 1999. *The Saffron Wave: Democracy and Hindu Nationalism in Modern India*. Princeton: Princeton University Press.

Hingle, G. S. 1999. *Hindutva Reawakened*. New Delhi: Vikas.

Irwin, R. 2006. *For Lust of Knowing: The Orientalists and Their Enemies*. London: Allen Lane.

Jeyaraj, D. 2005. *Genealogy of the South Indian Deities: An English Translation of Bartholomäus Ziegenbalgs Original German Manuscript with a Textual Analysis and Glossary*. London: RoutledgeCurzon.

Jones, K. W. 1976. *Arya Dharm: Hindu Consciousness in Nineteenth-century Punjab*. Berkeley: University of California Press.

King, C. R. 1994. *One Language, Two Scripts: The Hindi Movement in Nineteenth Century North India*. Bombay: Oxford University Press.

Leonard, J. G. 1991. *Kandukuri Viresalingam, 1848–1919: A Biography of an Indian Social Reformer*. Hyderabad: Telugu University.

Morris, H. 1904. *The Life of Charles Grant*. London: John Murray.

Murr, S. 1977. Nicolas Jacques Desvaulx (1745–1823) véritable auteur de Mœurs, institutions et cérémonies des peuples de l'Inde, de l'abbé Dubois? *Purusartha* III: 245–267.

———. 1987. *L'Inde philosophique entre Bousset et Voltaire*. Paris: École française d'Extrême Orient.

Noorani, A. G. 2002. *Savarkar and Hindutva: The Godse Connection*. New Delhi: Leftword.

Oddie, G. A. 2003. "Constructing "Hinduism": The Impact of the Protestant Missionary Movement on Hindu Self-Understanding." In R. E. Frykenberg (ed), *Christians and Missionaries in India: Cross-Cultural Communication since 1500*, 155–182. Richmond: Curzon.

———. 2006. *Imagined Hinduism: British Protestant Missionary Constructions of Hinduism, 1793–1900*. New Delhi: SAGE Publications.

Presler, F. A. 1987. *Religion Under Bureaucracy: Policy and Administration for Hindu Temples in South India*. Cambridge: Cambridge University Press.

Raghavan, V. 1957. "The Sarva Deva Vilāsa." *Adyar Library Bulletin* 21: 315–414.

———. 1958. "The Sarva Deva Vilasa: A Critical Historical Study." *Adyar Library Bulletin* 22: 45–118.

Robertson, B. C. 1995. *Raja Rammohan Ray: The Father of Modern India.* New Delhi: Oxford University Press.

Spellman, J. W. 1964. *Political Theory of Ancient India.* Oxford: Oxford University Press.

Sweetman, W. 2003. *Mapping Hinduism: "Hinduism" and the study of Indian Religions, 1600–1776.* Halle: Verlag der Franckeschen Stiftungen zu Halle.

Thapar, R. 1989. "Imagined Religious Communities? Ancient History and the Modern Search for a Hindu Identity." *Modern Asian Studies* 23: 209–231.

———. 1997. "Syndicated Hinduism." In Sontheimer G-D and Kulke H (eds), *Hinduism Reconsidered*, 2nd ed, 54–81. New Delhi: Manohar.

Ziolkowski, E. J. 1990. "Heavenly Visions and Worldly Intentions: Chicago's Columbian Exposition and World's Parliament of Religions (1893)." *Journal of American Culture* 13: 9–15.

# Chapter 6

## Media Hinduism

### Ursula Rao

Hinduism entertains a long relation with media. Religions have always used a wide range of media to communicate knowledge and stimulate experience. Religious texts, paintings, or ritual gestures and their activation in performances provide rich material for religious studies. Electronic media have opened a new chapter in this discussion. The new media are noted for their ability to increase the mobility of religious symbols, cutting across physical distances and circumventing, perforating, or reworking old social barriers (Babb, 1995: 3–4). The internet in particular motivates new forms of sociability and creates hierarchies that can be quite distinct from those in the offline world.

The following chapter explores the scholarly discourse of the religious and social reorientation of Hinduism in India and overseas that is linked to the rapid spread of electronic media. The general trend of the debate reinforces the notion that globalization promotes a paradoxical process of simultaneous homogenization and diversification, of new connectivity and fragmentation. The unifying force of a powerful and intolerant Hindu nationalist movement parallels the developing of new virtual communities of believers. On the other hand, we encounter religious cyber-wars, the individualization of religious experience in online rituals and the fragmentation of social spaces through religious specialization and quickly changing religious fashions. In the following chapter, political and devotional Hinduism are discussed separately, following a typical divide in the available literature. The chapter begins by examining the role of Hindu electronic media for the reworking of the political culture and public sphere in and beyond India since the 1990s. The second section investigates electronically mediated religious experiences, as well as the practices, traditions, and conflicts that shape these experiences and their interpretation. I will demonstrate how a traditionally generous acceptance of new technologies for religious communication in Hinduism is extended to electronic media. The omnipresence of religion in the new media has amplified opportunities for religious innovation and contributed to the re-circulation of Hindu image also outside traditional settings. It has produced new consumption practices and contentious negotiations about validity and meaning of religious experience and devotional activities.

## Moving Gods and the Nation State

1987 produced a sensation that awakened public interest in emerging forms of media Hinduism with a jolt. The year marked the first screening of the popular Hindu epic Ramayana as religious soap (also, *dharmic* serial) on Indian state television. Its extraordinary success took observers by surprise. The nation regularly came to a standstill on Sunday mornings, when people rushed to the next television set to follow the serial that was celebrated as a ritual event. The airing of the Ramayana and later the Mahabharata was, of course, not the first successful attempt at mass circulation of religious content through visual media. The making of religious soaps was only the latest chapter in a historical development of approximately 200 years that had seen the production of religious calendar art (Inglis, 1995; Lutgendorf, Smith, 1995; Beckerlegge, 2001a; Pinney, 2004), devotional comics (Pritchett, 1995; Hawley, 1996), and mythological films (Derne, 1995 in Babb; Das, 1980; Beckerlegge, 2001a). In the new millennium, we also witnessed the proliferation of DVDs with cartoon-animated versions of Indian mythologies (Maitra, 2008) and computer games that feature Hindu deities and demons.[1] The huge mass appeal of the weekly broadcast of the Ramayana in the 1980s sets this enterprise apart. There was an outcry by public intellectuals who feared that the television epic would reduce a rich performative tradition to a sleek consumer product (Thapar, 1989; Dalmia-Lüderitz, 1991). Others countered that the television version did not replace other narrative forms but enriched a plural religious universe (Lutgendorf, 1994). Both types of arguments were well rehearsed by the time electronic media entered the religious market. The worry about and the desire for a unified, standardized, and sanitized Hinduism was a key issue in all phases of the encounter between Hinduism and its Western "Other," Christianity. This time the debate was driven not so much by the anxieties over a changing religious practice but worries about the consequences the serialization of the popular epic would have for the secular texture and plural nature of Indian democracy.

The broadcasting of religious serials on state television foreboded an end to the Nehruvian area of secularism. Doordarshan[2] now officially presented Hindu epics as tales that speak for the nation, provide essential moral education, and ground collective identity (Lutgendorf, 1990; Lipner, 2001: 331–33; Rajagopal, 2001). The popularity of the serial did indeed locate the narration in the heart of the nation. But which narration? Visual codes, language, costumes, and chorography promoted a particular north Indian brahmanical interpretation of a widely consumed tale. The weekly ritual of viewing naturalized this version, establishing it in the center of a new religio-political aesthetic that provided the visual codes for the surging Hindu nationalist movement (Mitra, 1994).

Politics after television is fundamentally transformed, argues Rajagopal (2001) in his much cited interpretation of epic viewing. The serial was aired at a time when disillusionment with the Congress peeked. Slow development, massive social cleavage, political infighting, favoritism, corruption as well as Indira Gandhi's authoritarian rule, had thoroughly discredited the children of the freedom fighters. Hindutva[3] forces jumped into the void and promised a radical political renewal. They seized the historical opportunity to reverse their image from that of a communal alliance (charged with inciting religious violence and discredited by the murder of Mahatma Gandhi) to that of the forbearer of a new regime, that would be morally sound and distinctively Indian (read: Hindu). Hindu nationalist forces cultivated the fantasy of ancient India as an ideal golden age, governed by divine laws and blessed by the gods. The retrograde utopia was nurtured by the television serial about the adventures of a selfless god-king, his relatives, and adherence. The visual presentation in a sentimental soap made their world utterly attractive and let "sacrificial relationships, via personable Hindu icons, seem painless and even desirable" (Rajagopal, 2001: 138). The propaganda of the Hindu party, Bharatiya Janata Party (BJP) suggested that an army of devout servants of Lord Ram stood ready to bring about this ideal reign once their leaders were elected to the parliament. However, the tale of a new area, Mankekar (1999: 165) alerts us, was not the promise of a benign regime. The public images affirmed that the nation demanded sacrifices and barely concealed that the new order would be "predicated on violence, repression, and exclusions" (Mankekar, 1999: 165).

Both in its utopian and dystopian aspect the political mobilization of the Hindu Right was intricately linked to emerging forms of media Hinduism, also beyond the screening of the Ramayana and Mahabharata and outside the channels of state broadcasting (Rao, 2011). The Ayodhya movement[4] in particular forged a new symbolic language that reconfigured religious iconography to serve political propaganda. The staring example is an altered depiction of the God Ram. The popular calendar image of a benevolent and docile family father was turned into an angry, virile hero on the posters of the Ayodhya campaign (Kapur, 1993; Bhatt and Mukta, 2000). The new images were circulated in print and electronic form. Media mobilization through mobile video stations, Brosius (2002, 2005) demonstrates, complemented the technique of mass recruitment through grassroots organizations. In a circular movement, the electronic images were re-introduced into performative space. Actors of religious characters reincarnated as political leaders (Mitra, 1994) and politicians dressed as deities. The latter is exemplified dramatically by the chariot procession (*rath yatra*) of the powerful BJP leader Lal Krishna Advani (Davis, 1996). Moving in a Ram-like chariot, he deliberately blurred the borders between human and divine identity, mobilizing for political ends the Hindu notion of a porous human body that is open for divine manifestation. The political project borrowed the aura from divine heroes through extensive use of established religious visual codes and wooed the viewer-devotee as a voter (Farmer, 1996; Guneratne, 1998).

Electronic media produce new religio-political identities through which the always fluid boundary between religion and politics in India is renegotiated. While this happens on a new scale drawing ever more people into the project of national imagination it also re-produces some of the salient features of the religio-political mobilization of the independence struggle, when collective action in the public sphere conjured up a national imaginary with strong religious overtones (Freitag, 1989; Pandey, 1990). Yet, media Hinduism and a reinvigorated Hindu nationalism instituted a dramatic departure into a new temporality and an altered spatial arrangement. The mobilization of Hindu heroes no longer belongs to the anti-structure of ritual events (*katha*), festivals (Ramleela, Diwali), or even protests. It had become a mundane act of consumption firmly anchored in weekly routines. The new religio-political symbols and ideologies are present not only in public areas but in the intimate private sphere that partakes in a new media public (Rao, 2011).

There is another crucial change. Hindu fundamentalism has gone global. Worldwide anxious viewers consume news about the anti-Muslim, anti-Christian, or anti-secular actions of aggressive Hindus. More significant is the growing involvement of professional middle class Hindus living in the West in long-distance nationalism (Glick-Schiller, 2004). Political analysts (Mathew, 2000; Robinson, 2001; Kurien, 2005) have demonstrated how the search for cultural roots and identity can turn into a process of political affirmation. The internet provides seekers not just with portals for religious experiences but also with political propaganda and a well-packaged "truth" about Hindu fundamentals. Hinduism is presented as an integral and at the same time superior component of the multi-cultural landscapes of Western democracies. Migrants appropriate the orientalist notion of Hindus as embodying loft eastern spirituality, rendering Hindus simultaneously different from and ahead of all other ethnicities and nationalisms. The anonymity of the internet also provides space for the expression of such counter-racism as religious hatred (Mathew and Prashad, 2000; Robinson, 2001). It turns into an aggressive long-distance nationalism where it insists on the implementation of a dogmatic Brahmanical nationalism in India. Via membership in fundamentalist organizations and donations for "religious" and "educational" projects, migrants bolster Hindu Nationalists and support their project from a place comfortably removed from the suffering aggressive nationalism inflicts on the Indian public sphere (Hansen, 2001).

The substantial scholarship on media and Hindu politics convincingly demonstrates the close link between virtual deities, cyber-Hinduism and the ascent of Hindu nationalists to power in the 1990s. The conversion between mediated publics and politics in the 1990s has undoubtedly rung in a new area in Indian democracy. However, its character is far from decided. Years in and out of power (in the center and several North Indian states) has firmly established the Hindu nationalist party BJP in the Indian democratic system. Yet, the image of a heroic savior has crumbled under political pragmatism, ideological disputes, corruption, and inefficiency. Today no single religious soap or Hindu mass medium attracts the attention secured by the television screening of the Ramayana and the Mahabharata. The novelty has worn off and the authorial voice of Doordarshan has given way to a new plurality. What then remains today of the devotional energy and the nostalgic impetus that underwrote the political tremor of the 1990s? How do media and politics intersect at a time of rapid circulation of a profusion of new religious media products? Or, how has the prosperity of the new middle class and the celebration of neoliberal ideologies changed the parameters of this relation? While the study of Indian media enjoys unprecedented popularity, the topic of religion remains marginal and it might yet take time before we can read a political analysis of religious media during a period of disenchantment with Hindu real politics (Rao, 2011).

Overall, scholarship of political media Hinduism has tended to privilege the agency of propaganda over the analysis of complex reception processes. The discussion of religious conflict in India has only recently begun to theorize the complex links between a range of desires, traditions and connections that inform radical Hindu action (Rao, 2003b). Hansen (2001) and Eckert (2003) in particular analyze the interconnection of low caste assertion, class conflict, and performative politics for the success of aggressive Hinduism. Questions regarding the role of the media in this nexus remain largely unanswered. What motivates believers to join the ranks of Hindu fundamentalism? What are the links between devotion, religio-cultural traditions, and politics? Some evidence allows us to glean the complexity of the question at hand. Mankekar's survey of television reception makes plain that devotional viewing does not necessarily translate into approval of or interest in aggressive Hinduism (Mankekar, 1999: 180–184). Similarly, we know that cyber-Hinduism has many faces. Not all websites are saturated with Hindu nationalist propaganda and not every internet user searches for dogmatic certainties (Krien, 2005). More than being a political platform the internet also offers access to religious texts, portals for devotional activities, and also chat rooms for the discussion of specialized religious interests (Helland, 2007). It is time to move on from the discussion of the interrelations between religion, community, and politics, to trace some of the devotional practices infused by media and informing their production and circulation.

# Virtual Deities

The discussion of Hindu practice mediated by advanced technology is still in its infancy, empirically as well as theoretically. Once again, good starting points are the legendary television epics, which made public the devotional attitude believers bring to religious films in India. News reports informed that women in particular underwent ritual cleansing before watching the Ramayana. Devotees paid actor-deities respect by burning incense before the television or presenting food to the virtual deities (later redistributed as *prasad* [divine leaving], see Lutgendorf, 1990, 1994: 411–412; Mankekar, 1999; Rajagopal, 2001: 93–94; Beckerlegge, 2001a: 92). Performative elements of the television production support such "devotional viewing," through the use of popular iconographic codes, the playing of devotional music (*bhajans*) as soundtrack or the intersecting of photos from well-known temples and sacred sites (Mankekar, 1999: 187–204). The pious act of viewing is a form of *puja*, comparable to daily acts of devotion offered before images or at house shrines and temples (Fuller, 1992).

Like statues or photographs, actor-deities are treated as media that invite divine presence and allow humans to communicate with deities and receive their blessings through acts of superior seeing (*darshan*). Diana Eck aptly described *darshan* as an exchange. The devotional posture of the worshipper attracts the auspicious gaze of the deity, who showers on him the benevolence of his divine substance (Eck, 1981, see also Babb, 1981). In a strictly brahmanical sense, such viewing depends on the sacralization of the medium. A ritual act of installation turns a material object into an abode of a deity. However quotidian religiosity is not constrained by the theological deliberations of high caste priests and ancient scriptures. Hindus revere the divine in a wide range of forms, from stones, to statues and posters (Fuller, 1992; Rao, 2003).

The academic interest in media *darshan* goes back to the 1970s when a Bollywood blockbuster about the goddess Santoshi Ma (Goddess of Satisfaction) surprised observers (Derne, 1995). Within a short period the celluloid incarnation of a marginal regional goddess shot to national prominence. A large number of women began to observe her fast. Devotees undertook pilgrimages in her name and built dedicated temples. Das (1980) ascribes this success to the apt story line that hit a nerve by reflecting typical insecurities of lower middle class life in that period. The frustration of daily struggles in a nation with a stagnant economy was reflected in the diffuse and prolonged suffering of the heroine Satyavati, who is tested in her devotion for the goddess Santoshi Ma. A torment that lacks contours and a clear point of origin could not be eliminated by one grant battle of a powerful feminine force like Durga or Kali that in a brave stroke kills the source of evil. It needed a benevolent, patient, and dependable goddess who attends to innumerable daily ups and downs. Lutgendorf (2002) adds that the film echoed not only anxieties but also aspirations. The audiences' evaluation of their life was nurtured by longing for upward mobility. Like the goddess, lower middle class women desired membership in the inner circle of power, and like the heroine they struggled for a life less constrained by male authority. However, the film was more than a moral tale. It offered a solution to these common predicaments by prescribing a simple and inexpensive weekly fast, which viewers accepted as religious instruction to be taken literally.

While Das and Lutgendorf demonstrate how updating an ancient myth allows for popular recirculation, the medium remains unreflected in their analysis. There is the obvious issue of mass circulation and its effect. More vexing are questions about the spiritual quality of the medium. What are the deliberations that make new technologies acceptable for religious use, frame rules for auspicious usage, and guide the interpretation of the encounter (Campbell, 2005)? These questions have gained significance in recent years that saw the rapid proliferation of virtual deities and their spread across a wide terrain of electronic platforms. Consider the following evidence.

A growing number of temples in India acquire television sets. The transmission of images from the inner sanctum (Rao, 2003; Scheifinger, 2009: 281) or devotional films (Guneratne, 1998) increases the attractiveness of a religious site and helps control crowds, transforming an impatient mass into an attentive audience. Guneratne (1998: 264–265) reports that some youths in the famous Tirupati Temple (Andhra Pradesh) were so absorbed watching a religious soap that they stayed put even when called to enter the sanctum. There is a growing trend to record ritual procedures on video for local programming, home use, or community distribution (Beckerlegge, 2001b; Helland, 2007). Most recently, there is a proliferation of websites that offer online *puja* or ordering facilities for *puja* in Indian temples. Helland (2007: 11) reports about a website (www.westbengnal.com/puja/puya98) that exhorts exiled Bengalis to wallow in the joy of Durga Puja through visual consumption of the hectic festival activities in Calcutta. It will bring home closer to migrants, *Hinduism Today* claims (April 1999; cf. Helland, 2007: 11).

These virtual deities have provoked religious innovation. Take for example Gillespie's (1993: 53) comment about the reversal of attitudes toward the Mahabharata. Many Hindus consider the private consumption of the epic war as inauspicious and abstain from reading the verses about the battle that rips a family apart in their own homes. The same taboo has not been applied to the serial, which people comfortably view in their living rooms, thus integrating a formerly distant founding myth into the flow of everyday life. Scheifinger (2009) speaks about the ease with which the East Indian God Jagannath became available for global consumption. His temple in Bhubaneswar (Orissa) is jealously guarded against non-ethnic Hindus to prevent pollution and its potentially dire consequences. However, there is no ban on online *darshan* of the now easily available electronic image. These examples demonstrate that technical innovation promotes cultural change. The emerging debate about the role of electronic media for religious communication touches on three related perspectives: (1) the quality of the religious experience, (2) its position in changing community life, and (3) the impact of technology on authority structures.

The latter point is rather straightforward and little surprising. The harvest of new technologies catapults a novel class of technically savvy people into powerful positions, thus impacting social stratification. Scheifinger's (2010) description of ordering facilities for online *puja* beautifully illustrates the point. His case study is located in the famous Kalighat Temple in Calcutta, where tensions between priests and temple administration have a long history. In 1949, the priests lost a court case against the temple administration, and were stripped of the right to manage the temple, which they perceived as their hereditary duty. No longer able to access the huge temple income, priests incurred massive financial losses. Suddenly, their earning was confined to per-sonal donations and fees for commissioned rituals. The tables turned when enterprising members of the priestly families began operating websites. Overseas Indians became keen users of the online ordering facilities, connecting to their roots by leaving a material residue in their sacred homeland without having to undertake the expensive and arduous travel. The priests counter-balanced their structural disadvantage by successfully manipulating the internet. The new media breeds a new market place for religious competition, which sets in motion a recalibration of social relations pertaining to caste, class or gender in the offline world also.

The question of validity and efficacy of the new technology is socially contested and theoretically significantly more challenging. Scheifinger answers the question of efficacy with a broad stroke: "[F]or some of the authorities online *darshan* is identical to *darshan* at a physical site; for others there is a qualitative difference between the two practices—with the view being that the efficacy of online *darshan* is less" (Scheifinger, 2010). This seemingly redundant statement provides a mirror to the inherent logic of an excessively plural and fluid religious universe in which the significance, relevance, importance and validity of rituals is entangled with question of power and social belonging (Sontheimer and Kulke, 1989; Rao, 2003). The question of what is valid and for whom is never quite resolved and a perpetual reason for argument. Electronic gadgets and the internet provide new provocations that fuel contentious conversations about religious conduct, sacred objects, and ritual efficacy.

Karapanagiotis's (2010) study is a case in point. Vaishnava devotees in New Jersey treat virtual religious artifacts as sacred objects, yet consider their location (within the computer) as highly problematic. As a working tool and gadget for entertainment the computer offers lots of distractions. The simultaneous consumption of religious and non-religious content might pollute the sacred object or break religious concentration. These concerns can be addressed through "cleansing activities," such as shutting down of all secular, distracting or offensive windows or shifting the computer into a religious corner of the house. Such purposeful activities of narrowing down the functions of the multipurpose instrument are specifically adapted activities of framing that create the preconditions for a ritual to take place and announce its commencement (Rao and Köpping, 2000). It becomes apparent that the lack of universal Hindu doxa must not be mistaken for arbitrariness. Cultural context and religious enculturation provide crucial guidelines for distinguishing between sacred and profane, effective and non-effective, authentic and fake.

Karapanagiotis provides one example of many, demonstrating that devotees take for granted the portability of *darshan* from one medium to the other (Herman, 2010: 152). Thus judgments of efficacy tend to be unconcerned with the materiality of the medium, and focus on the attitude of the devotee and aptness of the situation. "Is the goddess present in a picture," I asked the president of the Kali Temple in Bhopal during research on urban Hinduism. His reply reveals the typical laissez-faire attitude of Hindus. Non-believers are like illiterate people who throw away a text because it does not confer any meaning to them. A believer, however, reads the signs of the divine and finds the presence of the goddess (Rao, 2003). Gillespie (1993) studied such devotional literacy among a Hindu family in London. Together with the Dhanis, Gillespie viewed two different versions of the Mahabharata. They started with the theatrical interpretation of the British film and theater director Peter Brooks, who used the Indian epic to create his own art piece, staged by an intercultural ensemble. His interpretation left the Dhanis bewildered and upset. Lacking the familiar cues, the story was rendered incomprehensible. For the Dhanis, it conveyed no deeper truth and showed an utter disrespect for their gods and ancient heroes. In contrast, the Indian television screening of the story evoked appreciation, pleasure, and devotion. The use of a popular iconographic lingua rendered the film readable within the parameters of an established religious discourse and thus communicated the vibrant subjectivity of the deities.

Dismissed as kitsch by art critics, the serial charms devotional viewers, who do not search for novelty or artistic refinement. Their esthetic judgment follows a "religious taste." The use of familiar visual images from calendar art and well-known ritual gestures motivates identification and moves the event into a spiritual realm ripe for divine communication. However, the film does not merely reproduce what is already known. The reiteration in serial format expands the parameters of a religious lingua. Repackaged as soap opera, the religious myth is turned into a melodramatic tale that emphasizes emotions and promotes personal identification with the characters. Ludendorf (1994 in Babb) argues that the new products advance a shift from the primacy of hearing of divine adventures through sacred words to viewing them.

The "realistic" films allow viewers to consume the actions of their gods, participate in their experiences, and identify with their predicaments (Rajagopal, 2001). This "participation" is shaped through the lens of a soapy production that lingers in "pure" emotions, thus creating the stereotypical deities as hyper-human. Baudrillard (1994) uses the prefix hyper to refer to a state of refinement, when an experience, quality, or product is cast into an ideal form that presents itself as uncontaminated by contradictions and complexities. I do not claim that Hindu media consumers live in Baudrillard's hyper-reality. I use his reference to draw attention to a process of translation that turns a philosophical ideal into a perfect life world doused in realism. The remodeling of theology as historical truth or idealized reality, inspires the longing for a pure space uncontaminated by the noise and mess of everyday life.

The disembodiment of the deities is followed by a progressive disembodiment of the devotee. The worshipper's *avatar* embarks on instantaneous pilgrimages in virtual landscapes and conducts online *puja* in cyber temples (Jacobs, 2007; Helland, 2007; Scheifinger, 2012). Literature on internet Hinduism is still sparse. The few available studies focus on topics typically found across the spectrum of research on digital religion. These are questions of ritual efficacy and religious authenticity, the changing character of communities and social hierarchies, and emerging new religious identities (Campbell, 2012). The proliferation of virtual religion advances also in Hinduism specialization, individualization, and pluralization. Above I have discussed concerns over the purity of internet rituals. Here I will add finding about new religious alliances through internet connectivity.

Herman (2010) argues that by rendering images mobile the internet not only uproots them from specific sites, but through circulation re-embeds them in new locations thus expanding the sphere of influence of religious networks. Examples are web-related activities of the Shree Swaminarayan Mandal in Downey, California. The temple committee maintains a popular website that transmits images and sounds of congregational activities through live streams. These arouse in viewers emotions of devotion and create a sense of presence without bodily immersion. Critics (Brasher, 2004; Jacobs, 2007) point out that such online activities lack the full sensual experience of temple rituals. This, Scheifinger (2012) counters, does not necessarily compromise the ritual experience, especially when it focuses on the inner stance as a central aspect of personal transformation.

In the new computer age, we can conclude with Herman (2010), that participation and emotional co-presence does not require going to the temple. The temple may simply come to the devotee, as it happens when the phone company AirTel sends live streams of *aarti* rituals (light rituals in temples) to the mobile phones of Indian customers (*Hitvana*, March 7, 2013). Distributed through Listserv, Swaminarayan's e-*darshan* reaches the mailboxes of followers punctually every Monday morning. Here the webmaster acts as nodal officer who establishes, maintains, and manages a community of believers and their exposure to ritual activities. Whether we can justifiably speak about such virtual co-presence as constitutive of a religious community is open for debate. For now it seems that the spectrum for possible participation from distant spectator to involved devotee is getting stretched. We also observe a growing specialization as a twin process accompanying increased connectivity.

The Hindu diaspora, Naryana (2006) asserts, has surpassed an early phase in which the distance to the homeland generated new generic forms of Hinduism. Today, migrants use technology to maintain contact with caste fractions, language groups, devotional sects, or other niche communities. Specialization is also a trend in chat rooms. Robinson (2004) evidences that religious internet forums concurrently split when conflicts between ideological fractions erupt. In these compartmentalized landscapes, devotion itself is transitory as Warrier (2003) points out. People with mobile lives regularly harvest the internet for changing spiritual needs. The study of sectarian groups, she suggests, needs to move from a focus on *guru–chela* (spiritual teacher–devotee) relation to discussing this relation within the context of life-trajectories marked by shifting devotional alliances.

## Conclusion

It is still early days and while evidence of change is plentiful, there is no bold attempt at theorizing the new condition, yet. However, there are recurring topics that challenge theoretical assumptions. Notably for Hinduism is the fact, that not much has changed. The discussion of electronically mediated Hinduism seems far removed from the concerns of early debate about new media and Christianity, which considered mainly developments in Western nations. Set against the theory that Western modernity and technological progress will continuously advance secularization; the beginning of the media age constitutes a great rupture. Late capitalism saw the re-enchantment of the media sphere and the proliferation of religious activities, both within and outside traditional religion. In India, public life has always been saturated with religious activities and the boundaries between politics and religion were never drawn with the same clarity as in Europe. Thus my first thesis is that electronic media produces more of the same. Seamlessly intergraded into a dazzling religious market, they create new platforms for religious competition, new conduits for divine communication, and new arenas for imagining and mobilizing the political community.

Yet, media Hinduism is more than old wine in new bottles. I concur with McLuhan (1964) that media have significant structuring effects. Scholars noted that technological innovation in religious narration has sentimentalized the relationship between humans and the divine. The new hyper-realism feeds a nostalgic longing for a utopian paradise. The viewers of Hindu soaps find themselves removed from this ideal world, constituting a mere audience that looks on from its position in the *kalyug* to gaze at an ideal transcendental space. This is a significant innovation in a religious universe that treats the human world as porous and expects divine presence in the here and now (Lipner, 2001). Media religion's capability to turn religious participants into spectators marks a new position that has become part of quotidian religiosity in sacred spaces that entertain with films, audio-animatronics, sound, and light shows. The transformation of amorphous village gods to anthropomorphic statues, and the mass circulation of the new religious esthetic of calendar art are historical moments that have significantly altered the religious imaginary. We now witness a novel innovation. The simulacrum has become an intimate part of the religious landscape.

The images of simulated Hinduism are highly volatile. They move rapidly between India and the diaspora, in and out of pop culture, fashion worlds, ideological communities, and devotional sub-cultures. Their consumption is not contained within an Indian cultural or ethnic space, or devotional and religious settings. Studies demonstrate that they perpetually re-perforate the ideal border between religion and politics. They also recalibrate the relation between religion and entertainment. My study of Hindu temples taught me that religion is thoroughly entertaining. Women eagerly awaited the morning routine of devotional singing that permits them to escape for a short while the constraining world of domestic duties. Kids nag their parents to take them on holidays to distant sacred sites and adolescents meet in the temple to engage in the titillating games of flirting.

In the world of virtual communication, devotional experience is reworked. It is no longer bound to specific sites or negotiated within ethnically structured social settings. Mobile religious symbols and virtual religious spaces can be activated anywhere and anytime. Hence, the potential for religious innovation is amplified.

## Notes

1. For example, http://www.computerandvideogames.com/article.php?id=213298 (accessed on February 4, 2010).
2. Doordarshan is the name of the state-run television channel. Literally it means seeing far. Doordarshan had a monopoly in Indian broadcasting before economic liberalization (1991) after which rules were gradually relaxed leading to a growing diversification of the Indian television landscape.
3. Hindutva is an umbrella term that refers to all those individuals and organizations that promote a Hindu nation. In the following text, I use it synonymously with Hindu Right, Hindu Nationalism, and Hindu Fundamentalism.
4. The conflict was triggered and kept alive by Hindu radicals fighting for the construction of a temple to Ram at the mythical birthplace of the god-king in Ayodhya. This is a highly controversial issue since the site belongs to the Muslim community and used to host a mosque, which was destroyed illegally by Hindu radicals. Despite archeological evidence to the contrary, Hindu fundamentalists maintain that a temple to Ram existed on the disputed site before it was destroyed by the Muslim invader Babar, who is said to have built the mosque.

## References

Babb, L. A. 1981. "Glancing: Visual interaction in Hinduism." *Journal of Anthropological Research* 37: 387–401.
Babb, L. A. and S. S. Wadley (eds). 1995. *Media and the Transformation of Religion in South Asia*. Philadelphia: University of Pennsylvania Press.

Baudrillard, J. 1994. *Simulacra and Simulation*. Michigan: The University of Michigan Press.

Beckerlegge, G. 2001a. "Hindu Sacred Images for the Mass Market." In G. Beckerlegge (ed.), *Religion Today. Tradition, Modernity and* Change, 57–116. Aldershot: Ashgate.

———. 2001b. "Computer-mediated Religion. Religion on the Internet at the Turn of the Twenty-first Century." In G. Beckerlegge (ed.), *Religion Today. Tradition, Modernity and* Change, 219–264. Aldershot: Ashgate.

Brasher, B. 2004. *Give Me that Online Religion*. New Brunswick, NJ: Rutgers University Press.

Brosius, C. 2002. "Hindutva Intervisuality. Videos and the Politics of Representation." *Contributions to Indian Sociology* 36(1 & 2): 265–295.

———. 2005. *Empowering Visions. An Ethnography of Hindutva Nationalism and New Media Technologies (1989–1993)*. London: Anthem.

Campbell, H. 2005. "Spiritualising the Internet." *Heidelberg Journal of Religions on the Internet* 1(1): 1–26

Campbell, H. A. (ed.). 2012. *Digital Religion: Understanding Religious Practice in New Media Worlds*. Hobocken: Taylor and Francis.

Dalmia-Lüderitz, V. 1991. "Television and Tradition. Some Observations on the Serialization of the Ramayana." In M. Thiel-Horstmann (ed.), *Ramayana and* Ramayanas, 207–228. Wiesbaden: Harrassowitz.

Das, V. 1980. "The Mythological Film and its Framework of Meaning: An analysis of Jai Santoshi Ma." *India International Centre Quarterly* 8(1): 43–56.

Davis, R. H. 1996. "The Iconography of Rama's Chariot." In D. Ludden (ed.), *Making India Hindu*, 27–54. New Delhi: Oxford University Press.

Derne, S. 1995. "Market Forces at Work. Religious Themes in Commercial Hindi Films." In L. A. Babb and S. S. Wadley (eds), *Media and the Transformation of Religion in South Asia*, 191–216. Philadelphia: University of Pennsylvania Press.

Eck, D. L. 1981. *Darshan. Seeing the Divine Image in India*. Chambersbury: Anima.

Eckert, J. 2003. *The Charisma of Direct Action. Power, Politics, and the Shiv Sena*. New Delhi: Oxford University Press.

Freitag, S. B. 1989. *Collective Action and Community. Public Areas and the Emergence of Communalism in North India*. Berkeley: University of California Press.

Fuller, C. J. 1992. *The Camphor Flame. Popular Hinduism and Society in India*. New Delhi: Penguin Books.

Gillespie, M. 1993. "The Mahabharata. From Sanskrit to Sacred Soap. A Case Study of the Reception of two Contemporary Television Versions." In D. Buckingham (ed.), *Reading Audiences*. Manchester: Manchester University Press.

Glick-Schiller, N. 2004. "Long-Distance Nationalism." In C. R. E. Melvin Ember and Ian Skoggard (eds), *Immigrant and refugee Cultures Around the World*, 570–580. New York: Kluwer Academic/Plenum Publishers.

Guneratne, A. R. 1998. "Mediating the Rise of Neo-Nationalism in India. Television, Cinema and Carnival." *Social Identities* 4(2): 263–281.

Hansen, T. B. 2001. *Urban Violence in India. Identity Politics, "Mumbai," and the Postcolonial City*. New Delhi: Permanent Black.

Hawley, J. S. and D. Wulff (eds). 1996. *Devi: The Goddess in India*. Berkeley: University of California Press.

Herman, P. 2010. "Seeing the Divine Through Windows. Online Darshan and Virutal Religious Experience." *Online—Heidelberg Journal of Religions on the Internet* 4(1): 151–177.

Helland, C. 2007. "Diaspora on the Electronic Frontier. Developing Virtual Connections with Sacred Homelands." *Journal of Computer-Mediated Communication* 12(3): 956–976.

Inglis, S. R. 1995. "Suitable for Framing. The Work of a Modern Master." In L. A. Babb and S. S. Wadley (eds), *Media and the Transformation of Religion in South Asia*. Philadelphia: University of Pennsylvania Press.

Jacobs, S. 2007. "Virtually Sacred. The Performance of Asynchronous Cyber-Rituals in Onone Spaces." *Journal of Computer-Mediated Communication* 12(3): 1103–1121.

Kapur, A. 1993. "Deity to Crusader: the Changing Iconography of Ram." In G. Pandey (ed.), *Hindus and Others*, 74–109. Delhi: Viking.

Karapanagiotis, N. 2010. "Vaishnava Cyber-Puja. Problems of Purity and Novel Ritual Solutions." *Online—Heidelberg Journal of Religions on the Internet* 4(1): 179–195.

Kurien, P. A. 2005. "Being Young, Brown, and Hindu. The Identity Struggles of Second' Generation Indian Americans." *Journal of Contemporary Ethnography* 34(4): 434–469.

Lipner, J. 2001. "A remaking of Hinduism? or Taking the Mickey Out of Valmiki." In H. D. Vries and S. Weber (eds), *Religion and Media*, 320–338. Stanford: Stanford University Press.

Lutgendorf, P. 1990. "Ramayan. The Video." *Drama Review* 34(2): 127–176.

———. 1994. *The Life of a Text. Performing the Ramcaritmanas of Tulsidas*. New Delhi: Oxford University Press.

———. 1995. "All in the (Raghu) Family. A Video Epic in Cultural Context." In R. C. Allen (ed.), *To Be Continued ... Soap Operas around the World*. London: Routledge.

———. 2002. "Evolving a Monkey. Hanuman, Poster Art and Postcolonial Anxiety." *Contributions to Indian Sociology* 36(1 & 2): 71–112.

Mankekar, P. 1999. *Screening Culture, Viewing Politics. Television, Womanhood and Nation in Modern India*. New Delhi: Oxford University Press.

Maitra, L. 2008. "Children's Oral Literature and Modern Mass Media in India with Special Reference to Gradual Transformation in West Bengal." *Indian Folklore Research Journal* 5(8): 55–64.

Mathew, B. 2000. "Byte-sized nationalism. Mapping the Hindu right in the United States." *Rethinking Marxism* 12(3): 108–128.

Mathew, B. and V. Prashad. 2000. "The Protean Forms of Yankee Hindutva." *Ethnic and Racial Studies* 23(3): 516–534.

McLuhan, M. 1964. *Understanding Media. The Extensions of Man*. New York: McGraw-Hill.

Mitra, A. 1994. "An Indian Religious Soap Opera and the Hindu Image." *Media, Culture & Society* 16: 149–155.

Pandey, G. 1990. *The Construction of Communalism in Colonial North India*. Mumbai: Oxford University Press.

140    Ursula Rao

Pinney, C. 2004. *Photos of the Gods: The Printed Image and Political Struggle in India.* New Delhi: Oxford University Press.

Pritchett, F. W. 1995. "The World of Amar Chitr Katha." In L. A. Babb and S. S. Wadley (eds), *Media and the Transformation of Religion in South Asia,* 76–106. Philadelphia: University of Philadelphia Press.

Rajagopal, A. 2001. *Politics after Television: Hindu Nationalism and the Changing of Indian Public.* Cambridge: Cambridge University Press.

Rao, U. and K.-P. Köpping. 2000. "Die Performative Wende. Leben—Ritual—Theater." In K.-P. Köpping and U.Rao (eds), *Rausch des Rituals,* 1–31. Münster: Lit.

Rao, U. 2003a. *Negotiating the Divine: Temple Religion and Temple Politics in Contemporary Urban India.* New Delhi: Manohar.

———. 2003b. *Kommunalismus in Indien. Eine Darstellung der wissenschaftlichen Diskussion über Hindu-Muslim-Konflikte.* Halle: Universität Halle.

———. 2011. "'Inter-publics' Hindu Mobilization beyond the Bourgeois Public Sphere." *Religion and Society* 2(1): 90–105.

Robinson, R. 2001. "Religion on the Net. An Analysis of the Global Research of Hindu Fundamentalism and Its Implications for India." *Sociological Bulletin* 50(2): 236–251.

———. 2004. "Virtual Warfare: The Internet as the New Site for Global Religious Conflict." *Asian Journal of Social Science* 32(2): 198–215.

Scheifinger, H. 2009. "The Jagannath Temple and Online Darshan." *Journal of Contemporary Religion* 24(3): 277–290.

———. 2010. "On-line Hinduism. World Wide Gods on the Web." *Australian Religious Studies Review* 23(3): 325–345.

———. 2012. "Hindu Worship Online and Offline." In H. Campbell (ed.), *Digital Religion,* 121–127. Hobocken: Taylor and Francis.

Smith, D. H. 1995. "Impact of 'God Posters' on Hindus and Their Devotional Traditions." In L. A. Babb and S. S. Wadely (eds), *Media and the Transformation of Religion in South Asia.* Philadelphia: University of Pennsylvania Press.

Sontheimer, G. D. and H. Kulke (eds). 1989. *Hinduism Reconsidered.* New Delhi: Manohar.

Thapar, R. 1989. "The Ramayana Syndrome." *Seminar* 353: 71–75.

# Chapter 7

## Modern Hindu Guru Movements

Michael James Spurr

## Introduction

Gurus have played a major role in Hindu religious life since Vedic times, but the modern era has more than its share of prominent examples of what some scholars have termed "great gurus—the *mahāgurus*" (Gold, 2005: 220). Facilitated by rapid transport, telecommunications and the ever-broadening Indian diaspora, these figures have garnered India-wide and even pan-global followings. Often, they are also controversial figures; to their critics, they are megalomaniacs, hypocrites, charlatans, and even felons. But this is at least partly in the nature of the role. The dichotomy of enthusiasm and scorn in accounts of gurus dates back to at least seventh century India (Smith, 2003: 168), and even modern scholars, while not usually extreme in their views, tend to have been divided between these two camps. Attraction and aversion are both powerful motivating factors, and in my own case at least, had I not been a follower of contemporary South Indian guru Sathya Sai Baba, I would have struggled to find the motivation necessary to complete my recent doctoral thesis on him.

Smith (2003: 168) laments that there is "no extensive academic survey of gurus," suggesting that scholars sympathetic to the notion of the guru tend to be drawn to one particular guru, producing studies focused on that guru to the exclusion of the wider phenomenon, and that unsympathetic scholars have a natural tendency to avoid the phenomenon altogether. Smith himself produces a good, if brief overview, referencing most of the previous scholarship, but in general his observation seems to hold true. Certainly even the years since

2003 have seen the production of several detailed studies of individual guru movements as well as a number of volumes of collected studies of individual gurus, but no comprehensive comparative analysis.

That said, the various collected volumes usually do contain some sort of introductory or concluding synthesis (e.g., Copley, 2000; Pechilis, 2004; Forsthoefel and Humes, 2005), and there are some genuine exceptions to Smith's rule. Jones (1989) contributes a reasonably comprehensive and often overlooked volume on Socio-Religious Reform Movements in British India. Aravamudan (2006), while not presenting the type of synoptic survey idealized by Smith, extensively references a significant number of modern gurus, cleverly explicating them via the episteme of Guru English. In shorter works, Shandip Saha (2007) surveys the influence of many Hindu gurus in the west and Angela Rudert (2010), while undertaking doctoral research on one particular guru, has truly broken Smith's mould in publishing an overview of recent scholarship on a broad set of modern Indian gurus who she classifies as "New-Age."

Now, in my own case, having focused my doctorate upon one guru, I have an opportunity to branch out in addressing the wider topic. An extensive survey is, however, beyond the scope of this chapter. There is in fact a sense in which, as Halbfass (1988: 218) puts it in relation to the many and diverse persons who significantly influenced the formation and various formulations of modern Hinduism, it would be "preposterous to attempt a complete or even representative account." And Halbfass is only referring to historical figures; he does not even consider the many thousands of living gurus. In a recent popular account, Ahuja (2006a; 2006b), fills two volumes with brief overviews of 40-odd high-profile 19th- and 20th-century Indian gurus, and a thorough analysis of even these figures would be a much bigger undertaking. Partiality is not the only reason that scholars generally choose to focus on only one guru.

What I can aim to do here, in keeping with the focus of this book, is to identify some key conclusions, broad themes and contrasts from the various approaches that scholars have taken in studies of modern Hindu guru movements, and attempt to point to some gaps or possible directions for future research. This in itself is no easy task, as scholars from a wide variety of disciplines have addressed the topic in a wide variety of ways. Jones (1989: 234) lists among his sources works on "history, political science, anthropology, sociology, comparative religion, and the history of religion," and I would add a multi-disciplinary dimension to this, variously incorporating additional elements from such diverse fields as economics (McKean, 1996; Urban, 2003a), literary criticism (Hatcher, 1999; Aravamudan, 2006), urban studies (Srinivas, 2008), cognitive science (Ketola, 2008), psychology (Storr, 1996), and even parapsychology (Haraldsson, 1997). Again, it will be impossible for me to do justice to all or even most of the elements of these works (and there are many others also), but I at least hope to reference enough major examples to facilitate further investigations by interested readers and researchers.

I will begin with questions of definition, for those who are "*mahāgurus*," or who speak "Guru English" do not necessarily fall within the definitions of "New-Age" or "socio-religious reform movements." And there are several other variously overlapping categories that scholars have applied to the phenomenon at hand. Even the highly conservative title that I have chosen for this chapter bears some close examination.

## Hindu Gurus

Traditional folk etymologies usually present the Sanskrit term guru as if it were an acronym of its two constituent syllables. The most popular variant associates "gu" with darkness (ignorance) and "ru" with removal of the same, producing the meaning "spiritual teacher."[1] Modern scholars tend to prefer derivations from the more literal meaning, "heavy," invoking the weight of authority vested in such teachers. There is also possibly a connection in this regard with the traditional "belief that mighty or holy persons have a spiritual attribute which is measured in quantity" (Ralston, 1989: 54), something which is taken to an extreme in the theories and practices of tantric alchemy (White, 1984).

The term guru has also been used for many centuries in India in a more general sense as descriptive of well-regarded authorities in a variety of fields of learning.[2] Its current widespread international usage in this sense, however, owes more to the impact on the modern imagination of the stereotypically flamboyant modern Hindu spiritual teachers typified by the narrower sense of the term.

Something of the aura of self-proclaimed expertise radiated by these figures obviously resonates with popular perceptions of high-profile experts on all manner of modern subjects, and it is likely that there are some genuine similarities in the psychodynamics underlying both phenomena. Storr (1996) presents a psychological study of a number of high-profile Western spiritual and psychological "gurus," and it would be interesting to expand this to include contemporary self-improvement, new-age healing, management, financial, and information technology gurus.

It is, however, the explicitly spiritual or religious and specifically Hindu dimensions of this phenomenon that form the subject of this chapter, and in this regard there is a gulf between these last figures and modern Hindu spiritual gurus, in that the latter are usually considered by their followers to literally be "descents" (*avatāra*) of one or more traditional deities. Gurus themselves may not always encourage this identification; their positions on the issue range from outright denial to forceful affirmation (Bassuk, 1987; Spurr, 2007). But to their followers the idea that the guru is more than just an exceptional human being is the rule rather than the exception. Such views might be dismissed as wishful thinking on the part of the followers or self-aggrandizement on the part of the gurus, but it should be noted that in the advaita (non-dualistic) traditions upon which most modern gurus draw, there is a strong sense in which categories such as avatāra or even guru are not accorded genuine ontological status, but are ultimately seen as dualistic constructs that must be transcended in order to comprehend the non-dual reality. Modern gurus of this persuasion often seem to use these concepts as vehicles for abstract philosophical or theological doctrine, rather than as simple identity statements, and in this sense, even when they sometimes choose to reject the term guru as inadequately descriptive of their spiritual self-understanding, they can justifiably be categorized as gurus nonetheless (Sharma, 1993: 3; cf. Rudert, 2010: 640).

Likewise, though they exhibit a range of beliefs in relation to their "Hindu" identity, and sometimes explicitly reject this also, they can, despite some inevitable cross-fertilization, generally be distinguished from non-Hindu Indian religious leaders (Gold, 1987: 173–199; Warren, 1999; cf. Aravamudan, 2006: 228; Rudert, 2010: 630, 635). While similar figures are found in Buddhism, Jainism, Sikhism (Sharma, 1993), Islam (Barth, 1990), and Christianity

(Ralston, 1989), these have their own distinctive features. This is not to deny that there is a good deal of diversity within modern Hindu movements. Smith (2003: 167–180) notes that "there are said to be tens of thousands of gurus" and "[g]urus are in fact difficult to summarize." But he is able to identify a number of common "general characteristics" nonetheless, and a number of other scholars have done the same. Babb (1986: 5, 206), for example, focusing on just three modern Hindu guru movements, writes that "if there is common ground between them, it is not a matter of 'beliefs'... [nor] a matter of what is sometimes called 'worldview,'" but he points out that "extreme diversity gives us the clearest possible contrast between varying externals and the constant inner core," and he proceeds to articulate a social psychology of common "loosely floating images" that embody definitively Hindu cultural and religious themes.

## Modern Movements

The term "movement" also bears some consideration in this connection, especially since, unlike the terms guru and "Hinduism," it has rarely itself been adopted by Hindu groups. In the present context, "movement" obviously refers to any guru or lineage of gurus with attendant teachings and followers, but its literal implication of an agenda for change—a movement—is also significant. As is often the case, an orientation toward "change" may simply be a fundamentalist desire to return to what are imagined to be earlier and more traditional means or standards of religiosity (cf. Jones, 1989: 2), or it may be a move to propagate genuinely traditional teachings to new audiences. But it is a change nonetheless. There is an alignment here with the broader category of "new religious movements" that scholars generally apply to groups that are either new to their geographic locale or that "rework older historical traditions with novel conceptual and ritual frameworks" (Srinivas, 2008: 338). In the present case, such "movements" could be contrasted with the followings of numerous, usually hereditary, family- or caste-specific gurus who are content to facilitate the *status quo* or who primarily adapt to change rather than actively promoting it. In addition to these, there are guru-led groups that represent continuities (albeit with some inevitable reinterpretation) of institutionalized pre-modern guru movements founded by the likes of Śaṅkara, Rāmānuja, Madhva, Vallabha, and Caitanya.[3]

The question of the meaning and scope of the term "modern" also arises in this regard. Some scholars find a convenient analogy with standard definitions of "modern" Western history (i.e., since approximately 1500 CE) in the fact that some features of the guru movements of this era, arising from the milieu of Hindu–Muslim encounters, parallel aspects of undeniably modern guru movements arising from the later Indian–European encounters. At the opposite extreme is a focus on just the last 50 years, as the profile of gurus in the West was raised via the cultural revolution of the 1960s and the intensification of the Indian diaspora to America and Europe (Rudert, 2010: 635, 639). But scholars most often seem to date the modern period in India from the time of the "full establishment of British rule in the late 18th century" (Vanita and Kidwai, 2000; cf. Beckerlegge, 2001: 68–69), and there seems to be reasonable justification for this.[4]

As Jones (1989: 1, 212–215) points out, the "colonial milieu" included such elements as the influence of British bureaucracy, which was reflected in Hindu "religious societies fully equipped with elected officials, weekly meetings, annual published reports, bank accounts, sophisticated systems of fundraising, annual meetings, executive committees, subcommittees, by-laws, and constitutions." The introduction of printing presses led to rapid "protestantization" as the "availability of the printed text encouraged the creation of creeds that summarized a complex set of teachings," the vernaculars stole the foreground from Sanskrit as media for religious expression, and religious truth was seen to reside in the resultant printed texts, depriving the Brahmans of their traditional monopoly in this area.

More controversial are claims that the substantial social service undertaken by the new Hindu movements was a response to Christian ideals (Beckerlegge, 2000a, 2000b; Srinivas, 2008: 143–144), but certainly the institutionalization of such service was a colonial-influenced novelty, and Christian missionary views undoubtedly drew responses and had influence in other areas. Copley (2000: 9) writes that Neo-Hindu movements "began to imitate the corporate life of Christianity, its communal prayer, its monasticism … its concepts of sin, guilt, the need for repentance and grace." The influence of

18th century European spiritualism as manifest especially in the Theosophy movement, of Unitarian Christian views, of English education and of the English language itself, along with the rise of romantic nationalism, further contribute to the distinctiveness of this time period (Aravamudan, 2006).

Dating the modern period in India from the late 18th century also makes it roughly contemporaneous with the advent of academic scholarship on Indian religions. This itself is a distinctive element, as the works produced by these scholars directly influenced a number of modern gurus as well as promoting a broader "Oriental renaissance" in the West, as "[w]riters, poets, and philosophers found inspiration in the Oriental classics and modeled some of their work on the new forms" (Singer, 1972: 24–26). The close temporal connection between scholar and guru also provides opportunities for contextualizing studies in ways that are impossible in relation to pre-modern movements. Mass media and popular culture references to gurus can be adduced for context (e.g., Smith, 2003; Aravamudan, 2006), as can census data and other government documents (e.g. Jones, 1989), and anthropological fieldwork often is invaluable (e.g., Babb, 1986; Srinivas, 2006). Members of guru movements can themselves even be asked to make a direct contribution, either by way of critical writing (e.g., Bryant and Ekstrand, 2004), or by contributing information. In one of the earliest scholarly accounts to focus exclusively on a modern guru, Müller (1898: 60–61) prefaces his translation of some of the sayings of the then recently deceased Ramakrishna (1836–1886) with a biographical sketch requested directly from Swami Vivekananda (1863–1902), Ramakrishna's most prominent disciple.

Further to this, scholars may themselves be followers of gurus, or may engage in debate with the objects of their study. Müller's writing on Ramakrishna was partly a rejoinder to views aired by the likes of the Theosophical Society (see below), and Charles White (also cited below) was himself a Theosophist. More recently, a number of scholars have attempted to write in 'discursive modes that are at once "insider" and "scholarly".' Care needs to be taken in this regard, but this at least provides a corrective to an unconscious propensity for "an implicit denigration of the Other … a denial of the fact that criticality, theory, and self-awareness are also concerns for religion(s) in general" (Cabezón, 2006: 32–34, 28–29). It also provides a number of other advantages (Spurr, 2007: 27–29), and my experience agrees with that of Hallstrom (1999: 12) when she writes: "my personal immersion in the philosophy and practices of the Hindu tradition has enhanced, rather than limited, my critical abilities as a scholar."

The fact that scholars directly participate in the construction of the "modernity" they profess to study is also significant and has been problematized. Some scholars theorize "multiple modernities" in which contemporary Indian modernity sits alongside rather than being derivative of Western modernity (Srinivas, 2008: 340–341). And this is a valid attempt to compensate for the "ethnocentric and Eurocentric assumptions" upon which early Western modernization theories were based. Smith (2003: 78–80) even goes so far as to discount seminal sociologist Max Weber's entire contribution to the study of Hinduism due to its Eurocentric presuppositions. But I would be hesitant to dismiss any early scholarly sources out-of-hand, for their closer temporal connection to the early modern period surely carries some advantage, and the prejudices that influenced them did not necessarily compromise their collation of factual information. Jones (1989: 228) points out, for example, that though "J. N. Farquhar's Modern Religious Movements in India (New York, 1919) …judged all groups in terms of whether or not they appeared to be moving toward English Protestant Christianity," it nonetheless "contains a vast amount of reliable data."

Smith also criticizes Weber's "decision to concentrate on the literate strata, on brahmans and monks," but this is again perhaps overly dismissive. While there certainly is much to be learned from subaltern strata and other means of study (Smith, 1978; Srinivas, 2008),[5] there surely remains at least some value in consideration of the textual antecedents of modern guru movements. As Sarkar (1997: 317–318) observes, there has been some scholarly interest in "ways in which elements of high textual culture could sink into and intermix with predominantly oral practices." He notes, for example, that, though illiterate, Ramakrishna, "could have relatively easy access to 'high' knowledge, despite poverty and lack of formal education, as he happened to be of Brahman birth … [and] could imbibe mainstream Hindu traditions through watching folk theatre performances of epic and puranic tales."

At least the latter part of this applies to most modern gurus, many of whom are not Brahmans. The textual outputs of the literate strata are in any case hard to ignore, and Smith goes on to cite in his chapter on gurus both Weber and one of his principal literate strata sources, Bhattacharyya (1850–1899), president of the brahman council of Bengal, author of one of the first modern appraisals of sects and guru movements.

Like that of Farquhar, Bhattacharyya's study is a valuable source of factual information, but it is inhibited by a distinct air of distain for gurus. The "meaningless" mantras and phallic idols promoted by tantric gurus and the repetitive recitations and erotic scriptures of their Vaiṣṇava counterparts evidently offend his Victorian and modernist sensibilities. He sees the modern guru phenomenon as something of an aberration, driven by greed, and finds "no mention of it in the ancient scriptures" (Bhattacharyya, 1896: 25–29). Clearly, from his perspective, there is little continuity between the earliest traditions and modern movements. But, however much of his views may be colored by his Vedic Brahman background and other prejudices, the question of the extent of continuity is an important one, and one which many subsequent scholars have addressed.

## Categories of Continuity

Weber (1916: 323–328), partly following Bhattacharyya, identifies the roots of modern guru movements in what he sees as a decline of earlier traditional (Sanskritic), hereditary and sectarian forms of guru leadership, the rise of emotionalist bhakti, and earlier bhakti displacement of the traditional role of the Brahmans, which paved the way for charismatic religious leadership to emerge from the middle classes in conjunction with their enhanced economic prospects under British rule. Mlecko (1982) traces a more detailed text-based history of Hindu guru concepts from ancient to modern times, and comes to a similar conclusion.

Some scholars have explicitly theorized this question. Jones (1989: 3, 211–212), divides modern movements into "transitional" and "acculturative":

> Transitional movements had their origins in the pre-colonial world and arose from indigenous forms of socio-religious dissent, with little or no influence from the colonial milieu …[and] made limited adjustments to that environment … The emergence of acculturative

movements within the colonial milieu was both a continuation of socio-religious dissent, and a modification of this tradition. The context
was new as South Asians, who came into direct contact with the English … adjusted to the realities of British dominance. Those, who could
not ignore these new rulers but who depended on them for their social
and economic position, found ways to restructure their own cultural
heritage in order to retain a place within that heritage.

Similarly, Halbfass (1988: 219–222) reiterates the ideas of Paul
Hacker, who "divided modern Indian thought … into 'Neo-Hinduism'
and 'surviving traditional Hinduism'," the main distinction between
which was not "any particular teachings," but, rather:

> the different ways in which they appeal to the tradition, the structures
> which they employ to interrelate the indigenous and the foreign, and
> the degree of their receptivity vis-à-vis the West …"Neo-Hinduism …
> always implies reinterpretation." … [Neo-Hindus] first adopt West-
> ern values and means of orientation and then attempt to find the for-
> eign in the indigenous: "… afterwards they connect these values with
> and claim them as part of the Hindu tradition."

A major focus of such "reinterpretation" is often identified in attempts to reconcile Hindu ideas with the modern theories of evolution that were a hot topic at the time (Bevir, 2000: 163).

Other scholarly theorizations draw analogies with Western history
in writing of a modern "Hindu Renaissance" or "Reformation" (e.g.,
Bharati, 1970: 272; Choudhary, 1981: 79). Beckerlegge (2004:140) cites
Sarkar's view that the "Hindu Renaissance" is largely a retrospectively
applied intellectual construct, and problematic for that reason, but
he does note that "reference was popularly made in 19th-century
Bengal to a 'new age' or 'awakening.'" And while "Neo-Hinduism"
is also an academic construct, Halbfass (1988: 219–222) notes that
the term "Neo-Vedantism" did have some currency in India at the
time. The difference between these last two terms is not without
significance, however, for the underlying theology of the vast majority
of acculturative, Neo-Hindu, Hindu Renaissance movements is
extrapolated from the canons of advaita vedānta, which, while
influential, is but one of the major traditional philosophical schools.

One reason for this emphasis rests on the obvious suitability of
non-dualism for the task of countering Christian derision of Hindu

polytheism. The most commonly adopted position in this regard is one that seminal Neo-Hindu Ram Mohan Roy (1772–1833) derived directly from traditional advaita, whereby polytheistic image worship is seen as an acceptable preliminary practice for those unable to comprehend the non-dual truth (Aravamudan, 2006: 43; cf. King, 1999: 132). Ironically, advaita was also encouraged by Christian missionaries as an "easy 'monistic' target" over and against which to promote "the moral superiority of Christianity." And more politically motivated British Orientalists, by whose works Ram Mohan was influenced, may have promoted it as an antidote to the advance of French Jacobinism (itself a potential prelude to French political expansion in India) or as a suitably quietist "indigenous ideological bulwark against social activism" (King, 1999: 120–131). Ram Mohan's significant monotheistic Sufi and Unitarian influences also perhaps made advaita an attractive choice. But, in any case, despite having almost no presence traditionally, advaita soon became equated with Vedanta in his Bengali milieu, and this milieu also gave rise to several other influential Neo-Hindu gurus. Beckerlegge (2004: 309) notes that "[i]n nineteenth-century Bengal, Vedanta was widely held to be synonymous with Advaita, and, by 1896, Vivekananda had come to identify 'Vedantist' with 'Hindu'."

Vivekananda's guru Ramakrishna, however, was not so much of this persuasion, and this indicates a problem with attempts to differentiate two types of modern Hindu movements. As Copley (2000: xiii) points out, "Jones speculates that quite often the leaders were transitional and the followers acculturative." But the fact of such anomalies would not be apparent without drawing a distinction in the first place, and it is often, as Halbfass (1988: 221) puts it, "useful and convenient" to do so (cf. Srinivas, 2008: 336–337). Without resorting to such categories, scholars would be forced always to deal in particular instances, and, while some would no doubt argue that this would be a good thing, it would put a limit on possibilities for creative and illuminating conjunctions. Jones's work is actually very conservative in this respect, consisting primarily of historical narratives constructed mostly from primary sources and broken down by religious movement and geographical location. Other scholars have reveled in being much less cautious.

One of the most creative scholarly works to reflect on gurus is Aravamudan's *Guru English*, in which he connects figures as diverse as Ramakrishna, Mother Teresa, and Salman Rushdie, skillfully situating them within a common linguistic milieu. He presents "Guru English" as, among other things, "a theolinguistics, generating new religious meanings ... [and] a literary discourse ... [using] multilingual puns, parody, and syncretism." He cites, for example, the "lame pun ... by Sai Baba," which 'suggests that bābā (colloquially, "father") ... is literally the Lamb of God, because lambs when they bleat, say "baa-baa"' (Aravamudan, 2006: 6, 36). But while these are new religious meanings, and while there is far more to Aravamudan's "Guru English" than mere punning, the phenomenon of folk etymology is obviously far from new (recall the definition of guru cited earlier). Similarly, while Aravamudan (2006: 50) cites influential Neo-Hindu Keshab Chandra Sen's criticisms of traditional theologies in which "[t]he disjunctive Or reigns supreme; the copulative And finds no place" as exemplifying 'the closest example of a grammatical rule for Guru English, a theolinguisitc prefiguration of E. M. Forster's liberal philosophy of "only connect,"' other scholars have suggested that "Neo-Hindu thinkers merely exploited the same "inclusivism" found within traditional Hinduism."[6]

Inclusivism is defined as "claiming for, and thus including in, one's own religion what really belongs to an alien sect" (Olivelle, 1986: 867, citing Hacker, the first scholar to apply this concept to Indian traditions). As Halbfass (1988: 411) notes, Hacker "suggests a deep affinity between non-dualism and inclusivism," and while there are some problems with applying this consistently to ancient advaita, the two certainly work together in Neo-Hindu movements. More generally speaking also, "inclusivistic arguments characterize the attitude of new and younger religious traditions vis-à-vis older and more established ones" (Olivelle, 1986: 867, citing Albrecht Wezler). And something of this is certainly evident among a number of gurus popularly and academically identified as belonging to the "Indian New Age," with their penchant for "adopting old, often foreign and 'other' traditions, ... co-opting, re-shaping, re-packaging, and commodifying ancient ideas from diverse sources for the current era" (Rudert, 2010: 629–630).

This "diversity" of sources should not, however, be overemphasized. Forsthoefel and Humes (2005: 8) contrast "egalitarian inclusivism," in which: "All [religions] go to the same goal," and "an inclusivism (all religions have value) with an exclusivist subtext (while all religions have value, all find their ultimate meaning and value in Hinduism)." And the latter is by far the more prominent in the Indian New Age. Palmer (2005: 105–106) writes for example that "while one may mistakenly gather that Satya Sai Baba is sharing a message of universal acceptance, he is, in essence, calling for a return to Vedic religion." This is, nevertheless, somewhat complicated by a sense in which some of the "Hindu texts and traditions" cited by many Hindu gurus are themselves "foreign and other."

Bharati (1981: 273–274) famously framed this as a "pizza-effect"—so named after the "new tastes" acquired by the pizza (originally a simple baked bread with no trimmings) in America, which contributed to a "new status" for it upon its return to Italy with Italian-Americans. The implication here is that the version of "Hinduism" expounded by many Neo-Hindu thinkers never really existed in its fully fledged sense until it was objectified via the Western Oriental Renaissance and provided with new status as it reimpacted on India. Bharati saw the beginnings of this "effect" with the emulation by Indian scholars of the early European Indologists, extending to include an unprecedented Hindu Renaissance emphasis on the Bhagavadgītā due to its popularity in the West.

White (1972: 878), perhaps influenced by his own inclusivistic Theosophical ideals, disagreed with this last point, arguing that the Bhagavadgītā was "important in ancient times, as exemplified by the commentary on it of Śaṃkara and other philosophers." And subsequent scholarship has questioned Bharati's more general conclusions (Hatcher, 1999). But the category of "Hindu Renaissance," which Bharati opposes to "grassroots" Hinduism, and other similar distinctions at least provide a vocabulary by which scholarly debate can proceed, even if (like the preliminary idols of traditional advaita) they must ultimately be transcended. Interestingly, White also took Bharati to task for presuming that a reputation for "miracles" garnered by Sathya Sai Baba is merely a testament to "[t] he seemingly boundless gullibility of the modern devotee." Again, whatever the ultimate conclusion may be, the idea of miracles is so prominent amongst modern gurus that it is deserving of at least some scholarly consideration.

# Miracles and Mischief

Something of a "pizza effect" is evident in the case of the Theosophical Society, founded in 1875 by Russian occultist Helena Blavatsky (1831–1891), and operating to this day from its headquarters in Chennai. Initially basing its teachings on Western esoterism, Theosophy adopted a number of Buddhist and Hindu ideas via their representations in the products of the Oriental Renaissance. It formed an early alliance in India with the Neo-Hindu Arya Samaj, founded by Dayananda Saraswati (1824–1883), finding resonance in his ideas of Vedic Hinduism as a comprehensive and universal religion, but Blavatsky and other Theosophy leaders soon struck out on their own, being unable to accept Dayananda's personalistic conceptions of the Godhead, intolerance of Buddhism, and aspirations to supreme guru status. They attracted large numbers of both Indian and European followers with their occult practices and syncretic appropriation of Hindu ideas (Johnson, 1994; Godwin, 1994; Bevin, 2000).

Not all were enamored of this new flavor of Hinduism however. Vivekananda, for example, was adamant that "Hindus … do not stand in need of dead ghosts of Russians and Americans," and he lamented the prominence of the Theosophical Society in representing Indian culture to the West (De Tollenaere, 2004: 40). And the Theosophists themselves were soon struck by internal controversy, with accusations of faked miracles, and an investigation by the London Society for Psychical Research concluding Blavatsky to be "one of the most accomplished, ingenious, and interesting impostors of history" (Aravamudan, 2006: 108). Blavatsky and other Theosophists claimed to receive remote guidance from spiritual masters, often referred to in a type of reverse Guru English ("Spiritualist Sanskrit" perhaps) by the Sanskrit term mahātmā ("great-souled"). If nothing else, this provoked a response from Müller (1898: 1), who chided them and others "whose powers of admiration are in excess of their knowledge and discretion" for their credulity in being swayed by "very silly miracles." Müller presented Ramakrishna by way of contrast as "A Real Mahâtman."

Not that Ramakrishna was without his own share of miraculous folklore, and Müller (1898: 60–61), in his request for a biographical account from Vivekananda, "warned him repeatedly" away from what he saw as the "mere fables" about Ramakrishna that he had read in other sources. Vivekananda, sympathetic to modern standards of objectivity, was only too happy to oblige, albeit that he finally fell short of the mark in Müller's estimation due to "a natural unwillingness, nay, an incapability, to believe or to repeat anything that might place his master in an unfavorable light." Fortunately, Müller could refer to other contemporary sources more "aloof from the propaganda carried on by Râmakrishna's disciples," although the worst he was able to come up with were frownings upon Ramakrishna's sometimes "abominably filthy" language and his "neglect" of his wife in favor of spiritual pursuits.

Many scholars would at least agree with Müller's ideal of attempting to penetrate beneath the layers of hagiographical reverence and tales of miracle-working that permeate popular accounts of modern gurus (cf. Srinivas, 2008: 334). In the case of living gurus, however, it is much more difficult to simply dismiss these as products of retrospectively applied devotional fancy. Indeed, they have attracted attention from academic parapsychologists. Haraldsson (1997: 222) studied Sathya Sai Baba's famous "miracles" over the course of a decade, repeatedly interviewing him and many eyewitnesses, and "in spite of a long lasting and painstaking effort … found no direct evidence of fraud." More aggressive, if less well-qualified skeptics have since come to the opposite conclusion, flooding the internet with much direct evidence, but it is difficult to generalize on the basis of either of these conclusions (Spurr, 2007: 41–54). For those versed in the appropriate methods and willing to undertake the necessary fieldwork, this remains an interesting and potentially fertile area for future research.[7]

When focus shifts from the guru to the movement as a whole, issues of the true biography of the guru and veracity of miracles become less important. Babb (1986: 162) observes that "[a]t this level, the extravagances of hagiography are not an impediment, but an important aid to discovery." His point is that it is primarily the persona of the guru and the meaning of purported miracles, rather than the question of their being miraculous, that animates devotees' beliefs and behaviors. He notes that many people who are neutral to Sathya Sai Baba and even many of his severest critics do not doubt the veracity of his supposed ability to perform miracles, but simply disagree with his followers that such miracles are valid evidence of spiritual greatness. Aravamudan (2006: 109) goes a step further, glossing over the Theosophical Society miracles as being akin to "special effects" in modern movies; that is, retaining some power and attraction even if revealed to be non-miraculous in nature.

At issue here is Weber's view that progress toward modernity is characterized by a progressive "disenchantment of the world"; Babb (1986: 200) suggests that, in the case of Sathya Sai Baba at least, miracles present "something of a Weberian reversal, an example of the re-enchantment of the world." McKean (1996: 20–23) puts this even more strongly: "Sathya Sai Baba's miracles offer India's monied consumers a self-indulgent, guilt-free experience of the magicality of objects." But Urban (2003a: 85) points out that,

> if Sai Baba appears on the one hand to be a kind of icon of materialism and consumerism—the magic and fetishism of the commodity incarnate—he is also quite strikingly on the other hand one of the greatest critics of Western materialism and consumerism.

My own research indicates that, far from promoting commodity fetishism, Sathya Sai Baba's "miracles" are usually angled at instilling in his followers a sense of the impermanence and worthlessness of worldly objects, as contrasted to the need for perpetual remembrance of the transcendent divine.

In addition to claims of faked miracles, accusations of sexual impropriety are also commonly leveled at gurus, and responses from followers range from outright denial to tantric rationalizations. Some scholars have addressed, and also failed to sufficiently address, this issue. Urban (2003b: 244–248) criticizes a number of scholarly practitioners of Siddha Yoga for ignoring in their collected volume on the movement "the intense controversy" and scandal" involving the "alleged sexual practices" of Siddha Yoga guru Swami Muktananda (1908–1982), "which, many claim, drew naïve young women into esoteric Tantric rituals." Rudert (2010: 640) notes that "the Siddha scholars' agenda to write a "theology" of the movement in which they were a part was entirely transparent," but at least some of the scholars involved have expressed regret at their omissions.[8] What is clear is that scholars who are also devotees tread a fine line in their writing when they combine their two identities. Srinivas (2008: 333–335), for example, a follower of Sathya Sai Baba, invokes the "ethics of studying a community of living believers" as setting "some limits" on the scope of her study, choosing to make no mention of the fact that Sathya Sai

Baba too is accused of (homo)sexual abuse, but admitting the existence of lesser allegations of fake miracles and "textual inconsistencies."

Reverent silence on such issues is perhaps less than ideal, but the opposite extreme, when scholars become the instigators of allegations, also has its problems. Srinivas alludes to scholarly portrayals of Ramakrishna as a latent homosexual (Kripal, 1995) as having "driven a wedge between outsiders and those within" the movement. The more serious issue for followers and scholars alike, however, seems to be with Kripal's questionable translations and neo-Orientalist approach (Urban, 1998). Nevertheless, sex scandals surrounding modern Hindu gurus are the rule rather than the exception, and there is a role for scholarship to play in elucidating some of the traditional paradigms that are sometimes invoked by guru movements and their critics in this regard (Hawley, 2004). More could also perhaps be done on the sociology and psychology of followers' reactions to scandals, including perhaps a comparative study of anti-guru movements started by former followers of scandalized gurus.[9] A lot has already been done on the more general socio-dynamics of guru movements.

## Charisma

Central to much debate in this area is the idea of "charisma" much popularized by Weber, who defined "charismatic authority" as being "based on the exemplary character, sanctity, and heroism of an individual person" (Ketola, 2008: 26). Von Stietencron (2001: 18–20) questions how applicable Weber's formulation of charisma may be to Indian traditions, in which

> the notion of charisma is first and primarily linked to the king … charisma was conceived of as a kind of subtle, luminous substance that could be conferred on a deserving person by a God or by ritual action … Later Indian mythology also sees royal charisma as a property of the divine, particularly of Viṣṇu.

But the two conceptions of charisma are not necessarily mutually exclusive, nor does the latter fall completely outside of Weber's scope (Riesebrodt, 1999: 2), and indeed both resonate with aspects of modern guru movements.

Smith (2003: 172) observes that the guru often "may behave like a king," be "addressed as 'Maharaj' ('Great King')," may "sit on a throne, and spend extravagantly." Von Stietencron (2001: 18–20) notes the relevance of the traditional "concept of prādurbhāva or avatāra, according to which the God Viṣṇu himself "becomes manifest" or "descends" and incorporates himself, or part of himself, on earth." Most modern Hindu gurus are regarded by their followers as avatāras, and there is a significant traditional overlap between the paradigms of king and avatāra (Spurr, 2007). To Smith's observations, I would also especially add those of Gonda (1969: 77–78), that the daily audiences granted by ancient Indian (divine) kings in some sense prefigure the daily darśan (lit. "viewing") given by many Hindu gurus, by which they are believed to optically bestow their grace upon their followers (see, e.g., Cornille, 2004: 136–138). Also perhaps significant is the phenomenon traditionally and popularly referred to as śaktipāt(a), a "descent of spiritual energy" via the touch of a guru, this being reasonably common within modern guru movements, and sometimes reported by followers as an experience of an influx of light. There is some scholarship on this phenomenon,[10] but room also for further investigation, especially in a contemporary comparative context.

While śaktipāt may in some sense be a direct transfer of charisma, the more general display of paranormal powers by a guru is seen by some scholars as "a secondary rather than a primary sign of charisma; it serves to validate and support a religious role, but cannot initiate it" (McDaniel, 1989: 262). Keyes (1982: 4–8) sees religious leaders' possession of intuitive religious knowledge as being more important than miracles in this regard, and he notes, further to this, that "[t]he actions of a person working against extraordinary odds to achieve some desirable social goal have from time to time been taken as signifying that the person is charismatic."

Both of these apply to most modern gurus, many of whom have undertaken significant social, educational and health projects. But "miracles" are also important, and certainly in the case of Sathya Sai Baba they served to initiate his religious role.

Also controversial is the common position articulated by Keyes that it is only "in the context of a crisis situation, [that] people are motivated to turn toward those who appear to embody a conjunction of the sacred and the worldly." As Warrier (2003: 222–229) notes, in the case of India's "urban middle class"—from whom Neo-Hindu gurus are usually considered to draw the bulk of their following—scholars "invariably point to a perceived lack of one kind or another in their lives which they purportedly seek to compensate [for] by participating in a guru faith." She gives various examples of this, including the suggestion that "[b]y invoking the certitudes and simplicities of an idealized past, religion bolsters the individual's capacity to face up to the uncertainties of fast-paced city life." She concludes, however, that any suggestions of a "lack" on the part of devotees are "sweeping generalizations," and do not apply to the followers of the contemporary guru Mata Amritanandamayi that she interviewed. Their quest, rather, is for deeper religious "meaning," beyond the "'mechanical' and 'ritualistic' religious observances and 'blind faith' of their parents."

Furthermore, rather than experiencing the fast-paced changes of modernization as stressful, Warrier's (2003: 231) informants testified to "the hope of increasing possibilities and multiplying opportunities … a growing awareness of multiple choices in every sphere of life, including that of religion." The spiritual crisis model proposed by Keyes is not at all in evidence here—Warrier (2005: 118) concludes that "[t]he appeal of popular gurus like the Mata lies in their ability to facilitate, rather than restrict, this process of individual creativity and innovation."[11]

A recent study of a number of prominent contemporary Hindu gurus with followings in America divides them into two basic types: "those taken to be basically an exceptionally wise human being, a respected teacher of age-old traditions, and those considered first of all to be an instance of the embodied divine, somehow superhuman and distinct from ordinary mortals" (Gold, 2005: 220–221).

This more or less parallels a distinction made by Weber between "traditional" and "charismatic" authority, the former being "based on an established belief in the sanctity of immemorial traditions" (Ketola, 2008: 26). Charismatic authority is by far the more prevalent in modern Hindu guru movements, but Weber never intended his ideal types to be mutually exclusive, and indeed some sort of mixture is usual. Ketola (2008: 6), for example, observes in relation to the founder of the Hare Krishna movement:

> Prabhupāda did not exemplify pure charismatic leadership. His authority rested to a great extent on his being properly initiated into the

tradition of Gauḍīya Vaiṣṇavism. He regarded himself as a missionary of a venerable tradition, not as a founder of a new religion ... yet in the eyes of his western followers, Prabhupāda did not gain legitimacy so much on the basis of tradition, but on the basis of his personal qualities. The new cultural context turned him into a charismatic leader ... He was not even a typical Hindu guru, since he rejected the monistic Advaita Vedānta taught by most of them. (Ketola, 2008: 6)

In this last regard, Prabhupāda lined his commentaries on traditional scriptures with a plethora of rejoinders to Neo-Hindu advaitic "impersonalism," while at the same time, ironically, heavily plagiarizing Neo-Hindu influenced English translations of the texts of traditional scriptures (Lorenz, 2004: 117–119). Weber (1922: 243) often characterized charismatic authority with words attributed to Jesus: "It is written ... but I say unto you," but Prabhupāda's discourse was more often of the form: "Worldly people or scientists or impersonalists think ... but it is written in the canons of Gauḍīya Vaiṣṇavism." As Ketola (2008: 139) puts it, "in the midst of a technological race to conquer space, Prabhupāda believed in Purāṇic cosmology with absolute certainty." Either way, it is the fact that the guru often seems to be a "counterintuitive being" that is attractive to followers,[12] along with the air of "unshakeable conviction" with which gurus are invariably imbued (Copley, 2000: 6). In Prabhupāda's case, the "pizza effect" is also significant, as his Indian followers are often drawn by "his success in bringing the Hindu tradition to the world" (Rochford, 2004: 188).

Ketola (2008: 30, 211–212) summarizes previous scholarly explanations of charisma as being of four kinds: "(1) those that put primary emphasis on the social situation or context of crisis; (2) those that emphasize the mental states of potential followers; (3) those that emphasize the message; and lastly (4) those that emphasize the leader." To this he adds his own approach, drawing on principles of cognitive science that operate independently of cultural conditioning. Gurus produce "frame violations," exposing followers' "deeply and unconsciously held expectations." They also evoke from their followers spontaneous essentialist conceptualizations of agency, as well as associations with ritual activities that produce "basic emotional responses and even more unusual forms of neural activity, resulting in some religious experience." While Ketola concludes that there is ultimately something ineffable about charisma, there is certainly more room for analysis in this area; cognitive science is a young and rapidly evolving field, and may yet produce more insights that add to our understanding of guru movements.

There are also opportunities here to shed some light on broader religious phenomena. Aravamudan (2006: 225) observes that "[i] f some religions are personality cults with centuries of institutional history, gurus are living instances of religions-in-the-making." Weber ultimately viewed charisma as "inherently unstable" and saw an inevitable tendency for new religious movements to become "institutionalized or routinized." This has already taken place to a large degree in some modern guru movements, prompted especially by the demise of the guru, but occurring also to some extent while the guru is alive (Collins, 2004: 215–216). Modern guru movements thus provide an opportunity for comparative studies of the ways in which this transition is made, and how this may reflect on or contrast with what we know of the history of older religious movements.[13] One significant difference lies in the awareness that the new movements may themselves have of the progression outlined by Weber, prompting them to deliberately seek ways of avoiding the negative aspects of institutionalization.[14] Another area in which it is likely that there will be significant differences, is in the treatment of gender, and this further presents its own opportunities for insight and study.

# Gender

It is notable, if hardly surprising given their strongly patriarchal cultural history, that most modern Hindu gurus are male. Some, such as Prabhupāda, are also overtly chauvinistic. Lorenz (2004: 122–123) concludes from a quantitative analysis of references to women in his works that:

56 percent of all statements concern women as sex objects
8 percent are statements about women's class, status or position
9 percent are restrictions that state that women should not be given any freedom
7 percent are statements about women having bad qualities

This of course needs to be balanced by attention to practical realities; Erndl (2004: 248) notes that Prabhupāda's "International Society for Krishna Consciousness (ISKCON) does not currently recognize women as gurus, but in response to a growing feminist voice within the movement now appoints women to its governing board and as temple presidents." Nevertheless, Lorenz's figures are representative of wider cultural prejudices, and Prabhupāda's views may generally be classified as traditionalist.

While there are some traditional precedents for a more elevated status for women and in particular for female gurus, the emergence into the public domain in the 20th century of a significant number of influential female gurus was a genuinely new development—even "the word guru does not accept a feminine form" (Pechilis, 2004: 6). Western influenced Neo-Hindu gurus like Dayananda, Vivekananda and the Theosophists, strongly promoted women's welfare, perhaps paving the way for this development, and Sarada Devi and "the Mother," wives of Ramakrishna and Aurobindo, respectively, took on prominent roles as guru figures for the movements that initially formed around their husbands (Srinivasa Iyengar, 1978; Rüstau, 2000). Pechilis (2004: 5–9) writes in the introduction to her edited volume on modern Hindu female gurus that many of them "participate in the classical guru tradition by taking instruction and initiation from a male guru." While some had female gurus or were self-initiated, "as a general rule female gurus follow established, male behavioral modes for *guruhood*, even if they did not take initiation from a male guru."[15] What is most challenging for female gurus, she says, is often not the fact that they choose to become gurus but rather the fact that they may not live up to "received social expectations ... the Hindu social norms of womanhood, which are marriage and bearing children."

One way in which this is overcome is through identification of the guru with the Goddess, or a specific goddess, and, even when not encouraged by the guru herself, such identifications are almost invariably made. Alternatively, a guru may be understood to be a reincarnation of an earlier female guru—contemporary guru Sree Maa is believed to be Sarada Devi reincarnate (Biernacki, 2004: 181). Received social expectations die hard, however, and even when a female guru or ascetic successfully rebels in creating a religious role for herself, she may promote to others "the dharmashastra ideal for women that her life contradicts" (Hallstrom, 2004: 104). And most of this also applies to males; it should not be forgotten that, especially in urban contexts with the rise of capitalism in the modern era, the dominant received social expectations for young men also point to career and family rather than *guruhood*. Sathya Sai Baba often encourages his male followers to marry and pursue worldly careers rather than following the path of early renunciation that he himself took, even when they express aspirations to renounce.

In any case, despite following predominantly male paradigms, some Hindu female gurus do fulfill a unique role in that, due to traditional cultural predilections for segregation of the sexes, they are more accessible to women than are male gurus (Hallstrom, 2004: 92–96). They may establish women's ashrams and schools for girls, minister to widows, and generally promote welfare for women, albeit usually retaining some traditional feminine ideals and restrictions (Anderson, 2004: 73–78). In spiritual matters, guru's themselves may sometimes disregard such restrictions; Raj (2004: 214–216) reports that Mata Amritanandamayi (Ammachi) "embraces, hugs, strokes, and kisses her devotees with total disregard to their gender, moral condition, and physical purity," although this may partly be a reflection of her own low-caste status. Raj nevertheless sees Ammachi's darśan guidelines as restrictive, in that they require women "to cover their shoulders and to wear dresses or skirts [and] not wear see-through dresses or tight dresses that reveal the shape of the body." But I would note that equivalent and often more extreme restrictions apply to the male followers of gurus who place an emphasis on the virtues of celibacy (Alter, 1997). This is not so much a case of restricting the freedom of one gender more than the other, as a case of seeking to minimize opportunities for sexual desire to manifest, and this in the interest of promoting focus on spiritual pursuits. Taken to an extreme, problems can arise in this regard (Bryant and Ekstrand, 2004: 352, 398), but these affect both males and females.

Another key issue facing female guru movements, and indeed guru movements in general, is that of succession. Erndl (2004: 247–249) postulates a typology of modes of succession for female gurus, and this again could apply equally to males: "succession from guru to disciple, what is in Sanskrit called a parampara, an unbroken lineage"; "sideways succession … a disciple become a guru of a lineage that is an offshoot"; "ambiguous succession … a disciple has received training from a recognized guru and may function informally, though not officially, as a guru"; "spontaneous succession ... the guru has no human guru ... divinity is revealed to her, and subsequently to others, spontaneously;" and the often overlapping category of "posthumous visionary succession ... the disciple is initiated and given transmission in a vision by his or her guru after the guru's death." Erndl also suggests that a number of other typologies be investigated as possibilities for future research: the international and ethnic makeup of the movement, "the degree to which feminine images of the sacred are privileged, and the degree to which feminist values and practices are emphasized."

## Out of India

Hindu gurus are not only found in India, and many who originated in India, also have followings elsewhere in Asia.[16] While interaction between India and the rest of Asia dates from ancient times, even in Southeast Asia, where other forms of Hinduism are common, it is only comparatively recently that anything resembling the modern Indian guru movement is in evidence, and this mostly due to offshoots of India-based movements. Such movements usually seem to find the bulk of their followings among ethnic Indians, to the extent that differences between them and their Indian counterparts are often minimal, especially if there is a constant flow of persons and communication to and from India. Inevitably, however, some degree of cultural, religious, or geographical localization takes place. Sathya Sai Baba, for example, has some Buddhist followers in Sri Lanka who consider him to be Maitreya—the next Buddha (Fuller, 1992: 179).

In 1880 CE, the Theosophical Society founded a lodge in Java, drawing its membership primarily from Dutch colonials and from the traditionally Hindu-inclined Javanese aristocracy, who were identified by the Theosophists with the supposed ancient Aryan invaders of Indonesia. The appropriation of Hindu terms and ideas by Theosophy was by no means always (or even mostly) in keeping with traditional Indian interpretations, and it drew some criticism at the time in this regard from other modern Indian religious groups. But, while its membership remained small, it nonetheless played a significant role in disseminating at least the semblance of Hindu ideas outside of India (De Tollenaere, 2004), and has followings today in most Asian nations.

The closest extra-Indian cousin of Indian Hinduism is found to this day in traditional Balinese religious beliefs and practices, but early Muslim and Christian missionaries and Indonesian government authorities, seeking to promote their own religious ideals, initially classified these as primitive "animism." This provoked a reaction from some Balinese Hindu intellectuals, who, inspired by Theosophy and a visit in 1927 by the famous Hindu poet Rabindranath Tagore, founded reform organizations in an effort to align Indonesian Hinduism more closely with Neo-Hindu visions of its Indian ancestry (Ramstedt, 2000). This cause was taken forward in 1950 by the Arya Samaj missionary Narendra Dev Pandit Sastri (1920–2001), who settled in Bali and was instrumental in founding the government-sanctioned "Parishad Dharma Hindu Bali" as a local analog of the Indian Vishva Hindu Parishad (Somvir, 2004). Other early Neo-Hindu groups also established contacts with Indonesia (Ramstedt, 2000), and more recent movements include ISKCON, the Sathya Sai Baba organization, and a couple of groups inspired by the ideals of Mahatma Gandhi (Somvir, 2004).

The emergence of the Sathya Sai Baba movement in Bali around 1980 was facilitated by decades of "Hinduization" of the pre-colonial Balinese traditions along the lines just described, but the emphasis on charisma and miracles in this movement presents a stark contrast and strong appeal in comparison to the highly ritualistic and impersonal forms of traditional worship. Howe notes that,

> [it] is represented as the rediscovery of an ancient religious tradition which focuses on the fundamentals of religious faith and belief by stripping away the allegedly superfluous accretions of customary religious practices ... But it is also seen as a modern form of worship, tailored to the demands of a fast-paced society and more in tune with new ideologies of individualism, democracy and personal achievement. (Howe, 2004: 182–183, n18)

Successful healings and exorcisms also seem to add to the attractiveness of the movement, as well as spiritualized exegesis of traditional rites and strong humanist elements, including criticisms of traditional caste hierarchies. Sathya Sai Baba followers tend to come from the educated classes and, in contrast to state-sanctioned Hinduism, Sathya Sai Baba's widespread international following creates the impression of participation in a wider global identity. Other factors not to be overlooked include simple curiosity and chance encounters with the Sathya Sai Baba movement (Howe, 2004).[17]

All of this, I would note, also applies to the Sathya Sai Baba movement in India and most other places, although there are a few notable contrasts in some of these. Ackerman and Lee (1988: 114) write that Sathya Sai Baba's movement in Malaysia is not "concerned with reforming or reinterpreting Hindu beliefs and practices," and Mearns (1995: 267), in another study of the Sathya Sai Baba movement in Malaysia, likewise suggests that many of "the rites pertaining to Baba reinforce and recodify familiar and accepted Hindu practices." But these perceptions are probably due to the fact that the movement's Malaysian Hindu milieu lacked the strong Brahmanical basis of Balinese Hinduism, and, drawing its following predominantly from middle-class ethnic Indians, had already been strongly influenced by earlier Neo-Hindu movements. There is, nevertheless, a growing contingent of Chinese Malaysian followers of Sathya Sai Baba, and this has already seen a rift in the movement as some Chinese followers are unwilling to subordinate themselves to the Hindu ideals of the somewhat overbearing middle-class Indian leadership of the movement (Kent, 2005: 30–31, 154–161).

Kent (2005: 157) notes that there is little data on the Chinese-educated Chinese Malaysian following of Sathya Sai Baba, and this therefore presents an opportunity for future research. Indeed, there is very little scholarship on Hindu guru movements in Asian cultures outside of India and Southeast Asia, and this thus provides a potentially interesting area for future research. There are, for example, Sathya Sai Baba organizations in China, Japan, Taiwan, South Korea, Nepal, Azerbaijan, Georgia, Kazakhstan, Russia, and the Ukraine. Another gap is in the lack of quantitative data on the size and spread of different movements. Srinivas (2008: 347–351) reproduces a list of overseas Sathya Sai Baba groups, giving numbers of members where available, but more research into the official statistics gathered by the Sathya Sai organization and other modern guru organizations could be illuminating.

# Conclusion

The number of modern Hindu guru movements is large and constantly increasing, presenting ongoing opportunities for novel scholarship. While modern Hindu gurus may not necessarily identify themselves as "Hindu" or as "gurus," they can usually be distinguished from non-Hindu religious leaders, and can usually be analyzed as taking on the role of a spiritual teacher. While they may not consider themselves to be "modern," or to found new religious "movements," they share a number of features that first appeared in India with the dawn of colonial rule, and they usually present an agenda of religious change—even if this is only an imagined fundamentalism. Scholars have approached this topic from a wide variety of disciplines and in a wide variety of manners, and there are unique opportunities in studying such a modern religious phenomenon. Scholars may contextualize their works with reference to popular culture, mass media, official statistics, and fieldwork. Or they may themselves even be followers of gurus, something that may both limit and enhance their studies.

Various typologies and characterizations of modern guru movements are proposed by scholars. Traditional, transitional, or grassroots gurus, are opposed to Neo-Hindu, acculturative, or Hindu Renaissance movements, exemplifying Weber's ideal types of traditional and charismatic authority, respectively. An "Indian New Age" is posited, alongside a "theolinguistic" episteme of "Guru English," and the idea of a "pizza effect," by which Hinduism became established and embellished in the West, enhancing its status back in India. True to their advaita underpinnings, modern movements may be strongly eclectic and "inclusivistic," adopting religious forms from diverse sources, yet may retain a privileged place for Hinduism among the world's religions. Common guru scandals involve allegations of faked miracles and sexual abuse, and scholars have been criticized for both avoiding and advancing issues in these areas. Properly considered, there is a role for scholarship to play in this regard, and there are opportunities in this for further study.

Ideas of "charisma" are perhaps the most theorized aspect of the study of modern guru movements, but even here there are opportunities for novel contributions—from advances in cognitive science to the simple fact that guru movements are prototypical "religions in the making." Similarly, while there has been a significant amount of recent scholarship, primarily undertaken by female scholars, focusing on female gurus and gender issues, there are opportunities to expand this to better categorize degrees of international and ethnic variety, feminine content, and feminist practices. Other opportunities in this and indeed all areas of our topic lie in more detailed quantification of the extent and spread of guru movements and in quantitative analysis of their textual outputs. As Srinivas and Lorenz show, these can provide some interesting characterizations and insights. Given that most modern movements keep membership records and that the literature produced by such movements is extremely prolific and often readily available on the internet in an easily searchable digital format, these are very promising means of future research. Finally, with a few major exceptions, Asian guru movements outside of India remain largely unstudied, and this presents another opportunity for research, especially for those able to undertake fieldwork or access written material in local languages.

## Notes

1. Scriptural touch-points for these etymologies include the *purāṇic Gurugītā*, the yogic *Advayatārako-paniṣad*, and the *Pāṇini sūtras* (see e.g., Mlecko, 1982: 33–34; Ralston, 1989: 54; Rigopoulos, 2005; and with due caution the Wikipedia article "Guru").
2. Martial gurus and gurus for music and other performing arts are probably the most common examples of this and, while there may be explicit spiritual elements to these disciplines, at a more popular level the term is also used of school teachers, parents, and other elders or seniors (cf. Storr, 1996: xi).
3. Saha (2007: 493–494) refers to a couple of good examples of such movements, further observing that because the gurus are orthodox Brahmans, they observe traditional scriptural injunctions forbidding travel across the oceans, but are still able to maintain significant diasporic followings through the use of television and the internet. On the "electronic presence" of gurus, see also Srinivas (2008: 104–108).
4. Aravamudan (2006: 17) presents a more sophisticated variant of this periodization.
5. For example, Srinivas (2008) analyses "Architecture as Rhetoric" and "Encrypted Spaces" in the Sathya Sai Baba movement; Smith (1978) critiques idiosyncratic gestures of Ramakrishna and Sathya Sai Baba in his "notes on a minor iconographic tradition."

6. Beckerlegge (2004: 308). Hatcher (1999) discusses this at length in a broader critical context and under the broader heading of "eclecticism."

7. For some of the traditional Indian context around paranormal phenomena, and a good overview of relevant research and methods, see Braud (2008). Perhaps the most famous popular account of guru miracles is Paramahamsa Yogananda's *Autobiography of a Yogi*, on which see Aravamudan (2006: 59–61).

8. Who Speaks for Siddha Yoga? A Book Review of Meditation Revolution (December 31, 1999), http://www.leavingsiddhayoga.net/book_review.htm (accessed on January 13, 2011).

9. Cf. Cowan (1999), who compares American Christian anti-cult groups.

10. White (1974); Williamson (2005: 150). For some of the traditional and modern theological background, see Sen Sharma (1990), Brooks et al. (1997).

11. Babb (1987: 186) suggests something very similar in relation to Sathya Sai Baba.

12. There is "oppositional charisma" at work here, see Waldman and Baum (1992).

13. Hatcher (1999: 166–169) comes at this from another angle when he casts charismatic gurus as "poets" and sees their followers (not necessarily institutionalised) as "literalists," lamenting that "Vivekananda's metaphors have today become 'axiomatic features' in the presentation of Hinduism."

14. For example, Brzezinski (2004) and Peter Heehs (2000: 221) notes that Neo-Hindu guru Sri Aurobindo (1872–1950) sought to avoid "the error of all 'Churches'" with the suggestion that his followers "remain open to 'new outpourings' of the founders' spirit."

15. An exception to this is the Brahma Kumari movement, which Babb (1986: 139) regards as being genuinely feminist (albeit founded by a man).

16. There are a number of studies of Hindu Gurus in American and other western settings, but this fall beyond the scope of this chapter.

17. Howe (2004: 267) contrasts the Sathya Sai Baba organization with a number of largely unstudied in-digenous (tantra-like) movements that arose in Bali around the same time. While language may be a barrier, he notes that some primary source material has been collected, and there is an opportunity in this also for further study.

# References

Ackerman, Susan and Raymond M. Lee. 1988. *Heaven in Transition.* Honolulu: University of Hawaii Press.

Ahuja, M. L. 2006a. *Indian Spiritual Gurus: Nineteenth Century.* New Delhi: Icon Publications.

———. 2006b. *Indian Spiritual Gurus: Twentieth Century.* New Delhi: Icon Publications.

Alter, Joseph S. 1997. "Seminal Truth: A Modern Science of Male Celibacy in North India." *Medical Anthropology Quarterly, New Series* 11(3): 275–298.

Anderson, Carol S. 2004. "The Life of Gauri Ma." In Karen Pechilis (ed.), *The Graceful Guru: Hindu Female Gurus in India and the United States,* 65–84. New York: Oxford University Press.

Aravamudan, S. 2006. *Guru English: South Asian Religion in a Cosmopolitan Language*. Princeton: Princeton University Press.

Babb, Lawrence. 1987. "Sathya Sai Baba's Saintly Play." In Jack Hawley (ed.), *Saints and Virtues*, 168–186. Berkeley; Los Angeles; London; University of California Press.

———. 1986. *Redemptive Encounters: Three Modern Styles in the Hindu Tradition*. L.A.: University of California Press.

Barth, Fredrik. 1990. "The Guru and the Conjurer: Transactions in Knowledge and the Shaping of Culture in Southeast Asia and Melanesia," *Man, New Series* 25(4): 640–653.

Bassuk, Daniel E. 1987. *Incarnation in Hinduism and Christianity: The Myth of the God-Man*. London: Macmillan Press Ltd.

Beckerlegge, G. 2004. "The Hindu Renaissance and Notions of Universal Religion." In John Wolffe (ed.), *Religion in History: Conflict, Conversion and Coexistence*, 129–160. Manchester: Open University; New York: Palgrave.

———. 2001. "Hindu Sacred Images for the Mass Market." In Gwilym Beckerlegge (ed.), *Religion Today: Tradition, Modernity and Change—From Sacred Text to Internet*, 57–116. Burlington, USA: Ashgate; Walton Hall: The Open University.

———. 2000a. *The Ramakrishna Mission: The Making of a Modern Hindu Movement*. Oxford, New York: Oxford University Press.

———. 2000b. "Swami Akhandananda's Sevavrata (Vow of Service) and the Earliest Expressions of Service to Humanity in the Ramakrishna Math and Mission." In Antony Copley (ed.), *Gurus and Their Followers: New Religious Reform Movements in Colonial India*, 59–82. New Delhi: Oxford University Press.

Bevir, Mark. 2000. "Theosophy as a Political Movement." In Antony Copley (ed.), *Gurus and Their Followers: New Religious Reform Movements in Colonial India*, 159–179. New Delhi: Oxford University Press.

Bhattacharyya, Jogendra Nath. 1896. *Hindu Castes and Sects: An Exposition of the Origin of the Hindu Caste System and the Bearing of the Sects Towards each other and Towards other Religious Systems*. Kolkata: Thacker, Spink and Co.

Bharati, A. 1981. *Hindu Views and Ways and the Hindu-Muslim Interface*. New Delhi: Munshiram Manohar Lal.

———. 1970. "The Hindu Renaissance and Its Apologetic Patterns." *Journal of Asian Studies* 29(2): 267–287.

Biernacki, L. 2004. "Shree Maa of Kamakkhya." In Karen Pechilis (ed.), *The Graceful Guru: Hindu Female Gurus in India and the United States*, 179–202. New York: Oxford University Press.

Bryant, Edwin F. and Maria L. Ekstrand (eds). 2004. *The Hare Krishna Movement: The Postcharismatic Fate of a Religious Transplant*. New York: Columbia University Press.

Braud, William G. 2008. "Patañjali Yoga and Siddhis: Their Relevance to Parapsychological Theory and Research." In K. Ramakrishna Rao, Anand C. Paranjpe, and Ajit K. Dalal (eds), *Handbook of Indian Psychology*. New Delhi: Cambridge University Press, Foundation Books.

Brooks, D. R., S. Durgananda, P. E. Muller-Ortega, W. K. Mahony, C. R. Bailly, and S. P. Sabharathnam (eds). 1997. *Meditation Revolution: A History and Theology of the Siddha Yoga Lineage*. South Fallsburg, New York: Agama Press, Muktabodha Indological Research Institute.

Brzezinski, Jan. 2004. "Charismatic Renewal and Institutionalization in the History of Gaudiya Vaishnavism and the Gaudiya Math." In Edwin F. Bryant and Maria L. Ekstrand (eds), *The Hare Krishna Movement: The Postcharismatic Fate of a Religious Transplant*, 73–96. New York: Columbia University Press.

Cabezón, José Ignacio. 2006. "The Discipline and Its Other: The Dialectic of Alterity in the Study of Religion." *Journal of the American Academy of Religion* 74: (1) 21–38.

Choudhary, K. 1981. Modern Indian Mysticism. New Delhi: Motilal Banarsidass.

Collins, Irvin H. 2004. "The 'Routinization of Charisma' and the Charismatic: The Confrontation between ISKCON and Narayana Maharaja." In Edwin F. Bryant and Maria L. Ekstrand (eds), *The Hare Krishna Movement: The Postcharismatic Fate of a Religious Transplant*, 214–237. New York: Columbia University Press.

Copley, Antony (ed.). 2000. *Gurus and Their Followers: New Religious Reform Movements in Colonial India*. New Delhi: Oxford University Press.

Cornille, C. 2004. "Mother Meera, Avatar." In Karen Pechilis (ed.), *The Graceful Guru: Hindu Female Gurus in India and the United States*, 129–47. New York: Oxford University Press.

Cowan, Douglas. 1999. Bearing false witness: propaganda, reality-maintenance, and Christian anticult apologetics. PhD Thesis. Calgary: University of Calgary.

De Tollenaere, Herman. 2004. "The Theosophical Society in the Dutch East Indies." In Martin Ramstedt (ed.), *Hinduism in modern Indonesia: A Minority Religion*, 35–44. London: RoutledgeCurzon.

Erndl, K. M. (2004). "Afterword." In Karen Pechilis (ed.), *The Graceful Guru: Hindu Female Gurus in India and the United States*, 245–249. New York: Oxford University Press.

Forsthoefel, Thomas and Cynthia Humes (eds). 2005. *Gurus in America*. Albany: State University of New York Press.

Fuller, C. J. 1992. *The Camphor Flame: Popular Hinduism and Society in India*. Princeton: Princeton University Press.

Godwin, Joscelyn. 1994. *The Theosophical Enlightenment*. Albany: State University of New York Press.

Gold, Daniel. 2005. "Epilogue: Elevated Gurus, Concrete Traditions and the Problems of Western Devotees." In T. Forsthoefel and C. Humes (eds), *Gurus in America*, 219–226. Albany: State University of New York Press.

———. 1987. *The Lord as Guru: Hindi Saints in North Indian Tradition*. New York: Oxford University Press.

Gonda, Jan. 1969. *Selected Studies: History of Ancient Indian Religion, Vol. 4*. Leiden: E.J.Brill, 1975.

Halbfass, Wilhelm. 1988. *India and Europe: An Essay in Understanding*. Albany: State University of New York Press.

Hallstrom, L. L. 1999. *Mother of Bliss: Anandamayi Ma (1896–1982)*. New York: Oxford University Press.

———. 2004. "Anandamayi Ma, the Bliss-filled Divine Mother." In Karen Pechilis (ed.), *The Graceful Guru: Hindu Female Gurus in India and the United States*, 85–118. New York: Oxford University Press.

Haraldsson, Erlendur. 1997. *Modern Miracles: An Investigative Report on Psychic Phenomena Associated with Sri Sathya Sai Baba*. Mamaroneck, NY: Hastings House.

Hatcher, Brian A. 1999. *Eclecticism and Modern Hindu Discourse*. New York; Hong Kong: Oxford University Press.

Hawley, John Stratton. 2004. "The Damage of Separation: Krishna's Loves and Kali's Child." *Journal of the American Academy of Religion* 72(2), 369–393.

Heehs, Peter. 2000. "The Error of All 'Churches': Religion and Spirituality in Communities Founded or 'Inspired' by Sri Aurobindo." In Antony Copley (ed.), *Gurus and Their Followers: New Religious Reform Movements in Colonial India*, 209–224. New Delhi: Oxford University Press.

Howe, Leo. 2004. "Hinduism, Identity and Social Conflict: The Sai Baba movement in Bali." In Martin Ramstedt (ed.), *Hinduism in Modern Indonesia: A Minority Religion*, 264–280. London: RoutledgeCurzon.

Johnson, K. Paul. 1994. *The Masters Revealed: Madam Blavatsky and the Myth of the Great White Lodge*. Albany: State University of New York Press.

Jones, K. W. 1989. *Socio-religious Reform Movements in British India*. Cambridge, New York: Cambridge University Press.

Kent, Alexandra, 2005. *Divinity and Diversity: A Hindu Revitalization Movement in Malaysia*. Copenhagen: NIAS Press.

Ketola, Kimmo, 2008. *Founder of the Hare Krishnas as Seen by Devotees: A Cognitive Study of Religious Charisma*. Leiden: Brill.

Keyes, Charles F. 1982. "Charisma: From Social Life to Sacred Biography." In Michael A. Williams (ed.), *Charisma and Sacred Biography*, 1–22. American Academy of Religion.

King, Richard. 1999. *Orientalism and Religion: Postcolonial Theory, India and "The Mystic East."* London: Routledge.

Kripal, Jeffrey J. 1995. *Kālī's Child: The Mystical and the Erotic in the Life and Teachings of Ramakrishna*. Chicago: University of Chicago Press.

Lorenz, E. 2004. "The Guru, Mayavadins and Women: Tracing the Origins of Selected Polemical Statements in the Work of AC Bhaktivedanta Swami." In Edwin F. Bryant and Maria L. Ekstrand (eds), *The Hare Krishna Movement: The Postcharismatic Fate of a Religious Transplant*, 214–237. New York: Columbia University Press.

Mearns, David. 1995. *Shiva's Other Children: Religion and Social Identity Amongst Overseas Indians*. New Delhi: SAGE Publications.

McDaniel, June. 1989. *The Madness of the Saints: Ecstatic Religion in Bengal*. Chicago: The University of Chicago Press.

McKean, Lise. 1996. *Divine Enterprise: Gurus and the Hindu Nationalist Movement*. Chicago: The University of Chicago Press.

Mlecko, Joel D. 1982. "The Guru in Hindu Tradition." *Numen* 29(1): 33–61.

Müller, Friedrich Max. 1898. *Râmakrishna: His Life and Sayings*. London: Longmans, Green and Co.

Olivelle, Patrick. 1986. "Review of 'Inklusivismus: Eine indische Denkform'" edited by Gerhard Oberhammer. *Journal of the American Oriental Society* 106(4): 867–868.

Palmer, Norris. 2005. "Baba's World: A Global Guru and His Movement." In T. Forsthoefel and C. Humes (eds), *Gurus in America*, 97–122. Albany: State University of New York Press.

Pechilis, K. 2004. *The Graceful Guru: Hindu female gurus in India and the United States*. New York: Oxford University Press.

Raj, S. J. 2004. "Ammachi, the Mother of Compassion." In Karen Pechilis (ed.), *The Graceful Guru: Hindu Female Gurus in India and the United States*, 203–218. New York: Oxford University Press.

Ramstedt, M. ed. 2004. *Hinduism in Modern Indonesia: A Minority Religion*. London: RoutledgeCurzon.

———. 2000. "Relations between Hindus in Modern Indonesia and India." *IIAS Newsletter* 23: 8–9.

Ralston, Helen. 1989. "The Construction of Authority in the Christian Ashram Movement." *Archives des Sciences Sociales des Religions* 67(1): 53–75.

Riesebrodt, M. 1999. "Charisma in Max Weber's Sociology of Religion." *Religion* 29(1): 1–14.

Rigopoulos, A. 2005. "The Guru-Gītā or 'Song of the Master' as Incorporated in the Guru-caritra of Sarasvatī Gangadhar: Observations on its Teaching and the Guru Institute." In Knut A. Jacobsen (ed.), *Theory and Practice of Yoga: Essays in Honour of Gerald James Larson*, 237–292. Leiden: Brill.

Rochford, E. Burke Jr. 2004. "Airports, Conflict, and Change in the Hare Krishna Movement." In Edwin F. Bryant and Maria L. Ekstrand (eds), *The Hare Krishna Movement: The Postcharismatic Fate of a Religious Transplant*, 273–290. New York: Columbia University Press.

Rudert, A. 2010. "Research on Contemporary Indian Gurus; What's New about New Age Gurus?" *Religion Compass* 4(10): 629–642.

Rüstau, Hiltrud. 2000. "The Ramakrishna Mission: Its Female Aspect." In Antony Copley (ed.), Gurus *and Their Followers: New Religious Reform Movements in Colonial India*, 83–106. New Delhi: Oxford University Press.

Saha, Shandip. 2007. "Hinduism, Gurus, and Globalization." In Peter Beyer and Lori Beaman (eds), *Religion, Globalization and Culture*, 485–502. Leiden; Boston: Brill.

Sarkar, Sumit. 1997. *Writing Social History*. Oxford; Delhi: Oxford University Press.

Sen Sharma, Debabrata, 1990. *The Philosophy of Sādhanā with Special Rreference to the Trika Philosophy of Kashmir*. Albany: State University of New York Press.

Sharma, Arvind. 1993. "Rajneesh and the Guru Tradition in India." In Susan J. Palmer and Arvind Sharma (eds), *The Rajneesh Papers*. New Delhi: Motilal Banarsidass.

Singer, Milton. 1972. *When a Great Tradition Modernizes*. New York: Praeger Publishers.

Smith, David. 2003. *Hinduism and Modernity*. Oxford: Blackwell Publishers.

Smith, H. Daniel. 1978. "Hindu 'desika'-figures: Some Notes on a Minor Iconographic Tradition." *Religion* 8(1): 40–67.

Somvir, Yadav. 2004. "Cultural and Religious Interaction between Modern India and Indonesia." In Martin Ramstedt (ed.), *Hinduism in Modern Indonesia: A Minority Religion*, 255–263. London: RoutledgeCurzon.

Spurr, Michael James. 2007. Sathya Sai Baba as Avatar: "His Story" and the History of an Idea. PhD Thesis. Christchurch: University of Canterbury.

Srinivasa Iyengar, K. R. 1978. *On the Mother: The Chronicle of a Manifestation and Ministry*. Pondicherry: Sri Aurobindo International Centre of Education.

Srinivas, Smriti. 2008. *In the Presence of Sai Baba: Body, City, and Memory in a Global Religious Movement*. Leiden: Brill.

Storr, A. 1996. *Feet of Clay: A Study of Gurus*. London: HarperCollins.

Urban, Hugh B. 2003a. "Avatar for Our Age: Sathya Sai Baba and the Cultural Contradictions of Late Capitalism." *Religion* 33(1): 73–93.

———. 2003b. *Tantra: Sex, Secrecy, Politics, and Power in the Study of Religion*. Berkeley: University of California Press.

———. 1998. "Review of Kālī's Child," by Jeffrey J. Kripal. *Journal of Religion* 78(2): 318–320.

Vanita, R. and S. Kidwai (eds). 2000. *Same-sex Love in India*. New York: St. Martin's Press.

von Stietencron, Heinrich. 2001. "Charisma and Canon: The Dynamics of Legitmization and Innovation in Indian Religions." In Vasudha Dalmia, Angelika Malinar, and Martin Christof (eds), *Charisma and Canon*, 14–40. New Delhi: Oxford University Press.

Waldman, M. and R. Baum. 1992. "Innovation as renovation: The 'prophet' as an agent of change." In Michael A. Williams, Collett Cox, Martin S. Jaffee (eds), *Innovation in Religious Traditions: Essays in the Interpretation of Religious Change*, 241–284. Berlin; New York: Mouton de Gruyter.

Warren, Marianne Elizabeth. 1999. *Unravelling the Enigma: Shirdi Sai Baba in the Light of Sufism*. New Delhi: Sterling.

Warrier, M. 2005. *Hindu Selves in a Modern World: Guru Faith in the Mata Amritanandamayi Mission*. London, New York: RoutledgeCurzon.

———. 2003. "Processes of Secularization in Contemporary India: Guru Faith in the Mata Amritanandamayi Mission." *Modern Asian Studies* 37(1): 213–253.

White, C. 1974. "Swāmi Muktānanda and the Enlightenment Through Śakti-pāt." *History of Religions*, 13(4): 306–322.

———. 1972. "The Sai Baba Movement: Approaches to the Study of Indian Saints," *Journal of Asian Studies* 31(4): 863–78.

White, D. G. 1984. "Why Gurus Are Heavy." *Numen*, 31(1): 40–73.

Williamson, Lola. 2005. "The Perfectibility of Perfection: Siddha Yoga as a Global Movement." In T. Forsthoefel and C. Humes (eds), *Gurus in America*, 147–168. Albany: State University of New York Press.

Weber, Max. 1922. *Economy and Society: An Outline of Interpretive Sociology, Vol. I.*, edited by Guenther Roth and Claus Wittich. Berkeley: University of California Press, 1978.

Weber, Max. 1916. *The Religion of India: The Sociology of Hinduism and Buddhism*. Translated and edited by Hans H. Gerth and Don Martindale. New York: The Free Press, 1967.

# Suggestions for Further Reading

Babb, Lawrence. 1986. *Redemptive Encounters: Three Modern Styles in the Hindu Tradition*. L.A.: University of California Press. (A comparative study of the Radhasoami, Brahma Kumari, and Sathya Sai Baba movements, drawing on anthropological fieldwork and theories of social psychology.)

Beckerlegge, G. 2000a. *The Ramakrishna Mission: The Making of a Modern Hindu Movement*. Oxford, New York: Oxford University Press. (An analysis of the early endeavors of this major modern guru movement.)

Forsthoefel, Thomas and Humes, Cynthia (eds). 2005. *Gurus in America.* Albany: State University of New York Press. (A collection of essays on a number of modern gurus, most of whom also have followings in Asia.)

Hallstrom, L. L. 1999. *Mother of Bliss: Anandamayi Ma (1896–1982).* New York: Oxford University Press. (This study of an important modern guru includes a good presentation of traditional understandings of the role of the guru.)

Haraldsson, Erlendur. 1997. *Modern Miracles: An Investigative Report on Psychic Phenomena Associated with Sri Sathya Sai Baba.* Mamaroneck, NY: Hastings House. (Based on more than a decade of fieldwork, this is a fascinating analysis of biographical, psychological, and parapsychological issues surrounding India's most influential modern guru.)

Hatcher, Brian A. 1999. *Eclecticism and modern Hindu discourse.* New York, Hong Kong: Oxford University Press. (Most modern gurus are eclectic; this is essential background reading for understanding their discourse.)

Heehs, Peter. 2008. *The Lives of Sri Aurobindo.* New York: Columbia University Press. (The definitive biography of this important modern guru.)

Jones, K. W. 1989. *Socio-religious Reform Movements in British India.* Cambridge, New York: Cambridge University Press. (A thorough descriptive history.)

Kent, Alexandra. 2005. *Divinity and Diversity: A Hindu Revitalization Movement in Malaysia.* Copenhagen: NIAS Press. (A study of issues faced by the Sathya Sai Baba movement in Malaysia.)

Ketola, Kimmo. 2008. *Founder of the Hare Krishnas as Seen by Devotees: A Cognitive Study of Religious Charisma.* Leiden: Brill. (Provides insights on religious leadership from the field of cognitive science. Includes an analysis of previous interpretations of charisma.)

Kripal, J. 1995. *Kālī's Child: The Mystical and the Erotic in the Life and Teachings of Ramakrishna.* Chicago: University of Chicago Press. (An important and controversial work to be read in conjunction with subsequent debate and its own second edition [1998].)

Pechilis, K. 2004. *The Graceful Guru: Hindu Female Gurus in India and the United States.* New York: Oxford University Press. (A collection of essays on the most prominent contemporary female gurus. Includes a general introduction and epilogue.)

Ramstedt, M. (ed.). 2004. *Hinduism in Modern Indonesia: A Minority Religion.* London: RoutledgeCurzon. (Includes a number of essays on Hindu guru movements in Indonesia.)

Srinivas, Smriti. 2008. *In the Presence of Sai Baba: Body, City, and Memory in a Global Religious Movement.* Leiden: Brill. (A diverse and interesting sociological study of the Sai Baba movement in Bangalore, Atlanta and Nairobi.)

Warren, Marianne Elizabeth, 1999. *Unravelling the Enigma: Shirdi Sai Baba in the Light of Sufism.* New Delhi: Sterling. (Insights into the life and teachings of an influential modern "Hindu" guru with a strong Muslim background.)

Warrier, M. 2005. *Hindu Selves in a Modern World: Guru Faith in the Mata Amritanandamayi Mission.* London, New York: RoutledgeCurzon. (A fieldwork-based analysis of the large transnational following of one of the most high-profile modern gurus.)

# Chapter 8

## Folk Hinduism: The Middle Ground?[*]

### Aditya Malik

While the study of Hinduism as a discipline within the field of religious studies began with the translation and interpretation of classical texts written in Sanskrit,[1] in recent years, there has been a turn toward a study of Hinduism in its modern manifestations. These latter scholarly interests are marked by a desire to understand Hinduism in its regional expressions, finding a focus on vernacular languages and literatures as well as on the alterations and new configurations within Hindu thought and practice that arise in the encounter with the West during the long period of colonization primarily by the British and other European imperial powers. These new or "modern" forms include Hindu reform movements or "neo-Hinduisms" of the 19th century, more recently in the 20th and 21st centuries, the rise of Hindu fundamentalism, or as the eminent historian Romila Thapar terms it "syndicated Hinduism" (Thapar, 1997: 54–81). These academic concentrations in Hinduism rooted, on the one hand, in the philological analysis of texts in the classical languages of India

---

[*] There is a degree of overlap in the use of "folk" and "popular" in the scholarly literature on Indian civilization and Hinduism. Clearly, while "popular" religion may refer to urban, even modern forms of religious narrative and practice and "folk" would seem to refer to "traditional," rural expressions of religion, the boundaries between the two categories are blurred at least in one direction. Thus, for example, "folk" can also refer to social classes, narrative forms, and ritual performance that occupy both urban and rural spaces in the South Asian context. It is because of the defining aspect of "folk" as a *nonelite* cultural and social form that spans both rural and urban contexts, as well as because of its accompanying ideas and practices that have a deeper regional and historical spread, that the term "folk" is being used in preference to the term "popular" in this chapter. See also, section entitled "Folk Hinduism: Contents and Communities."

and, on the other hand, in regional and "modern" manifestations are, to an extent, well entrenched in the way in which institutions of higher education teach Hinduism. Thus, for example, German universities, which have had a sustained interest in Indian culture and history since the early 19th century,[2] have departments that provide curricula and research opportunities in either "Classical Indology" or "Modern Indology," which in a British or North American context would translate into Classical and Modern Indian or South Asian Studies. This division is also reflected, for example, in the structure of the Handbook, whose first two sections broadly deal with ancient and modern manifestations of Hinduism. The present third section with its focus on "contemporary," "popular," or "folk" Hinduism steps outside of the usual framework in that it acknowledges that there is a vast variety of primarily oral narrative traditions and ritual practices that are not covered by the neat classification of Hinduism into classical or modern forms.

## Defining Folk Hinduism

The definition of what exactly constitutes contemporary and folk Hinduism is, however, a somewhat difficult and complex task. As Martin Fuchs, a sociologist and scholar of Indian Religions at the Max-Weber-Kolleg at the University of Erfuhrt in Germany, points out:

> [F]olk religion occupies an eccentric status. As a latecomer in the conceptual fold of Indian religious studies it forms a kind of residual, supplementary category. It is a category of a different kind than, for example, renunciation (*samnyasa*), devotion (*bhakti*) or even Brahmanism (priesthood), and it is still to find a secure place in the broader context of religious studies: it has to be located within a framework which it shares with those other concepts, within a common frame of reference. (Malik, 1997: 18)

Clearly, "folk" religion is a *conceptual* category, just as Hinduism itself is in part academic and in part social construction. As David Shulman, a scholar of southern Indian history, literature, and languages, writes:

> It is certainly true that "Hinduism" is an analytical construct, more
> an "etic" than an "emic" category. The very term is foreign and can be
> approximated in Indian languages by various modern neologisms …
> None of this need bother us unduly. The same could be said for many
> similar concepts … The more important questions relate to the proper
> content of the construct … it is not a "thing" out there … but genera-
> tions of scholars have shared an intuition of cultural unity. (1989: 7)

Thus, folk Hinduism, like its parent concept, is also an analytical
construct, emerging out of a particular appreciation that a large
area of religious practice and social life is excluded when we restrict
ourselves to the study of Hinduism through the categories of the
"classical" and "modern."

But where does folk Hinduism lie within the established conceptual
framework of the classical and modern? We could argue that folk
Hinduism, by default, is that aspect of Hinduism which is neither
classical nor modern. But saying this does not leave us with a concrete
understanding of the material contents, so to speak, of folk Hinduism
nor does it tell us anything about the interrelationships between
classical, modern, and folk Hinduism. Robert Redfield (1955), Milton
Singer (1972), and McKim Marriott (1955) from the University of
Chicago, who produced highly influential theoretical frameworks
for understanding Indian Civilization between the 1950s and 1970s,
used an important distinction between "Great and Little Traditions"
to understand complex cultural flows in South Asia. According to
this perspective, South Asian culture, society, and history could be
explained through movements between "Great Traditions" that had
certain linguistic, textual, and social signifiers like Sanskrit, written
texts, and compendiums such as the *Puranas*, *Dharmashastras*,
*Shrauta-Sutras*, and *Vedas*, and accompanying "pan-Indian" deities
such as Brahma, Vishnu, Shiva, Durga, or Lakshmi, and rituals
performed by high-caste Brahmans. "Little Traditions", on the
contrary, were marked by a different set of linguistic, textual, and
social signifiers: regional or vernacular languages and dialects, oral
narratives embedded in a local or regional landscape (rather than in a
distant "imaginary" divine or mythological landscape) that were told
and listened to by local singers and audiences, deities whose origins
and life stories were closely linked to smaller, local, or regional
communities, their language, and sense of social history, and a set of

rituals based again on local chronologies, conducted by priests and ritual mediators who did not belong to the high caste of Brahmans, but often to lower, nonelite communities, and even women. Redfield, Singer, and Marriott were prominent in creating the modern study of Indian civilization not only by identifying "Great and Little Traditions," but by offering a penetrating analysis of the dynamic and continuous linguistic, narrative, religious, ritual and social flows and exchanges between "Great" and "Little" traditions in an ever-changing, shifting, and adaptive, rather than bounded and fixed, landscape of cultural meaning, as pointed out by Kapila Vatsyayan.[3]

One crucial distinction between Great and Little Traditions, and indeed in our understanding of "classical" and "folk" traditions within Hinduism, is between written texts and oral narratives. Here again, the distinction is not absolute, as Indian civilization, while having an extraordinarily rich—perhaps even overwhelming in contrast to written texts—variety of oral narratives in different genres,[4] never was an exclusively oral culture: Writing and orality existed side by side, each exhibiting an awareness of the other, while producing a variety of vectors of interchange.[5] Yet, in pursuing an understanding of "Little Traditions" or what we are calling "folk" Hinduism, it is critically important to understand not only the intricate content of oral narratives but also their form, structure, delivery in performance and ritual, as well as who is telling them, for whom, and why they are being told. Thus, oral narratives, perhaps more so than written texts in Sanskrit, contribute intimately to the undulating creation and re-creation of local and regional, caste and community-based social, geographical, and historical identities. Any deep appreciation of folk Hinduism must, therefore, take into account the widespread existence through both time and region of oral narratives, without which neither the creation nor the dispersion, transmission, and transformation of ideas and practices within the broad context of Hinduism can be grasped.

Common sense would indicate that folk Hinduism is a contemporary phenomenon, signifying the existence of ideas and practices in what is sometimes called the "ethnographic present." But, then modern and even certain classical forms of Hinduism also occupy the present time. If the difference between these forms is not to be found in distinct temporalities, then where does the real difference lie? Is there a real difference? Or are we only creating divisions within something that has inner coherence for the sake of conceptual and academic clarity? As Kapila Vatsyayan, a scholar of Indian classical and folk dance, critically states:

> We have thus to re-examine both the Indian tradition as also critical writing in the English language which has constantly categorized the Indian tradition into the textual and the oral, the highly Brahmanized, Sanskritized and the vernacular, the sophisticated, the literate and the illiterate, and finally the classical and the folk. Our analysis will have shown that at no point within the tradition, were these seemingly binary categories really considered opposites. They were certainly differentiated categories but placed either into a continuum or, as I have said earlier, placed merely as segments of a circle rather than a line. (1994: 47)

Vatsyayan discusses the important Indian categories of *marga* and *desi* that would seem to translate into the classical and the folk. Marga, she points out, derives from the Sanskrit root *mrg* which means "to chase or hunt, especially by tracking." Marga, thus, denotes a *highway* along which, according to the earliest Hindu text, the *Rigveda*, one tracks the scent of hidden light, "hunting down" divinity in other words. Marga then is the highway or path that leads to the hidden light that elicits liberation. Desi, on the contrary, is derived from *dis* meaning "region," "quarter," or "local." Furthermore, terms derived from desi such as *desa-vyavahara, desacara*, and *desya* denote "local custom," "way of world," and "native," respectively. In sociological terms, marga can, in the view of Indian theoreticians, be equated with *nagara* or town/city and desi with *gram* or village (ibid.: 32–35). However, Vatsyayan, following the highly influential work of the art historian Ananda Coomaraswamy, states that there is a clear difference between the categories of marga and desi, on the one hand, and classical and folk, on the other:

> Coomaraswamy … clearly sees the logic of the *marga* as the dug path, a highway which is constantly on the move but in a particular direction with a specific purpose. It may perhaps be more appropriate to see what Coomaraswamy calls *desi* or a "by-way" … as the circumscribing or limiting of eternal universal paths into the mannerisms and styles of a region or a given time situation. Indeed, from this point of view the two terms appear to connote not levels of society but only universalization and specificity. This is certainly not what the terms

"classical" and "folk" in common parlance denote … The cognisance of the possibility of the *margi* becoming the *desi* at any given moment is inherent in the very nature of their relationship. (ibid.: 42)

Thus, according to the view outlined by Vatsyayan and Coomaraswamy, the marga and desi—loosely translated as classical and folk—have the capacity to swap around, replace each other, and to be related through equivalence rather than difference. There is no firm, impermeable boundary between classical and folk. To this list of "endocentric" categories can be added the well-known term dharma and its counterpart *desadharma* to, respectively, indicate universal or local "religion" and "duty"; the classification of deities and their rituals as being either *saumya* ("peaceful," "auspicious," "pleasant") or *ugra* ("strong," "fierce," "powerful"); and also *Sanskrit* to denote "refined," "perfected," "adorned," "ornamented," and *Prakrit* to mean "unrefined,' "vulgar," "provincial," "vernacular " (Sontheimer, 1997: 306).

## Context Sensitivity and Reflexivity

Following in the same vein as Vatsyayan, Ramanujan (1989, 1990), the late poet and linguist who taught at the University of Chicago, states that the interrelationships within different elements of Indian culture, in general, and between classical and folk streams, in particular, are organized around (a) context sensitivity and (b) reflexivity. Ramanujan borrows the idea of "context sensitive" and its contrasting notion of "context free" from the rules of grammar and applies it to explain cultural or civilizational attitudes found in India and in the West, and also in modernity as it takes hold in non-Western cultures. The idea of "context sensitivity" is particularly evident in the case of dharma in the sense of law, justice, or duty. The Dharmasastras or law treatises emphasize that the practice of justice, particularly in its punitive sense and in its sense as duty, is contextual, depending, for example, on social status, material and historical circumstance, and so on. This can be contrasted, for example, against the western (and modern) notion of the categorical imperative outlined in the highly significant work of the German philosopher Immanuel Kant (1724–1804) who states that there are intrinsically valid, and thus "context-free," moral actions based on unconditional obligations or duties. A similar view is echoed more recently in the "transcendental" view of justice developed by John Rawls (1921–2002), the Harvard philosopher of moral and political philosophy, who states that justice and its enactment are universal and independent of circumstance. However, according to Ramanujan:

> The main tradition of Judeo-Christian ethics is based on such a premise of universalisation—Manu will not understand such a premise. To be moral, for Manu, is to particularize ... In India the context-sensitive kind of rule is the preferred formulation ... In an illuminating discussion of the context-sensitive nature of dharma in its details, Baudhayana enumerates aberrant practices peculiar to the Brahmins of the north and those of the south. (1990: 47)

Thus, not only is the application of the idea dharma—roughly rendered as justice, duty, and morality—by definition in texts such as the Dharmasastras, "context sensitive," the meanings of so-called "endocentric" categories outlined above alter depending on the social, historical, and religious context we view them from. For example, a "low" or folk deity may be described by high-caste observers as being "ugra," that is, a deity which is "ferocious," "ogre like," "appalling," or "shocking." But from a low-caste devotee's perspective, the same deity, though may also be described as "ugra," would be considered "mighty," "noble," "high," and "powerful" (Sontheimer, 1997: 306).

According to Ramanujan, the second principle, reflexivity takes several forms: "awareness of self and other, mirroring, distorted mirroring, parody, family resemblances and rebels, dialectic, antistructure, utopias and dystopias, the many ironies connected with these responses, and so on" (Ramanujan, 1989: 189). From these two organizational principles of "context sensitivity" and "reflexivity," there constantly emerge new cultural, ritual, literary, and linguistic configurations:

> What we call Brahminism, Bhakti traditions, Buddhism, Jainism, Tantra, tribal traditions and folklore, and lastly, modernity itself, are the most prominent of these systems. They are responses to previous and surrounding traditions; they invert, subvert, and convert their neighbors. Furthermore, each of these terms, like what we call India itself, is "a verbal tent with three-ring circuses" going on inside them. Further dialogic divisions are continuously in progress. They look like single entities, like neat little tents, only from a distance. (ibid.)

Ramanujan critically points out that both scholars and nonscholars tend to reproduce the viewpoint of a single tradition, social community, literary stream that then results in a biased, monolithic conception of a cultural and religious tradition that is "indissolubly plural" even while it is conflicting and contested:

> Stereotypes, foreign views, and native self-images on the part of some groups all tend to regard one part (say, the Brahminical texts or folklore) as the original, and the rest as variations, derivatives, aberrations, so we tend to get monolithic conceptions ... Reflexivities are crucial to the understanding of both the order and diversity, the openness and the closures, of this civilization. One may sometimes feel that "mirror on mirror mirrored is all the show." (Ramanujan, 1989: 190f)

It should be apparent by now that not only is folk Hinduism a complex, if not problematic, category that we should resist trying to essentialize, but that the moot question is how the different expressions of Hinduism, whether folk, classical, or modern, interact with each other, creating an ongoing series of new reflexive configurations, although modernity and the processes of modernization create a rupture in the cultural flows of the subcontinent by upholding the "context free" over the "context sensitive," and compartmentalizing off interconnected realms: "Print replaced palm-leaf manuscripts, making possible an open and egalitarian access to knowledge irrespective of caste. The Indian constitution made the contexts of birth, region, sex and creed irrelevant, overthrowing Manu" (Ramanujan, 1990: 55). Similarly, even while such "context-free" trends may dominate today, it is important to keep in mind that there is no "privileged" or singular view from which to judge and define what Hinduism is, even though the perspectives of both scholars as well as members of diverse Hindu communities may seek to appropriate the meaning and scope of the religion, thereby producing skewed, monolithic conceptions.

## Folk Hinduism: Contents and Communities

Christopher J. Fuller, an anthropologist based at the prestigious London School of Economics, states that: "By 'popular Hinduism,'

I conventionally refer to the beliefs and practices that constitute the living, 'practical' religion of ordinary Hindus" (Fuller, 1992: 5). Again this brief definition involves categories that require further explanation. What is "practical" religion? Who are "ordinary" Hindus? "Practical" religion suggests a form of religion that is rooted in ritual practices that themselves are directed toward dealing with "practical" matters, that is, matters relating to the everyday concerns that people have such as health and well-being, material prosperity and success, the resolution of injustices, and so on. It also implies a form of religion that is not particularly concerned with concepts and ideas. In other words, the primary concern is with traditional practices rather than with being self-reflexive as are other, more theological elements of a religion. But the view that folk religion is in some way "unconscious" or "unreflexive" may itself mirror a bias that both scholars and "higher" elements of a religion carry toward "lower" or "folk" religion. The term "ordinary" Hindus can again mean different things. In simple terms, "ordinary" describes those Hindus who do not belong to an elite social group. "Ordinary" Hindus may be situated in rural or urban communities. Middle class Hindus living in sprawling urban centers by virtue of their social and financial status can also be classified as being "ordinary." But since they live in modern cities, are their religious practices to be considered "modern," "popular" (or "folk"), or perhaps both? In the modern Indian context, we must distinguish between the term "ordinary" as signifying a social *class* in the urban situation versus *caste* in both an urban and rural situation. Thus, while the term ordinary Hindus can mean middle or lower class members of urban communities, it can also in no insignificant terms mean members of low-caste communities that occupy a lesser status within the hierarchy of various *jatis* which, in a literal sense, means "species." Thus jati, while commonly translated as "caste," is primarily a Hindu institution in its origin, non-Hindus such as Muslims, Christians, and Sikhs are not only included but may also differentiate between various sub-groups within their communities based on the idea of sub-castes or jatis (Fuller, 1992: 13f). In theory, *jati* represents a system of social and cosmological classification that is universally encompassing. When we talk about popular or folk Hinduism as stemming from the practices of ordinary Hindus, we mean low-caste Hindus including communities that identify themselves as *dalit*, pastoral groups, farming, fishing and hunting communities, and even Muslims, Sikhs, and Christians that feature in the histories, narratives, and ritual practices of Hindu castes.

Fuller continues to point out: "Popular Hinduism can be distinguished from 'textual Hinduism,' the 'philosophical' religion set out and elaborated in the sacred texts that are the principle subject matter for Indologists, Sanskritists, historians of religions and other textual scholars" (1992). In a more emphatic tone, Fuller states:

> Obviously, I take it for granted that popular Hinduism is an authentic religion, equal in standing to any other, and that it would be sheer prejudice to dismiss it as superstition. In particular, the view that popular Hinduism is degenerate textual Hinduism ... is completely indefensible in the light of the ethnographic evidence. (ibid.: 6)

Although, as Fuller points out, the ethnographic reality clearly shows the existence of "popular" or "folk" Hinduism, the conceptual and material contents of this category remain tenuous. The late historian of Indian religions from Heidelberg, Gunther-Dietz Sontheimer, links folk Hinduism to four other "components" that, according to him, constitute Hinduism, namely, the teaching of Brahmans, bhakti or devotion, asceticism and renunciation, and tribal religion (Sontheimer, 1997). For each of these four components, he supplies descriptive criteria while positing the interconnectedness, both historically and in contemporary religious practice, of the components "as presenting a continuum and as interacting among themselves in a fluctuating process over thousand of years" (ibid.: 305). As in the case of the other four components, Sontheimer provides an outline of the elements of folk Hinduism. He emphasizes the fact that "a crucial ingredient in folk religion is the immediate presence and access to a god or a goddess in the form of a *murti* ... The god exists 'here and now', is earthbound, and does not live in some puranic *svarga*."[6]

The immediate presence of a folk deity is also noted in the observations of classical texts such as the *Purvamimamsasutras* that "define" a deity (*devata*) as possessing corporality (*vigrahatva devata*), consuming food offerings (*devata bhunkte*), being pleased by offerings (*prasadati devata*), rewarding the devotee (*prita sati phalam prayachati*), and being an owner of property (*arthapati devata*). The deity in the form of a murti seems "as it were a living personality and is treated as a living person" (ibid.).

Sontheimer points out that apart from the observations made on the nature of folk deities from the perspective of classical Sanskrit texts, there are other terms in regional languages that indicate a more extensive "checklist" of qualities. These terms "form an unwritten inventory of folk cults. They point to a pervasive, coherent and conservative system of folk religion which is spread all over South Asia and which can never be expected to have been reproduced in its original form in Brahmanical texts" (Sontheimer, 1997: 316). Among these terms are those that refer to the deity "possessing" the body of a devotee or medium, the participation of the deity in ritual performance or "play," and in ritual processions, and also terms that refer to a deity that is "alive, attentive, heedful and responsive." The deity responds to the material concerns or wishes of his or her devotees by way of granting children, cattle, and being instrumental in healing. Moreover, the deity is "attentive" by also responding to issues of jurisprudence facing his or her devotees by deciding on legal cases (Malik, 2010a; Sontheimer, 1997).[7]

## Folk Deities and Their Cults

An understanding of folk Hinduism can, as the discussion above shows, be successfully approached from the perspective of a folk deity involving an appreciation of several elements: (a) the communities who worship the deity, (b) the rituals performed for the deity, (c) the written and oral narratives told about the deity, and (d) the kinds of concerns or goals that are addressed and resolved by the deity. To this can be added the analysis of the connections that folk deities and their cults manifest toward both classical and modern forms of narrative, ritual, theology, politics, social justice, and governance. Thus, for example, a folk deity may, from the perspective his or her devotees, be a local or regional expression of a "classical" god or goddess such as Shiva, Vishnu, or Devi. The localization of the deity is invariably explained through orally transmitted narratives in a regional or local language told by priests or ritual specialists belonging to non-Brahmanical castes in specific ritual contexts.

Similarly, a folk deity may resemble the figure of a traditional Hindu king, presiding over a kingdom comprising of both a physical territory marked off by a region and a social territory marked off by a community of devotees usually consisting of several caste groups. The deity's relationship to his or her devotees is, like that of a king, defined horizontally as one between ruler and subjects, with the ruler providing protection and physical and mental well-being to his or her subjects, with the subjects in turn offering physical and emotional surrender in the form of devotion and loyalty and also in material offerings and gifts of money, grains, cooked and raw food, domestic animals for sacrifice, and so on. As mentioned earlier, the deity may also reside over matters of justice, the resolution of which is sought through ritual and other means providing an alternative route to the avenues of social and criminal justice supplied by secular courts of law that exist as part of the modern institutional framework of democracy in India. The multiple dimensions of folk deities and their cults are evident in many examples all over India, such as the worship of Khandoba in Maharashtra (Sontheimer, 1997), Draupadi and the Pandavas in Tamil Nadu and in Garhwal (Hiltebeitel, 1989; Sax, 2002), Pabuji and Devnarayan in Rajasthan (Malik, 2005; Smith, 1991), and Goludev in Uttarakhand (Malik, 2010a, 2010b; Sax, 2009). Thus, for example, Khandoba is a local manifestation or *avatar* of Shiva, Devnarayan of Vishnu, and Goludev of Bhairava, the terrifying, raging form of Shiva. Pabuji is a local manifestation of Lakshmana, one of the central characters from the Ramayana; Draupadi and the Pandavas are localized expressions of the main figures from the Mahabharata. While a particular community may identify itself as forming the "core" group of devotees of a folk deity—in the case of Khandoba and Devnarayan, for example, it is the pastoral communities of the Dhangars and Gujars, respectively— there are usually also other communities that identify themselves as devotees through narrative histories and ritual practices that bring these communities into relation with the deity and vice versa. Thus, in the case of Khandoba and Devnarayan, devotees also belong to merchant, "robber," warrior, leather-worker, potter, and even Brahman castes. In the instance of the widely worshipped, powerful goddess Draupadi in Tamil Nadu, her primary devotees, in terms of mythology and ritual space, are Pottu Raja, a "multiform" of Bhairava and Mahishasura (the buffalo–demon slayed by the Goddess in puranic texts such as the *Devi-Mahatmya*), and Muttal Ravuttan, a Muslim horseman or trooper (Hiltebeitel, 1989). Similarly, one of the important characters in the oral epic of Devnarayan is Kalu Mir Pathan, a Muslim general in the service of the former's arch-enemy, the Rana or Rajput chieftain of Ran Shahar (Malik, 2005). Devotees of the central Himalayan deity Goludev, once again, belong to various communities: Rajput, Brahman, and Dalit. Thus, although Goludev's main temples in Kumaon are managed by Brahman priests, rituals that are performed in order to embody the deity in human mediums are invariably conducted by members of Dalit communities. According to the deity's life story that is performed orally in a ritual context, Goludev himself belonged to the Rajput or Thakur community, being the son of a king. Goludev, like Khandoba and Devnarayan, is a king who rules over a territory, in this case, the "kingdom" or province of Kumaon in the central Himalayan state of Uttarakhand. But Goludev is also explicitly the "God of Justice" (*nyaya ka devta*). The adjudication of justice through the deity provides a significant example of how the classical, folk, and modern intersect, crossing themes and boundaries, creating "hybrid" forms of ritual, narrative, and justice. Thus, while Goludev as a folk deity is "modeled" along the classical notions of the Hindu king presiding over a kingdom of diverse subjects whose welfare is his primary responsibility, Goludev's temples are perceived along the lines of Indo-Persian courts of law. His temples are given the broad appellation of *darbar* meaning "court" in the sense of both royal court and court of law; quite specifically, however, his temples are classified according the hierarchy of modern, secular courts into "supreme," "high," and "district" courts. Devotees from towns and villages nearby his temples, and also from other districts within Kumaon and even far-flung places such as Delhi and Kerala offer written petitions to the deity. These are called *manauti* (surety, pledge) or *fariyad*, a Persian term denoting "plea," "complaint," "grievance," or "petition." The petitions are publicly accessible being hung on the outside of a temple. They deal with a variety of issues ranging from land and property disputes, health, marital well-being, financial success, careers, criminal cases, travel, business, relationships, and so on. In many cases, devotees offer the petitions in the knowledge that the secular courts may not expedite the perceived injustice in a timely or fair manner. The language of the petitions is also often a "hybrid" one, criss-crossing between devotional and legalistic terminology, as well between English, Hindi, and Kumaoni. An example of a petition is provided here:

[In Hindi]
    Victory to Goludevta
    at Chittai Temple[8]—my salutations to you.
    I heard your name and I am present in your court. I have heard that
    you sort out everyone's (problems), sort out mine too. I was told at
    the Jageshwar Temple about the Chittai Golu Temple. [I was told]
    you get rid of everyone's problems, get rid of mine as well.
    My problems (are):

[In English]
    Divorce.
    Health.
    Financial situation.
    Father's health.
    Love & affection amongst the two brothers.
    Job which would follow the divorce or as you wish.
    When all the *samasyas* [problems] are resolved I will return from
    Delhi and sacrifice a goat as liked by you, and hand [in] a bell, and
    give a shell. 6 months. First I will come to Jageshwar where I will
    complete the *Mahamritunja* [*puja*]. I will come to your temple. If I
    don't come after 6 months after completion of my work my witness
    is Rakesh Chand Verma.

                          Anand Sharma
                    [address in New Delhi]
                    [signature of witness]
                              25-2-08

The petitioner (whose name has been changed here) uses both English and Hindi for different sections of the petition. The first section in Hindi directly addresses the deity with salutations, indicating how the petitioner has come to know about Goludev while he was visiting another important sacred site in Kumaon. The petitioner also refers to the temple as a court and to Goludev's well-known ability to resolve difficulties. What follows is a section in English listing various matters, both personal and pertaining to family including divorce, financial circumstances, job, health, and well-being. The petitioner, who is from Delhi, promises to return within a stipulated time of six months to Jageshwar where he will first perform an elaborate puja, and then to Goludev's temple in Chittai where he will offer a goat, a bell, and a shell to the deity in return for the resolution of his problems. The petition is explicitly transactional: The petitioner pledges to make certain offerings in return for successfully obtaining what he wants from the deity. In keeping with its "legal" nature, the petition also carries the signature of a witness. The content and tone of the petition is, thus, both personal and devotional, but its format is public and legal, producing a document that is "hybrid" in its use of Hindi and English, and also in its usage of the language of religious and secular frameworks (Malik, 2015).

## Folk Hinduism and Modernity

Thus, we have here a continuation of classical and folk ideas concerning ritual, narrative, justice, and religion within the ideological framework of modernity and its secular institutions. Clearly, the modern instances of secular justice have not done away or dissolved the "traditional" or folk forms of justice. If anything, these continue to thrive alongside modern institutions while acutely critiquing the workability and viability of the latter to provide fair and expeditious justice. One of the important questions facing current and future scholarship is, therefore, how folk religious ideas and practices concerning justice, health, environment, medicine, community, history, and identity continue to exist and perhaps even flourish within the context of the modern nation state. The assumption being that modernity with its emphasis on technological growth, industrialization, democracy, egalitarian ideals, western medicine, rational thought and individualization would result in the gradual yet progressive displacement and disappearance of the nonrational, superstitious, nonsecular, religious, and traditional. However, while modernity and modernization have certainly brought about changes in "tradition," "traditional" practices of healing, social justice, ritual, narrative, community formation, and so on have not disappeared, as predicted in so-called modernization theory (Sax and Basu, in press). It is unconvincing and highly problematic to label these expressive forms as "premodern," "nonrational," "superstitious," etc., since this assumes that the universal validity and indeed teleological arrow of modernity and its institutions which in many senses, both theoretical and material, are confronted with failure and breakdown in today's world. As Ramanujan insightfully points out, modernity—rather than representing a rupture and ending of "tradition"—itself must be viewed as one of the many competing and fluid components of a reflexive, self-generating culture, of which folk and classical Hinduism are but parts.

# Notes

1. This interest was made evident in the translations of early Sanskrit works such as *Abhijnanasakuntalam* (the poet Kalidasa's famous play) by William Jones (1746–1794) whose research into classical languages brought about the new discipline of Indo-European Studies; the *Bhagavad Gita* by Jones's colleague Charles Wilkens (1749–1836); the *Upanisads* by Friederich Max Mueller (1823–1900) who subsequently initiated the mammoth 50 volume production of the "Sacred Books of the East" that consisted of English translations by various scholars of what were considered seminal texts of Hindu, Buddhist, Jain, Zoroastrian, Islamic, and Chinese traditions.

2. August Wilhelm von Schlegel held the very first chair in "Indological" studies at the University of Bonn in 1818. In the 19th century and the first half of the 20th century, culminating with the end of World War II, more research was conducted on India, particularly its textual traditions, at German universities than at other European and American universities combined. This research included the translation and analysis of works relating to Vedic, epic, and Puranic texts, grammars, classical poetry, science and medicine, law and politics, history, art, music, as well as Buddhism, Jainism, and "modern" or regional languages and literatures (Stache-Rosen, 1990).

3. See the following discussion for a further elucidation of Vatsyayan's perspective on this matter.

4. For example: oral epics, folktales, heroic ballads, children's stories, songs sung by women (for women), ritual chants, and so on.

5. See, for example, the excellent work of Ramanjan and Blackburn (1986).

6. *Murti* denotes an image; *svarga* means divine abode or heaven (Sontheimer, 1997: 315).

7. On the "juristic personality" of folk deities, see Sontheimer (1964) and Wagle (2005).

8.    This is the name one of the three main temples of Goludev, often referred to as his "supreme court."

# References

Fuller, Christopher J. 1992. *The Camphor Flame: Popular Hinduism and Society in India.* Princeton: Princeton University Press.

Hiltebeitel, Alf. 1989. "Draupadi's Two Guardians: The Buffalo King and Muslim Devotee." In Alf Hiltebeitel (ed.), *Criminal Gods and Demon Devotees,* 339–372. Albany: SUNY.

Malik, Aditya. 1997. "Hinduism or Three-thousand-three-hundred-and-three Ways to Invoke a Construct." In G. D. Sontheimer and H. Kulke (eds), *Hinduism Reconsidered,* 2nd revised edition, 10–31. New Delhi: Manohar.

———. 2005. *Nectar Gaze and Poison Breath: An Analysis and Translation of the Rajasthani Oral Narrative of Devnarayan.* New York: Oxford University Press.

———. 2010a. "In the Divine Court of Appeals: Petitions Before the God of Justice." In Timothy Lubin et al. (eds), *Hinduism and Law,* 207–214. Cambridge: Cambridge University Press.

———. 2010b. "Is Possession Really Possible? Towards a Hermeneutics of Transformative Embodiment in South Asia." In Fabrizio M. Ferrari (ed.), *Health and Religious Rituals in South Asia: Disease, Possession and Healing,* 17–32. London: Routledge.

———. 2015. "The *Darbar* of Goludev: Possession, Petitions, and Modernity." In William S. Sax and Helene Basu (eds), *The Law of Possession: Ritual, therapy, and the Secular State.* New York: Oxford University Press.

Marriot, McKim (ed.). 1955. *Village India: Studies in the Little Community.* Chicago: University of Chicago Press.

Ramanujan, A. K. 1989. "Where Mirrors are Windows: Towards an Anthology of Reflections." *History of Religions* 28(3): 187–216.

———. 1990. "Is There an Indian Way of Thinking? An Informal Essay." In Mackim Marriot (ed.), *India Through Hindu Categories,* 41–58. New Delhi: SAGE Publications.

Ramanujan, A. K. and Stuart H. Blackburn. 1986. *Another Harmony: New Essays on the Folklore of India.* Berkley/Los Angeles: University of California Press.

Redfield, Robert. 1955. *The Little Community.* Chicago: University of Chicago Press.

Sax, William S. 2002. *Dancing the Self: Personhood and Performance in the Pandav Lila of Garhwal.* New York: Oxford University Press.

———. 2009. *God of Justice. Ritual Healing and Social Justice in the Central Himalayas.* New York: Oxford University Press.

Sax, William S. and Helene Basu (eds). In press. *The Law of Possession: Ritual, Therapy, and the Secular State.* New York: Oxford University Press.

Shulman, David D. 1989. "Reconsidering Hinduism: What I might have said (in part) if…." In G. D. Sontheimer and H. Kulke (eds), *Hinduism Reconsidered,* 1st edition, 7–10. New Delhi: Manohar.

Singer, Milton. 1972. *When a Great Tradition Modernizes: An Anthropological Approach to Indian Civilization*. New York: Praeger Publishers.

Smith, John D. 1991. *The Epic of Pabuji: A Study, Transcription and Translation*. Cambridge (UK): Cambridge University Press.

Sontheimer, Guenther-Dietz. 1964. "Religious Endowments in India: The Juristic Personality of Hindu Deities." *Zeitschrift für vergleichende Rechtswissenschaft* 69(1): 45–100.

———. 1997. "Hinduism: The Five Components and their Interaction." In G. D. Sontheimer and H. Kulke (eds), *Hinduism Reconsidered*, 2nd revised edition, 305–324. New Delhi: Manohar.

Stache-Rosen, Valentina. 1990. *German Indologists: Biographies of Scholars in Indian Studies*. New Delhi: Max Mueller Bhavan.

Thapar, Romila. 1997. "Syndicated Hinduism." In G. D. Sontheimer and H. Kulke (eds), *Hinduism Reconsidered*, 2nd revised edition, 54–81. New Delhi: Manohar.

Vatsyayan, Kapila. 1994. "Sastra and Prayoga: Marga and Desi; On conceptual frameworks of Indian culture." In G. C. Tripathi and H. Kulke (eds), *Religion and Society in Eastern India*, 15–48. Bhubaneshwar: The Eschmann Memorial Fund.

Wagle, Narendra K. 2005. "Customary laws among the non-Brahman *Jatis* of Pune, 1824–1826." In Aditya Malik, Anne Feldhaus, and Heidrun Brueckner (eds), *In the Company of Gods. Essays in Memory of Gunther-Dietz Sontheimer*, 283–328. New Delhi: Manohar.

# Chapter 9

## Hinduism and Healing

### Fabrizio M. Ferrari

South Asia is home to a rich healing culture that, in different ways, has strived to preserve health and to counter the cultural, as well as personal, perception of sufferance. An immense corpus of rituals, narratives, and beliefs has been transmitted from Vedic times across South Asia to favor well-being and counter illness. Notions of health, however, are not universal, and the healing practices to which Hindus have recurred to may be radically different. While a study on the Hindu way of healing and Hindu understandings of health and disease is simply unrealistic, familiarity with some recurring patterns and distinctive features is essential to grasp how Hinduism developed in South Asia. The chapter will be divided into sections exploring medical knowledge, myths, and rituals in Veda, Āyurveda, Tantra, and in folk and devotional culture.

## Magical Medicine in the Vedas

References to healing practices in the Vedas are contained in the *Ṛgvedasaṃhitā* (ca. 1500–1000 BCE) and, more emphatically, in the *Atharvavedasaṃhitā* (ca. 1000–800 BCE). The *bhaiṣajya* (medical) section of *Kauśikasūtra* (the ritual part of *Atharvaveda* [AV]) is the main source of information on healing (Bahulkar, 1994).[1] Incantations are attributed to ritualists such as the *āṅgirasas*, *bhārgavas*, and the *ātharvaṇas*—three classes of priests initially unwelcome or unfit, to conduct Vedic śrauta (solemn) rituals and marginalized by the specialists of the *Trayī* (the Vedic "triad": *Ṛgveda* [RV], *Samaveda*, and *Yajurveda*).[2] Powerful mantras were later integrated with hymns and formulae from RV and "[w]ith the help of such 'acceptable' sorcery hymns, the Atharvavedins could gain a position as the fourth main priest at the śrauta rituals, where they silently watch over the whole procedure and rectify mistakes" (Witzel, 1997: 279).

Along with such classes of ritualists, the oral tradition preserved in the Vedas bears evidence to the presence of skillful medicine men: the *bhiṣáj*. They are described as male professionals whose work was aimed at mending men, animals (mostly cattle; see AVŚ 2.32 and 6.141), and crops (AVP 5.15.7) after the attack of demons. The *bhiṣájs* are variously called dancers or shakers (*vipra*), and are known as chanters or poets (*kavi*). Their diagnosis was seldom preventive, rather it was about casting away, or relocating, harmful demons/gods.

Illness was believed to be inflicted as a form of punishment for breaking vows, wrongdoing, failure to honor the gods and disrespect toward others. Negotiating health is a matter of contrasting the negative influence of presences such as gods, demons, evil eye, and aggressive spirits. The healing process is meant to identify a primary cause, to untie the knot between a powerful nonhuman force and its victim, and ultimately to relocate the demon/disease. This was primarily achieved by means of powerful and coercive incantations and the rituals accompanying them. The unfavorable god/demon was to be transferred in the bodies of competitors (e.g., by using love charms), enemies, or faraway people (AVŚ 5.22.1-14) in the waters, under the ground, or in the body of animals (RV 1.50.11-13).[3]

Although there are hymns that suggest that the practice of the medicine man included some sort of empirical knowledge of the human body and its anatomy (AVP 4.15), the duty of the healer was to assess symptoms, to identify their origin[4] and to make them go away by means of a complex ritualism made of mantra, dance, offerings (water and fire), preparations of amulets and remedies from herbs and animals (AVŚ 1.2.9; AVŚ 3.7.1; ŚB 3.2.2.20).[5] In Vedic medicine, health is defined by the absence of a particular demon. Early references to healing rituals confirm that in Vedic culture,

> the idea of health in a positive sense is wanting [...]. Any notion of the concept is to be found in the negative or the opposite of what was understood to be disease, or more specifically in the absence of particular disease-causing demons, of injuries and damages and of toxins. (Zysk, 2009: 8)

As per the healing process, this is built on three core elements, namely the power of mantra, ritual, and intentionality (Zysk, 2002). There is no evidence of transcendental aims. Magical medicine in the Veda is a function of the signifying activity of the human being who affirms himself as the subject in his history. Further, Vedic medical lore makes a case for a discussion on magic as a progressive performance whose place in society is a technical moment but, at the same time, competes with other social spaces.

Medicine men, primarily because of their association with fringe sectors of the population such as heterodox ascetics and tribal people (from whom they gathered and exchanged medical knowledge), were a dysfunctional presence.[6] Unlike the physicians of the post-Vedic tradition, bhiṣájs gathered their knowledge from the observation of animal sacrifices or natural phenomena (e.g., decomposition of bodies in the open)[7] (Jha, 2004: 30–37). Although Vedic literature abounds with passages where healers are disdained on virtue of their impure practice and inconvenient frequentations (ŚB 4.1.5.14), medicine men were an established presence, and a much needed one. In RV, a whole hymn (10.97) is dedicated to the therapeutic power of herbs and the skills of the bhiṣájs in managing them. Healers are mentioned in RV "in the middle of a threefold list of skilled professional that included carpenters (tákṣan), healers (bhiṣàj), and priests (brahmàn). Like the uneducated carpenters, healers repaired what was injure or broken, and like the learned priests, they commanded esoteric knowledge" (Zysk, 2010: 21).[8]

The training of the bhiṣájs is unclear. Vedic sources treat them as a professional class and mention healers as a corporation. With all probability, medical knowledge was transmitted by elders or more experienced healers to younger apprentices. Although we lack sufficient information to speculate whether being a bhiṣáj was an inherited profession or it was subject to the authority of teachers who initiated disciples, there is sufficient material in later sources pointing at a fairly clear understanding of their work (CaS. Sūtrasthāna 30.21).

The range of diseases treated by bhiṣájs is vast. In particular, AV highlights three groups of illnesses and their treatment: (1) external diseases, such as swellings, tumors, abscesses, fractures, and wounds; (2) diseases resulting from the assault of demons and "graspers," such as mental disorders and fevers; and (3) diseases resulting from poisoning. Furthermore, a number of unfavorable conditions required the intervention of the *bhiṣájs*, such as warms, dropsy, cough, epilepsy, the charm of sorcerers, frustration/depression, infertility, baldness, prevention of miscarriage, jealousy, love charms, irregular dentation, bad breath, war trauma, nightmares, protection from ominous animals, and so on.

The actions of the *bhiṣáj* were aimed at the identification of the disease, the pronunciation of the demon's name in either mantra or stories celebrating its might (and thus its dangerousness), and finally a coercive performance aiming at warding off its presence. Therapeutic exorcism required the use of herbs (RV 10.97), water (AVŚ 1.2.3; 1.6.24; 1.6.91), amulets (AVŚ 1.2.4; 1.6.85; 1.19.34-35; 2.4.10, 3.10.3; 4.6.81), sympathetic magic (AVŚ 1.1.22; 1.7.116), dancing, recitation of mantras, and the capacity to experience visions. Although Vedic mantras and hymns in both RV and AV suggest that healers were profoundly aware of the implications of diseases, these are believed to be nothing but living—nonhuman—presences.

Vedic charms do not just reflect a belief in magic. They show a concern with human suffering as a social issue. A member of the community who is stricken by a temporary lack of fortune, disability, or disease is a threat to the family, clan, etc., because he/she is no longer productive. The same applies to the householder under whose authority rest wife, offspring, land, cattle, etc. Especially in small-scale societies, the threats of poverty, malnutrition, indebt, expropriation, further diseases, and marginalization are frightful occurrences. Remedies were prepared to avoid the negative influx of gods, demons, and evil eye, whose action represented a threat not just to the individual but to his/her network (RV 10.42.10).

A wide range of nonhuman beings is believed to control, grasp, possess, break, scar, and devour the body. Vedic literature indulges in discussions and descriptions of dangerous gods, goddesses, and demons whose presence and attacks determine various diseases. Gods such as Takmán (Fever), Amīvā (a female domestic demon causing disease resulting from poverty and hunger), Rápas (a nonspecified infirmity), Hṛdroga (Angina Pectoris), Balāsa (Swelling), Harimán ("Yellowness"; Jaundice), etc., were feared but also praised as the mightiest gods for their power to heal (AVŚ 1.2.9.5-6).[9] Along with such demons, there exists a group of dangerous goddesses who are not specifically related to a particular symptom or disease: the three Nirṛtis (lit. disorder; *nir-ṛtám*).[10] These are defined by their overall destructive character and relation with the ineluctability of death. Another source of illness, and the object of powerful exorcism, is evil eye (*dṛṣṭi*),[11] almost invariably linked to the action of a human external agent (witch or sorcerer) who has the power to summon malignant forces and bind them to the chosen victim[12] and various malignant beings. These include *piśāca* (flesh-eating demons), *yakṣa* (semidivine beings who can turn into malignant demons), *asura* (demons, anti-gods), *rākṣasa* (ghouls), *kimīdin* (flesh eaters and Brahman haters), *yātudhāna* (sorcerers), *sadānvā* (female spirits infesting households), *arāya* (malignant spirits), and *durṇāman* (spirits acting like black magicians).

Although distant in cultural and historical terms, the know-how of Vedic medicine men will inform later empirical medicine, the establishment of the medical profession as a respectable sector in public life, and ritual forms of healing in Tantra, vernacular folklore, and devotional culture (*bhakti*).

## Classical Indian Medicine: Āyurveda

From ca. the 1st century CE, with the systematization of a vast *materia medica*, the "science of long life," Āyurveda, is paralleled to *śruti* (lit. "hearing," the Vedas) (CaS Sūtrasthāna 30: 21) and medical treatment is equated to mantra (SuS Cikitsāsthāna 1.75-76).[13] A series of innovative and original medical texts appear. Early compendia include *Carakasaṃhitā* (ca. 1st-2nd centuries CE), *Suśrutasaṃhitā* (ca. 3rd-4th centuries CE), and *Aṣṭāṅgahṛdayasaṃhitā* (attributed to Vāgbhaṭa, ca. 6th-7th centuries CE). Later works belonging to the classical tradition are: *Mādhavanidāna* (attributed to Mādhavakara, 8th century CE), *Śārṅgadharasaṃhitā* (ca. 13th-14th centuries), and the *Bhāvaprakāśa* of Bhāvamiśra (16th century).[14] Other relevant Ayurvedic compendia are the *Bhelasamhitā* (ca. 1st century) and the *Kāśyapa Saṃhitā* (7th century, almost entirely dealing with pediatrics and gynecology).[15]

In Āyurveda, health is primarily a matter of balance, or equilibrium, between bodily humors (*doṣa*). The human body (*śarīra*), it is posited, is crossed by three humors (*tridoṣa*): wind (*vāta*), bile (*pitta*), and phlegm (*śleṣman* or *kapha*).[16] The balance between these humors ensures the correct functioning of the body's digestive processes and development of bones, marrow, tissues, blood, etc. Healing is a process meant to achieve the state freedom from disease (*ārogya*) and longevity (*āyus*). Conversely, disease (*roga, vyādhi*) is a form of imbalance or chaos (*adharma*). The affirmation of medical practice as a respectable profession in Indian society had several social consequences. The consolidation of the profession of the physician (*vaidya*) as an occupation for *upajātis* (members of the three upper castes), more often *brāhmaṇas*, is one of them. Although social status seems not to be an issue, prospective physicians are male, should have sufficient wealth, and are recruited among *brāhmaṇas, kṣatriyas,* and *vaiśyas*. The profession of *vaidya* seems not to be a natural choice for *śūdras*, although Suśruta suggests that "*śūdras* may in fact be initiated into the profession, albeit without using mantras at the ceremony" (Wujastyk, 2012: 76). In practice, Āyurveda establishes social boundaries as per those who are welcome into the medical profession. However, medical science should neither be a trade nor a hereditary profession. Students must be accepted by a qualified teacher and prove themselves worthy by means of an irreprehensible moral conduct and commitment to study.

Along with physicians (and their trainees), medical personnel include the attendant (nurse), the wet-nurse, the midwife, other experienced women (Leslie and Wujastyk, 1991), staff kitchen, and "those who know plants" (ibid.: 59–67). Although there is no evidence of a specialized class of herbalists, Āyurveda bears witness to the valuable knowledge of people otherwise invisible in most medical literature. Such individuals are deemed necessary to medical practice for their knowledge of the territory, even though they were unmistakably reminded of their social subordination, illiteracy, or impurity (CaS Sūtrasthāna 1.120-123). Farmers, herders, hunters, and "forest-dwellers who eat roots" (SuS Sūtrasthāna 36.10) are invaluable sources of knowledge. This comes as no surprise, since villages of tribal people and also the retreats of ascetics and monasteries were well-known centers of medical knowledge and places where a rich pharmacopeia developed (Zysk, 2010).

From Vedic magic to the empirical study of medicinal plants in classical Āyurveda and the recent establishment of the National Medicinal Plants Board in India (AYUSH, i.e., Ayurveda, Yoga and Naturopathy, Unani, Siddha, and Homoeopathy), herbal medicine has continued to thrive (Khare, 2004).[17] But plants are not the only sources of medical treatment. Remedies obtained from animals abound in Āyurvedic compendia.[18] The duty of the physician is to ensure health and long life. If animal meat, or drugs derived from bodily parts of animals, is needed, then killing is inevitable (e.g., SuS Sūtrasthāna 46.53-138, but cf. Svoboda, 1992: 242 on side effects). As the Bengali commentator Cakrapāṇidatta says about CaS Sūtrasthāna 8.29: "For the rules of āyurveda do not teach the achievement of righteousness. Rather, they teach the achievement of health."[19] Early Āyurvedic literature records some 300 animals whose body parts or products were used in medicine (Jha, 2004: 98; Wujastyk, 2004: 833–836).[20] SuS is the most accurate compendium in terms of animal meat as medicine.[21] Although the vast majority of the animals listed were probably never used (hence the interpretation of the text as a "zoology"; Zimmermann, 2011: 98), there is an undisputable link between medicine and animals that goes back to the Vedic culture. The preparation of remedies containing animal blood and meat/fat or making of amulets from animal bones, horns, skin, and hair is justified in Indian medical culture. The rationale behind this practice is the belief that every species has qualities (guṇa) and savors (rasa). The animal, its flesh, parts of its body or its products are then used in a compensatory way, that is, to give what the patient (rogin, ātura, vyādhita) lacks.

Āyurvedic physicians distinguish themselves from ritual healers for their profound anatomical knowledge and a more empirical approach to diagnostics and therapeutics. With time, a medical ethos develops and it will inform the systematization of Āyurveda in India and beyond. Indian physicians "recognised a healthy life as being of fundamental, even primary importance, since without it no other goal of life would be possible. In various ways and with different arguments, they subordinated the quest for dharma to the quest for health" (Wujastyk, 2004: 838).

## Tantric Healing

Tantric medicine emerges from the early medieval Indian teachings in the Śaiva religion (c. 400–1300 CE) (Sanderson, 2009) and slowly penetrates various strands of Indic ritual culture. Early texts with a focus on healing include the Kriyātantras (sorcery texts) and its subgenres, like the Bhūtatantras (on demonic possession, e.g., Netratantra and Īśanaśivagurudevapaddhati), the Bālatantras (on childhood demonic possession, e.g., *Kumāratantra*)[22] and the *Garuḍatantra*s (on snakebites, e.g., *Yogaratnāvalī* of Śrīkaṇṭhapaṇḍita).[23] Unlike Āyurvedic compendia, Tantric texts are ideologically and politically constructed on influential philosophical traditions (Sāṃkhya, Yoga, and Vedānta) and theistic doctrines (Śaiva, Śākta, Vaiṣṇava, Bauddha, and Jaina). Suffering (*duḥkha*) is, thus, imputed to the lack of nondual awareness, which in turn permits to transcend limits. The liberating teaching underlying most tantric texts and practices is one culminating with the merging of the subject and the object, the overcoming of any oppositional vision, and the accomplishment of the supreme knowledge (*vimarśa*) that grants self-awareness.

Tantric texts combine ritual, alchemical, and medical elements (Meulenbeld, 1992: 107). Healing is a process leading to self-awareness by means of self-realization or accomplishment, and self-recognition (*pratyabhijñā*). Śiva himself is believed to be the highest expression of medical knowledge (MNT 4.7), and his teachings are essentially directed at correct envisioning, that is, awareness that suffering is generated by ignorance that the self is identical to God (Timalsina, 2012: 32). This knowledge implies an equation between the gross body (*sthūla śarīra*), the microcosm, and the universe (*brahmāṇḍa*), the macrocosm. To heal the body (an ever-changing reality called "mass," *piṇḍa*) and its components, the healer acts on its foundations (*ādhāra*) and voids (*vyoman*), and facilitates, or restores, the passage of winds or breath (*prāṇa*) through a series of channels (*nāḍī*) that intersect sites of energy (*cakra*) variously positioned in the human body (cf. Samuel, 2013: 40–41).[24]

Diagnostics responds to the idea that the subtle body (*sūkṣma śarīra*) is inhabited by several deities.[25] When the flow of various beings (*bhūta*) toward the central deity (Śiva, i.e., the self) is disrupted, an event signaled by various marks (*lakṣaṇa*), the tantric specialist intervenes. His performance is featured by *jñāna* (knowledge), *icchā* (volition), and *kriyā* (ritual action). Tantric healers are knowledgeable *siddha*s, accomplished teachers and masters in arts such as magic spells and *mantra*s, powerful diagrams (*yantra, maṇḍala*), gestures (*mudrā*), alchemy,[26] iatrochemistry, and (*haṭha*) *yoga*. Their practice is a coercive exercise of power and a ritual negotiation aiming at facilitating the flux of *prana* and the dispelling of unfavorable presences such as *rūpikā*s and *apasmāra*s (who cause the collapse of mental and physical equilibrium), *dūṣikā*s (blood poisoners), *cumbikā*s and *patralekhikā*s (vampire-like creatures), *grahas* and *rudraḍākinīs* (who cause madness and mood variations), *ḍāmarīs* (who suck vital breath), *piśācas* (predator demons who inhabit the cremation ground), and various classes of *yakṣas*, *rākṣasas*, *yoginīs*, *mātṛkās*, *vināyakas*, and *bhūtas* (here in the common acceptation of ghosts).

As we learn from the tantric literature, especially early grimoires, the remedial arsenal of healers is constructed on the knowledge of the power of plants, resins, and animal substances, and their use in a ritual context. In addition, from ca. the 13th century, tantric texts—*Kriyātantras* in particular—bear witness to the influence of the Indian and Tibetan alchemical tradition (White, 1996: 130; Mason, 2014), a trend which radicalizes with the medicalization of alchemy.[27] Along with an array of remedies made from various animal, botanical, and mineral substances, their combination and offering at powerful sites (e.g., cremation ground, crossroads, etc.), the installation (*nyāsa*) of mystic syllables or ritual shielding (*kavaca*) are among the most common practices. The healer is known as *mantrī*, or *mantra* practitioner, and his expertise is core to the healing process. *Mantras* are deities created by powerful gods (e.g., Śiva or Bhairava, his fierce aspect)[28] and manipulated by skillful mantrīs who use them as weapons or armors (Sanderson, 1986: 174–176).[29] Their role in a healing context is exemplified by the fights between Śiva and all sort of dangerous demons. Just like Śiva, the lord of *yogins*, the healer is a conqueror: fixing the flow of *prana* is a struggle that requires the acquisition of power (*siddhi*), withdrawal of the senses (*pratyāhāra*), and visualization (*dhāraṇā*) of Śiva as Bhūtanātha (lord of beings) and Mṛtyuñjaya (conqueror of death).

## External Agents of Illness: Health and Possession

An important aspect of South Asian healing culture, whether medical or ritual, is the belief that human beings can be possessed by benign and malevolent presences.[30] On the contrary, there is also a "positive" possession. Ritual specialists summon deities or benevolent spirits who enter their own body or that of health seekers and suggest therapeutic strategies, foretell the future, give practical advice, or help healers to counter the demonic presences (illness) afflicting their customers. Knowing how to be possessed is often conducive to various phenomena of social inclusion. The healer is considered a seat of a God/dess and, for that, is respected regardless of social status.[31] Negative possession, conversely, is an event explained as the unwanted visitation of a malignant entity (deity, spirit, ghost, demon, etc.) that causes sufferance, illness and, if not properly treated, death. Negative possession often generates social stigma and ostracism, which extends to the victim's kin (Dwyer, 2003; Barrett, 2008).

Earliest references to possession appear in the Vedic literature and are associated to mental illness. In AV, madness (*unmadita*) is caused by the infringement of social order and is believed to be treatable. Demonic possession (*unmatta*), conversely, is a negative event that can be controlled but not eliminated.[32] Descriptions of possessing presences can be found in early Vedic sources (RVid 1.101) and in a number of protective charms (AVŚ 3.1.16). This is a pervasive pattern in Indian medical culture. Āyurvedic physicians slowly, but resolutely, disengage from the divinization of disease and explain possession as *mānasika roga* (mental illness). Āyurveda substantially agrees in differentiating untreatable madness resulting from external agents (*āgantuka*) and madness imputable to internal (pathological) causes (*nija*), and therefore treatable. *Vaidyas* had charts listing: (a) the agents of possession responsible for the overpowering (*abhidarṣayanti*) of the individual; (b) their effects (symptoms); and (c) various therapeutic actions (CaS.Ci. 6.9.16-21; AHS.Utt. 4.1-44). In Āyurveda, possession is discussed within *bhūtavidyā*, the "science of the beings" or "demonology" and in the *bhūtatantras*, sections specifically investigating the doctrine of beings.[33] According to this tradition, the uncaring observation of one's *svadharma* (individual duty) attracts unfavorable presences (*bhūta*) and, particularly, a class of beings known as seizers or graspers (*grahas*).

Descriptions of the power and dangerous nature of graspers are ubiquitous in Indic texts and their pernicious affliction is variously called *graharoga* or *grahapīḍā*.[34] Graspers and seizers, who can be male (*graha*) or female (*grahī*),[35] are generally, but incorrectly, identified with "planets"[36] and are believed to manifest by means of negative possession.[37] Treatment varies. It is generally meant as a form of exorcism where powerful substances (blood, liquor), pungent herbs (KKG 30.79-82), and symbols of offence (blades, iron pegs, etc.) are presented in the dead of the night at crossroads, river confluences, or cremation ground (cf. SuS Uttarasthāna 27–36).

Given the popular identification of *grahas* with "planets," familiarity with astrology/astronomy (*jyotiṣā*) is mandatory for the knowledgeable healer. The origin of Jyotiṣa(from Sanskrit *jyotis*, "light") and its relation to health and wealth goes back to the first millennium BCE. A Vedic hymn for general well-being and prosperity praises celestial bodies and planets (AVŚ 19.9.7) and suggests that the idea of good health was somehow related to a correct (or auspicious) alignment of stars and planets.[38] In Jyotiḥśāstras, the observation of stars and planets serve to determine the features and character of the newborn (*jataka*), to foretell events related to a particular year (*varṣaphāla*); to investigate the influence of celestial bodies (*praśna*); to calculate the exact time when to perform rituals (*muhūrta*); and to predict astronomical events and their consequences (e.g., droughts, calamities, and epidemics). In both Āyurveda and Tantra, Jyotiṣa is functional to health and to protect from the unfavorable alignment of *grahas*. Two aspects are particularly emphasized: prediction of the duration of life (*āyus*) and the destiny of a person (*niyati*).[39] This is done by means of the study of natal horoscope (*kuṇḍali*).

Other applications of Jyotiṣa can be appreciated within the context of folk healing, where it survives in a simplified form in the practice of magicians, healers, oracles, and fortune tellers. While providing the authoritative background for the interpretation or prediction of the degree of inauspiciousness (*aśubha, amaṅgala*) of a particular moment in the history of the clients' current or past life, astrology is subsidiary to performance (dance, oracular possession, incantations) and the ritual presentation of offerings (including the sacrifice of animals). One of the main differences with *jyotiṣīs* is that folk astrologers are primarily specialists in horary astrology. Their performance is intended to answer the questions (*praśna*) of a customer on his/her past, present or future. The answer is derived from an interpretation of the alignment of planets, rather than on the consultation of the customer's *kuṇḍali*. Methods vary. Some astrologers are helped by trained animals (monkeys, bears, parrots, kites, etc.) or may associate the planets to particular stones, gems, cards, etc. It is, thus, not unusual that an astrologer is also a healer or works along with healers to establish a therapeutic strategy. Reading the destiny, inviting fortune, and countering evil eye have developed as important areas of specialism of folk astrologers and healers, who look at *grahas* as potentially dangerous deities and, at the same time, powerful allies.

## Folk Healing: Ritual, Magic, and Territorial Knowledge

Pluralism in South Asia has contributed to the implementation of multifarious healing strategies (Sujatha, 2007), each depending on territorial understandings and conceptualizations of illness (cultural discomfort) as opposed to disease (organic dysfunction) (Hahn, 1984: 2).[40] It seems, thus, appropriate when discussing folk or vernacular culture to stress the importance of localism. With this in mind, I will refer to folk culture as *āñcalik saṃskṛti*. The term, which is derived from the Hindi word *āñcal* (lit. "the hem" [of a sari]), is used to indicate both the peripheral position of a territory (village, district, and neighborhood) and its belonging to a wider map. In this way, I wish to stress the uniqueness of every *āñcal* and the impact of *āñcalik* culture, a reality built on regional and local mores (*ācār*), on Hinduism in general.

As per folk healing, this is a loose label, grouping together medical science, healing rituals, therapeutic narratives, territorial knowledge, and technological applications disseminated by modernization, colonialism, migration, urbanization, industrialization, and globalization. Hindu *āñcalik* culture is a reality defined by seats of power (*tīrtha*), human and divine hierarchies (*varṇa* and *jāti*), foundational narratives (*Purāṇas, kathā*), and a variety of ritual practices, from daily offerings (*pūjā*) to animal sacrifice (*balidāna*), vows (*vrata*), pageants (*yātrā*), and big festivals (*melā, utsava*). Local deities, often unique to the *āñcal*, are addressed in vernacular idioms. Although Sanskrit is the liturgical language of official occasions, folk culture highly values "the place to which one belongs" and emphasizes its order (*dharma*) with respect to the outside (Wadley, 2007: 429). The process of defining folk religion, folk culture, and folk logics is, thus, an exercise in pluralism and a way to understand the interplay of charisma exerted by human (gurus, sages, ascetics, devotees, saints, etc.), nonhumans (deities and spirits), and geographical sites (temples, places of burial, shrines, etc.) of power. In other words, it is a hermeneutics of dissonances.

The conceptualization of health and the production and transmission of healing strategies—including the modification, renovation, and obliteration of selected practices—in an *āñcalik* context is of the greatest importance. If folklore is "community life in which face-to-face relation predominate" (Chatterji, 2003: 567), then healing rituals make us reflect on the persistence of established norms and rules, their interaction with different sociocultural milieus, and the way in which they respond to times of crisis. Narratives, devotional practices, ritual offerings, and forms of renunciation (as in votive culture) reflect the need of health seekers to understand the source of pain. This is done by creating, enacting, and transmitting exemplary stories (myth), thereby, in turn, informing micro-history. The complex dynamics of presentation and counterpresentation core to ritual healing are forms of information exchange, ultimately aiming at control and satisfaction.

The healing process is a highly competitive one. This results in an actual medical market in which politics and strategies of self-promotion, and also of discredit,[41] are enacted at all possible levels and across all categories, that is, physicians, *vaidyas*, *tantrikās*, and folk healers such as *bhagat*s or *ojhā*s. By actualizing contingent and contextual needs through performances rooted in local language, logics, and aesthetics, folk healers give their clients the possibility to respond to what is perceived as injustice (i.e., pain). The authority exerted by "official" medical systems, however, is not to be underestimated. Health seekers and folk healers maintain a holistic approach where different specialists from different faith and scientific traditions work together in a frame defined by Mark Nichter as "masala medicine" (Nichter and Nichter, 2002: 206). The struggle against smallpox in India well serves to illustrate this.

One of the deadliest diseases ever, smallpox was endemic in India and—along with pneumonia, cholera, and malaria—it represented a major threat to the indigenous and colonial population. Indigenous and Western medical systems failed to develop an effective cure and, apart from quarantine, there was no prophylaxis. The only efficacious measure was variolation (or inoculation), a practice jealously administered by the *ṭīkādar*s (marking doctors), a class of folk healers from Hindu upper (*brāhmaṇa*) and lower classes (e.g., garland makers, *mālin*, and barbers, *nāpit*). This consisted in an intracutaneous injection of infected dried pus extracted in advance from human smallpox victims' scabs or pustules. The inoculation was expected to result in a milder form of smallpox and, ultimately, in the immunization of the patient (Coult, 1731 and Holwell, 1767 in Dharmapal, 2000). Although variolation enjoyed an enormous success among all religious communities of the Indian population (even among the British), from 1802, it was systematically replaced by the more effective Jennerian vaccination (Ferrari, 2014: 132–145).

Most Indians, however, especially in rural areas, refused vaccination and continued with the practice of inoculation even after its banishment in 1880. The reasons are manifold. It has been speculated that the less-educated population of villages looked at vaccination as an offence to a particular set of goddesses.[42] The rural population, however, was not adverse to vaccination per se. Arnold (1993: 156) and Bhattacharya (1998: 50–51) have demonstrated that a two-tiered system of vaccination was in place in India from 1850. While the urban vaccination scheme was informed by the latest technologies, the vaccination program in rural areas was less reliable. Calves' lymph was not always available, as cattle owners were reluctant to sell farming animals.[43] Further, when the lymph was extracted, this was often damaged during transportation or by the hot climate. When this happened, humanized unattenuated lymph was used. Side effects were inevitable, and peasants, who could not afford to miss work in a critical moment of the year (vaccination campaigns were generally scheduled during the harvesting season), refused vaccination (Ferrari, 2014: 136). Marking doctors too were concerned about the loss of prestige and income, and tried in all ways to resist the governmental ban. From around mid-19th century, variolation was increasingly presented as *pūjā*, an act of worship whose nonobservance—it was suggested—could cause the rage of the goddess (i.e., infection). Variolators were no longer healers, but became *pūjārīs*—or worked alongside with Brahman ritualists.

As the case of variolation in India illustrates, healing is a way to interpret and translate any catastrophe in the ways of the *āñcal*. Medical folklore promotes ways to challenge global forms of injustice (illness) and makes healing knowledge accessible and understandable.

But folklore is not just contents, it also is transmission. In South Asia, many categories of professional healers have formed. Different as their techniques may be,[44] illness is interpreted as a manifestation of power. A healer is an individual capable to control the power of imbalance by means of negotiation. The basic scope of healing is to recreate a situation of *acceptable* rather than absolute balance. Although there may be consensus on diagnosis, other etiologies converge in what can be explained as a competitive diagnostic process where the most successful performer gains social prestige and validation of his/her method and tradition.

Beside naturalistic explanations, many Hindus continue to believe that illness either results from wrongdoing or is the manifestation of an irate/disappointed deity. The academic literature has reported widely on such beliefs. Most works, however, have contributed to perpetuate a major error, that is, the identification of a disease with a deity (or vice versa). A quick survey on religion and disease in South Asia shows that goddesses like Śītalā, Māriyamman, Parṇaśavarī, Durgā Mahāmarī, Kālarātrī, etc., are almost invariably called "disease goddesses" or, more specifically, the "goddess of" pox fevers, plague, cholera, etc. The same applies to male deities (e.g., the "god of" fever, skin diseases, etc.). Such labels have been used so pervasively that Hindus too, when speaking in English, use them. In fact, this terminology does not fully reflect indigenous cultures. To paraphrase Lincoln (1996: 225), "The conjunction 'of' that joins the two nouns [god/dess and disease] is not neutral filler. Rather, it announces a proprietary claim and a relation of encompassment." Gods and goddesses are not disease. With the exception of Vedic literature, where—for instance—fever is Fever (the demon Takmán) (cf. AVŚ 1.6.20), diseases are manifestations of the power of deities and spirits. For instance, The Bengali goddess Olāi Caṇḍī is not cholera; she controls and protects from cholera (Ferrari, 2015). Similarly, the North-Indian "pox goddess" Śītalā is not the pox; she has power over pox viruses. Although her presence may cause pox fevers, she is a cooling goddess, as her name eloquently indicates, and a destroyer—or remover—of sufferance (*sarvaduḥkhāntakāriṇī* or *kaṣṭaharaṇī*) (SkP 7.1.135: 1–3. Cf. the *Śītalavijayastuti* and the songs included in the *Dasāśvamedhamāhātmya* which I translated in Ferrari, 2014: 15 and 32–33).

Healing narratives and rituals are not the incoherent response (common sense) to uneven development, as theorized by much Marxian anthropology. Folk healing gives voice to the need to control, and react to, what is perceived as iniquity. The healing process in *āñcalik* culture aims at countering relative injustice and negotiating balance so as to achieve relief at individual and social level.

## Beyond Magic and Empiricism: *Bhakti* as Medicine

Parallel to the development of medical knowledge, whether ritual, empirical, or spiritual, other therapeutic strategies have affirmed in Indian culture. The Indian narrative tradition shows us the affirmation of worldviews that borrow from the devotional culture (*bhakti*). Large sections in the *Purāṇas*, and also in the great epics (*Mahābhārata* and *Rāmāyaṇa*) and normative literature (*dharmanibandha*)[45] bear witness to a body of rituals and narratives revolving around the scheduled worship of gods and goddesses for the promotion of health and well-being. Such performances are given in the language of devotion (*bhakti*) and faith (*śraddhā*), and are primarily observed by women. Core to these practices is fasting (*vrata*), a mild form of renunciation attached to storytelling (*kathā*), singing (*gīti*), pilgrimage (*yātrā*), worship (*pūjā*), meditation (*dhyāna*), and mental resolutions in the form of promises to the gods (*mānasika*).[46]

Devotional *vrata* manuals and *pūjāpaddhati*s are central to what I have elsewhere discussed as "devotional medicine" (Ferrari, 2014). Unlike the various medical traditions discussed so far, *bhakti* healing requires no specialists. Auspicious gods and goddesses are healers, as clearly indicated in textual sources and a vast material culture. Devotional moods like love, piety, suffering, and repent—along with devotional possession—are cultivated and serve to the purpose of attracting the attention of a deity and to give voice publicly to personal sufferance. Unlike mystical or theological *bhakti*, devotees do not aim at various forms of liberation. In fact, they give voice to a belief system that objects—or is simply not concerned with—the teaching of non-attachment. Although the authors of law digests have tried to edit such popular culture by adventurously interpreting *mokṣa* (liberation [from rebirth]) as the ultimate aim of women's rituals, the materialism of devotional culture clearly transpires.

Equally important is the altruistic rationale of women's rituals. We know from legal texts that *strīdharma* is about taking care of male relatives, that is, father, brothers, husbands, and sons. But in a *vrata* context, women look at their performance as a total rite that gently heals their existence. This explains the active participation of women who are widowed or did not generate. Devotional healing should be read as the holistic manifestation of protective deities. The devotional service enacted on both scheduled festive occasions or voluntarily becomes a way to express various concerns. The social context should also be considered. *Vrata* culture, with its emphasis on healing, permits devotees to literally take a break from daily routine, domestic chores, labor and marital obligations. The mundane outcomes of devotional service are too important to be jeopardized. It is so that the space dedicated to Mā (the "Mother" [goddess]) becomes, quite literally, a safety net. Not only does it protect from disease and the fear of being ill, it also provides a niche for sanity and a place for one to be an actively critical individual (Ferrari, 2013).

## Conclusion

In this chapter, I have surveyed different aspects of healing culture within Hinduism. From early Vedic magic to the affirmation of indigenous medical systems and the spread of an enormous corpus of ritual tracts on health and well-being, the religious and philosophical traditions forming "Hinduism" have proved capable to variously, and efficaciously, respond to the crisis that is represented by disease, illness, and death. To this, one should add the ramification of *āñcalik* culture and the penetration of non-Indic diagnostic and therapeutic approaches. While there are aspects of well-being that are universal, others continue to be defined by culture and localism. As far as healing is concerned, four key aspects can be isolated. First, illness continues to be variously explained as a condition resulting from actions interpreted as contrary to the established norm. Second, the harm resulting from the above has been persuasively discussed as the presence of powerful other than human beings. Third, health is a precarious condition. Some illnesses are treatable, others are not. The efficacy of the remedies developed by knowledgeable medical practitioners and ritual specialists has limits. Fourth, the healing process—whether performed by human healers or gods—is always a pedagogical performance that intends to inform the community and transmit knowledge. In that, healing strategies in the Hindu context confirm themselves as an expression of social willpower, innovation, and tradition.

# Notes

1. AV contains non-*śrauta* rituals: (1) sorcery hymns (black and white magic, including healing instructions); (2) speculative hymns, often indicated as mystical; (3) discourses on *gṛhya* (domestic) and royal ritual (particularly marriage and death); and (4) appendixes of various genres (Witzel, 1997: 277–278).
2. The *ātharvaṇa* priest specializes in pacificatory (*śānta*) rituals but he also takes part in fire and *soma* sacrifices. The *āṅgīrasa*, conversely, is often discussed as a master of the art of black magic (*ghora*), witchcraft (*yātu*), and evil spells (*abhicāra*). Beneficial substances such as herbal remedies are, thus, listed as ātharvaṇic, whereas demonic—and therefore dangerous—preparations are āṅgīrasic (Rotaru, 2013: 17, n. 94).
3. Alternatively, healers summoned the gods for forgiveness. In this case, the *bhiṣáj* used to invoke the name of the afflicted person, the symptoms of illness, the names of the demon(s), and the name of the god(s). The rite was understood as an experience in which the grasp of the demon was simply neutralized (AVŚ 4.13.1-7).
4. In Vedic texts, there is no difference between the name of the demon/god and that of the disease.
5. Animals are also used to carry away disease (KauS 26.18 or 32.17).
6. The same criteria of exclusion were applied to the Aśvins twins, the physicians of the gods (TS 6.4.9.2).
7. The Vedic *bhiṣáj*, because of his impure profession, was not allowed to perform rituals (cf. Manu 3.152). The use of anatomical terminology was borrowed from the hymns pronounced by the *hotṛ* (the specialist of *ṛk* formulae) and the observation of their rituals.
8. With the normalization of dissenting categories (*saṃnyāsin*s [Vedic renouncers, Brahman by class] and *śramaṇa*s [lit. strivers, non-Vedic renouncers]) from ca. the 6th–4th centuries BCE, the *bhiṣáj*s joined various classes of mendicants and monks (Zysk, 2009: xiv–xv), thus facilitating the transmission of a large body of medical knowledge.
9. See the worship of Takmán (fever) in AVŚ 1.6.20. Zysks reports:

Homage is paid to it [Takmán] along with Rudra and King Varuṇa (AVŚ 6.20.2); it is called the son of Varuṇa (AVŚ 1.25.3); it is given the epithet the thousand-eyed immortal (P 5.21.7 = 13.1.4) which at AVŚ 11.2.3 is Rudra. It is associated with Yama (P 19.12.11); it accompanies the gods (P 1.45.1) and it is extolled and called breath at AVŚ 11.4.11. (2009: 34, fn 40)

10. The Nirṛtis are the Vedic goddesses of chaos. They are identified with destructive forces (RV 10.36: 2, 4; 10.59: 1-4) and invoked by those who seek revenge or the destruction of their enemies (AVŚ 7.70: 1-2). The Nirṛtis embody every evil aspect of nature as opposed to the principle of order itself, ṛtám. Men offer to them black pulses and black scarves (TS 1.8.1) to keep them away. In later Vedic literature, Nirṛti, one of the three Nirṛtis (or perhaps their embodiment), became prominent. Nirṛti, celebrated as the wife (or daughter) of *Adharma* (disorder) and mother of *Bhaya* (dread, fear) and *Naraka* (a sort of hell), is associated with oldness, barrenness, and diseases (AVŚ 1.2.10; 2.3.11.2; AVŚ 2.7.53.3). Along with *Mṛtyu* (death), Nirṛti is the regent of the southern direction (TS 4.2.5), the abode of the dead. The presence of Nirṛti is not a prominent one in Indic literature. References to this goddess are limited to the Vedas and she virtually disappears in post-Vedic Sanskrit and vernacular literature, although some of her distinctive features have been passed on to goddesses like Alakṣmī and Jyeṣṭhā (Leslie, 1991; Zeiler, 2008).

11. The dangerousness of evil eye is still dominant in South Asia. This is widely known in premodern and contemporary North India as *najar* (form Persian *naẓar*: "eye," "sight") and in South India and Sri Lanka as *tiṭṭi* or *diṣṭi*.

12. Formulae to contrast the evil charm of sorcerers and evil eye are scattered in AVŚ, particularly Book 3 (e.g., 1.7-8; 1.16; 4.17-19; 5.14; 5.31; 7.70).

13. Medicine becomes an *upaveda* (application) of RV, although SuS and BhPr indicate that medical science is the *upaveda* of AV. For a comprehensive study of Āyurveda, see the encyclopedic work of Meulenbeld (1999–2002).

14. From the 19th century, these texts will be divided in *bṛhattrayī* (great triad) and *laghutrayī* (little triad).

15. Āyurveda is not the only medical system in the subcontinent. The Siddha medical tradition of South Indian Tamil culture is a notable system built on the teachings of 18 mythical *yogi*s or *siddhar*. Their teaching is believed to be revealed, and therefore there is no date available. However, it has been posited that the Siddha medical tradition is not earlier than the 4th century CE (Weiss, 2009). Tibetan medicine, built on Buddhist principles and indigenous Tibetan culture (but heavily influenced by Tantrism and Āyurveda), developed across the Himalayan regions. Traditional Chinese medicine is also found across India. Unani Tibb is practiced by Muslim hakīms and is derived from the Greek–Arabic tradition (Attewell, 2007). Finally, "Western" biomedicine is now widespread and dominant across the Subcontinent. For reasons of space, this chapter will avoid a survey of the abovementioned medical traditions.

16. Along with *tridoṣavidyā* (science of the three humours), disease is also examined as resulting from heredity (*ādibala*), congenital fault (*janambala*), offence against wisdom (*prajñāparādha*), failure of the seven bodily supports (*saptadhātu*), divine wrath (*daivaroga*), contact (*upasarga*), and the ruler's immorality (*rājayakṣmana*). On contagion, see Das (2000) and Zysk (2000).

17. One of the earliest evidence of the importance of plants as well as those who knew their power is found in a late RV hymn (10.97). All sorts of plants are divine in Vedic culture. Yet, unlike soma, which is male and used in major rituals, the plants in this hymn are goddesses and mothers: *óṣadhīr íti mātaras tád vo devīr úpa bruve*

| *sanéyam áśvaṃ gāṃ vāsa ātmānaṃ táva pūruṣa* || (RV 10.97.4). Plants are also celebrated as healing goddesses in AVŚ 8.7.18-19, whereas soma is praised as a healing plant in RV 8.72.17; 8.79.2; 10.25.11 and 10.97.18—see Zysk (2010: 139).

18. Cf. Vedic literature where animals are food (TB 3.9.8) or indispensable offerings for sacrificial performances. In Manu too, animals can be killed, but only within the sacrificial arena (5.39).

19. Translated by Wujastyk (2004: 836).

20. CaS Cikitsāsthāna 6.10.39-40; 6.9.50-52; SuS Uttarasthāna 6.60.29-37.

21. Animals are divided in *jāṅgala* (living in arid terrains), *ānūpa* (living in presence of waters), and *sādhārana* (living in areas with mixed features), and classified as mammals, reptiles, birds, fishes, and insects.

22. See the extensive study conducted by Filliozat (1937).

23. For a detailed list of text dealing with Garuḍa medicine, see Slouber, 2012: 20–85.

24. The theory of the *cakras* is absent in the classical Indian medical tradition, just like yogic ideas at the base of much Tantric literature. The first reference to the cakras can be found in the *Mālinīvijayottaratantra* (ca. 10th century) and the *Kubjikāmātātantra* (11th century) (Heilijgers-Seelen, 1990; Flood, 2006: 158).

25. The subtle body in Tantrism is a practical rather than theoretical concept, and the flow of "breaths" impacts not just on the development of the body, but on mental processes, emotions, etc.

26. The āyurvedic term *rasaśāstra* is used to indicate mineral-based (mercurial) therapeutic practice, whereas ritual (tantric) alchemy is one aiming at the transformation of metals (*lohavāda*) and the use of elixirs (*dehavāda*).

27. See the study of Puri (2003) on medical *rasāyana* (the "path of *rasa*") as a process to purify and promote tissues and bodily components (*dhātu*).

28. Cf. the creation of the *mantra*-gods Krodheśvara, Khaḍgarāvaṇa, Aghora, and Jvareśvara from respectively Śiva's fury (*krodha*), roar (*rāva*), bellowing (*garjita*), and shaking limbs (*dhutagātra*) (KKG 9.28).

29. See the case of Bābā Kīnārām illustrated by Barrett (2008: 127).

30. The literature on possession is vast. Among recent studies, see Smith (2006) and Ferrari (2011).

31. This pattern is rapidly changing. Healers and their clients are often the target of nationalists (who promote one Hinduism for all Hindus) and radical socialists (who see in folklore the source of superstitions suffocating the emancipation of peasantry and the working class). The healing practices of Hindu minorities are under constant threat in Pakistan and Bangladesh, where the rise of Islamism is a consolidated phenomenon, in Sri Lanka, where state Buddhism is overly aggressive toward Hindu (Tamil) religious practices, and in Nepal, where Maoist groups show their intolerance toward folklore and religion.

32. Cf. Smith (2006: 477) who reports an unambiguous, yet isolate, hymn on the treatment of madness in Veda: "I, being skilled, prepare the medicine so that he, insane [*únmaditam*] because of a curse of the gods and demented [*únmattam*] because of the *rákṣas*-demons, may become sane" (AVŚ 6.111.3).

33. One of the earliest references to *bhūtavidyā* appears in CU 7.1.2.

34. In Āyurveda, possession often afflicts weak individuals. It is, thus, a condition primarily afflicting the sphere of children, and therefore it includes pregnant

women (especially, primiparae), puerperae, the fetus, and relatives of the newborn (Wujastyk, 2003a: xxi). (Vedic literature on miscarriage does not seem equally concerned with the possible wrongdoings of the mother-to-be. See RV 10.162.) This is epitomized in the 7th-century *Kāśyapasaṃhitā*, a later compendium specifically dealing with pediatrics (*kaumārabhṛtya*). The danger of demonic possession in the case of new mothers and the infant is famously told in the story of the demoness Jātahāriṇī, the "Seizer of the Born" (KāS. Kalpāsthāna 6: 8) (see Cerulli, 2012: 73–104).

35. Descriptions of nonhuman agents as dangerous "graspers" can be found in early Vedic sources (RVid 1.101), and in AV, a number of charms against this form of negative possession is listed (AVŚ 3.1.16).

36. The nine "planets"—Sun (*Surya*), Moon (*Chandra*), Mars (*Maṅgala*), Mercury (*Budha*), Jupiter (*Bṛhaspati*), Venus (*Śukra*), Saturn (*Śani*), the northern (*Rahu*) and southern (*Ketu*) orbital lunar node remain object of worship among Hindus of all backgrounds in that potentially dangerous Śani is with all probability the most feared, and revered, among the planets (Svoboda, 1997).

37. The Vedic goddess of chaos, Nirṛti, conserves a certain prominence in the "science of the beings" (bhūtavidyā) or demonology. Although there is no direct link between Nirṛti and the seizers, Āyurvedic compendia look at Nirṛti as the mother of all seizers (SuS Uttarasthāna 60.25–26).

38. Vedic people knew how to calculate solstitial and equinoctial points. This was particularly important to determine when to perform certain rituals or sacrifices and to secure health and well-being. VS 30.10 and TB 3.4.4.1 mention professional "observers of the lunar mansions" (*nakṣatra darśas*), although nothing suggests that the observation of planets and stars was used for divination purposes. Thought healers "who subsists by astrology" (cf. Manu 3.162) were with all probability considered impure, and therefore "to be diligently avoided," astrology/astronomy eventually became a major discipline listed amongst the sciences, or "limbs" (*aṅga*), of the Vedas.

39. The latter is one of the most popular aspects of folk astrology and its application to health issues.

40. Anthropological discourses agree in considering two forms of suffering: one based on the universal notion of pain as a response to bodily disruption (e.g., tissue damage) and one built on cultural notions (e.g., shame, impurity, mourning, etc.).

41. Healing is after all a business, often a profitable one, and the success of a healer depends on entrepreneurship.

42. All across the Subcontinent, smallpox was associated to particular *devī*s whose healing power was particularly sought after: Śītalā in north and central India, Pakistan, Nepal, and Bangladesh, Āi in North-eastern India, Ṭhākurāṇī in Odisha, Hāritī and Parṇaśavarī in the sub-Himalayan regions, Māriyamman in Dravidian-speaking India and Sri Lanka and, scattered all across the Subcontinent, local forms of Durgā and Kālī.

43. Separating cattle calves from their mother often resulted in the latter's infertility and incapacity to produce milk.

44. Healing specialists in *āñcalik* culture belong to different social sectors. They can be male, female, transgender, or with no gender (as in the case of *hijṛā*s); they can be celibate, householders, or renouncers, and they can belong to non-Hindu communities (e.g., Muslim Sufis or fakirs, Buddhist lamas, tribal shamans, etc.).

45. See the *vrata* sections in Hemādri's *Caturvargacintāmani* (late 13th century), the *Nirṇayasindhu* of Kamalakārabhaṭṭa (early 17th century), the *Vratārka* of Śaṅkarabhaṭṭa (late 17th century), and the popular *Vratarāja* of Viśvanātha (18th century).
46. On women's *vrata*, see McGee (1991) and Pearson (1996).

# References

Arnold, D. 1993. *Colonizing the Body: State Medicine and Epidemic Disease in Nineteenth-Century India*. Berkeley: University of California Press.

Attewell, G. 2007. *Refiguring Unani Tibb. Plural Healing in Late Colonial India*. New Delhi: Orient Longman.

Bahulkar, S. S. 1994. *Medical Ritual in the Atharvaveda Tradition*. Pune: Tilak Maharashtra Vidyapeeth.

Barrett, R. 2008. *Aghor Medicine. Pollution, Death, and Healing in Northern India*. Berkeley/London: University of California Press.

Bhattacharya, S. 1998. "Re-Devising Jennerian Vaccines?: European Technologies, Indian Innovation and the Control of Smallpox in South Asia, 1850–1950." *Social Scientist* 26(11/12): 27–66.

Cerulli, A. M. 2012. *Somatic Lessons. Narrating Patienthood and Illness in Indian Medical Literature*. Albany: State University of New York Press.

Chatterji, R. 2003. "The Category of Folk." In V. Das (ed.), *The Oxford India Companion to Sociology and Social Anthropology*, 567–597. Oxford: Oxford University Press.

Das, R. P. 2000. "Notions of 'Contagion' in Classical Indian Medical Texts." In L. I. Conrad and D. Wujastyk (eds), *Contagion. Perspectives from Pre-modern Societies*, 56–78. Aldershot: Ashgate.

Dharmapal (ed.). 2000. *Indian Science and Technology in the Eighteenth Century. Some Contemporary European Accounts* (reprint, 1971). Goa: Other India Press.

Dwyer, G. 2003. *The Divine and the Demonic. Supernatural Affliction and its Treatment in North India*. London/New York: Routledge.

Ferrari, F. M. (ed.) 2011. *Health and Healing Rituals in South Asia. Disease, Possession and Healing*. London/New York: Routledge.

———. 2013. "Alternative Yoginīs with Alternative Powers. Singing the Blues in the Causaṭṭī Yoginī Devī Mandir of Vārāṇasī." In I. Keul (ed.), *Yoginī in South Asia. Alternative Approaches*, 148–162. London/New York: Routledge.

———. 2014. *Religion, Health and Devotion in North India. The Healing Power of Śītalā*. London/New York: Bloomsbury.

———. 2015. "Devotion and Affliction in the Time of Cholera: Ritual Healing, Identity and Resistance among Bengali Muslims." In I. Vargas-O'Bryan and X. Zhou (eds), *Disease, Religion and Healing in Asia. Collaborations and Collisions*, 38–53. London/New York: Routledge.

Filliozat, J. 1937. *Étude de Démonologie Indienne: le Kumāratantra de Rāvana et les Textes Parallèles Indiens, Tibétains, Chinois, Cambodgien et Arabe* (*A Study of*

*Indian Demonology: The Kumāratantra of Rāvana and Indian, Tibetan, Chinese, Cambodian and Arab Parallel Texts)*. Paris: Imprimerie Nationale.

Flood, G. 2006. *The Tantric Body. The Secret Tradition of Hindu Religion*. New York: I. B. Tauris.

Hahn, R. A. 1984. "Rethinking 'Illness' and 'Diseases'." *Contribution to Asian Studies* 18: 1–23.

Heilijgers-Seelen, D. 1990. "The Doctrine of the Ṣaṭcakra According to the Kubjikāmata." In Goudriaan, T. (ed.), *The Sanskrit Tradition and Tantrism*, vol. 1 of Panels of the VIIth World Sanskrit Conference, 56–65. Leiden: Brill.

Jha, D. N. 2004. *The Myth of the Holy Cow*. London/New York: Verso.

Khare, C. P. (ed.) 2004. *Indian Herbal Remedies. Rational Western Therapy, Ayurvedic and Other Traditional Usage, Botany*. Heidelberg: Springer.

Leslie, J. 1991. "Śrī and Jyeṣṭhā: Ambivalent Role Models for Women." In J. Leslie (ed.), *Roles and Rituals for Hindu Women*, 107–128. London: Pinter.

Leslie, J. and D. Wujastyk. 1991. "The Doctor's Assistant: Nursing in Ancient Indian Medical Texts." In P. Holden and J. Littlewood (eds), *Anthropology and Nursing*, 25–30. London/New York: Routledge.

Lincoln, B. 1996. "Theses on Method." *Method and Theory in the Study of Religion* 8(3): 225–227.

Mason, A. (2014). *Rasa Shāstra. The Hidden Art of Medical Alchemy*. London/ Philadelphia: Singing Dragon.

McGee, M. 1991. "Desired Fruits: Motive and Intention in the Votive Rites of Hindu Women." In J. Leslie (ed.), *Roles and Rituals for Hindu Women*, 71–88. London: Pinter.

Meulenbeld, G. J. 1992. "The Many Faces of Ayurveda." *Ancient Science of Life* 11(3–4): 106–113.

———. 1999–2002. *A History of Indian Medical Literature*, 5 vols. Groningen: E. Forsten.

Nichter, M, and M. Nichter. 2002. *Anthropology and International Health: Asian Case Studies*. London/New York: Routledge.

Pearson, A. M. 1996. "Because it Gives Me Peace of Mind." *Ritual Fasts in the Religious Lives of Hindu Women*. Albany: State University of New York Press.

Puri, H.S. (2003). *Rasayana. Ayurvedic Herbs for Longevity and Rejuvenation*. London/ New York: Routledge.

Rotaru, J. 2013. "The Śantyudakavidhi in the Atharvavedic Tradition." *Electronic journal of Vedic Studies* 20(1): 1–38.

Samuel, G. B. 2013. "The Subtle Body in India and Beyond." In Samuel, G. B. and J. Johnston (eds), *Religion and the Subtle Body in Asia and the West: Between Mind and Body*, 33–47. London: Routledge.

Sanderson, A. 1986. "Mandala and Āgamic Identity in the Trika of Kashmir." In Padoux, A. (ed.), *Mantras et Diagrammes Rituelles dans l'Hindouisme. Équipe no. 249. L'hindouisme: textes, doctrines, pratiques* (*Mantras and Ritual Diagrams in Hinduism. Team no. 249. Hinduism: Texts, Doctrines, Practices*), 169–214. Paris: Éditions du Centre National de la Recherche Scientifique.

———. 2009. "The Śaiva Age." In Einoo, S. (ed.), *Genesis and Development of Tantrism*, 41–349. Tokyo: Institute of Oriental Culture.

Slouber, M. 2012. *Gāruḍa Medicine: A History of Snakebite and Religious Healing in South Asia*. Unpublished PhD dissertation, University of California, Berkeley.

Smith, F. M. 2006. *The Self Possessed: Deity and Spirit Possession in South Asian Literature and Civilization*. New York: Columbia University Press.

Sujatha, V. 2007. "Pluralism in Indian Medicine: Medical Lore a Genre of Medical Knowledge." *Contribution to Indian Sociology* 41(2): 169–202.

Svoboda, R. E. 1992. *Ayurveda: Life, Health and Longevity*. London: Penguin Books.

———. 1997. *The Greatness of Saturn. A Therapeutic Myth*. Twin Lakes, WI: Lotus Press.

Timalsina, S. 2012. "Body, Self, and Healing in Tantric Ritual Paradigm." *The Journal of Hindu Studies* 5(1): 30–52.

Wadley, S. S. 2007. "Grāma." In S. Mittal and G. Thursby (eds), *The Hindu World*, 429–445. London/New York: Routledge.

Weiss, R. S. 2009. *Recipes for Immortality. Medicine, Religion, and Community in South India*. Oxford/New York: Oxford University Press.

White, D. G. 1996. *The Alchemical Body. Siddha Tradition in Medieval India*. Chicago/London: The University of Chicago Press.

Witzel, E. J. M. 1997. "The Development of the Vedic Canon and its Schools: The Social and Political Milieu." In M. Witzel (ed.), *Inside the Texts, Beyond the Texts. New Approaches to the Study of the Vedas*, 257–346. Cambridge: Harvard Oriental Series, Opera Minora 2.

Wujastyk, Dagmar. 2012. *Well-mannered Medicine. Medical Ethics and Etiquette in Classical Ayurveda*. Oxford/New York: Oxford University Press.

Wujastyk, Dominik. 2004. "Medicine and Dharma." *Journal of Indian Philosophy* 32(5/6): 831–842.

———. 2003a. *The Roots of Ayurveda: Selections from Sanskrit Medical Texts*. London: Penguin Books.

———. 2003b. "The Science of Medicine." In G. Flood (ed.), *The Blackwell Companion of Hinduism*, 393-409. Oxford: Blackwell.

Zeiler, X. (2008). *Die Göttin Dhūmāvatī. Vom tantrischen Ursprung zur Gottheit eines Stadtviertels in Benares*. Unpublished PhD dissertation, Universität Heidelberg.

Zimmermann, F. 2011. *The Jungle and the Aroma of Meats. An Ecological Theme in Hindu Medicine*. New Delhi: Motilal Banarsidass.

Zysk, K. G. 2000. "Does Indian Medicine Have a Theory of Contagion?" In L. I. Conrad and D. Wujastyk (eds), *Contagion. Perspectives from Pre-modern Societies*, 79–95. Aldershot: Ashgate.

———. 2002. "Mantra in Āyurveda: A Study of the Use of Magico-religious Speech in Ancient Indian Medicine." In H. P. Alper (ed.), *Understanding Mantras*, 122–143. New Delhi: Motilal Banarsidass.

———. 2009. *Medicine in the Veda. Religious Healing in the Veda*. New Delhi: Motilal Banarsidass.

———. 2010. *Asceticism and Healing in Ancient India. Medicine in the Buddhist Monastery*. New Delhi: Motilal Banarsidass.

## Indian Texts

AHS: Shrikantha Murthy, K. R. (trans.). 2011. *Vāgbhaṭa's Aṣṭāṅga Hṛdayam*, Vol. 3. Varanasi: Chowkhamba Sanskrit Series Office.

AVP: Vira, R. (ed.). 1936. *Atharva Veda of the Paippalādas*. Books 1–13. Lahore: Arya Bharati Press.

AVP: Lubotsky, Alexander (Text, translation, commentary). 2002. *Atharvaveda-Paippaladā. Kāṇḍa Five*. Cambridge, MA: Harvard University Press, Harvard Oriental Series, Opera Minora Vol. 4.

AVP: Griffiths, A. 2009. *The Paippalādasaṃhitā of the Atharvaveda. Kāṇḍas 6 and 7*. A New Edition with Translation and Commentary. Leiden: Brill.

AVŚ. Whitney, W. D. (trans.). 1905. *Atharva-Veda Saṃhitā*. Harvard Oriental Series, Vol. VII. Cambridge, MA: Harvard University Press.

BhPr: Shrikantha Murthy, K. R. (trans.). 2008. *Bhāvaprakāśa of Bhāva Miśra*, Vol. 2. Varanasi: Chowkhamba Sanskrit Series Office.

CaS: Sharma, R. K., and Dash, B. (ed. and trans). 2011. *Caraka Saṃhitā*, based on Cakrapāṇi Datta's Āyurveda Dīpikā, Vol. 6. Varanasi: Chowkhamba Sanskrit Series Office.

CU: Olivelle, P. (ed. and trans.). 1998. *Chāndogya Upaniṣad. The Early Upaniṣad. Annotated Text and Translation, 166–287*. New York: Oxford University Press.

KāS: Tewari, P. V. (ed. and trans.). 1996. *Kāśyapa-Saṃhitā or Vṛddhajīvakīya Tantra* (Text with English Translation and Commentary). Varanasi: Chaukhambha Visvabharati.

KauS: Bloomfield, M. (ed.). 1890. "The Kāuçika-Sūtra of the Atharva-Veda, with extracts from the Commentaries of Dārila and Keçava." *Journal of the American Oriental Society* 14: i+iii+v–vii+ix–lxviii+1–305+307–373+375–424.

KKG: *Kriyākālaguṇottaratantra*. Muktabodha Digital Library, Catalogue number M00278; Manuscript: NGMCP 3/392 reel number B 25/32.

Manu: Olivelle, P. (ed. and trans.). 2004. *Manu's Code of Law: A Critical Edition and Translation of the Mānava-Dharmaśāstra*. Oxford/New York: Oxford University Press.

MN: Murthy, K. R. S. 2011. *Mādhava Nidānam (Roga Viniścaya) of Mādhavakara*, (Text with English translation). Varanasi: Chaukhambha Orientalia.

MNT: Avalon, A. (Introduction and Commentary). 1913. *Tantra of the Great Liberation (Mahanirvāna Tantra)*, a translation from the Sanskrit. London: Luzac.

RV: Jamison, S. W., and Brereton, J. P. (trans.). 2014. *The Rigveda. The Earliest Religious Poetry of India*, three vols. Oxford/New York: Oxford University Press.

RVid: Bhat, M. S. 1987. *Vedic Tantrism: A Study of the Ṛgvidhana of Śaunaka with Text and Translation*. New Delhi: Motilal Banarsidass.

ŚB: Eggeling, J. (trans.). 1882–1900). *The Śatapatha Brāhamaṇa According to the Text of the Mādhyadina School*, Vol. 5. Oxford: Clarendon Press.

SkP: Tagare, G. V. (trans.). 2003. *Prabhāsakhaṇḍa. The Skanda Purāṇa*, Part XX. New Delhi: Motilal Banarsidass.

SuS: Bhishagratna, K. K. (trans.) and Dwivedi, L. (ed.). 2003. *Suśruta Saṃhitā*, Vol. 3. Varanasi: Chowkhamba Sanskrit Series Office.

TB: Śāstrī, A. M. (ed.). 1908-1921. *Taittirīyabrāhmaṇa with the Commentary of Bhaṭṭa Bhāskara Miśra*, Vols 1-3. Government Oriental Library, Biblioteca Sanskrita Series 36, 38, 42, and 57. Mysore: Government Branch Press. (Reprint, New Delhi: Motilal Banarsidass, 1985).

TS: Āgāśe, K. S., N. Talekar et al. (eds). 1900-1908. *Taittirīyasaṃhitā with the Commentary of Sāyaṇācārya* [*Kṛṣṇāyajurvedīyataittirīyasaṃhitā*], Vols 1-10. Pune: Ānandāśrama.

VS: Paṇśīkar, V. L. (ed.). 1929. Śuklayajurveda-Saṃhitā (Śrīmad-Vājasaneyi-Mādhyandina*). With the Mantrabhāṣya of Uvaṭācārya and the Vedadīpabhāṣya of Mahīdhara*. Mumbai: Nirṇayasāgara Press.

# Chapter 10

## Possession

### Elisabeth Schömbucher

Performances of possession have fascinated scholars by their very intensity. Watching a person in a state of trance, in which he/she is talking (or rather shouting) in a kind of singing recitation for sometimes more than an hour in front of a considerable audience, is one of the most impressive events that can be encountered in any field research in rural India. Such a possessed person might act as if completely out of control and bystanders take care to prevent serious injuries. The possessing entity might shout, cry, threaten, or insult the audience. After the entity has left its human vessel, the person seems normal again, just a little bit exhausted. Such observations have resulted in questions like: "What exactly happens, when a person is believed to be possessed by a spirit or a deity?" or "How do we explain that possession is still a common phenomenon in South Asia, whereas in Western countries it is of marginal importance at the most?" As a topic of research, possession is far from being outdated. As recent publications show, modernity does not make possession obsolete. The different forms of possession get integrated into a pluralistic system of social, ritual, and medical practice in today's India (Schömbucher, 1999).

When we speak of possession, usually two forms are distinguished: the term *spirit possession* refers to unwanted, uncontrolled states of possession by ghosts and demons, which are harmful for the possessed person, whereas the terms *possession mediumship* or *oracular possession* refer to ritually induced and controlled states of possession by deities or ancestors. Indian languages distinguish between the two forms, for example, *bhut badha* (harmful effect of the spirit) and *angat yene* (to come into the body) in Marathi (Stanley, 1988: 57), or *upadra* (trouble) *happened to so and so* and *darsana* (seeing the divine) *happened to so and so* in Tulu (Claus, 1984: 62). In the Himalayas, *jagar* (awakening) refers to a session of oracular possession in which the god comes or sits on the head (*sir pe ana/baithna*) of a *nacnevala* (dancer) and speaks through him/her to an audience (Malik, 2009: 83; Sax, 2009: 47). In South India, a person in or on whose body a deity comes is called *bhakturalu* (devotee) in Telugu and *camiyati* (god dancer) in Tamil (Schömbucher, 1999: 39). One might add a third form of possession that is enacted on stage by a ritual performer, such as in *teyyam* performances in Kerala, in which the deity is impersonated by a ritual specialist cum performer (Freeman, 1993: 114, 1998). Smith (2006) has shown that various forms of possession are already described in the Vedic and classical literature of India. The Sanskrit term *avesa* (entrance into) is used for the benevolent, controlled, self-induced form of possession, whereas the terms *pravesa* (to enter toward) and *grahana* (to grasp, to seize) refer to the uncontrolled, harmful form of possession by malevolent spirits.

The dichotomy between uncontrolled spirit possession and a more controlled and enacted form of oracular possession has been overemphasized by the Western thought. In Western societies, spirit possession nowadays belongs to the realm of psychiatry and possession mediumship to the realm of esoteric rituals. In India, on the contrary, spirit possession can and often does develop into possession medium- ship, as is shown in many case studies (Schömbucher, 1994a). One example is the story of Somavati, who as a young woman had been possessed by various malevolent spirits for several years. Obeyesekere (1977: 240ff) met Somavati in 1969 at a local shrine in a Colombo suburb in Sri Lanka where she was to be exorcized by a priest. She was as that time 29 years old, and during the previous two years had been possessed by several *pretas* and demons. Somavati was the eldest daughter of a poor farmer. Her father owned no land, so he left his natal village and earned his livelihood as a day laborer. Somavati was given to her maternal grandmother when she was just a few months old. At the age of 7, she was taken home by her parents, where she was to take care of a number of smaller siblings. At the age of 18 years, she married a 25-year-old mason despite the initial objections of her parents. In the coming years, Somavati gave birth to two children. She was frequently beaten by her husband who had turned out to be an alcoholic. Finally, she went back to her parents and got divorced.

Back in her parents' home, her situation became eventually unbearable. She had no income of her own and depended completely on her parents. In this situation, she became possessed for the first time. This first possession by a preta did not occur arbitrarily, but during an exorcistic ritual, in which the preta had been exorcized from another woman. It is considered extremely dangerous to attend such a ritual, since it is well known that an exorcized spirit tries to find another victim immediately. Somavati, however, had been asked to be present by her father's employer and could hardly object. Her situation was indeed perfect for the attack of a spirit. Her state of mind was extremely unbalanced. In terms of social status, she was in a liminal state (divorced, a mother of two children, and still dependent on her parents); moreover, she was asked to go out at dusk (a favorable time for malevolent spirits) and attend an exorcistic ritual. Thus, she predisposes herself to become the victim of a spirit's attack. In the following two years, other pretas took possession of Somavati. Eventually, she was also possessed by demons, such as Riri Yaka, the blood demon, and Mahasona, the great demon of the graveyard. Different exorcists had tried to rid her of these spirits and demons, but had succeeded for only short periods of time. The same or other spirits had come back. Finally, it was decided that the demons and all the pretas should be exorcized at a temple. An exorcistic ritual was arranged for Somavati and another possessed woman at a local temple of the goddess Pattini. It lasted the whole night and attracted a fairly large audience who had come to witness the struggle between the pretas and demons, impersonated by Somavati on the one side and various gods and goddesses impersonated by two priestly media on the other side. The media were possessed by the deities Skanda, Dadimunda, and Kali, who finally succeeded in convincing the demons to leave. Despite this successful exorcism, Somavati stayed on at the temple. One week after the exorcism, the goddess Pattini announced through the priestly medium that she would take possession of Somavati and prevent malevolent spirits from tormenting her as long as she worshiped the goddess. Pattini also announced the exact date, and four months after the exorcism, Somavati was initiated into the Pattini cult, becoming possessed by the goddess during the ritual. Somavati was now able to become possessed by Pattini regularly. She was also entitled to have her own shrine in the temple compound and to act as a priestly medium and oracle of the goddess Pattini. This brought Somavati high social prestige but obliged her to lead a somewhat ascetic way of life. In point of fact, Obeyesekere noted that in the four years following her initiation, she became irregularly possessed by Pattini. She worshiped her as her protective deity, but did not develop medial and divinatory abilities (Obeyesekere, 1977: 235–295; Schoembucher, 1993: 239–267). Somavati's story is unusually long when compared with other anthropological case studies. It shows that there is, of course, a distinction between the two forms of possession, which is also made by the people themselves, but there is also continuity rather than a dichotomy between the two forms. Somavati was first "patient" or "victim" and then became "medium" or "oracle." What looked at first like illness turned out to be a potential for ecstatic religious experience that could be developed into divine possession. The emphasis on dichotomy has had an effect on the anthropological interpretation of possession in other cultures. It is rooted in the cultural notions of possession among Western observers. Anthropologists, who are supposed to represent a culture from its indigenous point of view, are so much entangled in their own cultural concepts of person that it is difficult for them to consider other ideas of personhood. The notion that a person can be "possessed" by external, supernatural beings runs counter to Euro-American concept of person. The Western, pathological model of possession, which has played the most important role in the interpretation of possession, cannot comprehend developments such as those in Somavati's life story. The concept of person in South Asian culture sees the self as an unbounded entity that can be interspersed with equally unbounded divine or demonic entities (Schömbucher, 2006: 45f). In order to show how Euro-American ideas about possession have changed over time and how they have influenced the interpretation of possession cults in India, I will present the most famous possessed woman in Europe and then go on to discuss possession in South Asia.

## Possession and Religion

The most well-known European possessed woman is Soeur Jeanne des Anges, who lived in the 17th century in France. In the year 1632, Soeur Jeanne des Anges was possessed by a demon for the first time. She was then 27 years old and the prioress of the convent of the Ursulines founded in 1627 in the town of Loudun in central France. She was the highly educated daughter of a wealthy and influential family belonging to the higher nobility. After two years of suffering, which manifested itself in convulsions, hallucinations and fainting, as well as pain in different parts of her body, it was beyond doubt that seven demons had possessed Jeanne des Anges. They were Asmodi, Leviathan, Behemot, Isaakaaron, Baalam, Gresil, and Haman.

Two years later (1634), the bishop of Poitiers ordered that the Jesuit Father Jean-Joseph Surin, a well-known mystic of the time, should be her exorcist. In the following years, numerous exorcisms were held in the churches of Loudun. Her exorcisms were large, impressive public performances. An elevated stage was erected in front of the altar, so that the audience could see the spectacle of the battle between God and Satan. The stage was padded with mattresses so that the possessed woman would not hurt herself during her convulsions. After only seven weeks, in an exorcism attended by 6,000 people and in the presence of the bishop and other high-ranking persons, the first three demons (Asmodi, Gresil, and Haman) left her body, leaving three wounds beneath her heart (Soeur Jeanne, 1989: 83). The exorcisms of the other demons took another three years and were marked by severe illness and suffering. Isaakaaron, the demon of unchastity, was felt to be the most pertinent intruder. He came at night, and "he invoked the most indecent images to be imagined" (ibid.: 104). Isaakaaron's nocturnal attacks caused a false pregnancy, which lasted several months. During an exorcism where the bishop, several doctors and "a mass of other people" were present, the demon was forced to throw up the "whole amount of blood that he had accumulated in her body." After this exorcism, all signs of her pregnancy disappeared immediately (ibid.: 102).

With ascetic exercises, such as flagellation, fasting, sleep deprivation, sitting in cold water, extended prayers, wearing an iron belt, and rolling over hot coals, Jeanne des Anges fought against her demons. Her strict daily penances were finally successful. On November 5, 1635, during a great exorcism, Leviathan, the demon of arrogance and vanity, left her body, leaving a red cross on her forehead, which was visible for a few weeks. In the course of the following weeks, two other demons left her body. Behemot, the demon of blasphemy, was now the last remaining demon in her. He tried to prevent her from praying, and during the exorcisms uttered blasphemies against God. Another year of exorcisms, penances, flagellations, fasting, and bulimic attacks followed. On January 1, 1637, another exorcism was performed, despite her reservations because of her bad health. After this exorcism, she contracted a "lethal illness," with high fever, blood vomiting, and chest pain, which was diagnosed as pleurisy (Soeur Jeanne, 1989: 167–169). Five weeks later, Extreme Unction was performed for her. At death's door, Jeanne describes, she fell into ecstasy and again had a vision of St Joseph, who put a fragrant ointment on the parts of her body that hurt. Jeanne des Anges got off her death bed and was cured immediately—to the amazement of the doctors.

Her life now changed completely. After the miraculous cure, Jeanne had received a reliquary: On her chemise, there remained five stains of the fragrant oil with which she had been healed. When applied to the body of sick persons, it could perform miracles. She also had permanent stigmata—the sacred names of Jesus, Mary, Joseph, and Francis de Sales, written bloodred on her left hand—which renewed themselves from time to time. She made a long and triumphant journey through northern France and to Paris, where thousands of people wanted to see her stigmata. For that purpose, she was seated in a specially constructed wooden container-like room where she could display her hand on a pillow through a small window. In Paris, she was received by King Louis XIII, his wife Queen Anne of Austria, and Cardinal Richelieu. After the public excitement about her miracles and stigmata had calmed down, Jeanne des Anges spent quiet years in her convent. Her stigmata were renewed regularly, and she had almost daily visions of a beautiful, blond young man, whom she refers to as her "good angel," who acted as a mediator in her desire for mystical unity with God. She wrote her autobiography as well as numerous letters about her mystical experiences. After her death in 1665, the Ursuline nuns of her convent constructed a shrine, in which were kept her head, her chemise, and a drawing of her last exorcism. She was venerated as a quasi saint. Only in 1750, 85 years after her death, did the Bishop of Poitiers order that the shrine be dismantled.

What does the story of Jeanne des Anges, her demonic possession, her exorcisms, her miracles, and her mysticism tell us? It tells us first of all, that, like today, in the 17th century, people were fascinated by possession. To an outside observer, it was not possible to comprehend the experience of possession. It was not possible to know exactly what it meant and how it felt to be "possessed." Exorcisms were spectacular performances that attracted the nobility as well as the masses. Jeanne's accounts of her experiences made her an exotic other for her listeners. The degree of fascination is made obvious by the fact that not only did the publications on the events of Loudun increase during her lifetime, her possession again became the object of several publications in the 20th century: Huxley (1952) wrote *The Devils of Loudun*; Certeau (2000) wrote a historical treatise on *The Possession at Loudun*; several translations of Jeanne des Anges' autobiography were published (Ewers, 1989); Oesterreich (1921) described her life in great detail in his work *Possession*. Films such as Ken Russell's popular movie *The Devils* (1971) prove that she still inspires the fantasies of people in our times.

Second, the story of Jeanne des Anges tells us that there is not *one* *true* explanation of possession. In fact, there were several possibilities for society to deal with her's. Jeanne's possession states were not judged unanimously. Different possibilities were considered. It could have been a disease, which would have had to be cured with medical treatment; it could have been fraud (which would have been punished); it could have been a (negative) religious experience. In her case, it was the royal court and the Catholic Church that protected Jeanne and established the authoritative discourse. Jeanne des Anges' time was that of the Thirty Years' War of religions between Protestants and Catholics. It was a time when Huguenots constituted a majority in Loudun and when the Catholic king in Paris decided to impose centralist authority in the provinces. It was a time of plague epidemics, when 3,700 out of 14,000 inhabitants of Loudun died in 1632 between May and September. And it was still the time when political enemies were convicted as sorcerers and sentenced to death on the pyre. The priest Urbain Grandier was accused of publishing libertine ideas about celibacy, of having sexual relationships with daughters of the best families of Loudun, and of acting as a sorcerer, sending devils to Jeanne and her nuns. He was burnt in Loudun on August 18, 1634. Under these circumstances, Jeanne's exorcisms were an opportunity to strengthen Catholic and royal power. During her exorcisms, representatives of the high clergy and high nobility not only displayed curiosity, but also rendered political significance to possession and exorcism. But at the same time, Jeanne was examined by a whole series of physicians and surgeons from the famous medical faculties of Paris and Nantes, and she was treated with drugs, purgatives, and bleeding. Despite a few skeptics who saw the cause not in demons but in a mental disorder, such as melancholy, hysteromania, erotomania, and the force of imagination (Certeau, 2000: 134f), the authoritative religious discourse was confirmed by several doctors of medicine who declared that "we judge (given the excesses that surpass the natural) that there is possession by evil spirits, which appeared to us by divers signs that we deduce as requested" (Certeau, 2000: 114–115).

Third, spirit possession was and is always "the attempt to free oneself from it." Such attempts may consist in "transposing it, repressing it, [or] transferring it elsewhere" (ibid.: 227). After various unsuccessful attempts to repress it, Soeur Jeanne's possession was finally transferred from a demonic possession to mysticism, from a negative to a positive religious experience.

## Possession and Anthropology

With Jeanne des Anges in mind, let us turn to anthropological studies of possession in South Asia. An overview of the anthropological literature on the topic shows that the possessed person is the paradigmatic "exotic other." The possessed person, especially if it is a woman, looking fierce and acting wild, her eyes rolling and her hair flying, appears exalted and dangerous to the observer. She performs a role that is the opposite of what the decent, or even submissive, Indian woman is supposed to play. Questions as to whether this behavior is to be considered as pathological, or a genuine ecstatic experience, or merely a performance enacted for an audience have occupied researchers for generations (Bourguignon, 1976). As early as 1711, Bartholomaeus Ziegenbalg (1926 [1711]), the first Danish protestant missionary in South India, mentioned "devil dancers" in his *Malabarisches Heidentum*. He and other missionaries could still imagine that personified evil powers, such as the devils of Jeanne des Anges, could enter into human beings and then had to be exorcized by ritual specialists. The missionaries had no difficulties in seeing possession as an ecstatic religious experience, although they condemned the belief in Hindu deities as superstitious and pagan. Since the missionaries could not acknowledge Hindu deities as gods, and since according to Christian demonology, only "devils" could intrude into human beings, the *camiyati* (god dancer) in Tamil Nadu had to be called a "devil dancer." However, Ziegenbalg and other missionaries of his time were convinced that "devils" exist, that they can possess human beings, and that they are quite powerful and destructive. Missionaries, who are frequently perceived as the first anthropologists, provided comprehensive reports on possession. Although their cultural translation was restricted due to their Christian notion of demonology, they shared the belief that supernatural entities existed and could enter human beings.

Social anthropologists have had a much more ambiguous attitude toward possession. Their search for a deeper meaning of possession has resulted in a series of different interpretations (Boddy, 1994: 412). In the following survey, it becomes obvious that "translations" of possession from one culture to another run the risk of oversimplifying or even misinterpreting the phenomenon. Anthropological interpretation of possession cults started with the medical paradigm, according to which possession is seen as an expression of mental disease or stress. Jeanne's possession took place on the verge of several epistemological transformations. In her times, medical discourse was not yet dominant. Religious discourse was still valid. But she was the last possessed person to be treated in a religious manner. Her successors were all treated (unsuccessfully) in psychiatric wards. Today, anthropological studies on possession are also confronted with different epistemologies, but the other way round. For a long time, anthropologists have preferred medical discourse to religious discourse.

Many anthropological studies on possession can be subsumed under the heading "rationalistic reduction," in the sense that they are reducing a phenomenon to a single aspect (Oesterreich, 1921). Starting from a rational world view with the premise that nobody "really" can get possessed by spiritual entities, for spiritual entities do not "really" exist, possession is interpreted in medical terms—as a mental disease, such as hysteria, epilepsy, or neurosis in the case of spirit possession or as an indigenous therapy in the case of possession mediumship, with the possessed medium acting as an indigenous healer.

Often-quoted publications on spirit possession by Freed and Freed (1964, 1990), Kakar (1983), and Lewis (1989) argue that young women are especially likely to become possessed by evil spirits because they are oppressed by a dominant male society. In situations of stress, such as marrying into a new family or the breakup of a marriage, women take refuge in possession. This is seen as an "oblique strategy of attack" to fight against oppression (Lewis, 1989: 105)—or as the manifestation of mental disturbances due to severe stress (Kakar, 1983). These examples display anthropology's skepticism about native explanations. When people of another culture say that a young woman is possessed by spirits, in the eyes of anthropologists, she really undergoes some mental crisis, which she enacted in accordance with cultural concepts of spirit possession.

The American anthropologist Peter Claus, who carried out research on possession in south India, demanded in the 1980s that ethnography on possession should not be problem oriented, but should concentrate on the explorative method (Claus, 1984). This demand resulted in a number of ethnographies in which indigenous interpretations of possession and corresponding actions are presented. The most important aspect is the recognition of different concepts of person. Ideas of personhood vary widely among cultures. In India, possessed persons usually are not perceived to behave "as if" (although there are of course cases of fraud). A different concept of person provides a different experience of the world. Deities and demons are not perceived as "disembodied symbols" but are considered to be "divine persons" (Moreno, 1985: 119). Accordingly, essential aspects or elements of human and divine persons "can disaggregate, transmute and relocate back and forth among various kinds of animate and inanimate embodiments" (Freeman, 1999: 151).

In the interconnectedness of divine and human spheres, possession is one of several possibilities of divine manifestation in humans. On all levels of religious practice, not only priests are filled with divine substance or consciousness (*caitanyam*) during rituals (Kjaerholm, 1982: 191), but divine power is also highly present and accessible to devotees during festivals or rituals. Anybody can be possessed by divine power during festivals, although not all qualify to be a medium (Sontheimer, 1976: 139–140). Performers in the sacred theatre in South India, for example, are transformed into the deity by gazing into a mirror (Freeman, 1998). Similarly, the demonic can manifest itself in humans if certain preconditions (such as neglecting the gods, ritual impurity, or sorcery) are fulfilled.

Another important aspect in these explorative ethnographies is a different attitude toward the state of trance. Trance, the altered state of consciousness, is an important (and obvious) feature of possession. Since it is accompanied by amnesia, it has been seen for a long time as a state of dissociation, in which self-control and a sense of reality get lost. Several studies have shown that altered states of consciousness need not be pathological. Neurophysiological changes that induce trance states can be evoked with certain stimuli. Overstimulation by hyperkinetic mechanisms, such as music, dance, rhythm, or drums, or understimulation by monotony or meditation, can induce trance states. However, neurophysiological alterations are only a common basis; different cultural concepts are more important for the individual psychological reaction, as has been shown with peyote experiments (Ludwig, 1968; Prince, 1966; Walker, 1972: 146). In many non-western societies, so-called "normal" people can easily enter altered states of consciousness. Numerous examples of spontaneous trance states during rituals or religious processions show that this is not an exceptional (or pathological) behavior (e.g., Inglis, 1985; Kapadia, 1995, 1996; Sontheimer, 1976; Stanley, 1988).

Ethnographies on possession in South Asia show that when a young woman gets possessed, certain actions are taken to free her from this unwanted condition. We can distinguish three different types of attempts to free a person from possession: exorcism, medical treatment, and the acknowledgement of ecstatic abilities and their development into controlled possession or possession mediumship. A woman who shows symptoms such as fainting, hearing voices, speaking insultingly, or other strange behavior is not necessarily assumed to be possessed by unwanted and harmful spirits. The possibility of a mental illness is always considered. Bruce Kapferer has provided many examples of young women who were treated simultaneously in hospitals and by exorcists, as the story of Asoka's possession shows. She was eight years old when she suddenly awoke close to midnight, complaining of a headache and severe stomach cramps. She also heard a voice. Her mother identified this voice as the ghost of her deceased elder sister who had died almost exactly on this day a year ago. She summoned a local exorcist to her house. He supported her interpretation and also elaborated it. He suggested that Asoka could also be possessed by the demon Mahasona, since she had eaten prawns for dinner before the onset of her illness. He tied a thread to keep away ghosts and demons that would be effective for three days. In the meantime, Asoka's mother's elder sister came by and insisted that Asoka be taken to a hospital. Medical tests for meningitis and other diseases proved negative. While Asoka was in hospital, her mother summoned another exorcist. He reconfirmed the initial diagnosis and tied another thread for three days. Asoka's symptoms reappeared after three days. At this point, another elder sister of Asoka's mother intervened. She supported the exorcist's diagnosis of an attack by the demon Mahasona. She also raised the possibility of sorcery. She could convince everybody that not only Asoka was affected by the demon, but that the whole family would be suffering unless an exorcism for Mahasona would be performed. In the end, the family started preparing for an elaborated and expensive exorcism ritual (Kapferer, 1991: 89–96). With many similar examples, Kapferer could show that the diagnosis is a complex process of negotiations among exorcists, the patient, family members, relatives and neighbors on how to interpret a "demonic illness." Different interpretations compete with each other for some time, and it is in this discursive process that the demonic eventually is shaped and constituted within a certain context (ibid.: 105).

If neither exorcism nor medical treatment is successful, the possession states are controlled in a different way. Gananath Obeyesekere has provided us in *Medusa's Hair* with many examples of women like Somavati, described above, who were initially possessed by unwanted and harmful spirits, such as pretas and *bhuts*. After several unsuccessful exorcisms to banish the spirits, they were converted from malevolent into protecting beings. The possessed women could eventually, after an initial period of suffering and crisis, develop their potential for divine possession. As ecstatic priests, they are able to control their possession states. Thus, in Obeyesekere's words, "[i]n a ritual of exorcism demon, priest, patient, god, parents, and community are all involved in a grand cosmic drama put together from existing myth models into a larger grammar of meaningful action" (1981: 102). Another example is the Siri cult in south India. The initial possession of the goddess Siri is perceived as a threatening new experience by the affected young woman. Only after her family acknowledges her as a vessel for the deity and makes arrangements for regular worship of the deity in her temple does this negative experience develop into a positive one (Claus, 1984).

New insight into the phenomenon of possession has been provided by Smith's (2006) book *The Self Possessed*. In this comprehensive study, Smith analyzes Indic literature from all ages—the earliest Vedic texts, the epics, devotional literature, and Sanskrit drama, to mention just a few. He identifies several forms of possession in Vedic and classical literature that correspond with the distinction made in modern Indian languages: the benevolent, controlled, self-induced form of possession (avesa) and the uncontrolled, harmful form of possession by malevolent spirits (pravesa and grahana). A comparison of Sanskrit texts and modern ethnographies shows a long tradition of consistent experiences of possession in the cultural tradition of South Asia. Smith shows that possession occurred in all regions and in all social strata of the subcontinent. He also found that already in Vedic texts, more women got possessed by evil spirits, whereas the positive self-induced form of possession was mainly reserved for men. There is no reason given for that in the texts and Smith's cautious interpretation agrees with the anthropological findings: As weaker persons, women are more susceptible to negative possession, whereas men have more access to ritual practices, and therefore self-induced possession. With his diachronic study of possession, Smith is able to show that, for thousands of years, positive possession is the most common form of spiritual expression in India. It exists side by side with the negative, disease-producing possession. For Smith, possession, in the widest sense, is a "state of mind characterized by intensity, emotional excitement, and desire" (2006: 590).

## The Cultural Translation of Possession

With these examples in mind, let us turn to the level of cultural translation. We have to ask, how can we interpret possession in the 21st century without reducing it to the symbolic manifestation of some psychic disorder, and without saying that "the other" is superstitious, irrational, unsophisticated, using folk concepts, or acting "as if"? What are possessed persons? Are they hysterical, oppressed, and manipulative—or are they religious specialists, ecstatics, mystics, who are sensitive to a different reality that manifests itself as a positive or negative religious experience?

Ethnography has shown that the interpretation of possession is a complex undertaking. It is not enough to consider the individual psychology; the social context and especially the concept of the person have to be considered as well. Even then, the cultural translation of possession is accompanied by a process of desacralization. In analogy to an icon, which is God for a devotee (Davis, 1997) but an art object with aesthetic qualities for an outside observer, we tend to say that a woman possessed by a spirit undergoes a crisis, and that a possessed medium or oracle is a person (with communicative competence and poetic talents) who, acting *as if* possessed, interprets problems of others and can be considered as an indigenous healer. Does this mean that the cultural translation of possession is not possible without desacralization? Would it be more adequate to say that the possessed medium has access to supernatural entities whose existence remains opaque to ordinary people in their normal waking consciousness? Lévi-Strauss (1965: 297) once said, "No common analysis of religion can be given by a believer and a non-believer, and from this point of view, the type of approach known as 'religious phenomenology' should be dismissed."

To answer the question about cultural translation and desacralization, I will consider my own research on possession mediumship among the Vadabalija, a Telugu-speaking south Indian fishing caste (Schömbucher, 1994a, 1994b, 1998, 1999, 2001, 2006). Whenever, after a possession séance where the goddess spoke through her medium to an audience of about 20 people, I asked, "What did the goddess say?" more than one hour of recitation could be summarized with just one or two sentences: "She said, you didn't worship me. Therefore, I have made your child sick. You have to worship me and make offerings." Although the answers were always correct and although similar answers are obviously the basis of most anthropological writings on possession, cultural translation has to take into consideration what else is being said and how is it said in possession séances.

A performative approach to language as social action can avoid desacralization (Schömbucher, 2003). It has been overlooked that possession is expressed verbally, as stated by Nuckolls (1991, 1992). As a speech event, it has to be seen as a cultural praxis in which contexts of human lives are constructed and performed by linguistic means. According to speech–act theory, language not only represents or refers to reality, it also creates it (Austin, 1962). Divine or demonic presence is created verbally, based on the assumption that gods or demons exist as persons (not merely as symbols). Words in performances are not only referential but they construct meaning. According to Foley (1995: 208), the power of words is derived from the performance as enabling event and a certain tradition as enabling referent. Foley has created the term *performance arena* as "the locus where an event of performance takes place, where words are invested with their special power" (Foley, 1995: 209). Words spoken through a possessed medium do not convey meaning on their own. One important factor of the *performance arena* is the audience, which gives words their illocutionary power. What is spoken during states of possession is interpreted through listening. Besides speaking, listening should be considered a cultural practice influenced by cultural concepts (Burghart, 1996).

What do listeners hear when deities speak to them? As a performative event, a possession séance among the Telugu-speaking Vadabalija consists of three sections, which I call evocative, narrative, and directive (Schömbucher, 2011: 83). Divinities are not just present in humans, divine presence has to be created. Among the Vadabalija, it is created in the evocative section with panegyric elements in which the goddess praises her power and guarantees that she and all the other deities have always protected the devotees. The language is highly formulaic and repetitive. In the narrative sections, the goddess recounts the reasons for individual misfortune, illness, etc. This has to be specific. It has to fit individual experience as well as cultural models of misfortune. In the directive passages, the goddess gives instructions for future actions, very often saying that people should worship her more or make specific offerings.

While the evocative passages bestow the power of the divine utterances, it is the narrative passages that make the divine words true. In the narrative passages, the goddess proves that she knows everything and that everything she says is correct. The third section, in which the goddess gives directives to her devotees, is developed in a dialogue with the audience. The audience may protest at the beginning against the demand of a sacrifice and it is negotiated between audience and goddess to what extent her demands are justified and acceptable. Only mutual agreement makes the divine demands obligatory (Schömbucher, 2006, 2011).

It is the audience who gives authority and efficacy to the divine words. When the Vadabalija summarized the divine words for me, they would mention the directives, the demands of the goddess. If I insisted long enough, they gave an account of the narrative passages in which the causes of misfortune were explained. Interestingly, here, the audience heard more and different things than what I could find in the translations of the texts. Often, their own versions were mixed with the divine version. They never mentioned the evocative and panegyric elements with which divine presence had been created. There was no need for that because divine presence and power are accepted beyond doubt.

In the course of the "linguistic turn" in the social sciences during the 1990s, possession has come to be perceived as a performance in which meaning is created with verbal and other performative devices. The new approaches allow us to look at possession not as an event in which the possessed person acts "as if," but as one in which a certain reality is created by the performer as well as the audience. In their studies on possession cults in the Himalayas, both Sax (2009) and Malik (2009) add a new dimension to performativity. According to their observations, it is not only the words of the songs that cause possession, but the appearance of the God is also a matter of embodiment rather than of language: The God dances (*nacna*) or is made to dance (*nacana*) by the exorcist in the body of the oracle. Therefore, Sax concludes that an interpretation of possession would need a hermeneutics of the body rather than a hermeneutics of the text (Sax, 2009: 47). Similarly, Malik concludes from his fieldwork on possession rituals:

> [T]hat the *jagar* can be more fruitfully described as a ritual of embodiment rather than a ritual of possession or trance—since the category of possession itself carries within it a considerable amount of cultural bias and theoretical implications suggesting a duality of body and consciousness or spirit. (Malik, 2009: 92)

## New Approaches to the Study of Possession

Possession is still a widely prevalent cultural practice in the Indian subcontinent. A wide range of different forms of possession can be witnessed. Regarding spirit possession, the tormented person shows various signs of physical or mental disorders. Regarding the more controlled forms of oracular possession or spirit mediumship, we can observe various processes. In some instances, language might be the most important medium for invoking the deity into the human body, in others, it is the rhythm of drums, and again in others, looking into a mirror completes the transformative process by which a divine entity enters the human body of a performer. Naturally, each researcher stresses as important what he or she has observed. A comparative approach that encompasses different forms of possession enables us to crystallize some common features.

Each form of possession needs two protagonists. In the case of spirit possession, there is always a victim possessed by spirits and an exorcist who is trying to free the tormented person from malevolent spirits (Schömbucher, 2004a). In the case of oracular possession or spirit mediumship, there are ritual specialists, priests (or gurus, as in the central Himalayas) who invoke and control the possessing entities and oracles or mediums who are able to embody these entities (Schömbucher, 2004b). A guru, according to Sax,

> is summoned in order to control spirits of affliction; to exorcize them, to turn their curses into blessings, to compel them to do his client's bidding. He must show no fear, [he must be] self-assured and in control of himself as well as the gods and spirits. (2009: 112)

Possession cults are cults of affliction and healing in which the disturbed family unity is restored. The typical object of ritual healing is the group and not an individual (Kapferer, 1991; Sax, 2009). Still, as Krengel observes:

> [S]pirit possession is a very complex institution, which is simultaneously concerned with a whole range of issues [...] *jagars* are not just held for the purpose of healing, but provide a stage for active discourses on past, present and future affairs of the local society. A *jagar* resembles a journey, for which an actual problem or symptom is just the starting point. The oracular communication with the divine (evil spirits and deities) leads to misdeeds that have no connection with the symptoms and deeds of the person suffering. (1999: 287)

Despite its dramatic appearance, which at first sight is emotionally overwhelming to an outsider, possession states are verbally constructed events whose structures are well ordered and can be anticipated by the audience. Besides the two types of protagonists mentioned above, a third element is needed in possession, the audience. Words spoken in a state of possession cannot be efficacious on their own. Despite the ritual setting in which they are spoken and the communicative competence of the possessed person, they need an addressee who makes them efficacious. Speaking alone does not provide words with illocutionary power, but merely acts as a presupposition for listeners to do so (Schömbucher, 2011: 82–85).

From the perspective of an indigenous listener, possession mediumship is an occasion in which human beings (medium and audience) can create divine presence for a short while. From the perspective of an external listener who acknowledges speech–act theory, the possessed media are extraordinarily gifted persons who are able to create divine presence and interpret the world by their specific communicative competence and poetic talent. Their interpretations are only efficacious if acknowledged by the audience.

For both kinds of listeners, possession is not primarily a healing ritual, although illness is a frequent topic; possession is not primarily divination, although questions concerning the future are answered. For indigenous listeners, possession is an occasion to worship the gods, be near them, and talk with them. Accordingly, in a case of spirit possession, indigenous listeners create a performance arena where the demonic words are invested with special power. Viewed this way, possession is not a *premodern* way of explaining things, but one of several possible discourses to explain personal misfortune, illness, etc. In terms of efficacy, divine words are comparable to other forms of discourse.

Is possession really possible? How does it work? Are possession rituals efficacious? If so, why? Anthropological research still revolves around these crucial questions (Goodman, 1988, 1990). One way of answering these questions is the performative approach to language, according to which, divine presence is created verbally. Another way of answering the same questions is Malik's proposal of a hermeneutics of embodiment or rather embodied consciousness, instead of considering "trance," "ritual," and "oracle" as the center of investigation (Malik, 2009: 80). If we perceive possession as rituals of embodiment, we could speak "of a system of 'knowledge and practices' rather than 'beliefs and practices,'" since embodied consciousness is knowledge (ibid.: 92). Both approaches have brought us closer to the events experienced by the actors themselves, with fewer Western presuppositions about the reality of the experience.

# References

Austin, John L. 1962. *How to Do Things with Words*. Oxford: Oxford University Press.

Boddy, J. 1994. "Spirit Possession Revisited: Beyond Instrumentality." *Annual Review of Anthropology* 23: 407–434.

Bourguignon, E. 1976. *Possession*. San Francisco: Chandler.

Burghart, Richard. 1996. *The Conditions of Listening*. In C. J. Fuller and J. Spencer (eds), *Essays on Religion, History and Politics in South Asia*. New Delhi: Oxford University Press.

Certeau, Michel de. 2000. *The Possession at Loudun*. Chicago/London: University of Chicago Press.

Claus, Peter J. 1984. "Medical Anthropology and the Ethnography of Spirit Possession." *Contributions to Asian Studies* 18: 60–72.

Davis, Richard H. 1997. *Lives of Indian Images*. Princeton: Princeton University Press.

Ewers, Hanns Heinz. 1989. "Vorwort zur ersten Auflage der deutschen Ausgabe (1911) (Foreword to the first German edition [1911])." In Soeur Jeanne (ed.), *Memoiren einer Besessenen (Memoirs of a Possessed)*. Hg. v. Michael Farin. Nördlingen: Greno Taschenbuch Verlag.

Foley, John Miles. 1995. *The Singer of Tales in Performance*. Bloomington/Indianapolis: Indiana University Press.

Freed, R. S. and S. A. Freed. 1990. "Ghost Illness in a North Indian Village." *Social Science and Medicine* 30(5): 617–623.

Freed, S. A. and R. S. Freed. 1964. "Spirit Possession as Illness in a North Indian Village." *Ethnology* 3: 152–171.

Freeman, Richard. 1993. "Performing Possession: Ritual and Consciousness in the Teyyam Complex of Northern Kerala." In H. Brückner, L. Lutze, and A. Malik (eds), *Flags of Fame. Studies in South Asian Culture*. New Delhi: Manohar.

———. 1998. "Formalised possession among the Tantris and Teyyams of Malabar." *South Asia Research* 18(1): 73–98.

———. 1999. "Dynamics of the Person in the Worship and Sorcery of Malabar." In J. Assayag and G. Tarabout (eds), *Possession in South Asia. Speech, Body, Territory* (Special Issue of Puruùàrtha 21), 149–182. Paris: Collections Purusartha. Éditions de l'École des Hautes Études en Sciences Sociales.

Goodman, Felicitas. 1988. *How About Demons? Possession and Exorcism in the Modern World*. Bloomington/Indianapolis: Indiana University Press.

———. 1990. *Where the Spirits Ride the Wind*. Bloomington/Indianapolis: Indiana University Press.

Huxley, Aldous. 1952. *The Devils of Loudun*. New York: Harper and Row.

Inglis, Stephen. 1985. "Possession and Pottery: Serving the Divine in a South Indian Community." In J. P. Waghorne and N. Cutler (eds), *Gods of Flesh, Gods of Stone. The Embodiment of Divinity in India*. Chambersburg, PA: Anima Publications.

Kakar, Sudhir. 1983. *Shamans, Mystics and Healers. A Psychological Enquiry into India and its Healing Traditions*. Oxford: Oxford University Press.

Kapadia, K. 1995. *Siva and Her Sisters: Gender, Caste, and Class in Rural South India.* Oxford: Westview.

——. 1996. "Dancing the Goddess: Possession and Class in Tamil South India." *Modern Asian Studies* 30 (2): 423–445.

Kapferer, Bruce. 1991 [1983]. *A Celebration of Demons. Exorcism and the Aesthetics of Healing in Sri Lanka.* Bloomington: Indiana University Press.

Kjaerholm, Lars. 1982. "Possession and Substance in Indian Civilization: Thoughts Emanating from Field-work in South India." *Folk* 24: 179–196.

Krengel, Monika. 1999. "Spirit Possession in the Central Himalayas. Jagar-rituals: An Expression of Customs and Rights." In J. Assayag and G. Tarabout (eds), *Possession in South Asia: Speech, Body, Territory* (Purusartha 21), 265–288. Paris: Collections Purusartha. Éditions de l'École des Hautes Études en Sciences Sociales.

Levi-Strauss, Claude. 1965. "The Bear and the Barber." In William Lessa and Evon Z. Vogt (eds), *Reader in Comparative Religion,* 2nd ed, 289–297. New York/London: Harper and Row.

Lewis, I. M. 1989. *Ecstatic Religion. A Study of Shamanism and Spirit Possession.* New York/London: Routledge.

Ludwig, Arnold. 1968. "Altered States of Consciousness." In Raymond Prince (ed.), *Trance and Possession States.* Montreal: R.M. Bucke Memorial Society.

Malik, Aditya. 2009. "Dancing the Body of God: Rituals of Embodiment from the Central Himalayas." *Sites:* New Series 6(1): 80–96.

Moreno, Manuel. 1985. "God's Forceful Call: Possession as a Divine Strategy." In Joanna P. Waghorne and Norman Cutler (eds), *Gods of Flesh, Gods of Stone. The Embodiment of Divinity in India.* Chambersburg, PA: Anima Publications.

Nuckolls, Charles W. 1991. "Deciding How to Decide: Possession Mediumship in Jalari Divination." *Medical Anthropology* 13: 57–82.

Nuckolls, Charles W. 1992. "Divergent Ontologies of Suffering in South Asia." *Ethnology* 31: 57–74.

Obeyesekere, Gananath. 1977. "Psychocultural Exegesis of a Case of Spirit Possession in Sri Lanka." In V. Crapanzano and V. Garrison (eds), *Case Studies in Spirit Possession.* New York: Wiley.

——. 1981. *Medusa's Hair. An Essay on Personal Symbols and Religious Experience.* Chicago/London: University of Chicago Press.

Oesterreich, Traugott Konstantin. 1921. *Die Besessenheit (Possession).* Langensalza: Wendt und Klauwell.

Prince, Raymond. 1966. *Trance and Possession States.* Montreal: R.M. Bucke Memorial Society.

Sax, William S. 2009. *God of Justice. Ritual Healing and Social Justice in the Central Himalayas.* Oxford: Oxford University Press.

Schömbucher, Elisabeth. 1993. "Gods, Ghosts and Demons: Possession in South Asia." In H. Brückner, L. Lutze, and A. Malik (eds), *Flags of Fame. Studies in South Asian Culture.* New Delhi: Manohar.

——. 1994a. "When the Deity Speaks: Performative Aspects of Possession Mediumship in South India." In J. Kuckertz, Hg. (ed.), *Jahrbuch für musikalische Volks- und Völkerkunde (Yearbook of Musical Folklore Studies and Ethnology)* (Band 15). Eisenach: Karl Dietrich Wagner.

Schömbucher, Elisabeth. 1994b. "The consequences of not keeping a promise: Possession Mediumship among a South Indian Fishing Caste." *Cahiers de Litt,rature Orale* 35: 41–64.

———. 1998. "Death as the Beginning of a New Life. Hero Worship among a South Indian Fishing Caste." In E. Schömbucher and C. P. Zoller (eds), *Ways of Dying. Death and its Meanings in South Asia*. New Delhi: Manohar.

———. 1999. "A Daughter for Seven Minutes: The Therapeutic and Divine Discourses of Possession Mediumship in South India." In J. Assayag and G. Tarabout (eds), *Possession in South Asia: Speech, Body, Territory* (Purusartha 21), 33–60. Paris: Collections Purusartha. Éditions de l'École des Hautes Études en Sciences Sociales.

———. 2001. "Inviting Deities into Lord Jagannath's Town: The Religious Practice of the Vadabalija Fishermen of Puri." In H. Kulke and B. Schnepel (eds), *Jagannath Revisited: Studying Society, Religion and the State in Orissa*. New Delhi: Manohar.

——— (with Heidrun Brückner). 2003. "Performances." In Veena Das (ed.), *The Oxford India Companion to Sociology and Social Anthropology*, S. 598–624. New Delhi: Oxford University Press.

———. 2004a. "Exorcism." In Peter J. Claus and Margaret A. Mills (eds), *South Asian Folklore: An Encyclopedia*. New York: Garland Publishing Inc.

———. 2004b. "Possession." In Peter J. Claus and Margaret A. Mills (eds), *South Asian Folklore: An Encyclopedia*. New York: Garland Publishing Inc.

———. 2006. *Wo Götter durch Menschen sprechen: Besessenheit in Indien* (*Where Gods Speak through Humans: Possession in India*). Berlin: Dietrich Reimer Verlag.

———. 2011. "Divine Words, Human voices: Listening to the Female Voice in Performances of Possession." In Heidrun Brückner, Hanne M. de Bruin, and Heike Moser (eds), *Between Fame and Shame. Performing Women—Women Performers in India*. Wiesbaden: Harrassowitz.

Smith, Frederick M. 2006. *The Self Possessed. Deity and Spirit Possession in South Asian Literature and Civilization*. New York: Columbia University Press.

Soeur Jeanne. 1989. *Memoiren einer Besessenen* (*Memoirs of a Possessed*). Hg. v. Michael Farin. Nördlingen: Greno Taschenbuch Verlag.

Sontheimer, Günther Dietz. 1976. *Biroba, Mhaskoba und Khandoba: Ursprung, Geschichte und Umwelt von pastoralen Gottheiten in Maharashtra* (*Biroba, Mhaskoba and Khandoba: Origin, History and Environment of Pastoral Deities in Maharashtra*). Wiesbaden: Franz Steiner Verlag.

Stanley, John M. 1988. "Gods, Ghosts, and Possession." In Maxine Berntsen and Eleanor Zelliot (eds), *The Experience of Hinduism: Essays on Religion in Maharashtra*. Albany: State University of New York.

Walker, Sheila. 1972. *Ceremonial Spirit Possession in Africa and Afro-America*. Leiden: E.J. Brill.

Ziegenbalg, Bartholomaeus. 1926 [1711]. *Ziegenbalg's Malabarisches Heidentum* (*Ziegenbalg's Malabarian Heathenism*), edited and published by W. Caland. Amsterdam: Verhandelingen der Koninklijke Akademie van Wetenschappen te Amsterdam.

# Chapter 11

## The Urban Hindu Arranged Marriage in Contemporary Indian Society

### Reshmi Lahiri-Roy

The Hindu arranged marriage is one of the oldest surviving cultural practices in the world. In this chapter, I have ventured to explore the dominant sociocultural discourses[1] that have shaped and are currently shaping the urban Hindu arranged marriage. This chapter discusses the importance of the traditions of the Hindu marriage amongst urban middle- and upper middle-class Hindus. It briefly traces the roots and origins of the ideals in conjunction with the ideological constructs shaping the Hindu woman. While examining the strategic role played by the institution of marriage in the functioning of the Indian social system, the chapter simultaneously discusses the importance of the extended family system in India. The influence wielded by the extended family within the Indian social discourses has to be understood in relation to arranged marriages, as they are usually inextricably linked. The roles of caste and class within the urban Hindu arranged marriages are also focal points within the chapter. This analysis is conceptual, and therefore based completely on literary study. In no way does this discussion claim to have covered all required ground; but it attempts to give a broad general idea of the social, historical, cultural, and other factors that go into the making of a contemporary Hindu arranged marriage. It also briefly touches upon possible directions for contemporary and future research scholars with regard to this ancient institution.

Examining the often paradoxical nature of the Hindu marital culture in urban India and the traditional norms governing the origins of marriage as a social institution, the use of cultural sanctions as means of patriarchal control through social and religious traditions is touched upon within the discursive analysis. This research is focused on India's urban middle and upper classes, and generally the upper castes. It lays no claims to scholarship with regard to arranged marriages amongst Dalits, rural Hindu India, or the economically disadvantaged dwelling across India. This has been done keeping in mind the limitations of scope of the analysis and, most importantly, the insufficiency of my scholarly knowledge with regard to the abovementioned issues. This study delves into historical comment but does so only to connect its relevance to the contemporary discourse regarding marriage that is the issue under analysis.

## The Traditional Hindu Marriage

In India, marriage or *vivaha*, as it is termed in Sanskrit, is the single most important event in the lives of individuals. It continues to contain almost all the ancient features from its time of origin. The history of Hindu marriage can be traced back a few millennia. H. N. Chatterjee (1972), the Sanskrit scholar and historian, in his study, *Studies in the Social Background of the Forms of Marriage in Ancient India*, comments:

> Marriage to the Hindus is a religious institution to which the famous definition of marriage in Roman Law is fully applicable. It is indeed, as in ancient Rome, an association for life and productive of full partnership, both in human and divine rights and duties.[2] To them marriage involves sacred and onerous duties. (Chatterjee, 1972: 4)

The Vedas set out in detail the ritualistic importance of the nuptial ceremony and the significance of each ritual attached to it.[3] The rites of the Hindu marriage ceremony are very complex and have not undergone much simplification over the years. Pandit Bhaiyaram Sarma, the Indian historian and classical scholar, writes:

> Ceremonial rites and rituals occupy a place of utmost importance in the life of a devout Hindu ... any average religious Hindu Society, however urbanized and unorthodox, has not been able to ring out the old when every little work in the Hindu home, sacred or profane, begins with the performance of appropriate rites according to the prescribed code. (Sarma, 1993: vii: Introduction)

Ancient scriptures outline various forms of marriage. Some are not totally acceptable; others are very much in evidence even with the passage of a few thousand years.[4] Within the rituals of the traditional Hindu marriage were embedded certain concepts that are very much a feature of the contemporary Hindu nuptials. The wife as *Ardhangini* is one such important concept within Hindu norms. In ancient Hindu tradition, a man's life was not considered complete without a wife, his ardhangini or other half. H. N. Chatterjee writes:

> The high conception of marriage in India may be traced back to the age of the Vedas ... the *Satapathabrahmana* emphatically declares that a wife is half of one's person and therefore before getting a wife, a man cannot be said to be complete. (Chatterjee, 1972: 13)

Contained in Reverend J. E. Padfield's 1908 book, *The Hindu at Home: Being Sketches of Hindu Daily Life,* one of the earliest books on the subject and now increasingly rare and expensive, is Sir Monier Williams' (who was Boden Professor of Sanskrit at Oxford University) translation of a passage from the Hindu epic, *Mahabharata*:

> *A wife is half the man, his truest friend;*
> *A loving wife is a perpetual spring*
> *Of virtue, pleasure, wealth; a faithful wife*
> *Is his best aid in seeking heavenly bliss;*
> *A sweetly-speaking wife is a companion*
> *In solitude, a father in advice,*
> *A rest in passing through life's wilderness.*[5] (Padfield, 1908: 48)

The occasionally paradoxical nature of the traditional Hindu view of marriage is observed when one compares the above translation with the assertion from the *Manusmriti*[6] that contradictorily states that a wife is subordinate to husband's will at all stages. In Chapter 5 of Professor George Buhler's (1886) translation of the *The Laws of Manu*, one comes across a decree stating, "Though destitute of virtue, or seeking pleasure (elsewhere), or devoid of good qualities, (yet) a husband must be constantly worshipped as a god by a faithful wife" (ibid.: 154). In contrast is a proclamation by the female goddess in the *Rigveda* that goes, "I am the banner and the head, a mighty arbitress am I: I am victorious, and my Lord shall be submissive to my will."[7]

Also, according to R. C. Majumdar and Pusalker, the marriage hymn in the *Rigveda* (RV 10.85.26) claims that the wife "should address the assembly as a commander" (1951: 424). They also suggest that Rigvedic verses indicate that women were free to enter marriage at a mature age (Majumdar and Pusalker, 1951: 394). But again in the *Manusmriti*, there are Rigvedic verses demeaning to women. For instance, in the *Rigveda*, one comes across a verse that proclaims, "Indra himself hath said, the mind of woman brooks not discipline. Her intellect hath little weight."[8] These Rigvedic hymns are probably the earliest references to the position of women in the Hindu society. A. L. Basham, the noted Indologist, refers to the *dharmashastras* (Instructions in sacred law) in his book, *The Origins and Development of Classical Hinduism,* and with regard to the status of women in ancient India comments that "the woman's status in ancient India was always inferior to that of the man, her punishment for wrongdoing being, according to the law books, equivalent to that given a *sudra*" (1989: 105).

Another important feature of the Hindu marriage was the concept of *Stridhana*. In ancient India, women were given gifts that were termed Stridhana and were her property alone. As Basham (1967: 179; 1989: 105) explains, they were passed on to her female offspring. Stridhana was not property received by the wife from either her father-in-law or her husband. Kautilya, the ancient Indian philosopher in the court of the Mauryas, in his political treatise, *Arthashastra,* discourses on the woman's right to property or Stridhana, as does the self-contradictory *Manusmriti.* Such property belonged to the wife alone and was not to be touched by the groom or his parents except in emergencies such as ill-health, famine, performing religious ceremonies, and so on. But simultaneously, the *Manusmriti* confusingly declares that a wife has no property and the wealth earned is for the husband (Buhler, 1886: VIII.416).

## The Marriage Rituals

The Hindu marriage bond is considered unbreakable and amongst most Hindus there exists a spiritual belief that if the couple remain true to each other, marriages being preordained like all things, the same couple will reunite in all births through eternity. Although customs vary according to factors such as region, caste, community, sect, and such other factors, there are certain basic features of any Hindu marriage such as the *Kanyadaan* or giving away of the virgin bride by the father to the groom, the *Panigrahana* or the acceptance of the bride's hand by the groom, as well as the very essential *Saptapadi,* the seven steps around the holy fire that with cited promises and vows bind man and woman together as husband and wife for all eternity. But present within these rituals are many complexities and ambiguities, demonstrating the existing pitfalls, if a layman attempts to practice the rituals without the presence of the priests, who are considered to hold all keys to the ambiguities.[9] Chatterjee (1972: 3) is of the opinion that the extreme complexity of the rituals of Hindu marriage has evolved because of the contribution of "the great masses of people and races with divergent levels of culture" whereas Paul B. Courtright, scholar of Religious and Asian Studies, in his introductory essay on the section on Hinduism in *Sex, Marriage and Family in World Religions* states:

> Constructing a history of Hinduism in general or its views on sex, marriage, and family in particular, presents important challenges. While Hinduism is arguably the oldest continuing religion in the world, dating back to at least 1500 BCE, it has developed in many directions while maintaining a core identity. (Courtright, 2006: 227)

The Hindu marriage ceremony is dominated by traditional mores that wrap the wedding ritual in excessive pomp and ceremony. Very few brides or grooms undergoing the ceremony have prior knowledge of the scriptural meanings. A specific feature of the Hindu marriage is the ritual of conducting the entire ceremony in Sanskrit. The mantras are chanted by Brahman priests and the Saptapadi are the seven steps taken around the fire by the bride and groom together, their garments joined, citing vows, symbolizing their unbreakable future ties. The urban Hindu couple mechanically intones the mantras after the priest. C. J. Fuller's view in his anthropological study on Hinduism, *The Camphor Flame*, is that although the Hindu man–wife relationship reflects "hierarchical ideology" and is "institutionalized inequality," yet a sexually mature woman as wife exercises "ritual power" over a man akin to that of the goddess in Hindu mythology (1992: 24). Courtright also observes:

In the context of family lineages and social identity passed through males, the female's capacities and powers in shaping marriage are often more difficult for outsiders to see. Traditionally, the outer world of field, commerce, sacrifice, and battle has been the locale of men; the inner world of the home, food, children, and health has been the province of women. (Courtright, 2006: 229–230)

Dr A. S. Altekar, historian, archeologist, and numismatist from Maharashtra, and one of the earliest Indian experts on Hinduism, in his work, *The Position of Women in Hindu Civilization: From Prehistoric Times to the Present Day*, explains that a father who does not get his daughter married at the right age is considered a sinner in traditional Hindu ideology (1956: 8). A daughter's marriage based on factors of caste status and social prestige, accompanied by rigid rituals to solemnize the union, did and still does occupy immense importance within Hindu discursive ideology. Altekar, like Basham, bases his research of Classical Hinduism within the ideological discourses of the upper castes. Similarly, Courtright commenting on premodern India states, "the parents of the bride and groom have the obligation to arrange the marriage on behalf of the family, a family that includes ancestors long deceased and descendants yet unborn" (2006: 271). It is important to note that the concept of marriage led to the presence of settled homes, curtailing the instability in society. Sarma (1993: x) comments that "the Hindu society, though thoroughly superstition-laden was not promiscuous, it was a society well-regulated and strictly ordered."

The basic philosophy governing Hinduism has always stressed the importance of the stage of householder and family relations in an individual's life. A. L. Herman, philosopher and author of *A Brief Introduction to Hinduism*, explains the householder or *Grhastha* stage in a person's life as dictated by Hindu rituals:

> The householder takes wife and children and since he supports the other three *asramas*,[10] lives out the prescribed period of his life working at the vocation inherited from his father ... The *asramas* were also open to qualified women. (Herman, 1991: 76)

A young Hindu girl is traditionally reared on myths of Savitri[11] and Sita,[12] and not really on tales of Kali's destruction of the oppressive demonic world, and is thus socioculturally indoctrinated into accepting the man as her superior. C. J. Fuller points out that "the status of her family and caste also depend heavily on a woman's sexual conduct. An unmarried girl who is unchaste and wife who is unfaithful bring dishonor" (1992: 21).

In his highly regarded work, *The Wonder that was India: A Survey of the History and Culture of the Indian Subcontinent Before the Coming of the Muslims* concerning marriage rules in ancient India, Basham (1967: 167) writes that "the couple were usually of the same caste and class, but of different *gotras* and *pravaras*,[13] if they were of high class." After studying certain Hindu ideas on the subject, the anthropologist Mary Douglas, in her study titled *Purity and Danger: an Analysis of the Concepts of Pollution and Taboo*, observes that within many social groups, the woman is considered the entry point of all pollution; thus, her purity appears to ensure the purity of the race. With regard to Hindu social groups, she comments:

> The caste membership of an individual is determined by his mother, for though she may have married into a higher caste, her children take their caste from her. Therefore women are the gates of entry to the caste. (Douglas, 1966: 126)

It has to be noted that this system is not so prevalent now, as the current Hindu social system is distinctly patrilineal. The lineage of the offspring is traced from the father.

Growing instability within the Hindu society in the 6th century due to rise of other religions such as Buddhism led to increasing Sanskritization[14] and the growing dominance of Brahmanism lead to further subordination of women and the need to protect family property and lineage through the birth of sons. Basham states, "From the earliest hymns of the *Rigveda* sons were looked on as great blessings. At least one son was almost essential, to perform funeral rites for his father and thus ensure his safe transit to the other world" (1967: 161).

The historical subordination of the Hindu woman is commented upon by International Studies scholar Anand A. Yang in his essay "Whose Sati?: Widow Burning in Early-Nineteenth-Century India," as he writes, "although the characterization of the Vedic Age between 1700 and 500 BC as a 'golden age for women' is debatable, the decline in their status in the centuries thereafter is a matter of dispute"

(2008: 21). In her study on the Indian women across all walks of life, the American journalist, Elisabeth Bumiller, discusses the importance of a woman's fertility and the insistent need for male progeny, even in the India of the late 20th century. Bumiller's (1990: 10) account takes its title from the traditional blessing still used for a new bride, "May you be the mother of a hundred sons."

The concept of the *pativarata*, the ideal devoted Hindu wife, though often satirized in modern India through media and cultural mores, was and to some extent is a fundamental concept within the Hindu marriage. C. J. Fuller writes, "Throughout India, the ideal Hindu woman is symbolized as auspicious Lakshmi, who as Vishnu's consort, is commonly represented as the perfect woman and wife" (1992: 201). The figure of the mother goddess looms large in the Hindu psychoanalytical and sociocultural patterns prevalent at all times. Although the idea of the modern Hindu woman as an idealized pativarata may sometimes be a subject of mockery within the contemporary social discourses in urban India, Courtright's assertion still holds validity that "stage of life, social position, occupation, and gender shape what dharma is appropriate at a particular moment" (2006: 228).

## Caste and the Traditional Hindu Marriage

Basing his discussion on the historical perspective in *Caste and Race in India,* sociologist G. S. Ghurye observed that "castes were groups with a well-developed life of their own, the membership whereof ... was determined not by selection but by birth" (1969: 2) and in her essay, "Caste in Contemporary India," historian Eleanor Zelliot writes, "the classic texts also offered an explanation for one's birth into a certain caste" (2004: 243). The caste system maintains its stranglehold, even in urban areas, using the traditional discourse of purity as opposed to pollution. It plays on the psychological need of the upper caste Hindus to maintain what they consider their unpolluted or in case of Brahmans their "twice-born" status. On the basis of the theories[15] of the French anthropological scholar Louis Dumont, whose specialization was Indian cultures and societies, the Reverend Professor Frank

Whaling, a Religious Studies and Gandhi scholar, in his recent work, *Understanding Hinduism*, observes:

> The Brahmins are the highest and purest *varna,* and the Dalits are the lowest, in that they are outside *varna* and are impure altogether. The other *varnas* rank in between. Pollution occurs in different ways ... Thus marriage and sex have to function within the correct set of *jātis* in the correct *varna.* (Whaling, 2010: 75)

The issue of the upper castes' deeply ingrained fear of pollution is further explained by Zelliot's statement that "a *chandala* is the offspring of a Brahmin woman with a Shudra man and the lowest of the low" (2004: 245).

In the historical context, the lower caste woman enjoyed more physical freedom than the upper caste ones; but Fuller (1992: 22) notes, "high caste women derive the benefits of subordination," like the aristocratic women of Europe in earlier days. Even today, the upper caste urban Hindu woman has definitely benefited most from the empowerment of women that has taken place in post independent India. Fuller also observes that although higher caste women maintain a deferential veneer of subordination to patriarchy, many vital decisions within the homes are actually in the hands of the wife (ibid.: 21–22).

Caste-endogamy perpetuates a system whereby individual subjugation to societal and group needs is paramount. Caste has rigid rules that often facilitate a high degree of familial patriarchy. Within the Indian social structure, marriage is considered a union of two families rather than individuals with factors such as lineage, heredity, dowry amongst others to be considered. Therefore, intercaste or interreligious marriages are not the norm in arranged marriage situations, as they constitute a loss of status in the caste hierarchy. Fuller stresses that "castes are normally endogamous" and intercaste marriages are usually hypergamous (ibid.: 14).

## Social Discourse within the Urban Hindu Marriage

Within the traditional Hindu marital discourse, the Hindu male is habitually supposed to display a lack of interest in his newly wedded wife. Yet, the often contradictory scriptural discourse tradition decrees that a man's life is not considered complete without a wife, his ardhangini or other half. Such ideals are not really seen in practice in average urban Hindu lives. In fact, Sudhir Kakar and Katharina Poggendorf-Kakar in their psychoanalytical work, *The Indians: Portrait of a People,* have found that within the modern Hindu marriage, the average Indian woman is left with the fantasy of the perfect couple that never manifests itself in reality:

> The central image of this dream is the couple or *jodi*. The couple, of course, exerts a universally powerful pull on the human imagination, given our deeply buried wish to be seen by the spouse as god might have done—that is, with absolute love and total understanding. It is telling that in spite of the social consensus in favour of joint family and widespread praise of its virtues, the couple continues to remain a lodestar in the cultural imagination of Indian women. Iconically represented   as *mithuna* (sexual intercourse) couple in medieval temple structures, its highest manifestation is *ardhanarishwara*—the Lord who is half woman, visualization of the jodi as a single two-person entity. (Kakar and Poggendorf-Kakar, 2007: 64)

Certain sections of the Hindu urban middle-class society are strong advocates of hegemonic norms. This is also observed through certain discourses in such families, which regulate behavior patterns between married couples along rather unnatural and stifling patterns. In the course of her study of Punjabi families, titled "Masks and Faces: An Essay on Punjabi Kinship," anthropologist Veena Das comments:

> a newly married couple ignore each other completely during the day. For instance on arriving home in the evening, the husband may exchange greetings with everybody except his wife. Similarly, the wife is required to abstain from showing any interest in his presence. The myth is sustained that his wife is a stranger for a man. (Das, 1994: 207–208)

Das's ideas are supported by Kakar's analyses in *The Inner World: A Psycho-analytic Study of Childhood and Society* wherein regarding Indian family situations, he observes:

> Any signs of a developing attachment and tenderness within the couple are discouraged by the elder family members by either belittling or forbidding the open expression of these feelings. Every

effort is made to hinder the development of an intimacy within the couple which might exclude other members of the family, especially the parents. Oblique hints about "youthful infatuations," or outright shaming virtually guarantee that the young husband and wife do not publicly express any interest in (let alone affection for) each other; and they are effectively alone together only for very brief periods during the night. (Kakar, 1981: 74)

The contemporary urban Hindu couple would be justified in questioning the religious discourse that considers man and wife to be inextricably intertwined for all time. Why is the husband supposed to display a lack of interest in the wife whose presence completes him spiritually? Such contradictions are visible in the scriptures themselves, as most religious texts have been formulated over centuries and are thereby confusing. Courtright observes that "While individual love and attraction are worthwhile, one of the goals of life, they are subordinate to the larger concerns of the family and lineage" (2006: 230). Within families advocating a very conservative arranged marriage system, the opinion of the younger generation is sometimes not solicited on the grounds that for children, parents personify living gods and respect for elders follows automatically. This socioreligious hegemony continues to ensure the obedience of the younger generation and the women, by inculcating a culture of discouraging critical analysis of time-honored sociocultural traditions. Even in postmodern India, the "commodification" of women is an intrinsic aspect of the Indian sociocultural value system.

## Family in India

Within the arranged marriage system, the extended family as a whole exercises enormous control over most aspects of the lives of a young married couple. Patricia Uberoi, the Australian-born Indian sociologist, in her essay "Family, Household and Social Change" explains that a joint or extended Hindu family, in legal terms, is an Indian sociocultural concept deriving from "Hindu legal texts and is concerned with defining coparcenary property relations and regulating matters of ritual, marriage and inheritance" (1994: 387). In sociological terms, it implies "a household composed of two or more married couples" (ibid.) including the offspring of the couples and mostly the spouses of the male offspring. India is one of a handful of nations where many marriages are still arranged. The Indian society distinguishes sharply between "arranged" versus "love" marriages. In the context of this discussion, the term "extended family" does not always refer to a joint family, as living in the same premises is not a prerequisite for the exercise of cultural hegemony. This chapter also examines the patriarchal control exercised by extended families over young married couples. The Canadian sociologist, Aileen Ross, in her work, *The Hindu Family in its Urban Setting*, commented that there was evidence that city life does not always lead to disintegration of the joint family system (1961: 21). Half a century later, in spite of growing industrialization and urbanization, the urban Hindu marriage still labors under the cultural hegemony of extended family pressures.

A close scrutiny of the above arguments substantiates the idea that in the life of a Hindu, family and community are prioritized over marital bonds. This seriously compromises the position of the Hindu woman in the contemporary society. In their study, "Introduction: On Hindu Marriage and Its Margins," anthropologists Lindsey Harlan and Paul Courtright emphasize the importance of the works of Louis Dumont in shaping the contemporary understanding of Hindu society:

> Dumont argues that whereas Western society tends to be individualistic in outlook, Indian society tends to be holistic: it understands the cosmos as a whole, of which society is a constituent part. As society plays its role within the natural order of the universe, so people play roles within society, but these people are not individuals with strictly discrete identities. Rather, they are  interdependent parts of society. (Harlan and Courtright, 1995: 5)

Harlan and Courtright further explain that "because a marriage affects the status of the entire family and its lineage, it is deemed too important a decision to leave to the persons actually getting married" (ibid.).

The strength of patriarchy is further observed in the complaisant manner in which most educated Hindu urbanites undergo the wedding ceremony. The older generation, particularly the parents of the individual spouses, can be viewed as perpetrators and staunch upholders of this system. The motivational factor appears to be an urgent desire to control the lives of their offspring in order to consolidate their own superior position within the cultural tradition, relegating their offspring to a subordinate status. The patriarchal Hindu discourse has always functioned along such lines. The Sociologist Murray Milner in his study, *Status and Sacredness: A General Theory of Status Relations and An Analysis of Indian Culture*, provides relevant insights, as he states that "since status is relatively inexpansible, some must lose status if others are to gain status" (1994: 112). Similarly, Kakar and Poggendorf-Kakar (2007: 45) also point out that the Indian society at large is undemocratic and all relationships are automatically conducted on lines of superiority and subordination.

Even in modern urban India, the older women in the family often have a vital role in the initial shaping of a new marital relationship. Veena Das's analysis of these women as "female patriarchs" is highly relevant:

> Despite the patriarchal character of the Indian family, there exists an independent community of women which evolves as a result of the taboo on the interaction between the sexes. This community which has already internalized patriarchal values now ensures the conditioning of the female child into her social role of docile daughter/wife/mother ... Das, describes these women as "female patriarchs," old women who may often speak on behalf of men. (Das, 1985: 3)

In an extended family situation, the older Hindu women often become the main advocates and executors of patriarchal hegemony. As Kakar and Poggendorf-Kakar (2007: 60) observe, "The much-maligned mother-in-law, besides (or even because of) being animated by her own possessiveness in relation to her son, is no more than the family's designated agent preventing the build-up of a 'foreign' cell in the family body."

## Marriage and Family within a Contemporary Discursive Ideology

In extended families, the older generation often use the already stressed lives of the younger generation to further manipulate them. A fear of criticism from elders also leads to younger married couples passively accepting the hegemonic pressures in order to maintain domestic harmony. In an extended family situation, if a boy disobeys parental dictates, the blame is immediately transferred to the wife. "Attractive young women are often accused of having done *tona* or *jadu* (magic or spells) to their husbands" (Das, 1994: 208). The Hindu arranged marriage does not stress the union of two different entities, namely the bride and groom who are discouraged from forging themselves into an independent and mutually supportive unit. As discussed earlier, the core feature of the Hindu marriage is the supreme importance of the extended family.

For newly wed Hindu couples, marriage usually implies taking on further duties and responsibilities, especially within the framework of arranged marriages. Pleasure in most forms is considered a negligible aspect of the new marital relationship. Familial attitude makes it clear that marriage is for fulfillment of duties and obligations. As Aileen Ross points out "romantic love" between husband and wife "could be a disruptive element" (1961: 154) in the context of extended family ties. Kakar's 2007 study of Indian society shows how the situation remains largely unchanged within the contemporary cultural discourse when compared with the past. This is ironic within a culture that supports the second largest film industry in the world churning out endless tales of romantic love. Within urban educated families, constant monitoring of the lives of young married couples is often disguised as attempts to alleviate the loneliness of the new bride and incorporate her as a member of the family. As Kakar (1981: 73) reminds us that she occupies the lowest rung of the family hierarchy, and therefore it is easy to prevent her forming a close bond with her new husband.

The anthropologist Henrike Donner in her ethnographic study, conducted in Kolkata, titled *Domestic Goddesses: Maternity, Globalization and Middle-class Identity in Contemporary India*, has observed that

> In private discussions young people in particular would speak very emotionally about their expectations regarding love and marriage and would often use a lot of vocabulary that is associated with companionate marriage, for instance the English word "soulmate" (or its local equivalent *sathi* lit. a companion) representing an ideal partner. (Donner, 2008: 65)

But in reality, the strong opposition faced by married couples in their efforts at identifying strongly with each other as partners and fostering their own unit, with privacy and space being allotted for the strengthening and growth of the marital relationship, is highly visible within the cultural system. In particular, the prime importance of the groom's natal extended family is constantly stressed. In certain instances, this role is usurped by the bride's family, especially if it occupies higher rungs of the socioeconomic hierarchy. The consequence in both cases is that the husband–wife relationship lags behind in order of importance, and hence may not emotionally deepen at all, leading often to hidden depression or strife between the married pair. Sometimes, both families in different ways exercise equal controls over the man and woman.

In such circumstances, coupled with the shortage of suitable and adequate accommodation in India's larger metropolises, it is sometimes nearly impossible to nurture a nuclear unit with strong ties between the spouses and their own children. Das in her studies of Punjabi joint families observes:

> One of the very noticeable facts of life in a joint family is that parents of young children hardly ever fondle them in the presence of others … to fondle one's own children and to respond to their demands immediately, is also to cast aspersions on the ability of the family to love them or look after them. (Das, 1994: 209)

So that extended family may remain socially intact, young children are often deprived of much-needed physical contact with their parents. If the parents attempt to transgress norms laid down by the family, it may lead to exhibition of great displeasure in the form of taunts, snide comments, and even lead to family quarrels.

The Hindu sociocultural structure presents many arguments stressing the need for the constant presence of extended family in the lives of newlyweds or younger married couples, as that entails help with childcare, housework, finances, and so on. But many such arguments are rendered null and void, as a large number of children reared under grandparental supervision are usually very spoilt and often feature as booty in the conflict between warring generations, paying a heavy emotional price in the process. In her 1961 study of Indian families, Aileen Rossstated, "[c]hildren … can be just as unhappy in joint families as in smaller ones" (1961: 17). Five decades later, Indian child psychologist, Dr Sushma Mehrotra asserts that "most 'unhealthy' children come from joint families because they live together out of compulsion and not out of choice." She further comments that children reared in joint families are not really adept at sharing. "It is always assumed that children from joint families are more likely to share their things as they interact on a daily basis with so many people. However, if the family atmosphere is hostile, it can have an adverse effect on children."[16] Housework is rarely ever decreased with additional family members, but the cultural myth is perpetuated as is a pattern of exploitation. The interests being served are usually those of the extended family, and those of younger married couples suffer the most.

But reverting to the analysis of the "exclusion" treatment meted out to the daughter-in-law, it can be considered that it often stems from the fact that she is regarded very much as an outsider in her husband's family. Cultural dissimulation is finely tuned to lay constant stress on the daughter-in-law's faults coupled with complete denial on the part of her in-laws that they have ever made her feel like an interloper within their family. In an interview with Martin Jacques, cultural theorist Stuart Hall says, "We never acknowledge that tight-knit communities are founded on exclusion."[17] The Indian family and kinship system works on a similar principle, which shifts into place with greater force, with the presumably 'threatening' presence of a new bride.

## Cultural Burdens of Obligation

Hindu children, rarely if ever, escape the debt of birth. Most offsprings come into the world carrying what can be termed the "cultural milk debt." Here, as a "cultural insider," I am paraphrasing from cultural phraseology in Bengali (my mother tongue) whereby a child always has to fulfill his/her *dudher hrin* (*dudh* = milk; *hrin* = debt). Bollywood cinema resounds with instances of the traditionally garbed self-sacrificing Hindu mother claiming back her *doodh ka karz* (in Hindi, *doodh* = milk; *karz* = debt) from her grown offspring. The father and extended family also reap the benefits of this debt by default. The young Hindu male, in particular, carries this burden with him all his life. This debt originates in the very act of being born, as this act puts the child in debt to those who have given him/her the gift of life. Within the sociocultural discourse, it would be considered highly improper if the offspring ever raised the issue of the parents deriving satisfaction from the birth and rearing of children. It insists that parents be accorded a semidivine status as people who have undergone endless sacrifice to ensure their children's welfare. Duty is the key phrase in these interactions and these cultural norms are mostly thematically validated by the Bollywood cultural discourse and are often ably supported by the regional Indian cinematic discourse as well. The ideology inherent within this discourse refuses to acknowledge the gratification found in the act of parenting. This denial raises a cultural paradox in a society in which lack of offspring is a matter of social and emotional disgrace.

This discourse accords the Hindu male a definite social status, generally superior to his female counterpart. As a consequence, the males within the family develop a clear sense of self and sometimes during the entire process, selfishness to an unusual degree. Kakar's studies conclude that

> custom, tradition and the interests of the extended family demand that in the realignment of roles and relationships initiated by marriage, the roles of the husband and wife ... be relegated to relative inconsequence and inconspicuousness. (Kakar, 1981: 74)

As observed earlier in the chapter, the notion of shame is used very strongly in the effort to weaken the marital bonds, so that family control over the couple may remain intact.

## Social Changes in Urban India

There is an ongoing struggle in the urban Hindu woman's mind between inherited traditions and the constant flux of social changes. She is torn between the education and new knowledge available to her and the equally strong pull of ingrained patriarchal dictates. While studying Indian arranged marriages of the 1990s and women's roles in India, Elisabeth Bumiller noted:

> The "new" Indian arranged marriage is something of a breakthrough after all. The middle class has essentially created an odd hybrid by

grafting the Western ideal of romantic love onto the traditions of Hindu society—yet another example, perhaps, of the Indian talent for assimilating the culture of a foreign invader ... In the end, the result is something completely and peculiarly Indian, including the notion that it "works." (Bumiller, 1990: 42)

The matrimonial columns in the leading English dailies provide ample proof of the eternal cycle of human demands and expectations controlled by hegemony. New terms such as "convented" have been coined by Indian advertisers in their intensive search for the right match. The term "convented" contains within it many nuances. Its technical interpretation is that it is desirable for the bride to have completed her schooling at a convent/missionary school where English is the medium of education, and girls hailing from such schools have greater fluency in English. Also, the fees charged by such schools are higher than ordinary state-run schools and this denotes the secure financial status of the family and this is also a matter of prestige. Furthermore, the so-called "convented" girls are more conversant with Western customs and norms of behavior, thus making themselves suitable spouses for educated boys, especially for the upcoming "yuppies" and prospective Indian grooms based in Western countries.

The dichotomy inherent in such requirements by the grooms' families is that there is an assumption that the girl's exposure to Western education and knowledge of English has not in any sense led to an intellectual application of such learning and infused her with liberalized ideas moving beyond the dictates of cultural urban hegemony. Such parochial pragmatism coupled with an emphasis on financial considerations exposes the negative aspects of the discourse governing urban arranged marriages. Kamala Ganesh in her essay, "Patrilineal Structure and Agency of Women: Issues in Gendered Socialization," analyzes that:

The capacity to adjust, given so much importance in the socialization of girl and women, does not consist of acceptance alone, but includes the acquisition of negotiatory skills. The overall outcome of such negotiation may not often be in their favour due to the relations of power in patriarchy, relations which are reflected in patrilineal kinship and operationalized in the household. (Ganesh, 1999: 236)

Bumiller (1990) details interviews she conducted with young urban Indian women about to enter marriage, shedding further light on certain common factors influencing particularly the female psyche in India with regard to arranged marriages. She recounts the acceptance in the attitudes of the young, qualified urban women whose marriages had been arranged by family:

> Women routinely told me that they had decided to marry a man-half-an-hour after the first meeting because they felt it was "meant to be." "It's the biggest gamble of one's life," said Ritu Nanda. "So why not just leave it to destiny?" (Bumiller, 1990: 33)

At times, it is also total acceptance of an immensely subordinate status in another family and a complete subjugation of individual will and desire, a total surrender through consensual control. This acceptance is what drives the belief in destiny; the first is used as a rationalization for the second. "Destiny" is easier to openly accept than one's explicit subservient status. It is also a disavowal of personal responsibility. Even in contemporary India, the sociocultural discourse assumes that a daughter is born to be married, bring honor to her family, and yet be culturally subordinated unless she becomes the mother of sons. Across all strata of Indian society, the male offspring is the most coveted. Nobel laureate and economist Amartya Sen in his essay, "Economics and the Family," emphasizes that "the low female–male ratio in the Indian population and the lower life expectancy of women are matched by evidence of serious extra deprivation of women in terms of other basic capabilities" (1994: 459).

A modern twist is lent to the issue of female "commodification" when the urban Hindu woman's qualifications and earnings serve to enhance her worth as a commodity in contemporary India. As Rama Bijapurkar, one of India's most respected leaders of thought on market strategy, wryly observes:

> While it is true, by women's own admissions, that mothers-in-law are more tolerant and husbands less repressive, and she has equal voting rights on family issues, it isn't social evolution that is driving this change as much as the state of the economy. In other words, we have God (or Goddess?) EMI or equated monthly instalment to thank for driving this change. The concept of family has changed from a predominantly social unit to an economic unit. The new truth about

Indian marriages is the old truth—that its business model is around a pragmatic "life business" partnership rather than around romance.[18]

With regard to the urban Hindu arranged marriage, economic interests are, unfortunately, often a vital motivating factor. In postmodern India, they occasionally tend to override other traditional governing factors such as caste or subcaste membership. In a society devoid of welfare benefits, parental expectations often focus on male offspring as sources for future social security. While daughters have traditionally been treated as subservient upholders of caste and class endogamy, with the recently changing socioeconomic factors, families without male progeny often burden daughters with similar expectations of being able to contribute to the overall family income.

## Changes in Urban India

Young Hindu women from the urban middle classes face enormous challenges due to constant changes within the urban Indian socioeconomic discourse. There are large numbers of Indian girls and women from the cities and towns pursuing academic qualifications and financially lucrative careers in India and overseas who feature as "favorites" in the "matrimonial market." Urban Hindu women today have carved a niche in most professions. In "The Family and Reproduction of Inequality," Andre Beteille, one of India's leading sociologists and writers, says that "Change is also coming about in attitudes toward the education of girls; certainly they continue to be prepared for marriage, but more and more of them are being prepared simultaneously for careers" (1994: 443). But these women face a real dilemma. They are culturally coerced into "Superwomen" moulds, which are highly stressful on both personal and professional levels. It is very much the norm for urban Indian women of particular age groups to combine highly competitive careers in medicine, management, engineering, and other demanding professions with marriage and motherhood, simultaneously juggling the eternal roles of the docile, hardworking daughter-in-law and dutiful daughter. It is, yet again, another sacrifice of personal needs and time on the part of the Hindu woman within a discourse that commits them from birth to constant adjustment and compromise.

Education for women has become a very important issue in India. But it does not always guarantee certain fundamental rights that women, especially married women, have often been denied. Bride-burning by in-laws or suicide due to dowry harassment is an extant social evil in India. A *Times of India* report on February 21, 2011 reads:

Recently, 28-year-old R Sushila was admitted to the burns ward of the Kilpauk Medical College Hospital (KMCH), Chennai after she tried to immolate herself. When she died a week later with 90% burns, it was recorded as a suicide. However, nurses said she had told them she committed suicide unable to bear the pressure and harassment from her husband and in-laws for dowry. We get around eight burns cases every day and of those five are women and they are mostly reported as cases of accidents or suicide.

As per a *TIME* magazine report, dowry deaths in India have gone up 15-fold from 400 cases in 1980s to 5,800 in 1990s. National Crime Bureau of the Government of India reported 6,000 dowry-related deaths in 1995. These are official figures, reality must be petrifying.[19]

An educated woman is definitely at an advantage in her marital home in comparison to her uneducated counterparts. In urban India, within certain sections of society, education of both sexes has assumed a position of paramount importance. Sadly enough, for the Hindu women, the focus is not always on positive reform; it is often the mere addition of a bargaining tool in the matrimonial situation or a creation of a parental pension fund in the event of lack of sons.

In a recent article, the feminist thinker and academic, Vrinda Nabar highlighted the modern woman's dilemma originating from the hegemonic cultural discourses:

What is more remarkable is how little attitudes have changed even among the middle class ... I ran into an old school friend who told me her daughter was doing occupational therapy. "She couldn't get into medical school, but it's just as well. Girls should do what they can make time for once they're married ... This woman was herself a trained doctor. Was something of her own frustration contained in that statement? Or was she submitting to the juggernaut of social conditioning? Why is it that the older generation has done little to promote a paradigm shift in such perceptions though many of us came of age during the most rebellious and iconoclastic phase of the post-War era? (Nabar, 2009)

Certain traditional patterns are now being rearranged with the onset of urbanization, the influence of westernization, and increasing levels of female education. But on certain levels, change has not really occurred so much as the same pattern has merely refashioned itself along different lines. Discourses of expectations and control systems are still very much in place, sometimes under different headings with altered subtitles. The occasional impatience of the better-educated and highly stressed younger generation is usually dubbed as insensitivity and a total lack of consideration for elders.

## Hindu Marriages in the Diaspora

With regard to the urban diasporic Hindu arranged marriage, Donner writes:

> [T]he idea that virtual strangers can be matched is currently experiencing a revival of sorts, as many parents of young, well-educated but not affluent women cannot resist the temptation, if the opportunity of marrying a daughter to a migrant  working either in the Gulf or in the US, presents itself. In these cases, the so-called "dollar brides" are often not able to meet the precious groom before he flies in before the wedding, and whether or not parents arrange for virtual contact via video links or at least email, depends entirely on the individual case. (Donner, 2008: 70–71)

Diasporic marriages amongst Hindus open up an entire new field of study which in turn contains many multicolored cultural strands. Some of these marriages that take place amongst Hindu migrants in the first worlds are very tradition bound, whereas others are completely outside the scope of parental desires. Others might be exogamous but not interreligious conducted with parental blessings. Many urban diasporic Hindus are caught in the usual conflict between the first- and second-generation migrants. Cultural anthropologist and economist, Professor U. Kalpagam, in "'American Varan' Marriages among Tamil Brahmins: Preferences, Strategies and Outcomes" (2008: 98), discusses the neglect in Indian sociological studies of the "diasporic terrain' as well as changing forms of marriage and "transgressive behaviors" such as intercaste marriages. She also goes on to state that in a study of arranged marriages, it is vital to focus on "community specific matrimonial studies" and "how diasporic opportunities redefine social status within cultural groups" (ibid.).

When we speak of the diasporic Hindus, it has to be remembered that we are dealing with a vast majority of people of different castes, classes, and communities influenced by individual family cultures. Again, the term urban Hindu marriage in the context in which it is discussed in this chapter may not apply to many of them. With regard to the second- and third-generation Hindu migrants, in *Hinduism Today,* Stephen Jacobs (2010), media and cultural studies theorist, comments that the question to be addressed is whether the relationship with the "perceived homeland/sacred land" for the second-generation or third-generation or later-generation migrants becomes so attenuated that the term "diaspora community" does not really apply to them. He also indicates the formation of other distinct Hindu identities such as British Hindus and American Hindus, and so on (ibid.: 107). These issues are being focused on in sociological and other studies and there remain enormous research possibilities in these arenas.

## The Future of the Arranged Marriage and Family in India

In the 21st century, social discourses in urban India have undergone significant changes and in order to strengthen the social fabric and better the conditions for women and families in general, it is necessary that conditions are facilitated for the formation of strong marital relationships within arranged marriages without undue family interference. Within many sections of urban Hindu society, there is already a positive attitude to "love marriages," wherein the individuals choose their own future partners. As Courtright observes:

> Maybe because of co-education or other social opportunities, the boy or girl may have thought of someone else to be their spouse. Parents

are usually inclined to consider the situation favourably unless there is something that they feel is undesirable. (Courtright, 2006: 271)

Another new phenomenon is the evolution of what can be referred to as the "new Hindu urban male," educated, not fixated on gender models, and open to new ideas, who along with the "new urban Hindu woman" is challenging and slowly bringing alterations within the traditional discourses, helping them evolve into positive stabilizing not stifling forces. These nontraditional, yet culturally aware, individuals are making themselves strongly heard in metropolitan India. It is not that they do not exist in smaller towns or villages. It is just that the hegemonic discourse holds greater sway within smaller communities in nonmetropolitan areas. The rise of this new urban youth has seen changes in many social mores. For instance, with noted Indian designers and chefs such as Tarun Tahiliani and Sanjay Kapoor around, fashion designing and the culinary arts have begun to be coveted careers for males without hindering their matrimonial prospects in arranged marriages. Similarly, girls doing MBAs also are no longer dubbed "bad wife material." But Bijapurkar's analysis seen earlier in the chapter answers many questions regarding such changes.

Meanwhile, vital issues such as marital rape and emotional abuse are slowly being prioritized, especially after changes in Indian laws during 2005–2006. India was one of the last countries to pass laws on marital rape. Sociologist Kalpana Kannabiran points out that the 19th century "problematized" women's issues within Hinduism. Prepubescent marriage, female infanticide, restitution of conjugal rights, and marital rape were central issues (Kannabiran, 2004: 275) and they still are major factors within the Hindu sociocultural discourse. New research is bringing fresh perspectives to bear on these matters, but there are vast opportunities for exploration of these issues within the Indian cultural discourse.

In the words of American Indologist, Wendy Doniger, "Hindus nowadays are diverse in their attitude to their own diversity, which inspires pride in some and anxiety in others. In particular it provokes anxiety in those Hindus who are sometimes called Hindu nationalists or … right-wing Hindus…" (2009: 14). The rising phenomenon of Hindutva, a movement which Amartya Sen terms "the promoters of a narrowly Hindu view of Indian civilization" (2005: ix–x) as well as a militant and fundamentalist aspect of Hindu culture is a relatively new phenomenon in Indian society. It has caught the popular imagination in urban areas and while it is instrumental in fostering communal tensions, it also opens up a research direction for future scholars, as this social discourse is bound to be detrimental the status of the Hindu woman and have a regressive impact on the Hindu discourse in the long run. This is because exponents of this dogmatic ideology prefer the rigid and fundamental aspect of man–woman relations that arose due to the Sanskritization of ancient India after 500 BC.

In conclusion, it can be said that the ancient system of the Hindu arranged marriage has proved its strength by surviving centuries of political, cultural, historical, and social change and upheaval. But it faces its biggest challenge in contemporary Indian society. Whether it can adapt and survive, and perhaps even find enrichment in a rapidly changing world remains to be seen. But as an institution it offers challenges, sometimes unfair ones, especially from a female perspective. In such a situation, the convention-bound hegemonic discourses can often stifle the efforts of couples working hard at building a strong relationship. A fulfilling and loving relationship between married couples is always an inspiration to their future generations. Any obstacle in the course of such a path should be tackled and resolutions to problems sought by logically analyzing the sociocultural discourses. But Kakar and Poggendorf-Kakar issue a warning:

> Only the future will tell whether the Indian woman's long cherished wish to constitute a 'two-person universe' with her husband will not degenerate ... into a mutual ego boosting, a joint self-centredness, a folie a deux of a special kind. (Kakar and Poggendorf-Kakar, 2007: 70)

## Notes

1. "[D]iscourse" is widely used in social theory and analysis, for example in the work of Michael Foucalt, to refer the different ways of structuring areas of knowledge and social practice ... Discourses do not just reflect or represent social entities or relations, they construct or "constitute" them. Different discourses constitute key entities ... in different ways, and position people in different ways as social

subjects ... and it is these social effects of discourse that are focused upon in discourse analysis. Another important focus is upon historical change: how different discourses combine under particular social conditions to produce a new, complex discourse. (Fairclough, 1993: 3–4)

2. H. N. Chatterjee (1972/1974: 4) provides as a footnote, no. 11 of the Chapter on general observations (1–91), the Roman Law in Latin: "*Nuptiae sunt conjunctio maris et feminae et consortium omnis vitae divivi et humani juris communicatio.*"

3. Vedas are the earliest of the Indian scriptures and are collated into four volumes, namely, the *Rigveda, Yajurveda, Samaveda,* and *Atharvaveda.* They were later overcome by the *Upanishads.* The word "Veda" means knowledge. The Vedas generally stand for rituals.

   The *Rigveda* is only the first constituent of a great body of literature known as Vedic by Western scholars and classed by Hindu tradition as "sruti", "that which has been directly heard", as distinct from later religious literature, such as the epics, the *Puranas* and the *Dharmashastras,* which are known as "smriti", "that which has been remembered" The latter class is considered less sacred than the former. (Basham, 1989: 27)

4. In Indian sources, most information about marriage as an institution is found in the *Dharmasutrasv* and *sastras,* or the manuals of religious law, of duties and rights and of castes and life stages. The ritual manuals (*Grhyasutras*) give a detailed exposition of the ritual of marriage according to different Vedic schools. Here, the most important piece of information is that in addition to the basic Vedic rites, various customs of different countries and social groups must be observed.

   The *dharma* authors defined eight different forms of marriage, variously acceptable to different classes. Most often, these are quoted from the *Manavadharmasastra,* but these are also found, for instance, in the *Yajnavalkyadharmasastra,* and even in the *Asvalaynagrhyasutra.* According to Manu, the first four are permissible to the Brahmans and include the rites of Brahman (*brahma*), the *gods (daiva),* the *rsis (arsa)*, and *prajapati (prajapatya),* that is, giving the daughter to a man learned in the Veda, to an officiating priest, against a formal gift of cow and bull, and to a suitable bridegroom. The Ksatriyasv are also permitted the rite of *Raksas* or the forcible abduction of the girl and that of the *Gandharvas* or mutual agreement of the bride and the groom. The rite of the *Asura* or purchase of the bride is hesitatingly allowed to the lower classes, while that of the *Pisacas (paisaca)* or seduction of the girl during her sleep, intoxication, or confusion is proclaimed forbidden. It has been pointed out that the less acceptable sorts of marriage are perhaps included in the system to give the status of married women to the victims of such acts. This is the classification of the *Dharmasastra,* but even these eight forms are by no means exhaustive. One immediately thinks of the *Swayamvara,* a contest of warriors with the bride's hand as the reward (Kattunen, 1998).

5. *Brahminism and Hinduism,* p. 389 cited in Padfield (1908).

6. *Manusmriti or Manusamhita* are the ancient law books that formed the basis of the Hindu law. The *Laws of Manu* from somewhere between 200 BCE and 200 CE is considered the oldest and one of the most important texts of this genre.

Scholars are now quite well agreed that the work is an amplified recast in verse of a "Dharmasutra," no longer extant, that may have been in existence as early as 500 BCE. Manusmriti (Laws of Manu) is considered by some Hindus to be the law laid down for Hindus (Buhler, 1886).

7. Rigveda Book 10 Hymn CLIX *Saci Paulomi*. Available at: http://www.sacred-texts. com/hin/rigveda/rv10159.htm (accessed on September 29, 2011).

8. Rigveda Book 8 Verse 17 Hymn XXXIII *Saci Paulomi*. Available at: http://www. sacred-texts.com/hin/rigveda/rv10159.htm (accessed on September 30, 2011).

9. It is indeed difficult to determine which of the ceremonies is essential and conclusive. The task is fraught with further complications, as there are diverse customs, varying from place to place and even from family to family. But there are common features. Asvalayana accordingly states in his Grhyasutra that most common of the ceremonials should be observed in marriage. Manu is of the opinion that mantras of marriage ( as are pronounced at the time of Panigrahana—grasping of the hand of the bride by the husband) lead to wifehood no doubt, but marriage finds completion in the performance of the rite of the Saptapadi. Medhatithi stresses the importance of the verse of Manu when he observes that consequent to the observance of the rite of Saptapadi, a marriage cannot be annulled even if the bride is found to be insane (Chatterjee, 1972–1974: 18).

10. *Asramas* denote stages.

11. "Savitri … like the Greek Alcestis, followed her husband Satyavant when he was being carried away by the death-god Yama and so impressed the god with her loyalty that he released her lord" (Basham, 1967: 182).

12. "Sita … faithfully accompanied her husband Rama into exile and endured great hardships and temptations for his sake" (ibid.).

13. Gotras: "The Brahmans of the later Vedic period were divided into exogamous septs (*gotras*), a system which was copied in part by other classes and has survived to the present day" (Basham, 1967: 140). Pravaras: "In the Brahman's daily worship he mentioned not only the name of the founder of his gotra, but also the names of certain other sages who were believed to be the remote ancestors of his family" (ibid.).

14. The caste system is far from a rigid system in which the position of each component caste is fixed for all time. Movement has always been possible, and especially in the *middle regions of the hierarchy*. A caste was able, in a generation or two, to rise to a higher position in the hierarchy by adopting vegetarianism and teetotalism, and by Sanskritizing its ritual and pantheon. In short, it took over, as far as possible, the customs, rites, and beliefs of the Brahmins, and adoption of the Brahminic way of life by a low caste seems to have been frequent, though theoretically forbidden. This process has been called "Sanskritization" in this book, in preference to "Brahminization", as certain Vedic rites are confined to the Brahmins and the two other "twice-born" castes. (Srinivas, 1952: 32)

15. Based on Dumont's classical work *Homo Hierarchus: The Caste System and its Implications* (1980).

16. Available at: http://www.indiaparenting.com/raising-children/129_256/parenting-in-joint-families.html (accessed on August 21, 2010).

17. Martin Jacques' Interview with Professor Stuart Hall. 21.5.03. Available at: www. usyd.edu.au/su/social/papers/hall1.html
18. Available at: http://www.ramabijapurkar.com/indiamyland/new_ind_women. php (accessed on March 19, 2007).
19. Available at: http://www.youthkiawaaz.com/2011/03/dowry-deaths-in-india-the-story-of-the-powerless/ (accessed on September 14, 2011).

# References

Altekar, A. S. 1956. *The Position of Women in Hindu Civilization: From Prehistoric Times to the Present Day*. Banaras: Motilal Banarsidass.
Basham, A. L. 1967. *The Wonder That Was India: A Survey of the History and Culture of the Indian Sub-continent Before the Coming of the Muslims*, 3rd rev. ed. London: Sidgwick and Jackson.
———. 1989. *The Origins and Development of Classical Hinduism* (edited and annotated by K. G. Zysk). New Delhi: Oxford University Press.
Beteille, Andre. 1994. "The Family and Reproduction of Inequality." In P. Uberoi (ed.), *Family, Marriage and Kinship in India*, 435. New Delhi: Oxford University Press.
Buhler, George, trans. 1886. *The Laws of Manu*. Available at: http://oaks.nvg.org/pv6bk4.html (accessed on October 5, 2011).
Bumiller, Elisabeth. 1990. *May You Be the Mother of a Hundred Sons: A Journey Among the Women of India*. New York: Random House.
Chatterjee, H. N. 1972. *Studies in the Social Background of the Forms of Marriage in Ancient India*, Vols 1 and 2. Calcutta: Sanskrit Pustak Bhandar.
Courtright, Paul B. 2006. "Hinduism." In D. S. Browning, M. C. Green, and J. Witte, Jr. (eds), *Sex, Marriage and Family in World Religions*, 226–291. New York/Chichester: Oxford University Press.
Das, Veena. 1985. "The Body as Metaphor: Socialization of Women in Punjabi Urban families." *Manushi* 28: 2–6.
———. 1994. "Masks and Faces: An Essay on Punjabi Kinship." In P. Uberoi (ed.), *Family, Marriage and Kinship in India*, 198–224. New Delhi: Oxford University Press.
Doniger, Wendy. 2009. *The Hindus: An Alternative History*. New York: The Penguin Press, 2009.
Donner, Henrike. 2008. *Domestic Goddesses: Maternity, Globalization and Middle-class Identity in Contemporary India*. Aldershot, Hants, England/Burlington, VT: Ashgate.
Douglas, Mary. 1966. *Purity and Danger: An Analysis of the Concepts of Pollution and Taboo*. New York/London: Routledge.
Fairclough, Norman. 1993. *Discourse and Social Change*, 3–4. Cambridge, Oxford, UK: Polity Press in association with Blackwell Publishing.
Fuller, C. J. 1992. *The Camphor Flame: Popular Hinduism and Society in India*. Princeton, NJ: Princeton University Press.

Ganesh, Kamala. 1999. "Patrilineal Structure and Agency of Women: Issues in Gendered Socialization." In T.S. Saraswathi (ed.), *Culture, Socialization and Human Development: Theory, Research and Applications in India*, 235–254. New Delhi/Thousand Oaks, Calif/London: SAGE Publications.

Ghurye, G. S. 1969. *Caste and Race in India*, 5th rev. ed. Mumbai: Popular Prakashan.

Harlan, Lindsey, and Courtright, Paul B. (eds). 1995. *From the Margins of the Hindu Marriage: Essays on Gender, Religion and Culture*. New York: Oxford University Press.

Herman, A. L. 1991. *A Brief Introduction to Hinduism: Religion, Philosophy and Ways of Liberation*. Boulder, Colorado: Westview Press.

Jacobs, Stephen. 2010. *Hinduism Today*. London/New York: Continuum.

Kakar, S. and Poggendorf-Kakar, K. 2007. *The Indians: Portrait of a People*. New Delhi/ New York: Penguin, Viking.

Kakar, Sudhir. 1981. *The Inner World: A Psychoanalytic Study of Childhood and Society in India*, 2nd ed. New Delhi: Oxford University Press.

Kalpagam, U. 2008. "'American Varan' Marriages among Tamil Brahmins: Preferences, Strategies and Outcomes." In Rajni Palriwala and Patricia Uberoi (eds), *Marriage, Migration and Gender*, 98–124. New Delhi/Thousand Oaks, Calif: SAGE Publications.

Kannabiran, Kalpana. 2004. "Voices of Dissent: Gender and Changing Social Values in Hinduism." In R. Rinehart (ed.), *Contemporary Hinduism*, 273–309. Santa Barbara, California: ABC_CLIO.

Kattunen, K. 1998. "Mutual Agreement or Auction of Brides: Ancient Indian Marriage in Greek Accounts." *Studia Orientalia* 84: 31–38. Previously published in: A. Parpola and S. Tenuhen (eds), *Changing Patterns of Family and Kinship in South Asia*, 33. Helsinki: University of Helsinki.

Majumdar, R. C. and Pusalker, A. D. 1951. *History and Culture of the Indian People: The Vedic Age*, Vol. 1. Mumbai: Bharatiya Vidya Bhavan.

Milner, Murray. 1994. *Status and Sacredness: A General Theory of Status Relations and An Analysis of Indian Culture*. New York: Oxford University Press.

Nabar, Vrinda. 2009. "Femmepowerment." Featured in *Harmony Magazine*, India. Available at: http://www.harmonyindia.org/hportal/VirtualPrintView.jsp?page_id=10452 (accessed on August 21, 2010).

Padfield, J. E. 1908. *The Hindu at Home: Being Sketches of Hindu Daily Life*. Verpery, Madras: SPCK Press.

Ross, Aileen D. 1961. *The Hindu Family in its Urban Setting*. Toronto: University of Toronto Press.

Sarma, Bhaiyaram (trans. R. C. Prasad). 1993. *The Vivaha, the Hindu Marriage Samskaras*. New Delhi: Motilal Banarsidass Publishers.

Sen, Amartya. 1994. "Economics and the Family." In P. Uberoi (ed.), *Family, Marriage and Kinship in India*, 452–466. New Delhi: Oxford University Press.

———. 2005. *The Argumentative Indian: Writings on Indian History, Culture and Identity*. England: Allen Lane (an imprint of Penguin Books).

Srinivas, M. N. 1952. *Religion and Society Amongst the Coorgs of South India*, 32. Oxford: Clarendon Press.

Uberoi, Patricia. 1994. "Family, Household and Social Change in India." In P. Uberoi (ed.), *Family, Marriage and Kinship in India*, 383–392. New Delhi: Oxford University Press.

Whaling, Frank. 2010. *Understanding Hinduism*. Edinburgh: Dunedin Academic.

Yang, Anand A. 2008. "Whose Sati?: Widow Burning in Nineneteenth-century-India." In Sumit Sarkar and Tanika Sarkar (eds), *Women and Social Reform in Modern India*, 15–37. Bloomington, Indianapolis: Indiana University Press.

Zelliot, Eleanor. 2004. "Caste in Contemporary India." In Robin Rinehart (ed.), *Contemporary Hinduism*, 243–272. Santa Barbara, California: ABC_CLIO.

# Chapter 12

## On Hinduism and Caste

Vinay Kumar Srivastava

With reference to the relationship between Hinduism and caste, one hears from Indians, lay and academic, two sets of opinions.

The first is that the "spine of Hinduism is caste system"; without it, it is nothing but a battery of abstract propositions and spiritual thoughts about divinity and the ways of life, beyond the wisdom and comprehension of laypersons, of interest principally to the literati, philosophers, and religious scholars. Many consider Hinduism, a term gaining popularity in the 19th-century British India, as a "school of metaphysics" whose objective is to transform a person into "a perfect human being" and to make "him one with the ultimate reality (paramātmān)" (Basu, 1990: 3–4; Sarma, 1953: 3). The centrality of Hinduism to the present-day discourse, in academic world as well as the popular, owes to the practices and considerations of inequality that have come to prevail, and are also regarded as legitimate, as a result of the adherence of Hindus to the caste system.[1]

Here, we may recapitulate the oft-quoted Srinivas's (1952: 213) opinion that caste system is the "structural basis" of Hinduism, meaning thereby that it is the principle of Hindu social organization. To escape unequal treatment, sometimes horrendous and gruesome, at the hands of the upper castes, many communities of lower castes in the past have embraced the religions, both indigenous and externally introduced, promising the equality of all humans before the divinity, but, to their utter dismay, they have found that their preconversion social status has continued to haunt them along with their new identity. They may be equal before god, but not so in the world of men. Moreover, even the converts to the other religions have caste-like gradations among them. So, there are "upper caste Muslims" (barī zāt ke musalmān) as well as "lower caste Muslims" (chotī zāt ke musalmān); although members of both these categories share the same platform in the mosque, they neither have the ties of matrimony nor commensality among them; in fact, the general interaction between different groups is highly limited and instrumental. Ipso facto, each of these categories—or the subdivisions among each one of them—constitute(s) a bounded unit in a hierarchically arranged system. Equality in some social spheres does not automatically guarantee equality in the others. Against this backdrop, Srinivas (1952: 231) notes that the caste system "survives conversion to Christianity or Islam." Although Srinivas mentioned these two religions, the story of the other religions in India (Buddhism, Jainism, Sikhism, Judaism, Zoroastrianism, and "tribal practices") is also the same; castes (and groups akin to caste) have been ethnographically reported among each one of them, and one of the research interests of students from different social science disciplines is to describe caste system among non-Hindus and enunciate their differences in practices and thoughts from Hindu communities (Ahmad, 1973; Mandelbaum, 1962; Singh, 1977).

The other opinion, expressed vociferously, is that caste has brought disrespect to Hinduism. We are so overwhelmingly embroiled in understanding caste system that the other salient aspects of Hinduism have been relegated to the backseat.[2] The excessive importance that caste received from the outsiders, particularly the colonial administrators, has led many to believe that "Hinduism is nothing but caste religion, the religion that decrees inequality between people," which may not be true. Although caste is not a colonial construct, as tribe is, the colonial discourse about India (and South Asia) made it a central institution of Hinduism. The legacy of the colonial administrators and scholars was carried forward by their counterparts of Indian origin, with the consequence that not only people from other countries but Indians also believe that caste is pivotal to Hinduism. The whipping that Hinduism has received from various quarters, particularly the social workers and activists, is all because of caste.

This line of argument takes two forms: one, to rebut with the authority of the textual tradition the centrality of caste to Hinduism (Nadkarni, 2003; Sharma, 2000: 132–180) and, second, to eliminate caste and its practices from everyday life. Subscribing to the idea that change comes from below and people should themselves harbinger change, instead of depending upon the state and the other agencies of the civil society, there are cases of Indians refraining from using their surnames, for these may reveal their respective caste identities. Many Indians also avoid any public discussion on caste, for they think it is a sensitive issue capable of fueling the emotions of people, leading to a state where daggers may be drawn between communities; and some believe that caste can be transcended by encouraging intercaste marriages.

Some also believe that when we speak of a subject, we create its "discourse," and the more it is talked about and discussed, thus, becoming a part of the public parleys, the more conscious we become of its existence. I have heard sociologists and social anthropologists say that they became aware of caste and its reality after reading about it in their books and articles. Before that, they told me, having been brought up in cities and metropolises, they were hardly aware of their respective castes as well as of the others. They scarcely followed the particularistic criteria (of caste or any other primordial tie) in evaluating the others or establishing their relations with them. Being mutual interpretations of cultures, the disciplines of sociology and social anthropology help one know oneself in relation with the others. The general implication of this argument is that once we stop talking about caste—consciously avoiding it from our discourse—the "subject of caste" will bear a retreat.

Whichever opinion we subscribe to, the truth is that caste continues to be an important institution and also, a subject of discourse, in contemporary India, although it may have taken a new *avatāra* (incarnation), a new form, as Srinivas (1996) summed it up in the title of his edited book. Being Hindu automatically implies that one is born in a caste, whether or not one follows its occupation or the way of living and whether or not one is aware of one's caste identity, its history, and its place in the hierarchy. This, however, is not the case with those born to the folds of those religions that do not have caste or those that emerged as a vehement reaction to caste. For instance, a Muslim is born to a religion and a Hindu to a caste. An Indian Muslim acquires a caste because of his "historical mooring"— the preconversion status—a Hindu, because of his religion. This relationship between Hinduism and caste—whether caste is the structural principle of Hinduism or has discredited Hinduism—is of tremendous research interest and is being explored below.

Each society is organized in accordance with one or the other principle, or a set of several principles.[3] Traditional societies—and India is one of these—hold the principle of birth (or what is technically termed "ascription") in high esteem. Distinction between the gentry and the commoner or the patrician and the plebeian is on the basis of birth, and it can be seen in many parts of the world; but nowhere in the world has the principle of birth gone to such an extent as it is in India and also in some parts of south Asia (Beteille, 1977).[4]

The Indian society displays social inequality in its most explicit, extreme, elaborate, and manifest form, the outcome of which is that the Indians are most conscious about their rank and position in the society, which they unabashedly flaunt in public gatherings and expect obeisance from those inferior to them.[5] This would also explain why certain social practices in India systematically "exclude" the lowly placed groups and communities from the "mainstream," that largely comprises the superiorly graded, advantaged, and privileged sections, the decision-makers, who monopolize key positions in coveted professions, bureaucracy, business, corporate sector, academics, army, and politics.

A set of concepts that has gained considerable currency in contemporary political and intellectual discourse in India is of "exclusion and inclusion." The goal of development and planning is defined as bringing within its fold, as early as possible, the hitherto-deprived and excluded people of the country (Sen, 2000).[6] An oft-quoted phrase that has acquired popularity with the present United Progressive Alliance (UPA) government is of "inclusive development," which means that directed and planned changes should bring all, unexceptionally, within its fold. The critics of the contemporary model of development in India often say that it is "exclusionary," as the upper crusts largely monopolize its benefits, which do not percolate to lower and deprived sections of the society.

What has made India a hierarchical society? Why are Indians overly conscious of their rank? Why in some parts of the country, children, since beginning, are tutored that the only worthy job in India is of a civil servant and they should aspire to clear the prestigious Indian Civil Services Examination, for it would give them power, status, wealth, and renown?[7] One may agree with Kakar and Kakar (2007) that inculcation of the principle of hierarchy has its origin in early socialization, when children interiorize the subtleties of rank and titles and the concomitant behavioral patterns. However, the question remains: Which principle of social organization makes Indians "ranked beings," "status-conscious," and "status-contestant"?

The answer to this may be explored against the background of two paradoxes. First, whilst Indians have become fully aware of the fact that they are hierarchical and want the disabilities concurrent with the system transcended, they are dead against sacrificing a modicum of their own privileges, the advantages, and profits that accompany their status. Second, whilst they wholeheartedly support that discriminations in society be alleviated, they want their private worlds to remain intact, as these have been from the past.

Many scholars think that the key to understand India—and particularly, why Indians are *Homo hierarchicus*—is to examine its system of social organization and stratification famously known as "caste," a term derived from the Portuguese word *casta*, first used in 1563 by Garcia de Orta (Mathur, 1964: 59).[8] Meaning "species" and "breed" in biology and "tribe," "clan," "race," "family," or "kind" in social study, this term was used for groups found among Hindus where distinction was made between people of "greater or lesser dignity" (Basham, 1988: 148; Marriott and Inden, 1985: 348). In addition, the early travelers noted an important fact about the hierarchical system in India: It was not only Hindus who were so divided but even people professing other faiths were also treated similarly. For example, the Christians were accorded a low status and a Hindu of higher caste refrained from eating or drinking with them (Hutton, 1946). Khushwant Singh (1966: 568), a leading Indian *littérateur*, noted that in Punjab, as the converts to Christianity were mostly from low castes, Christians came to be almost synonymous with the category of scavengers (those who were called "sweepers"). That the Hindu lower castes embraced Christianity and Islam is commonplace knowledge among higher caste people, so instead of viewing the converts as the followers of other religions, equal to their own, they see them as downwardly placed "lower castes," with whom they behave as if they were in the Hindu caste system (Beteille, 1972; Mandelbaum, 1962).

This tells us that the word "caste," and the behavior associated with it, is extended to encompass the other non-Hindu groups. The Hindus view the world around them, including both the coreligionists and the others, as divided into castes, and each one of them is ranked, that is, occupies a place in the hierarchy. It is not only the Hindus but the others also view the world as ordered into strata, one placed upon the other. However, it is not a situation of mechanical placing, as is the case with the earth. Each stratum defines its position with respect to the one placed above and below it, and enjoys a differential combination of privileges and deprivations. Those placed high are far more advantaged than those occupying the lower rungs of society. The caste system is a system of social inequality.

The early scholars were interested in finding out the geographical spread of the caste order (Blunt, 1931; Dubois, 1906; Hutton, 1946; Ketkar, 1909). In a narrow sense, it was described as pan-Indian; in a broad sense, it was seen as occurring in several parts of south Asia and also in all those areas of the world where the Hindus had settled down. So, castes would be found in Fiji, Mauritius, the islands that constitute the West Indies, the Indian neighborhoods in Great Britain, the United States of America, and the continents of Australia and Africa. Within India, caste profiles and practices differed greatly when we moved from one part of the country to the other. For instance, stringency of caste system was highly pronounced in the states of south India.[9] A practice wherein the lowest castes were expected to carry bells and ring them periodically, announcing their arrival in public places, lest they caused defilement to castes superior to them, thus earning their wrath and reprimand, was reported from south India, so was the consignment of lowest castes to a nocturnal existence. They emerged out of their households when people above them in the ranked order had retired to bed and would not be in public places to risk an exposure to ritual contamination that might entail their excommunication from their community. Castes were also classified as of the "right hand" and the "left hand," and they had "factious rivalry, leading to frequent clashes" among them sometimes on trivial matters (Bayly, 1999: 107–108; Hutton, 1946: 59, 143–144).[10] In north India, caste system was far from being so severe; and many areas in northeast India were free from the grasp of caste. In Punjab, the rise of Sufi cults frontally attacked caste practices and rituals. The result was a weakening of the caste system, despite the fact that today's Punjab has the maximum population of the Scheduled Castes in India.

One of the anthropological interests was to describe the institution of caste in different parts of India and also in the world. In the latter, the aim was to discover what happened when castes were planted elsewhere. In research works dealing with Hinduism abroad, one of the domains of study was caste, and we learnt that people who participated in the secular and caste-free world as "individuals" became "caste-beings" (or "collective beings," to use words from Dumont [1980]) when home or in the midst of the others from their caste (see essays in Burghart, 1987). All this led to the conclusion that an obituary on caste would not be written, since this practice and its way of thinking have a resilience of its own and would thrive notwithstanding the vast changes in the other institutions of society. Caste would never be an artifact of the bygone time; it would endure in the consciousness of people, influencing and, in some cases, conditioning the quarters of their lives.

The point to be stressed here is that the multifariousness of caste, which intensive studies brought to the fore, poses problems about its definition and conceptual understanding.[11] Moreover, the model of caste constructed on the basis of an objective understanding of intercommunity interactions is different from a people's comprehension of their caste. If the former is an "external" perspective, based on "what people do," the latter is "intrinsic," for it rests on "what people think." The positivists have emphasized the former, since behavior can be observed but not the thoughts and ideas of people; the interpretive thinkers have given an equal attention to people's notion of their grouping and how they think it differs from that of the others.

As the matters become complicated because of the diversity of caste system and the dialectics of the "lived-in" order, as opposed to the "thought-out," many scholars of caste have avoided entering into the quagmire of the definitions and attempting a suitable one, but deal with what caste does and the form it has taken in present-day India. They begin with the assumption that India has a large number of communities, most of which are castes; they are viable and demand a particular kind of behavior, deportment, and attachment from their members.[12] Although castes have weakened in urban India, they play an assertive, and sometimes aggressive, role in villages and small towns; and this nature and vehemence of caste demands an intensive study.

The other opinion, to which I also subscribe, "what caste is"—its definition—is as important as "what it does" (Dube, 1968: VI). Just because a phenomenon is complex and diverse does not imply that the attempts to define it are given up. Definitions, it is well known, systematize investigations. Keeping this in purview, caste should be distinguished from the other principles of social ranking found in India and elsewhere. Notwithstanding the fact that the word caste continues to be used loosely to denote any "closed" or "homogeneous" category, by social scientists as well as biologists, we may not be able to make any headway in social studies unless we have a clear conception of what it is and the manner in which its bearers use it.[13]

India is a literate civilization (Das, 1982: 1–2). A vast corpus of the literature dating back to not less than 1500 BCE is available on Indian institutions and thoughts (Kane, 1946). Before all this was committed to writing, it was orally transmitted in families and temples from one generation of learners to the next. Before printing press came into existence, one of the foremost meritorious duties (especially of priests, seers attached to temples and monasteries, and religious apprentices) was to copy the texts and make its multiple copies, with the result that today, in archives and museums as well as repositories of the places of worship, we have a rich collection of texts that tell us about India, its people, their institutions and thoughts. Even today, when printing technology has advanced a great deal, in Jain *upasharey* (places where renouncers stay, particularly during the monsoon) and Hindu *mandir* (temple), one may see the newly initiated members meticulously copying the religious and moral texts in their spare time.

Although sociologists and anthropologists are overwhelmingly concerned with the "field view" of the society, its existential reality, in the context of India, they cannot ignore the "book view," which is central to the historian's craft. In fact, Dumont (1980) says that a proper understanding of Indian society lies at the confluence of Indology (the "book view") and sociology (the "field view"). In case of literate civilizations, the questions to be answered are: How far does the "book view" influence the conceptualization and functioning of the institutions at the ground level? And, does the "book view" of a society change over time against the backdrop of the actual functioning of institutions?

Historians tell us that caste emerged in the middle of the 1st millennium BCE not as a description of the actual society at that time but as an intellectual idea of what the ideal society should be, which tasks (vocations, duties) should be performed by its members, and how they should aspire to live (Omvedt, 2003). A term used in *Rigveda*

(1500–900 BCE), *varna*, meaning "color," initially used to distinguish the speakers of Indo-Aryan language, who being of Caucasoid stock were fair complexioned from the dark-complexioned Dravidian speakers, also called *dāsa* (slave) and *dasyu* (robber), was employed in *Satapatha Brahmana* and subsequent texts for the four categories of humans who emerged from the body of the primeval (the "first") being in an act of sacrifice.

Let us expand on this theory of the creation of caste. Consisting of 1,028 hymns and composed somewhere in northwest India, *Rigveda*, the first in the category of Vedic literature, is divided into 10 books (*mandala*) (O'Flaherty, 1988). The 10th book is of particular importance, for here we come across the "Hymn of the (Primeval) Man (*purusasukta*)" (*Rigveda* 10, 90). It begins with the conception of a "mighty giant" (*Purusa*, the "first Purusa"), a cosmogenic figure, the first being to come into existence, who is believed to be larger than the entire universe. In the course of time, this being suffers from a feeling of loneliness and solitariness, and resolves to divide itself, and thus produces its feminine component, one who comes to be known as Viraj. Basham (1989: 24) tells us that a verse in the *Brhadaranyaka Upanishad* says that Purusa (the "first Purusa") and Viraj mate, producing another Purusa (the "second Purusa"), and then are produced the gods.

At one point of time, the gods decide to offer a sacrifice to their father, the "first Purusa," and for this they choose his eldest son, the "second Purusa" (ibid.). This another "gigantic victim," the "second Purusa," is slain and dismembered, and from the parts of his body, the universe, including its human dwellers, is created. The "Hymn of the (Primeval) Man" informs us (ibid.: 25):

> When they divided the Man,
> into how many parts did they divide him?
> What was his mouth, what was his arms,
> what were his thighs and his feet?

> The Brahmin was his mouth,
> of his arms was made the warrior (Rajanya, Kshatriya)
> his thighs became the Vaishya,
> of his feet the Sudra was born.

The *Rigveda* initially mentions two elite sorts—the poet priests (Brahman) and the warrior chiefs (*Rajanya*); the rest are the commoners called *Vish*, who are later divided into Vaishya and Sudra (Das, 1982). Each of these four types is called varna; and the model of Hindu society, religiously and textually ordained, is known as *chaturvarna* (four varna). It may be noted here that the term varna has also been translated as "caste" in some works, whilst some have retained varna as it is and translated the term *jāti* as "caste." My submission is that both these concepts provide a key to understand Hindu hierarchy—varna is textual (book view), for the idea of four social categories is laid out in texts; jāti is contextual (field view), for it is the term that people use for different occupational and endogamous groups in their everyday life. Thus, instead of utilizing the blanket term "caste" for them, we should use the local words that the texts and the people employ, and the mutual interpretations of these terms would guide us how ideas and actions are actually ordered. To sum up: By jāti, we understand the "locally structured endogamous and occupational group that stands in a hierarchical relationship with other such groups"; and by varna, the "religiously sanctioned professional division of labour in society culminating in the emergence of hierarchically placed groups for cosmic perpetuity and fulfillment."

Building up on the *purusasukta* hymn (in *Rigveda*), *Manusmrti* (or *Mānava-Dharmasāstra*) (1.31) says that after creating the world, its resources, and inhabitants, "for its growth and prosperity" (1.31), "for the protection of this whole universe" (1.87), the Lord "produces from his mouth, arms, thighs, and feet, the Brahmin, the Kshatriya, the Vaishya, and the Shudra (1.31)" (Raghavan, 1953: 280–281).[14] Besides human forms, there emerge from the body of the primeval being gods, plants and animals, elements, seasons, planets, and others (Marriott, 2005), all those which have been created and those which would be created. I once saw a calendar that carried a pictorial representation of the vision of the cosmic form, the colossal image (*virāt swarūp*), that Krishna manifested before Arjuna, based on Chapter XI of the *Bhagavad Gita*. It showed the entire cosmic manifestation. From the mouth of the god, the Brahman (shown as a man carrying sacred book in his right hand) was shown emerging along with fire and cow, implying the equivalence of all the objects that were caused by the same part of the body. The Kshatriya (or Rajanya) was shown as carrying a weapon (*pharsā*) in his hand, the Vaishya, with a long account book (*bahī*), and the man materializing from the feet, the Shudra, was shown half-bent, almost at an angle of 90 degrees. The calendar pictorially signified the professions (or the duties) that each of these humans was expected to perform.

*Manusmrti* (1.88–91) delineates the activities of each of these varnas (Table 13.1).

**Table 13.1: Activities of Varnas**

| S. No. | Varna | Activities |
|---|---|---|
| 1. | Brahman | Reading and teaching the Veda, offering and officiating at sacrifices, receiving and giving gifts (or alms) |
| 2. | Kshatriya | Protecting the subjects, giving gifts, offering sacrifices, reciting the Veda, avoiding attachment to sensory objects |
| 3. | Vaishya | Tending cattle, giving gifts, offering sacrifices, reciting the Veda, trade, money lending, cultivation of land |
| 4. | Shudra | To serve meekly and ungrudgingly the above three classes |

Common to the first three varna are three activities: reciting Veda, offering sacrifice, and giving gifts, and distinctive about Brahman is teaching Veda, officiating at sacrifices, and receiving gifts (or alms). The upper three varna share the concept of "dual birth," the biological and the social, the latter marking the commencement of the process of learning, because of which they are called "twice-born" (*dwija*); they are also termed *suvarna* (good varna). The Shudra have only one birth—the biological. *Manusmrti* also clearly says that there is no fifth varna.

According to *Manusmrti* (1.92), a man is believed to be "purer above the navel." The Lord, therefore, has declared "the purest part of him to be his mouth." As the Brahman springs from the "loftiest part of the body," and he is also the first-born, possessing the Veda, he is the "lord of the whole creation" (*Manusmrti*, 1:93-5).[15] The chief good of the subservient classes—particularly the Shudra—lies in serving the Brahman with their full might. About the Shudra, *Manusmrti* says that they may earn their living by working for a powerful Kshatriya and a wealthy Vaishya, but the reward in terms of an elevation of his status in the following birth will result from his serving the Brahman dedicatedly (9.334-5; 10.121-3).

That the Brahman priest is a representative of God on earth is one of the popularly shared beliefs in rural India (Babb, 1975; Lewis, 1958). Honorifically addressed as "Brahman *devtā*" (a form of god), before the commencement of any ritual, his feet are washed with water and this water that supposedly carries the "purity of his feet" is euphemistically called the "nectar of the feet" (*charanamrita*). Ideally, it is meant to be drunk by the receivers of his ritual services.[16] The Brahman priest's feet are touched by all classes of people, barring those who fall below the line of purity, irrespective of their economic and political statuses.[17] To quote *Manusmrti* (2.135) in this context: "A ten-year-old Brahmin and a hundred year old king, one should know, stand with respect to each other as a father to a son; but of the two, the Brahmin is the father." It is because for *Manusmrti* (2.136-7), the grounds of respect arranged in a hierarchy are knowledge, ritual life, age, kin, and wealth. Not only because of the theory of creation, but also since the Brahman is the fountainhead of knowledge, carrying out the functions of teaching, contemplation, and cogitation, he occupies the highest position in the universe and is worthy of worship. Obviously, as one goes down, the privileges are reduced; in Table 13.2, some of the sociological parameters from *Manusmrti* that show how different classes are distinguished are presented.[18]

**Table 13.2: Differences in Classes**

| S. No. | Parameters | Brahman | Kshatriya | Vaishya | Shudra |
|---|---|---|---|---|---|
| 1. | Name given to the male child should connote (2:31-2) | auspiciousness, happiness. | strength, protection. | wealth, prosperity. | disdain, service. |
| 2. | Vedic initiation to be carried out in the (2:36) | eighth year from conception. | 11th year from conception. | 12th year from con-ception. | no Vedic initiation. |

*(Continued)*

*(Continued)*

| S. No. | Parameters | Brahman | Kshatriya | Vaishya | Shudra |
|---|---|---|---|---|---|
| 3. | Water purifies when (2:62) | it reaches the heart. | it reaches the throat. | it is taken into the mouth. | it touches the extremity of his lips. |
| 4. | When meeting a person of a particular varna, one should ask whether (2:127) | he is doing well. | he is all right. | his property is secure. | he is in good health. |
| 5. | Seniority depends upon (2:155) | knowledge. | valor. | wealth in grain (and other goods). | age. |
| 6. | A man can have (3:13) | four wives, one each from the lower three varna and one from his own. | three wives, one each from the lower two varna and one from his own. | two wives, one from the lower varna and one from his own. | one wife, from his own varna. |
| 7. | When marrying a man of upper class, the bride of lower class should take hold of (3:44) | not applicable (Brahman woman only marries endogamously.) | an arrow, indicating her status. | a goad (spiked stick). | the hem of her husband's garment. |
| 8. | Period of impurity lasts for (5:83) | 10 days. | 12 days. | 15 days. | one month. |
| 9. | The judge administers oath to a class by (8:113) | making him swear by his veracity. | by his chariot or the animal he rides on and by his weapons. | by his cattle, seeds, and gold. | by all the sins causing loss of caste. |

(Continued)

| S. No. | Parameters | Brahman | Kshatriya | Vaishya | Shudra |
|---|---|---|---|---|---|
| 10. | (1) Punishment for assailing a Brahman (8:267) | (1) not applicable. | (1) fined 100 panas (copper coins). | (1) fined 150 or 200 panas. | (1) to suffer corporal punishment. |
| | (2) Fine imposed on Brahman for abusing (8:268) | (2) not applicable. | (2) 50 panas. | (2) 25 panas. | (2) 12 panas. |

Besides being religiously proclaimed, what distinguishes the varna and jāti system from the other systems of ranking found in the world is that it is holistic, and as Dumont (1980: 43) says, the *"whole is founded on the necessary and hierarchical coexistence of the two opposites,"* the pure and the impure. Temporary states of purity and impurity have been reported from many communities (Dumont, 1980: 50–51; Sinha, 1965). People are expected to acquire purity when approaching their pantheon and they lapse into pollution when death occurs in their family or a birth takes place. In some communities, pollution is incurred on seeing a corpse or on sighting a bird (such as the crow) or a functionary (such as the funeral priest [*mahābrahmin*]) associated with death. Women are also polluted during their menstrual periods; some communities also have outhouses for confining menstruating women for the entire period of their pollution. The period and the kind of pollution terminate with the performance of the purificatory rituals but it does not imply that after the ritual is over, the participants enter into a state of purity. The states of "temporary purity" and "temporary pollution" are polar categories, which persons occupy depending upon the context they are in; when performing ritual, they are in a state of purity, and at the time of death, it is the state of impurity; both purity and impurity are ephemeral deviations. Ordinarily, they are in what Srinivas (1952: 106) calls, the "normal ritual status."[19]

By comparison, cardinal to caste is the belief that certain communities are "permanently pure" and some "permanently impure," in a system of relationships, and no ritual or transcendental practice can have any effect on these states, that is nullifying the effect of any one of them. As one moves down the hierarchy of castes, purity decreases, becoming cipher at the bottom, whereas impurity increases; and as one moves up, increase in purity accompanies a concomitant decrease in impurity, although all are equally affected by the circumstances of temporary purity and impurity. For instance, a Brahman may lapse into a state of "temporary impurity" when death occurs in his family, but even then he is pure with respect to the castes below him. His "temporary impurity" exists independently of the status of "permanent purity." However, when in a state of "temporary impurity," he will not perform any rituals (including the funeral) for his clients, for ritual performance demands sacredness on the part of the performer. To distinguish marriage rituals (or any other that are auspicious) from the funeral (or those that are inauspicious), since both of them require sacredness, Srinivas (1952) distinguishes between two forms of sacredness: One that accompanies marriage rituals is "good sacredness" and one that goes with death is "bad sacredness," but the Brahman priest, who officiates at these rituals, should not be in a state of "temporary impurity."

It is not just human beings, but all entities in the world—animate and inanimate—are arranged hierarchically on a scale of purity and pollution. Dumont (1980: 34) says that it is not only an outsider's understanding, rather the bearers of caste view the universe around them in terms of this central opposition of the pure and the impure; "caste is a *state of mind*." It is an ideological system built upon the Hindu ideas of the accumulation of the deeds of the past birth (karma) that determine one's present birth and living staunchly according to the duties (*duties*) of one's caste.

Within each of these groups, there are subgroups, which are also hierarchically arranged. With respect to the Brahman, the Shudra constitutes a monolithic group, but within it, there are several groups that are arranged on the axis of purity and pollution. Beteille (1972: 418) observes that untouchability is practiced by the lowest castes themselves. Giving an example from Tamil Nadu, he says "Pallas do not draw water from Paraiyan wells, nor do they allow Paraiyans to use their wells." Both the Palla and the Paraiyan are lower castes in Tamil Nadu.

There have been a plethora of debates with Dumont's position. Although my intention is not to take up these here, I wish to point out that one of the major issues in these debates pertains to the place Dumont gives to power (economic and political) in his highly ambitious thesis, which presented the Brahmanical perspective on caste, pivoted on rituals and purity. Yes, the *power* the Brahmans wield is "to perform rituals," "to offer the exegeses of texts," "to indulge in occult lore such as astrology and palmistry," "to teach the wider public the ideas of morality, ethics, and spirituality," and "to cosmically legitimize the Kshatriya rule." The Brahmanical power—despite the fact that the rulers kowtow before the priests—is highly confined, for all its decisions are limited to the domains of religion and ritual. The kings exercise what may be called "general or overarching power," take decisions about all ambits of social and spiritual life, direct priests to perform rituals to vouchsafe their interests and maintain cosmic harmony, and for all this, the rulers render expensive gifts (including land and villages) to Brahman priests (Nath, 2000). Although Brahmans become fabulously rich because of Kshatriya patronage, they as well as the rulers know that once the Brahmans start managing the wealth, they will be distracted from the nontransferable intellectual and ritual functions, and if this ever happens, the entire universe will lapse into disarray. Keeping this in mind, the rulers advise the Vaishya and Shudra to look after the wealth of the priests (Das, 1982). Albeit the power of the Kshatriya, the varna model places the Brahman's ritual power over all the other powers (political or economic).

Those outside the scheme of varna were called *Panchama* (the "fifth"), a put-all-it-in category that comprised the excommunicated groups, those who had depressed in this for violating the duties (dharma) assigned to them in the varna order, or who did not abide by the rules of marriage and pollution, and those who lived in jungles, away from the centers of civilization, such as the tribal populations. The varna model (which also includes those outside it, the Panchama) may be summarized in the Table 13.3.

**Table 13.3: The Varna Model**

| Varna Hierarchy | Within/Without Varna Category | Twice-born | Power | Ritual Performance | Points Earned |
|---|---|---|---|---|---|
| Brahman | + | + | + (religious) | + | 4 |
| Kshatriya | + | + | + (temporal) | − | 3 |
| Vaishya | + | + | − | − | 2 |
| Sudra | + | − | − | − | 1 |
| Panchama | − | − | − | − | 0 |

*Notes:* + denotes yes; − denotes no.

Those who earn the maximum points occupy the summit of the hierarchy. The designation "caste Hindu" applies to those who are within the varna scheme; the Panchama are the "out-caste."

By contrast, as was spelt out previously, jāti is a "lived-in" system—caste as practiced and experienced in everyday lives of people. Indians (including those in remote villages) know about the four (five)-fold division of their society and also that there are multiple jātis and in future, many more may be created.

In the past, historians tell us, before the formal structuring of Hindus in four varna took place, there existed a myriad of servicing groups, each trying to acquire some sort of specialization over an occupation, in a system where groups were interdependent. Thus, varna was a paradigmatic attempt to think about the functions that must be performed to create a society in balance with the entire cosmos (the natural and heavenly forces), which could guarantee salubriousness to human survival. An ideal society would require the lawgivers, law executioners, and the goods producers, in this hierarchy, and there should be a class of people (the service renderers) to serve them. In this theory of social structure, the lawgivers (and Manu was one) are religious personnel, specializing in performing rituals that are expected to have cosmogenic effects; and since religion is the principle of social organization, they are at the top of the hierarchy, although they may lead a life of flagrant poverty, and ideally they are supposed to renounce the world (Biardeau, 1989; Dumont, 1980).

The "field view," however, acquaints us with a different picture. Those who control economic resources also get their hands on political power. The varna-wise supreme, Brahman priests, succumb to their instructions and commands, abbreviating their rituals if they so desire. The political and economic facts may be "residual" and "secondary" in varna hierarchy, but not in jāti, the understanding of which will require concepts like "secular status" and "dominant caste" that Srinivas (1959) had given in his study of the village of Rampura in Karnataka.

Both varna and jāti have a set of similarities. As pointed out earlier, why a person is born in a particular caste is explained in terms of his deeds (karma) in the last birth. If in this birth, one adheres to one's caste duties and follows the righteous path, doing well to others, one will improve upon one's position in the next birth.[20] The aim of life should be to consistently improve upon one's position in subsequent births, so that finally one is released permanently from the incessant cycle of birth and death. The world (*sansār*) is seen as a theatre of sorrows (*dukh*), from which one should aim to seek liberation forever to be in a state of eternal bliss.

The jāti system has multiple social categories, some of which are only locally found, whereas some have an all-India representation. Brahmans, for example, are an all-India caste; the *Shakka* (those bearing water in leather bags) is highly local. Each region, therefore, has its own hierarchy, and one of the occupations of field anthropologists is to determine it making use of the principles of attributes and diacritical signs that castes use and the actual interaction and the norms of proximity that operate between them (Marriott, 1959, 1960).

This middle level of jāti hierarchy shows a lot of blurring, with each of these castes claiming to be "slightly superior" to the other (Marriott and Inden, 1985). In both varna and jāti hierarchies, the Brahmans are the "purest'" and at the lowest level are those who are believed to be the permanent abettors of impurity; Gandhi called them the "children of god" (Harijan), and today, the term *dalit* (meaning "suppressed," "crushed," "broken to pieces"), coined by Jyotirao Phule in the 19th century, is used for them (Mendelsohn and Vicziany, 1998: 4). They, in villages, where there are no latrines, remove dead animals, work with leather, clean public spaces and remove garbage, carry petroleum lights on ritual occasions, and produce music. In small towns and cities, where flush latrines have yet not been installed in houses, these castes (often termed "sweeper," *mehtar*, *bhangī*, *achuta*) remove excrement from dry latrines and carry it in buckets or baskets as loads on their heads, which is the main reason of their being treated as an "untouchable group," in spite of the legal abolition of the practice of untouchability. According to a recent survey that the Safai Karamchari Andolan (Movement of Manual Scavengers) conducted, there are not less than 1.3 million people engaged in cleaning of other people's excreta, often with bare hands, of which 95 percent are women. The worst aspect of this is the discrimination meted out at schools to the children of manual scavengers, where they are made to perform cleaning and scavenging work. They are so demoralized because of the stigma that continues that they drop out from schools and start helping their parents in their work.[21] More than 50 years ago, Dr Bhimrao Ramji Ambedkar, the "architect of the present reservation policy" (Thorat and Kumar, 2008: 1), had said that the first step toward the liberation of the untouchables was to withdraw collectively and permanently from menial occupations. In this context, he gave the slogan: *bhangī, jhārū choro* (the sweepers, leave the broom) (Prashad, 2000: 168).

In a nutshell, the mutual opposition of purity and impurity is explicit in both varna and jāti.

The important observation is that people are aware of the existence of both the hierarchies, of varna and jāti. Although they may not use, they are not unaware of the term varna, thanks to its use (and of many other words of Sanskrit origin) by priests and discoursers (*kathāvāchak*).[22] For instance, *Manusmrti* is hardly read by general populace, by comparison to the epic of *Ramacharitmanas* and the *Bhagavad Gita*, but its salient ideas are known to them, for they figure in various religious discourses. The attempts to fit a wide mass of jātis in different varna categories, to make the grotesquely diverse order of jātis look neat and nonoverlapping as varna, have taken place in past, but hesitancy surfaced when the jātis that were neither ritual technicians, nor warriors, nor agriculturists, and businesspersons had no option but to be classified as Shudra. So, the caste of the scribes— the Kayastha—became Shudra, so did the caste of the genealogists (Rav, Jagga, Bahi-bhat) and so did the caste of the goldsmith—the Sunar; such a "refugee status"—since one cannot be accommodated in the first three, the only option is the last category—was not acceptable to them.

Over a period of time, jātis have become conscious of their identities; in the contemporary politics of assertion, jātis opt for solidifying their unity, rather than seeking a place in varna system or trying to move up in ritual hierarchy. The process of upward ritual mobility, which Srinivas (1952) called Sanskritization, is on decline.[23] Caste has moved into the realm of politics: From a socioreligious institution, it has become political, and it seems that its ties with Hinduism have become tenuous. Beteille (2012: 135) writes, "It would not be too much to say that democratic politics has given a new lease of life to caste." Castes are alive in contemporary India, but if it still is the "structural basis" of Hinduism, as Srinivas (1952: 213) said, and I quoted him earlier, is a question that demands close attention.

India is so diverse that any attempt to give a set of general propositions about it is fraught with risk. City dwellers (particularly those from the metropolises) experience caste differently than those from villages, especially interiorly located. Take two instances.

For Punjabi-speaking families in Delhi, which are not from the merchant caste, the social universe is divided into two types: the Khatri and the Arora. If you ask the Punjabis what these groups are, some would regard them as jātis, whilst others may be skeptical of using this term, although they would say that these are "like jātis." The Khatri consider themselves as superior to the Arora and the latter also concede this. The Khatri also say that they are not just confined to Punjab, their brethren are also dispersed in Uttar Pradesh, where their lingua franca is Hindi, not Punjabi. They prefer endogamy, but would not resist marriage with the Arora.  Barring that these two groups have different surnames and think in terms of biological differences between them—the Khatri are believed to be fair complexioned, tall, with sharp features—there are no other social and cultural indices—purity and pollution included—that distinguish one from the other.

When I interviewed middle-aged and old respondents from these communities about their experiences of caste, two points surfaced. First, they recalled that separate vessels (made of glass rather than metal) were kept for offering food or water to "touchable" servicing castes (such as laundry persons, house and utensil cleaners, barber), which also had access to the houses. Second, the manual scavengers, the latrine cleaners, were out of bounds of the main house. They were expected to finish their work in the morning and then return in the early afternoon for a daily gift of a couple of leavened bread (rotī) from each house they served. At the end of a month, some little monetary compensation was also made. On ritual contexts, they were gifted money and clothes, and on occasions of feast, their work was to remove leaf plates in which food was served, collect the garbage, take away any leftover food, and at the conclusion of the communal eating, food and money were also given to them.

I learnt that whilst the first practice still continued in some households, the second had become a relic of past. Its decline began after flush latrines were installed, but even after that, for some time, the manual scavengers used to come to clean, for which they were monetarily paid rather than in kind also. Then came a time when the householders started cleaning the toilet pots themselves. Great improvement had also taken place in the quality of detergent liquids and the technical gadgets for cleaning the toilets. All this led to a situation where service relationships with the caste of sweepers have almost ended once and forever. Today, the erstwhile sweepers who served individual houses are largely employed by the municipal corporations for cleaning the public spaces. The paternalistic ties between the individual households and the sweepers working for them are now a social fact of the departed time.

This was the caste experience of my urban respondents. Compare it with the situation from the villages of Rajasthan, where each jāti has a separate quarter comprising all its households. Aside the law, the practice of untouchability is rampant in rural India and also in small towns (Jodhka and Shah, 2010; Sheth, 2004;).[24] Lower caste people are expected to pay deference to the dominant caste of the Rajput. Lower caste men and women are supposed to remove their shoes when they walk through the streets where Rajputs live.[25] In the past, I learnt the lower caste men were supposed to bow, with their torso bent, whenever they passed through Rajput neighborhoods. In a wedding procession, the bridegrooms from lower castes were not supposed to mount the mare. If they did, they must dismount the animal when they reached closer to Rajput houses. In earlier days, the use of gold ornaments was also denied to lower castes.

Many of these practices have changed in some villages as a consequence of the efforts of the local leaders, but in many, they still continue. Stories of the crusades led by nongovernmental organizations to fight the disabilities are well known. Nevertheless, the cases of discrimination and injustice abound.

For urban Indians, caste is an artifact that enlivens at the time of searching a spouse, as the other institutions (such as clubs, pubs), where young men and women may meet up and decide about their "living together" and marriage, have yet not developed the way they have done in west. The hold of families on the matrimonial alliances of their children, particularly girls, is still robust. However, at the same time, matrimonial advertisements that appear in national newspapers frequently mention "caste no bar," implying their readiness to marry intercaste; and such marriages have become common in upper, educated, and professional classes. Still, a bulk of marriages is parentally arranged from within the caste, although a meeting of the prospective spouses is arranged so that they have an opportunity to "see" each other before they are bonded in matrimony;

in this way, the families accommodate to the individualism of their children. Intercaste and intercommunity marriages may not be so rare, but to the best of my knowledge, marriages between "twice-born" persons and those at the lowest rungs of caste hierarchy (such as leatherworkers, manual scavengers) are quite infrequent.

When our attention turns to village India, three facts strike us. First, people are *conscious* of their caste as well as of the others, although intercaste relations (or, the *jajmānī* ties) have declined in comparison to what used to be, say, 50 years ago.[26] With the rise of the backward class movements, many occupational castes have started withdrawing from hereditary relations of interdependence (Raheja, 1988; Singh and Harit, 1960). Against this backdrop, Srinivas's conclusion in his posthumously published paper of 2003 that contemporary India has castes but not "caste system" (a system of interdependent castes) is worth examining. Second, castes are emerging as "cultural bodies," each having its own congregation of "artifacts, structures, and agencies" that endeavors to create its integration and unity.[27] This is happening against the setting of castes playing decisive role in local and state politics. In addition to each jāti emerging as a "cultural body," jātis sharing the same location in the local social structure come together to form what may be termed a "cluster" or "bloc" of castes, and such a federation also creates its own set of distinguishing cultural characteristics.[28] This would also explain the rise of the cults of several caste-linked deities.

Third, the policy of compensatory discrimination, in accordance with which the Scheduled Castes and Scheduled Tribes get material benefits from the state, has led to a refiguring of jātis into two grids— the "beneficiaries" and the upper strata, those who are not covered by this provision. Relations between these two groups have become acrimonious over time, especially after 1991 when the government accepted the Mandal Commission Report that recommended measures of positive discrimination for the "Other Backward Classes" (Bayly, 1999: 294–300). Cases of caste antagonism and hostility are reported from different parts of the country. In private conversations, one group heaps vitriol on the other.[29] Atrocity on lower, depressed castes is increasing; about one hundred thousand of its cases are pending action (*The Indian Express*, May 17, 2012). It is also increasingly seen that in some parts of India, upper castes find it difficult to digest the fact that the lower castes are able to do well, and surpass them, in various activities.[30] What was considered at one time as an exemplification of organic solidarity is now a system in which jātis compete and conflict, consolidating them as "vote banks" against the others. The process of upward ritual mobility has been replaced by the twin processes of creating one's cultural identity and participating in the democratic politics, for in this way, one's interests might be met.

Caste associations have emerged in all parts of India, but the functions they perform in cities and villages are different. In former, they are truly voluntary, lacking sanction. Unthinkable in Indian cities and metropolises today is an episode like the one Gandhi (1927: 37–39) described in his autobiography. Gandhi's caste (Modh Bania) folks were agitated about his travel abroad for study. The headman of the community argued that since his religion forbade voyages abroad, Gandhi was instructed to abandon his plan; but when he resisted the interference of caste in this matter, he was excommunicated.

That was century before last. Caste associations in cities today work toward building the "social capital" of people, extending their networks and providing them with a readymade group to choose their spouses, besides instilling in them a sense of identity. Many of these associations also publish their respective periodicals, some regularly, some, erratically, all depending upon their financial situation, to be sent out to their members and dignitaries of the area, free of cost. The content of these magazines may be conveniently divided into four sections. The first deals with write-ups on the caste's glorious tradition and past; the second, its prominent people and their achievements; third, the matrimonial advertisements, for the insertion of which the community people make nominal or no payment; and lastly, short articles and poems that members contribute. Besides being viewed as an act of social service, these periodicals apprise its readers with the happenings in the community, thus strengthening their sense of belongingness.

In villages (and small towns), caste bodies take the form of a "council," involuntary and punitive, and in some cases, repressive. Not only do they take up the cases of dispute among its members, providing them with solutions that are binding, but also reinforce the cultural practices that the caste believes to be of its definitional value. Umpteen instances can be cited from north India where caste panchayats have prohibited *sagotra* (intraclan) marriages, village endogamy, intercaste marriages, and cases of hypergamy and hypogamy, with dreadful consequences. These councils have also prohibited the use of western dresses, especially by women.

Caste is one of the few institutions of the world that has received severe criticisms and denigrations in the last two and a half thousand years. At the center of these appraisals has been the question: How can God—the most merciful and just—create a system in which a large mass of people is consigned to lead a despicable existence at the brink of dehumanization? By definition, God cannot be unfair, so the texts that legitimize caste system, making it sacrosanct, were de facto composed by people—the priest intellectuals—who wanted to ensure their supremacy, control over resources and labor, in times of come. The foul the text composers played was their claim that the division of labor and the hierarchy of orders were divinely decreed. Human beings share the same life, pass through similar stages of existence, and have common predicaments and fortitudes, and therefore an ideology that causes discrimination among God's highest creation (that man is) is rebuttable.

This was the tenor of arguments that the critics of caste have launched right from 600 BCE when Buddhism and Jainism started making their presence felt. The protagonists of religions that came to India from outside (such as Christianity, Islam, Judaism, and Zoroastrianism) attacked caste system, making available an alternative, where all could attend the place of worship without prohibition. The 15th-century religion, Sikhism, reiterated the same point about human equality and equality of all before God. The desire to be treated at par with all humans attracted several lower castes to embrace religions that promised equality. The devotional (bhakti) saints and movements also criticized caste system, contending that it has brought disrepute to the otherwise transcendental religion of Hinduism. Some of these saints—like Kabir—distanced them from formal and institutionalized religions, and spread the message of human equality. Sur Das, a 16th-century devotional poet and singer, cited umpteen examples in his poems in which Lord Krishna preferred the "company of the lowly and outcaste to that of the pure and well-placed" (Hawley, 1984: 137).

The interesting observation is that whilst these saints rejected caste, they expressed their profound love for Hindu gods and goddesses, implying that the glory and veracity of Hinduism were eclipsed by caste system. The 17th-century Marathi poet, Tukaram, says the following in one of his *abhangs* (verses in devotional poetry):

> Brahmins do not lead their lives according to the tradition;
> They commit thefts and instigate others.
> Like Muslims, they wear *pyjama* and [things made of] leather.
> They occupy high positions and let the people die of hunger.
> They even punish the innocent,
> Kings torment the ruled; unhesitatingly loot them at pilgrim centres,
> Vaishya and Shudra are lowly placed [so they cannot do anything],
> O Lord! Aren't you seeing the oppressors, the Brahmins and Kings?
> Are you sleeping? Come soon [to save us from the state of oppression].[31]

In another abhang, Tukaram says that God's (Ram) name (*nām*) can be recited by everyone, irrespective of his varna, and by "sailing in the boat of god's name, one can go across the world of birth and death and seek oneness with god" (Seth, 1979: 144).

Against this backdrop, another important change is in terms of the consolidation of the caste-specific deities of the lower castes (Srivastava, 1997). Since all-India Hinduism (or Sanskritic Hinduism) has been solely responsible for generating and legitimizing inequalities, the lower castes intend to distance them from it. Thus, instead of worshipping the deities of caste Hindu, they want to repose their firm faith in their own caste deities. This would explain the popularity of Balmiki, the dacoit-turned-saint, who composed the *Ramayana*, among the Dalit communities in India, or the rise of the cult of Ramdev among the Meghwal (the weaver caste) of Rajasthan. Exhibiting the properties of both hydra and banyan tree, Hinduism has the ability to branch out, incorporate in its womb multitudinous pantheons, and allow its adherents to follow any sect, cult, god-figure, folk hero, depending upon their likes and historical traditions.[32] Those who worship Balmiki describe them to be so, but they do not call them "non-Hindu"; they are, thus, Hindus who worship Balmiki and not the upper-caste gods and goddesses.

Against this ethnographic backdrop, my submission is that in these discourses, caste system was dissociated from Hinduism. Disrespect to Hinduism, which is an ancient religion, has primarily been caused by caste practice. This line of submission is discernible among both medieval and modern thinkers, and has been summarized well by Swami Vivekananda (1893) in the following sentence: "everyone made the mistake of holding caste to be a religious institution and tried to pull down both religion and caste all together and failed." Since many scholars thought that caste and Hinduism are inextricable, they have favored renouncing the portals of Hinduism to embrace one or the other caste-free religious stream. Dr Ambedkar, for instance, "turned to Buddhism as personal faith and as an ideology that offered an alternative to Hinduism" (Rodrigues, 2002: 16). Caste system, he thought, annihilated the individualism and stripped people of the ability to judge a person on merit (Ambedkar, 2002a: 275). Hindu society needed to be reorganized on the basis of the principles of liberty, equality, and fraternity, and for achieving this objective, Ambedkar (2002b: 307) thought, "caste and Varna must be destroyed."[33]

Many Indians would agree with Dr Ambedkar. They want freedom from caste. Mass media are leaving no stone unturned in familiarizing people with the evil of caste practices. That an Indian Administrative Service (IAS) officer was constrained to resign from the coveted service because of caste discrimination was recently in news when this officer appeared on national television and said that in the service he was "first a member of the caste of leatherworkers, then an officer."[34] Also in the same program was a college lecturer narrating the practice of untouchability and discrimination in the hostel of a prestigious university where she read for a higher degree. Such episodes fill Indians with revulsion. They want, as said previously, a caste-free society. However, the fact of having been brought up in a caste society, and internalizing it for a long time, hues one's consciousness, which would explain why there are caste-based matrimonial advertisements or why in a sperm bank in Bihar, tubes filled with spermatic fluid carry caste stickers (Tewary, 2012), because caste figures as one of the considerations in people's decision-making ventures. In the television program mentioned above, one of the dignitaries said "*jāti kabhī jāti nahīn hai*" (jāti is one that does not go away).[35]

Caste awareness is also age related. Young Indians are comparatively free from caste scourges. Caste has come a long way from being a principle of social organization to be an element of one's consciousness, which is largely activated on life-cycle occasions. A common observation in urban India is that when people meet for the first time, they usually enquire about the place (region) from where they hail rather than the castes to which they belong. Since caste has an adaptive structure (Gould, 1963: 429–430), it has been able to find a place in politics, but more and more people are realizing its perils for India's future development and democratic tradition.

## Notes

1. Although I have not done a survey on the number of articles and books published on caste each year, my general impression is that hardly a day passes in India when a case of caste atrocity does not occur and is not reported in national newspapers. Academic writings on caste have not declined as was speculated when the study of agrarian structures was gaining prominence; however, the body of contemporary works "interrogates" caste from the perspective of inequality (Jodhka, 2012: X), rather than just dealing with a description of "caste systems in different parts of India."

2. One may quote Mahatma Gandhi (1987: 12) here, "Caste has nothing to do with religion … it is harmful both to spiritual and national growth."

3. It is not only a sociological way of putting the ideas. People in India often speak in terms of the *niyam* (principle, rule) according to which they think their social living is (or should be) organized. Many ills in society (such as crime against women, financial corruption, telling lies, female feticide and infanticide, etc.) are explained as caused by a feebleness of the niyams; so, when a council (*panchayat*) in Uttar Pradesh decided that women below the age of 40 would not use mobile phones, a violation of which would lead to their punishment, it justified its decision as a "return to the rule of tradition," one that has weakened in the face of "western modernity" (*pashchami ādhuniktā*) (*The Hindu*, July 17, 2012). Notwithstanding their limitations, the concepts of tradition and modernity help us greatly in understanding contemporary India.

4. Many early writers on India were struck by caste practices in India. Baines (1912) writes, "It needs but a very short time in the country to bring home to the most casual observer the ubiquity of the institution [caste]."

5. Kakar and Kakar (2007: 8) write, "Indians are perhaps the world's most undemocratic people, living in the world's largest and most plural democracy."

6. Incidentally, one of the units of research and specialization, funded by the University Grants Commission, which has been added to Indian universities in the last seven years or so, is the Centre for Study of Social Exclusion and Inclusive Policy. The aim of this center is to understand the process of exclusion in society, critically examine the inclusive policies that have come into existence, thus contributing to the creation of a just and egalitarian society.

7. Civil servants are sometimes tauntingly called in India "modern Brahmans."

8. Gupta (2005: 409) says, "Although tribes and religious distinctions exist in other societies as well, what sets India apart is the prevalence of the caste order."

9. Ghurye (1932: 8) writes, "The ideas about the power of certain castes to convey pollution by touch are not so highly developed in Northern India as in the South."

10. Castes grouped in "right hand" would regard themselves as superior to those in the "left"; thus, a lower caste person in "right hand" would place him/her as superior to the Brahman of "left hand."

11. "[A]ny attempt at definition [of caste] is bound to fail because of the complexity of the phenomenon" (Ghurye, 1932: 1).

12. The People of India Project that the Anthropological Survey of India undertook in the 1980s counted 4,635 communities in India, of which 461 were tribal. See Singh (1994).

13. Barth (1960), for instance, translates *quam* as "caste"; but these quams are devoid of rituals and religious status. If there are crucial differences between Hindu castes and the Swat "castes," as Barth has also noted, then one would wonder why the term caste is used for the Swat case. Why cannot term like "ethnic group," "social class," or "social category" be used for stratification among the Swat? All this directs us to delineate the diacritical characteristics of caste. I have also come across zoological writings wherein the term "caste" is used for the species of ant.

14. For *Manusmrti*, I have relied upon its translations by Bühler (1886) and Olivelle (2006). Prabhu (1940: 286) says that Purusha—in the *purusasukta* hymn—is "described as being himself 'this whole universe, whatever has been and whatever shall be.'"

15. Hutton (1946: 60) says that in South India, the Brahmans are spoken as *mahajanan* (of great birth) and they are regarded as belonging neither to the "right" nor to the "left" hand castes. However, that is not true of all areas of South India (Srinivas, 2003: 456).

16. In both rural and urban India, I have seen the performance of this ritual—I have myself done it on umpteen occasions—but I have never come across people drinking the "nectar" that follows from washing the Brahman priest's feet. However, water (or any other liquid preparation) in which idols of gods are bathed (or washed, dipped) is commonly drunk by the devotees. I think the conception of hygiene is there at the back of the mind of people; they know that the priest's feet are soiled and the water collected after washing these is unsuitable for consumption, but since it is "sacred," it should not be drained out. A common practice is that this water—the "nectar of the feet"—is offered to a plant. In this way, the sacredness of the water is kept intact. Idols, by comparison, are least soiled, and so the liquid in which these have been dipped is less threatening to health and can be consumed without fear.

17. In case those who "fall below the line of purity," that is, the untouchables, touch the Brahman, it is the latter who is defiled rather than the untouchable acquiring purity. The belief is that impurity is highly contagious.

18. In addition to these, there are many others. I have selected these to give an idea of the nature of differentiation and hierarchy. Prabhu (1940: 289) notes that there are variations with respect to how different "twice-born" castes should recite the Gayatri Mantra, a hymn, and how, for instance, sacrifice should be conducted.

19. Srinivas (1952: 106) defines the "normal ritual status" as the "status which a person enjoys most of the time."

20. Marriott (2005: 357) says, "The idea that acquired characteristics are heritable aligns Hindu thought with Chevalier de Lamarck rather than Charles Darwin and distinguishes it from purely genetic racism."

21. The Safai Karamchari Andolan is a voluntary association concerned with the total implementation of The Employment of Manual Scavengers and Construction of Dry Latrines (Prohibition) Act, 1993, which has banned manual scavenging. See *The Tribune* (September 6, 2000), *Frontline*, 26 (3), (2009), *The Hindu* (March 24, 2012).

22. Freed and Freed (1966: 679) note that in a north Indian village, people know Veda; they read *Ramayana* and *Mahabharata*. The village also has formal religious storytelling sessions. Households often invite the priest to recite the *Satyanārāyan kathā* (the story of Satyanarayan, i.e., Vishnu). Also see Babb (1975).

23. Lynch (1969: 213) writes that the "Jatav [the caste of leatherworkers in Agra] may give up Sanskritization for political participation." Mobility on the "axis of power" (politicization) has replaced one on the "axis of status" (Sanskritization) (Beteille, 1967).

24. The state of Rajasthan recorded the highest incidence of registered atrocities against *dalits* across the country in 2010 (*The Hindustan Times*, May 3, 2012). Also see Mendelsohn and Vicziany (1998).

25. I observed this during my fieldwork in Rajasthan in the 1980s; a recent report from a village in Karauli district (Rajasthan) shows that this practice is still existent (*The Times of India*, August 12, 2012).

26. When speculating the caste of an outsider becomes difficult, the villagers unhesitatingly ask his/her caste, for this will direct future interactions with him/her.

27. Atal (1968: 235) recorded a verse that was the highlight of a pamphlet that the leatherworkers issued in one of their meetings. It ran like this: *jisko nā nij gaurav tathā nij jāti kā abhimān hai/voh nar nahin, hai pashu nirā aur mritak samān hai.* (One who is not proud of his honor and of his caste/is not a man; he is mere beast and like dead.) The aim of such meetings is to create unity among caste members and make them acutely aware of their problems so that they can all join hands.

28. It is not individual jātis that contest elections, rather it is an alliance of different jātis, formed for political purposes. It is quite likely that these jātis may have relations of hostility among them. Ishwaran (1968: 155) observed that in Shivapur (a village in Karnataka) "when, by political maneuvering, one caste is in the process of dominating the village, the other castes tend to combine against it." Individual jātis have a smaller size; that is the reason why they join with others for political goals. See Gupta (2000: 171–176).

29. Sometimes it becomes public. On Rahul Gandhi's visits to the colonies of *dalits*, Mayawati, the former chief minister of Uttar Pradesh and a *dalit* leader, said, "I have also come to know that when this prince [referring to Rahul] returns to his home in Delhi after meeting and eating with *dalits*, he is given a bath with a special soap and he goes through purificatory rituals with incense and incense sticks" (*India Today*, July 19, 2008).

30. See Jodhka (2010) on *dalit* businesspersons. *The Hindustan Times* (July 19, 2012) carried a news item on the incidents of violence in a Punjab village after an upper caste man was defeated in the game of wrestling by a lower caste person.

31. See Seth (1979: 244). The English translation is mine. *Pyjama* is like a pair of trousers and is believed to have been introduced by Muslim rulers.

32. About Hinduism, Gandhi (1987: 5) wrote, "One and indivisible at the root it has grown into a vast tree with innumerable branches."

33. The inaugural issue (February 11, 1933) of *Harijan*, the weekly journal of Harijan Sevak Sangh (Servants of the Untouchables' Society), founded by Gandhi, carried Dr Ambedkar's statement, which succinctly summed up his position:

> The out-caste is a by-product of the caste system. There will be out-castes as long as there are castes. Nothing can emancipate the out-caste except the destruction of caste system. Nothing can help to save Hindus and ensure their survival in the coming struggle except the purging of the Hindu faith of this odious and vicious dogma.

34. The Aamir Khan's Satyamev Jayate, Star Plus Television Channel, July 8, 2012. The officer, Balwant Singh, resigned in 2000 from the civil service and later wrote a book titled *An Untouchable in the I.A.S.* (*The Tribune*, September 6, 2000).

35. The word *jāti* means "caste" in this context; as a verb, it means "to go," and is used with feminine gender.

# References

Ahmad, Imtiaz (ed.). 1973. *Caste and Social Stratification among Muslims in India* (Edition 1978). New Delhi: Manohar.

Ambedkar, B. R. 2002a. "Annihilation of Caste." In Valerian Rodrigues (ed.), *The Essential Writings of B.R. Ambedkar*, 263–305. New Delhi: Oxford University Press.

Ambedkar, B. R. 2002b. "Reply to the Mahatma." In Valerian Rodrigues (ed.), *The Essential Writings of B.R. Ambedkar*, 306–319. New Delhi: Oxford University Press.

Atal, Yogesh. 1968. *The Changing Frontiers of Caste*. Delhi: National Publications.

Babb, Lawrence A. 1975. *The Divine Hierarchy: Popular Hinduism in Central India*. New York: Columbia University Press.

Baines, Athelstane. 1912. *Ethnography (Castes and Tribes)*. Strassburg: Trübner Verlag.

Barth, Fredrik. 1960. "The System of Social Stratification in Swat, North Pakistan." In Edmund R. Leach (ed.), *Aspects of Caste in South India, Ceylon, and North-West Pakistan*, 113–146. Cambridge: Cambridge University Press.

Basham, A. L. 1989. *The Wonder that was India*. London: Sidgwick & Jackson.

Basu, D. D. 1990. *The Essence of Hinduism (A Discourse on Comparative Religion on the Background of Hinduism)*. New Delhi: Prentice-Hall.

Bayly, Susan. 1999. *Caste, Society and Politics in India from the Eighteenth Century to the Modern Age. The New Cambridge History of India (IV-3)*. Cambridge: Cambridge University Press.

Beteille, Andre. 1967. "The Future of Backward Classes: The Contemporary Demands of Status and Power." In Philip Mason (ed.), *India and Ceylon: Unity and Diversity, A Symposium*, 83–120. London: Oxford University Press.

———. 1972. "Pollution and Poverty." In J. Michael Mahar (ed.), *The Untouchables in Contemporary India*, 411–420. Arizona: The University of Arizona Press.

Beteille, Andre. 1977. *Inequality among Men*. Oxford: Basil Blackwell.

———. 2012. *Democracy and Its Institutions*. New Delhi: Oxford University Press.

Biardeau, Madeleine. 1989. *Hinduism, The Anthropology of a Civilization*. New Delhi: Oxford University Press.

Blunt, E. A. H. 1931. *The Caste System of Northern India, With Special Reference to the United Provinces of Agra and Oudh*. London: Humphrey Milford and Oxford University Press.

Bühler, G. 1886. *The Laws of Manu*. Oxford: Oxford University Press.

Burghart, Richard (ed.). 1987. *Hinduism in Great Britain, The Perpetuation of Religion in an Alien Cultural Milieu*. London: Tavistock.

Das, Veena. 1982. *Structure and Cognition, Aspects of Hindu Caste and Ritual*. New Delhi: Oxford University Press.

Dube, S. C. 1968. "Foreword" to Yogesh Atal. *The Changing Frontiers of Caste*, V–IX. New Delhi: National Publications.

Dubois, Abbe J. A. 1906. *Hindu Manners, Customs and Ceremonies* (Third Edition). Oxford: Clarendon Press.

Dumont, Louis. 1980. *Homo Hierarchicus, The Caste System and Its Implications*. Chicago/London: The University of Chicago Press.

Freed, Ruth S. and Stanley A. Freed. 1966. "Unity in Diversity in the Celebration of Cattle-curing Rites in a North Indian Village: A Study in the Resolution of Conflicts." *American Anthropologist* 68 (3): 673–692.

Gandhi, M. K. 1927. *An Autobiography or the Story of My Experiments with Truth* (Translated from the Gujarati by Mahadev Desai). Ahmedabad: Navajivan Publishing House.

———. 1987. *The Essence of Hinduism*. Ahmedabad: Navjivan Publishing House.

Ghurye, G. S. 1932. *Caste and Race in India*. Bombay: Popular Prakashan. (Reprint 2011).

Gould, Harold A. 1963. "The Adaptive Functions of Caste in Contemporary Indian Society." *Asian Survey* 3(9): 427–438.

Gupta, Dipankar. 2000. *Interrogating Caste, Understanding Hierarchy and Difference in Indian Society*. New Delhi: Penguin Books.

———. 2005. "Caste and Politics, Ideology over System." *Annual Review of Anthropology* 21: 409–427.

Hawley, John Stratton. 1984. *Sūr Dās: Poet, Singer, Saint*. New Delhi: Oxford University Press.

Hutton, J. H. 1946. *Caste in India. Its Nature, Function, and Origins*. Cambridge: Cambridge University Press.

Ishwaran, K. 1968. *Shivapur, A South Indian Village*. London: Routledge & Kegan Paul.

Jodhka, Surinder S. 2010. *Dalits in Business: Self-employed Scheduled Castes in Northwest India* (Working Paper Series, IV (2)). New Delhi: Indian Institute of Dalit Studies.

———. 2012. *Caste*. New Delhi: Oxford University Press.

Jodhka, Surinder S. and Ghanshyam Shah. 2010. *Comparative Contexts of Discrimination: Caste and Untouchability in South Asia* (Working Paper Series, IV [5]). New Delhi: Indian Institute of Dalit Studies.

Kakar, Sudhir and Katharina Kakar. 2007. *The Indians, Portrait of a People*. New Delhi: Penguin Books.

Kane, Pandurang V. 1946. *History of Dharmasastra*. Pune: Bhandarkar Oriental Research Institute.

Ketkar, S. V. 1909. *History of Caste in India*. New Delhi: Low Price Publications. (Reprint 1990.)

Lewis, Oscar. 1958. *Village Life in Northern India: Studies in a Delhi Village*. Urbana: University of Illinois Press.

Lynch, Owen M. 1969. *The Politics of Untouchability, Social Mobility and Social Change in a City of India*. New York/London: Columbia University Press.

Mandelbaum, David G. 1962. *Society in India*. Mumbai: Popular Prakashan.

Marriott, McKim. 1959. "Interactional and Attributional Theories of Caste Ranking." *Man in India* 39: 92–107.

———. 1960. *Caste Ranking and Community Structure in Five Regions of India and Pakistan*. Pune: G.S. Press.

———. 2005. "Varna and Jati." In Sushil Mittal and Gene Thursby (eds), *The Hindu World*, 357–382. New York/London: Routledge.

Marriott, McKim and R. B. Inden. 1985. "Social Stratification: Caste." In *Encyclopaedia Britannica* (Fifteenth Edition) 27: 348–356.

Mathur, K. S. 1964. *Caste and Ritual in a Malwa Village*. Mumbai: Asia Publishing House.

Mendelsohn, Oliver, and Marika Vicziany. 1998. *The Untouchables: Subordination, Poverty, and the State in Modern India*. Cambridge: Cambridge University Press.

Nadkarni, M. V. 2003. "Is Caste System Intrinsic to Hinduism? Demolishing a Myth." *Economic and Political Weekly* 38 (45): 4783–4793.

Nath, Vijay. 2000. "From 'Brahmanism' to 'Hinduism': Negotiating the Myth of the Great Tradition." Presidential Address, Section-I, Ancient India, Indian History Congress, Sixty-first Session, Kolkata.

O'Flaherty, Wendy Doniger (with Daniel Gold, David Haberman, and David Shulman) (ed.). 1988. *Textual Sources for the Study of Hinduism*. Manchester: Manchester University Press.

Olivelle, Patrick. 2006. *Manu's Code of Law: A Critical Edition and Translation of the Mānava-Dharmaśāstra*. New Delhi: Oxford University Press.

Omvedt, Gail. 2003. *Buddhism in India, Challenging Brahamanism and Caste*. New Delhi: SAGE Publications.

Prabhu, P. N. 1940. *Hindu Social Organization, A Study in Socio-psychological and Ideological Foundations*. Mumbai: Popular Prakashan.

Prashad, Vijay. 2000. *Untouchable Freedom: A Social History of a Dalit Community*. New Delhi: Oxford University Press.

Raghavan, V. 1953. "Introduction to the Hindu Scriptures." In Kenneth W. Morgan (ed.), *The Religion of the Hindus*, 265–398. New York: The Ronald Press Company.

Raheja, Gloria Goodwin. 1988. *The Poison in the Gift. Ritual, Prestation, and the Dominant Caste in a North Indian Village*. Chicago/London: The University of Chicago Press.

Rodrigues, Valerian (ed.). 2002. *The Essential Writings of B.R. Ambedkar*. New Delhi: Oxford University Press.

Sarma, D. S. 1953. "The Nature and History of Hinduism." In Kenneth W. Morgan (ed.), *The Religion of the Hindus*, 3–47. New York: The Ronald Press Company.

Sen, Amartya. 2000. *Social Exclusion: Concept, Application, and Scrutiny*. Asian Development Bank, Office of Environment and Social Development, Manila.

Seth, Ramesh. 1979. *Tukaram avam Kabir, Ek Tulnatmak Adhyan* (in Hindi) (Tukaram and Kabir: A Comparative Study). New Delhi: Sahitya Shodh Sansthan.

Sharma, Arvind. 2000. *Classical Hindu Thought: An Introduction*. New Delhi: Oxford University Press.

Sheth, D. L. 2004. *Caste, Ethnicity and Exclusion in South Asia: The Role of Affirmative Action Policies in Building Inclusive Societies*. United Nations Development Programme, Human Development Office.

Singh, Harjinder (ed.). 1977. *Caste among Non-Hindus in India*. New Delhi: National Publishers.

Singh, Indera P. and H. L. Harit. 1960. "Effects of Urbanization in a Delhi Suburban Village." *Journal of Social Research* 3 (1): 38–43.

Singh, Khushwant. 1966. *A History of the Sikhs* (Two Volumes). Princeton: Princeton University Press.

Singh, K. S. 1994. *The Scheduled Tribes* (National Series, Volume III). Kolkata/New Delhi: Anthropological Survey of India/Oxford University Press.

Sinha, Surajit. 1965. "Tribe-Caste and Tribe-Peasant Continuua in Central India." *Man in India* 45: 57–83.

Srinivas, M. N. 1952. *Religion and Society among the Coorgs of South India*. New Delhi: Oxford University Press. (Reprint 2003.)

———. 2003. "An Obituary on Caste as a System." *The Economic and Political Weekly* XXXVIII (5): 455–459.

——— (ed.). 1996. *Caste, Its Twentieth Century Avatar*. New Delhi: Penguin Books.

Srivastava, Vinay Kumar. 1997. *Religious Renunciation of a Pastoral People*. New Delhi: Oxford University Press.

Thorat, Sukhadeo and Narender Kumar (eds.). 2008. *B.R. Ambedkar, Perspectives on Social Exclusion and Inclusive Policies*. New Delhi: Oxford University Press.

Tewary, Amarnath. 2012. "At a Sperm Bank in Bihar, Caste Divisions Start Before Birth." *The New York Times* (India Ink: Notes on the World's Largest Democracy), July 12.

Vivekananda, Swami. 1893. Letter to Alasingha of 2 November 1983. "The Vivekananda Letters." Available at: www.angelfire.com/ma/Vivekananda/Vivekanandaletters. htmi (accessed on February 20, 2012).

# Further Readings

Beteille, Andre. 1969. "A Note on the Referents of Caste." In Andre Beteille (ed.), *Castes: Old and New, Essays in Social Structure and Social Stratification*, 146–151. Mumbai: Asia Publishing House.

———. 2002. "Varna and Jati." In Andre Beteille (ed.), *Equality and Universality, Essays in Social and Political Theory*, 59–69. New Delhi: Oxford University Press.

Galanter, Marc. 1984. *Competing Equalities, Law and Backward Classes in India*. New Delhi: Oxford University Press.

Ghurye, G. S. 1972. *Two Brahmanical Institutions, Gotra and Charana*. Mumbai: Popular Prakashan.

Gough, Kathleen. 1960. "Caste in a Tanjore Village." In Edmund R. Leach (ed.), *Aspects of Caste in South India, Ceylon, and North-West Pakistan*, 11–60. Cambridge: Cambridge University Press.

Inden, Ronald B. 1976. *Marriage and Rank in Bengali Culture: A History of Caste and Clan in Middle Period Bengal*. New Delhi: Vikas Publishing House Pvt Ltd.

Leach, Edmund R. 1961. *Pul Eliya, A Village in Ceylon, A Study of Land Tenure and Kinship*. Cambridge: Cambridge University Press.

Leonard, Karen Isaksen. 1978. *Social History of an Indian Caste, The Kayasths of Hyderabad*. New Delhi: Oxford University Press.

Quigley, Declan. 1993. *The Interpretation of Caste*. Oxford: Clarendon Press.

Risley, H. H. 1915. *The People of India* (Second Edition). London: W. Thacker and Co.

Srinivas, M. N. 1959. "The Dominant Caste in Rampura." *American Anthropologist* 61: 1–16.

———. 1962. "Varna and Caste." In M. N. Srinivas (ed.), *Caste in Modern India and Other Essays*, 63-69. Mumbai: Media Promoters and Publishers Pvt. Ltd. (Reprint 2002.)

Tambiah, Stanley J. 1985. "From Varna to Caste through Mixed Unions." In Stanley J. Tambiah (ed.), *Culture, Thought, and Social Action. An Anthropological Perspective*, 212–251. Cambridge, MA: Harvard University Press.

Wiser, William H. 1936. *The Hindu Jajmani System: A Socio-economic System Inter-relating Members of a Hindu Village Community in Service*. Lucknow: Lucknow Publishing House.

# About the Editors and Contributors

## Series Editor

**Geoffrey A. Oddie** is Honorary Senior Lecturer, Department of History, University of Sydney. He is a graduate of the Universities of Melbourne and London where he received his PhD in the School of Oriental and African Studies. He has lectured in the History department since 1964 and has been a Visiting Fellow at the Australian National University (1982); Visiting Fellow at the Jawaharlal Nehru University, New Delhi (2007); and Visiting Professor at the United Theological College, Bengaluru. Two of his books are *Popular Religion, Elites and Reform: Hook-Swinging and Its Prohibition in Colonial India, 1800–1894* (1995) and *Imagined Hinduism: British Protestant Missionary Constructions of Hinduism, 1793–1900* (SAGE, 2006).

## Editors

**Will Sweetman** is Associate Professor of Asian Religions, University of Otago, New Zealand. He studied philosophy, religious studies, and theology at the Universities of Lancaster and Cambridge. He has taught at universities in London and Newcastle, and held research fellowships at the University of Halle, Germany, and the University of Cambridge. He has published three books and several articles on historical and theoretical aspects of the study of Hinduism.

**Aditya Malik** is Professor and Dean in the School of Historical Studies at the newly established Nalanda University, India. He was trained in philosophy, archaeology, history, social anthropology, and religious studies at St Stephen's College, New Delhi; Deccan College, Pune; and the South Asia Institute of the University of Heidelberg, Germany. He received his PhD and Habilitation (professorial degree) in Modern Indian Studies at the University of Heidelberg. He has taught at the Universities of Heidelberg and Canterbury in New Zealand. He was Head of Religious Studies (2002–2004) at the University of Canterbury. He has been Senior Fellow of the German Research Council, Heidelberg; Visiting Faculty, Institute for Advanced Studies, Hebrew University, Jerusalem; Visiting Professor, University of Delhi; and Fellow at the Max Weber Centre for Advanced Social Science Research, Erfurt. He was founding Deputy Director of the New Zealand South Asia Research Centre (NZSAC) and Associate Director of the New Zealand India Research Institute (NZIRI). He has numerous publications on pilgrimage; oral traditions, ritual embodiment and performance; religion, law, and justice; medieval and contemporary historiography; and secularism, religion, and modernity in South Asia.

## Contributors

**Thomas Birtchnell** is Lecturer in Geography and Sustainable Communities, University of Wollongong, Australia.

**Fabrizio M. Ferrari** is Faculty, Department of Theology and Religious Studies, University of Chester.

**Robert Eric Frykenberg** is Professor Emeritus of History and South Asian Studies, University of Wisconsin, Madison.

**Reshmi Lahiri-Roy** is Faculty, School of Education, Faculty of Arts and Education, Deakin University, Australia.

**Timothy Lubin** is Professor, Department of Religion, Washington and Lee University, and Adjunct Professor of Law, Washington and Lee University School of Law.

**Ursula Rao** is Director, Institute of Anthropology, University of Leipzig, Germany.

**Elisabeth Schömbucher** is Adjunct Professor, Department of Indology, University of Wuerzburg, Germany.

**Michael James Spurr** is Faculty Member, University of Canterbury, New Zealand.

**Vinay Kumar Srivastava** is Professor, Department of Anthropology, University of Delhi.

# Index